MARKETING
MANAGEMENT
STRATEGIES AND PROGRAMS

McGRAW-HILL SERIES IN MARKETING

MARKETING MANAGEMENT
STRATEGIES AND PROGRAMS
FIFTH EDITION

JOSEPH P. GUILTINAN
University of Notre Dame

GORDON W. PAUL
University of Central Florida

McGraw-Hill, Inc.

New York   St. Louis   San Francisco   Auckland   Bogotá
Caracas   Lisbon   London   Madrid   Mexico City   Milan   Montreal
New Delhi   San Juan   Singapore   Sydney   Tokyo   Toronto

This book was set in New Baskerville by Better Graphics, Inc.
The editors were Bonnie K. Binkert, Jim Nageotte,
and Bernadette Boylan; the designer was Karen K. Quigley;
the production supervisor was Paula Keller.
New drawings were done by Hadel Studio.
R. R. Donnelley & Sons Company was printer and binder.

Cover credit: Michael Melford/The Image Bank

MARKETING MANAGEMENT
Strategies and Programs

Acknowledgments appear on pages 460–461, and on this page by
reference.

This book is printed on acid-free paper.

   4 5 6 7 8 9 0 DOC DOC 9 0 9 8 7 6

ISBN 0-07-048971-8

Library of Congress Cataloging-in-Publication Data

Guiltinan, Joseph P.
   Marketing management: strategies and programs / Joseph P.
Guiltinan, Gordon W. Paul.—5th ed.
     p.   cm.—(McGraw-Hill series in marketing)
   Includes bibliographical references and index.
   ISBN 0-07-048971-8 (alk. paper)
   1. Marketing—Management.   I. Paul, Gordon W.   II. Title
III. Series.
HF5415.13.G84   1994
658.8—dc20   93-22754

INTERNATIONAL EDITION

ABOUT THE AUTHORS

JOSEPH P. GUILTINAN is Professor of Marketing and Associate Dean, College of Business Administration, University of Notre Dame. He holds the BBA degree from Notre Dame and both the MBA and DBA degrees from Indiana University.

Dr. Guiltinan has served on the faculties of the University of Massachusetts–Amherst and the University of Kentucky. He was department chair at both Kentucky and Notre Dame.

Dr. Guiltinan's other books include *Marketing* (now in its fourth edition) published by Allyn & Bacon and *Pricing Bank Services* published by the American Bankers' Association. His research has appeared in the *Journal of Marketing, Journal of Consumer Research, Journal of Retailing,* and many other publications.

GORDON W. PAUL is Professor of Marketing at the University of Central Florida–Orlando. Professor Paul received his Ph.D. in marketing from Michigan State University. He has been on the faculty at Louisiana State University–Baton Rouge and the University of Massachusetts–Amherst. He has been a Fulbright lecturer in Greece and Portugal and has published numerous articles in a variety of journals and proceedings. Professor Paul has co-authored *Consumer Behavior: An Integrated Approach* (Richard D. Irwin, Inc.) and *Readings in Marketing Management: Strategies and Programs* (McGraw-Hill).

To Our Families

Sharon, Joanna, Jennifer,
and Shannon Guiltinan

Gloria, Christopher, and Bradley Paul

CONTENTS

PREFACE

This book is specifically designed for advanced undergraduate students and for those MBA students with some previous coursework in marketing. It is intended for use in those courses in which the application of marketing concepts, tools, and decision-making processes is emphasized.

We have conscientiously written this book to accommodate a variety of teaching approaches. For those instructors who favor the lecture or discussion approach, there is ample material and coverage for the course. For those who prefer to use cases, simulations, or other pedagogy, the book provides the basic foundation for such an approach. In addition, practicing managers will find it useful in providing guidelines for developing marketing plans and programs.

As with previous editions, this book presents concepts from a decision-making perspective rather than from a descriptive point of view. For example, it does not include survey chapters on consumer behavior or marketing research. Instead, these topics are covered in the context of their relevance to managers, so that students will gain an appreciation of their importance in making product, price, distribution, and promotional decisions.

This approach reflects our emphasis on the middle-management marketing decisions that students are most likely to confront in their careers. Accordingly, top management's strategic decisions have been distinguished from the strategic and operating decisions that middle managers make for a specific product or product line. Additionally, because marketing managers are held accountable for profits as well as sales, the budgetary considerations of marketing decisions are given extensive coverage.

The book has been organized around the **marketing planning process** to clearly delineate the relationship among marketing decisions. In Part One we present the marketing planning process, and we examine the corporate marketing planning decisions that top management must make to provide direction for middle-management decisions. Part Two presents the analytical tools that middle managers must use in analyzing the situation confronting the products or product lines for which they are responsible. Included in this section are chapters on market analysis (presenting approaches for analyzing the buying process and market segmentation), market measurement, competitive analysis, and profitability and productivity analysis (for budgeting decisions). Part Three presents systematic planning approaches for developing a marketing strategy for a product and for program decisions needed to implement the overall marketing strategy. The programs discussed include product development, pricing, advertising, sales promotion, and sales and distribution. Part Four examines the coordination and control mechanisms available to marketing managers. Included in this section are chapters on organizing and managing marketing and sales activities and on the annual marketing plan.

Users of previous editions will note that in terms of philosophy and perspective, this edition follows that of previous editions. However, we have made some important changes. For one, we have incorporated coverage on quality and customer service throughout the book. Another important addition is the coverage of direct marketing. In both cases we have attempted to incorporate material that reflects and addresses these recent marketing trends. As the importance of international markets continues to expand, marketing managers find they cannot examine multinational concerns as appendages to strategy. As in the previous edition, we have integrated the international dimensions of marketing throughout the text and given emphasis to this important aspect of many marketing decisions.

In addition to these changes, we have added numerous up-to-date examples that illustrate marketing practices as they are applied to a variety of organizations. We have enhanced existing chapters by incorporating new material. In particular, we have made a number of important additions useful when defining market segments. We have combined the previously used five-step approach to competitive analysis into four steps and incorporated Porters' five competitive forces shaping strategy into the discussion. Materials on the use and benefits of utilizing internal databases for targeting high potential markets have been added to the chapter on market measurement. Additionally, issues such as category management, strategic alliances, changes in distribution, organizational downsizing, and flexibility are given prominent attention in this edition. Additional emphasis has been given to services and industrial marketing practices in this edition. New end-of-chapter discussion cases and questions have been added to reflect this emphasis as well as to help integrate the international perspective.

To a large extent, the modifications reflect the comments and suggestions of faculty members who have used previous editions as well as the insightful evaluations by several reviewers. For their support and constructive comments we are especially indebted to the following individuals: Sharon E. Beatty, University of Alabama; Cathy Cole, University of Iowa; Edward F. Fern, Virginia Polytechnic Institute and State University; Craig A. Kelley, California State University, Sacramento; Ronald T. Lonsdale, Loyola University of Chicago; Daryl McKee, Louisiana State University; Kenneth L. Rowe, Arizona State University; Mark Spriggs, University of Oregon; H. Rao Unnava, Ohio State University; and Larry K. Yarbrough, University of Arkansas.

We continue to be particularly appreciative to Sam Gillespie of Texas A&M University who has provided us with constructive suggestions and materials throughout several editions. Our thanks are due, too, to our editor Bonnie Binkert who has been an enthusiastic booster of the approach we have taken.

In addition, Jim Nageotte has provided us with many useful suggestions as well as ensured that deadlines were met. We are most appreciative to Jim and Bernadette Boylan, who once again was a pleasure to work with. Our thanks are due to Pat Koers and Jeanna Knowles for their assistance in preparing the manuscript for publication. Their skill and attention to detail are most appreciated.

Joseph P. Guiltinan
Gordon W. Paul

PART ONE

MANAGERIAL PERSPECTIVES ON MARKETING

In today's world it sometimes seems that change is the only constant. Managers of both profit-oriented and not-for-profit organizations face an environment characterized by rapidly changing technology, by competition that is increasingly multinational in scope, and by shifting political and economic forces such as the economic unification of Europe, an international trend toward the deregulation of key industries, and dramatic growth in international trade and foreign investment.

These changes have important implications for marketing decisions in an organization. Decisions on the design of products and services, on prices, and on appropriate promotional methods and distribution systems must be made after considering environmental constraints and opportunities. Because the environment is dynamic and complex and because the range of marketing decisions, issues, and positions is extensive, organizations must develop processes for coordinating various decisions and activities to ensure a common purpose and direction. This is particularly important at what is generally called the *middle-management* level of an organization. The term *middle management* is generally applied to the vast area between first-line supervisors and vice presidents. In marketing, middle-management personnel include individuals with titles such as product or brand manager, advertising manager, market manager, and sales manager.

This book provides the concepts, tools, and decision-making approaches that prospective middle-level managers need to carry out their specialized job roles and responsibilities. However, each of these job roles represents only one or, at most, a few elements of the total marketing effort. Accordingly, so that a middle manager can fully appreciate and effectively utilize these concepts and tools, it is important to understand the relationship between top-management and middle-management decisions.

In Part 1, which includes Chapters 1 and 2, we examine the broad organizational setting in which the marketing function is performed, and we discuss the ways in which the organization as a whole can attempt to deal with broad environmental changes. Both of these issues are important to ensure that middle-management activities are integrated and well focused.

Chapter 1 presents the marketing planning process, which serves as the basis for *integrating* the various marketing activities. Chapter 2 discusses the role of top-management decision making, which is to develop a corporate marketing plan that establishes a basic *direction* for middle-management actions.

CHAPTER 1

THE SCOPE OF MARKETING MANAGEMENT AND THE MARKETING PLANNING PROCESS

OVERVIEW

Perspectives on what constitutes marketing and on the place marketing holds in the firm have undergone substantial change over the last fifty years. In the middle of this century, the term "marketing" was viewed as more or less equivalent to the term "selling." Many companies believed that with enough effort and expense, almost any product could be sold by high-powered selling and aggressive advertising. In effect, this "selling concept" implied that marketing's role was to help dispose of whatever goods or services a firm decided to produce.

In the 1950s, leading marketing practitioners and scholars began to develop a different view. The business environment became increasingly complex as products became more sophisticated, growing personal incomes permitted the purchase of more discretionary items, and competition began to increase. From his observations about success and failures in this new marketplace, former General Electric executive John B. McKitterick concluded:

> So the principal task of the marketing function in a management concept is not so much to be skillful in making the customer do what suits the interests of the business as to be skillful in conceiving and then making the business do what suits the interests of the customer.[1]

McKitterick's arguments are considered by many scholars to be the first widely known statement of what has evolved into the *marketing concept*. The essential elements of the marketing concept are

---

[1] John B. McKitterick, "What Is the Marketing Concept?" *The Frontiers of Marketing Thought and Action*, American Marketing Association, Chicago, 1957, pp. 71–82.

1. Carefully analyzing markets to understand needs,
2. Selecting target groups of customers whose needs match up with the firm's capabilities, and
3. Tailoring the product offering to achieve customer satisfaction.[2]

The goal of this book is to enable prospective middle-level marketing managers to understand the decision-making concepts and tools that can be used in carrying out the three elements of the marketing concept. However, marketing managers do not operate in a vacuum and must have a perspective on the role of marketing in all parts of the organization. Accordingly, in the remainder of this chapter we will examine

- The meaning of customer satisfaction and its relationship to quality management,
- The characteristics of a market-oriented organization,
- The relationship between middle-management and top-management decisions, and
- The marketing planning process as a systematic approach for developing and coordinating marketing decisions.

CUSTOMER SATISFACTION AND QUALITY

A buyer's degree of satisfaction with a product is the consequence of the comparison a buyer makes between its actual performance and the performance the buyer expected prior to use or consumption.[3] The stronger the claims a marketer makes on behalf of a product, then, the better the level of performance needs to be to satisfy the customer. In delivering customer satisfaction, an organization has to understand the significance of quality.

When the word quality is mentioned, most people think first of defect-free products. This traditional manufacturing-oriented view of quality has been broadened considerably in recent years by the rise of the total quality management philosophy. Today, high quality means pleasing customers—going beyond merely protecting them from annoyances. For example, North American automotive manufacturers have nearly eliminated the manufacturing defects that created a quality gap between themselves and Japanese firms. But the Japanese producers have continued to lead in offering fine touches, such as computer-driven "active" suspension systems and uniform sets of buttons and levers for controlling lights, stereos, and directional signals. This

---

[2] Frederick Webster, Jr., "The Rediscovery of the Marketing Concept," *Business Horizons*, May–June 1988, p. 31.
[3] Ralph Day, "Modeling Choices Among Alternative Responses to Dissatisfaction," in *Advances in Consumer Research*, Vol. II, Thomas Kinnear, ed., Association for Consumer Research, Ann Arbor, Mich., pp. 466–469.

philosophy is called *miryoku-teki hinshitsu*, or "things gone right."[4] Put another way, a truly quality-oriented view of customer satisfaction is one that subscribes to providing a level of performance that *exceeds* rather than just matches expectations.

In seeking to provide this level of customer satisfaction, organizations can pursue any of eight dimensions of quality.

1. *Performance*: the basic operating characteristics of a product, such as the prompt delivery of an express package or the clarity of a television picture
2. *Features*: the special supplemental characteristics that heighten the use experience, such as free drinks on an airplane trip or optional seat-cover materials in an automobile
3. *Reliability*: the probability of product failure within a given time frame
4. *Conformance*: the degree to which a good or service meets established standards, including the timeliness of an airplane arrival or how close a shirt comes to its stated size
5. *Durability*: the amount of use a product can take before it must be replaced
6. *Serviceability*: the speed, courtesy, competence, and ease of repair, and the courtesy and competence of service personnel
7. *Aesthetics*: how a product looks, feels, sounds, tastes, or smells
8. *Perceived quality*: the quality that is inferred from a seller's reputation (for example, Maytag washers, Rolex watches)[5]

For marketing managers, it is important to assess the dimensions of quality that are most important to buyers and to understand the levels of their expectations. Then they must find ways to meet or exceed these expectations. But decisions on the target levels of performance for each dimension are seldom the sole responsibility of a marketing manager. Certainly operations, manufacturing, and research and development people (among others) have equally important roles in delivering quality.

THE MARKET-ORIENTED ORGANIZATION

While attention to customer needs and satisfaction is essential to an organization's success, it will not be sufficient. As we saw in the preceding section, the delivery of quality and satisfaction will require contributions from many parts of the organization—especially operations and research and development. Marketing managers alone may be unable to assess whether the firm has the requisite abilities to meet certain needs and may lack information about the costs of tailoring products to achieve customer satisfaction. Additionally, most

---

[4] David Woodruff, Karen Lowry Miller, Larry Armstrong, and Thane Peterson, "A New Era for Auto Quality," *Business Week*, Oct. 22, 1990, pp. 85–96.
[5] David Garvin, "Competing on the Eight Dimensions of Quality," *Harvard Business Review*, November–December 1987, pp. 101–109.

firms operate in environments consisting of multiple organizations that compete for the customer's business.

The concept of *market orientation* thus incorporates the notion of customer satisfaction, which should be the basic philosophy of doing business, but is broader. Specifically, market orientation consists of five elements:

1. *Customer orientation*: having a sufficient understanding of the target buyers to be able to create superior value for them continuously
2. *Competitor orientation*: recognizing competitors' (and potential competitors') strengths, weaknesses, and strategies
3. *Interfunctional coordination*: coordinating and deploying company resources in a manner that focuses on creating value for the customer
4. *Long-term focus*: adopting a perspective that includes a continuous search for ways to add value by making appropriate investments in the business
5. *Profitability*: earning revenues sufficient to cover long-term expenses and satisfy key constituencies[6]

Figure 1-1 summarizes the components of market orientation.

An example of a market-oriented company that has achieved notable success recently is Motorola.

> Motorola has experienced success in recent years in a number of telecommunications and electronics markets. The company is the world's largest maker of modems (which enable computers to "talk" to each other over telephone lines) and has emerged as a leading innovator in cellular phones and electronic pagers. The MicroTac cellular phone which fits into a coat pocket and the company's wristwatch pager have both received technical as well as market acclaim. Additionally, Motorola is a leader in automotive electronics and in microprocessors and memory chips used in products such as computers and cameras.
>
> Motorola's success has been ascribed in large part to the firm's continuing, long-term emphasis on research and development which has enabled it to be responsive to customer demand. As Motorola sees things, customers want improved benefits, better quality, and lower prices. To achieve all of these first requires an understanding of the market. Consequently, Motorola customer service personnel work closely with customers, sometimes even helping to design customers' products (such as Canon's EOS 35mm camera). Moreover, design, manufacturing, and marketing personnel work together on new product projects so that products are designed at the outset to be cost-effective to build and to provide the benefits and features customers want.[7]

Thus, Motorola has responded to the market with innovative products that satisfy target customers. The key to Motorola's success, however, lies in its market-oriented organization. Research and development still has a primary

---

[6] John Narver and Stanley Slater, "The Effect of a Market Orientation on Business Profitability," *Journal of Marketing*, October 1990, pp. 20–22.

[7] Lois Therrien, "The Rival Japan Respects," *Business Week*, Nov. 13, 1989, pp. 108–118.

FIGURE 1-1
Market orientation. (*Source:* John C. Narver and Stanley F. Slater, "The Effect of a Market Orientation on Business Profitability," *Journal of Marketing,* October 1990, p. 23.)

goal of enhancing technology, and manufacturing must meet high-quality goals as well as lower costs. By identifying which needs the company can serve, given its manufacturing and design capabilities, Motorola is able to coordinate the marketing requirements posed by the marketing concept with its internal technical and manufacturing constraints and capabilities to achieve significant competitive advantages in its markets.

As the Harvard professor Benson Shapiro has pointed out, however, achieving the interfunctional coordination necessary to implement the marketing concept is not easy. Effective coordination requires that information on buyer needs be known throughout the organization and that each functional department appreciate the constraints faced by other units.[8] Additionally, there must be a strong commitment to the goals of customer satisfaction and profitability. The importance of an organizationwide commitment to the customer cannot be overstated. Firms may need to develop extensive training programs or other innovative mechanisms for building commitment. Consider, for example, the actions taken by Inland Steel.

Inland Steel executives developed a plan to enhance long-term growth by becoming stable, preferred suppliers to leading firms in the various steel-consuming industries. One of the target companies was Whirlpool, a leader in the appliance business. But Whirlpool was unwilling to make large commitments to Inland until they saw improved product quality. One of Inland's strategies for building quality was to take busloads of steel workers and supervisors to Whirlpool's production facilities so they could meet Whirlpool's manufacturing personnel and gain a better understanding of *why* high quality steel was important in appliance manufacturing. The result was

[8] Benson Shapiro, "What the Hell Is 'Market Oriented'?" *Harvard Business Review*, November–December 1988, pp. 119–125.

a substantial improvement in product quality and vastly expanded sales to Whirlpool.[9]

Probably the most controversial aspect of being market-oriented revolves around its applicability to not-for-profit organizations such as colleges, arts organizations, political groups, and social-action causes. Hospitals, for example, have begun to recognize that patients expect more than just basic health care. Increasingly, hospitals are emphasizing pleasant extras: friendly nurses and staff, faster service and attention, nicely decorated rooms, and even gourmet meals in some cases.

The primary controversy, however, revolves around the degree to which an organization should focus on customer or client satisfaction when the essential mission of the organization cannot be changed (for example, an anti-abortion or environmental group) or where production is based on personal norms and values (as would be the case with arts-based organizations). Businesses can move across products and markets to satisfy customers and still retain their core purpose of providing economic exchanges. But not-for-profit organizations must consider their market orientation within the limits imposed by their purposes.[10]

LEVELS OF MARKETING MANAGEMENT

Because the marketing concept requires a customer orientation, middle managers' activities focus on specific customer needs and on adapting the firm's products, prices, promotional effort, and other activities to meet these needs. The marketing concept, however, is also a philosophy that provides long-range direction and purpose for the organization, and in a market-oriented organization, marketing must be coordinated with other functional activities. Therefore, marketing decision making takes place also at the top-management level. We should emphasize that the distinction between top management and middle management is found in the types of decisions they make, not only in their job titles. In small- and medium-sized organizations, the same individual may have both kinds of responsibilities. (See Table 1-1 for a brief outline of the two levels of marketing management.)

Top-management decisions are those that provide the long-term direction of the organization regarding the markets and needs that will be served and the kinds of products that will be produced. Essentially, top management decides which businesses to enter (or exit) and how to allocate resources across these businesses.

---

[9] Based on discussions between one of the authors and sales and marketing personnel at Inland Steel.

[10] For example, Elizabeth Hirschman, "Aesthetics, Ideologies and the Limits of the Marketing Concept," *Journal of Marketing*, Summer 1983, pp. 45–55.

TABLE 1-1	**THE TWO LEVELS OF MARKETING MANAGEMENT**		
THESE PERSONNEL	**AT THIS LEVEL**	**MAKE THESE DECISIONS**	
Chief executive officer	Top management	Markets to be served	
Comptroller		Products to offer	
Vice president of marketing		Product objectives	
Other vice presidents		Allocation of resources	
Marketing managers	Middle management	Product design	
Product and brand managers		Prices	
Sales managers		Advertising	
Advertising managers		Sales promotion	
Promotion managers		Selling and distribution	
Customer service managers		Customer service	

Consider, for example, the information in Table 1-2. The three well-known corporations listed in this table are typical of most business organizations in that they operate in multiple markets with multiple products (both goods and services). Moreover, the chosen mix of businesses and the allocation of resources among these businesses are continually being evaluated. For example, in recent years Sears entered the credit card business, and IBM left the typewriter business (although it allows its former typewriter division, now a separate company, to use the IBM name). Quaker sold its Mattel toys subsidiary and has shifted marketing spending to give more support to Gatorade and its cereal brands.

As a general rule, middle-management decisions focus on the sales and profitability of individual products, brands, or lines of closely related products marketed as a group (such as Quaker Oats cereals). Action-oriented programs regarding advertising campaigns, sales promotions, prices, and product development, as well as sales-force activities directed at buyers or distributors, are generally the responsibility of middle managers. Thus, the product manager at Gatorade must develop a plan for effectively using any increased resources made available by top management to build the product's business.

Although top-management and middle-management marketing personnel focus on different decisions, their activities depend on and influence one another.[11] First, middle managers can and should provide top management with information on sales and profit trends and on problems and opportunities existing in the marketplace for each product. This information is useful to top management in developing the overall corporate strategy. Second, the decisions made by top management will influence the difficulty of the tasks faced by middle managers. Top management will set goals and general directions for middle managers, and middle managers must establish the detailed plans for achieving these goals.

[11] Paul F. Anderson, "Marketing, Strategic Planning and the Theory of the Firm," *Journal of Marketing*, Spring 1982, pp. 15–26.

TABLE 1-2	**SOME MAJOR BUSINESSES AT LARGE CORPORATIONS***

IBM

Mainframe computers
Minicomputer systems
Personal computers
Printers
Software for computer users

QUAKER OATS

Quaker cereals
Ken-L-Ration pet food
Aunt Jemima breakfast products
Gatorade
Van Camp beans
Celeste pizza
Rice-A-Roni

MINNESOTA MINING & MANUFACTURING (3M)

Medical products
Traffic control and security systems
Imaging systems
Information systems
Data storage products
Video and audio products
Industrial tapes
Automotive systems
Industrial abrasives
Consumer products

* The rapid rate of change in corporate strategies all but assures that some of these businesses will be eliminated and new ones added every year or so.

THE MARKETING PLANNING PROCESS

Planning is merely a systematic way for an organization to attempt to control its future. A plan is essentially a statement of *what* the organization hopes to achieve, *how* to achieve it, and *when* it will be achieved. Virtually every marketing manager acknowledges the importance of planning, because the logic behind it is undeniable. In practice, however, planning often does not take place. One reason for this is that the results of planning are often long-term, and top management places a premium on immediate results. Another is that, because they are under considerable time pressure, the middle managers are more action-oriented than planning-oriented. Some organizations still lack a decision-making structure that facilitates planning.

In other organizations, however, planning is the *basis* of the management process. In general, these firms believe that planning

- Encourages systematic thinking about the future,
- Leads to improved coordination,
- Establishes performance standards for measuring results,
- Provides a logical basis for decision making,
- Improves the ability to cope with change, and
- Enhances the ability to identify marketing opportunities.

Marketing planning is the systematic process for developing and coordinating marketing decisions. Because marketing decisions are made at two major levels—top management and middle management—the marketing planning process must operate at two levels (see Figure 1-2). Corporate marketing planning provides overall direction for the organization by specifying the products the firm will make and the markets it will pursue and by establishing the objectives to be achieved by individual products. Often, firms use the term *strategic business units* (or SBUs) to represent these products and product lines. Middle-management planning specifies the details for implementing the corporate marketing plan on a product-by-product basis. Note that the corporate marketing planning process should provide the basic *direction* for middle management, and the middle-management planning process should *integrate* the various specialized marketing decisions made on behalf of each product.

FIGURE 1-2

Linking corporate marketing planning to middle-management planning.

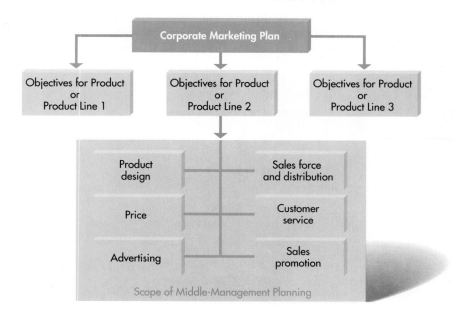

Corporate Marketing Plan

| Objectives for Product or Product Line 1 | Objectives for Product or Product Line 2 | Objectives for Product or Product Line 3 |

Product design

Price

Advertising

Sales force and distribution

Customer service

Sales promotion

Scope of Middle-Management Planning

In other words, all marketing decisions should be made in the context of marketing plans. Only in this way can a firm coordinate the specialized middle-management roles and achieve its objectives.

Basic Steps in Planning

Although marketing planning takes place at both the corporate level and the middle-management level, four basic steps are involved at each level (see Figure 1-3).

1. *Conducting a situation analysis.* Before developing any action plan, decision makers must understand the current situation and trends affecting the future of the organization. In particular, they must assess the *problems* and *opportunities* posed by buyers, competitors, costs, and regulatory changes. Additionally, they must identify the *strengths* and *weaknesses* possessed by the firm.
2. *Establishing objectives.* Having completed the situation analysis, the decision makers must then establish specific objectives. Objectives identify the level of performance the organization hopes to achieve at some future date, given the realities of the environmental problems and opportunities and the firm's particular strengths and weaknesses.
3. *Developing strategies and programs.* To achieve the stated objectives, decision makers must develop both strategies (long-term actions to achieve the objectives) and programs (specific short-term actions to implement the strategies).
4. *Providing coordination and control.* Plans that are fairly comprehensive often include multiple strategies and programs. Each strategy and each program may be the responsibility of a different manager. Thus, some mechanism

FIGURE 1-3
Basic steps in planning.

Conduct a Situation Analysis

Establish Objectives

Develop Strategies and Programs

Provide Coordination and Control

must be developed to assure that the strategies and programs are effectively implemented.

Organizational structures and budgets are the primary means for coordinating actions. Control is also essential because the success of strategies and programs can never be predicted with certainty. The purpose of control is to evaluate the degree to which progress toward an objective is being made and to pinpoint the causes of any failure to achieve objectives so that remedial actions can be taken.

One further point about planning must be noted. Planning is a *process*. Organizations operate in complex and dynamic environments. Therefore, as the situation changes, managers must be prepared to modify objectives and strategies to deal with those changes.

Marketing Management and the Marketing Planning Process

Marketing management encompasses all the decisions involved in designing and executing marketing plans in order to implement the marketing concept. As we have indicated, marketing decisions are made by top management and by middle managers, and decisions made at these two levels influence one another. Accordingly, both levels will be examined in this book, although our focus is primarily on decision making at the middle-management level.

More specifically, subsequent chapters will examine the kinds of information, concepts, tools, and procedures marketing managers can employ in decision making. As Figure 1-4 indicates, these decision areas are treated within the framework of the marketing planning process. Chapter 2 examines procedures for developing the situation analysis, objectives, and strategies at the corporate level. Additionally, a major outcome of corporate marketing planning is the development of product objectives that guide decision making at the middle-management level. This is also covered in Chapter 2.

In Chapters 3 to 6 we will examine techniques and procedures for conducting a situation analysis at the individual-product level.

Our primary focus in Chapters 7 to 13 is on developing marketing strategies and programs that will achieve the product objective and that take into account the problems and opportunities uncovered in the situation analysis.

Finally, Chapters 14 and 15 present procedures for coordination and control at both the middle-management and top-management levels.

In examining Figure 1-4, the reader should note the direction of the arrows linking the major sections. That some arrows go in both directions between two sections reflects two important points. First, in a well-managed organization, top management will use the insights of middle management as an important input to corporate strategy. Information on the situation analysis for a given product and on the feasibility of developing a successful marketing

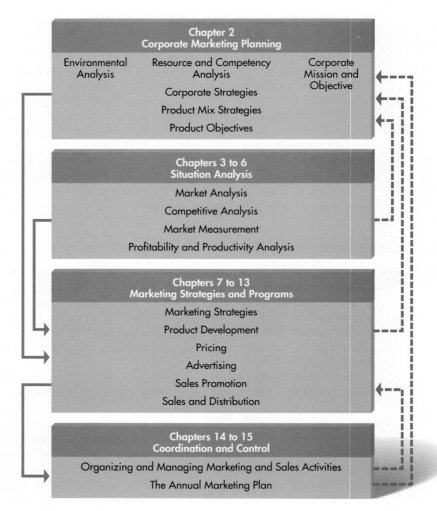

FIGURE 1-4
Marketing management and the marketing planning process: an overview.

strategy for a product is usually more detailed at the middle-management level and should be communicated to top management.

Second, the control function has a primary purpose of alerting managers to the need for changes in objectives, strategies, or programs. This feedback is denoted by the dashed lines.

CONCLUSION

The marketing concept serves as our starting point for examining marketing management because this concept reflects the basic purpose of a business. Without giving effective attention to customer needs, marketing and the other business functions will lack the direction needed for success.

SCHWINN BICYCLE CO.: THE DECLINE OF A LEADER*

In August of 1991, Schwinn Bicycle announced it was closing its Greenville, Mississippi, production plant and would henceforth import all its bikes (except for a small line of premium bikes) from China Bike in Hong Kong or a joint venture bicycle plant in Hungary. At the time of the announcement, Richard Schwinn, the vice president for manufacturing and product development, said he would not mind resuming domestic manufacturing if Schwinn could get a competitive advantage.

For decades, Schwinn was the most famous U.S. bicycle brand, and the company held about 25 percent of the market in the 1950s and 1960s. By 1992 the company's share had declined to about 8 percent and, sadly for Schwinn, most of this decline occurred during the 1980s—a decade that witnessed an explosion in industry bicycle sales from 6 million units per year to 12.6 million. Throughout the decade, Schwinn sales stuck at 900,000 units.

Schwinn's decline has been attributed to a variety of causes. For one, while mountain-bike sales boomed and new rivals like Trek USA and Specialized Bicycle Components won over bikers with lighter, sleeker models, Schwinn stuck to producing the same durable but bulky models. As one dealer suggested, "Their image has kind of aged. It's not considered to be the cool product anymore."

Another questionable tactic for a company selling in the mid-price range was the move to overseas manufacturing. The strategy proved ill-fated when quality-control problems emerged. Moreover, as one competitor noted, "Anyone manufacturing bicycles offshore is going to find it difficult to come up with anything but a me-too product."

1. What dimensions of quality are likely to be most important in the bicycle market? Given Schwinn's position prior to the 1980s, on which dimensions could Schwinn possibly have been viewed as offering superior value?

2. What aspects of a market-orientation appear to have been absent from Schwinn's business practices?

3. What are the pros and cons of having the same person in charge of manufacturing and product development? What impact might this have on market orientation?

4. Do you agree with the following statement or not? (Explain your reasoning.)

   "In a business that focuses on a single product category like bicycles, corporate-level planning is not so important."

---

* Developed from Timothy O'Brien, "Beleaguered Schwinn Seeks Partner to Regain Its Luster," *Wall Street Journal*, May 20, 1992, p. B2; Adam Lashinsky, "Schwinn Fighting to Keep On Rolling," *Crain's Chicago Business*, May 31, 1992, p. 4; "Schwinn Finds Overseas Lure Potent," *Chicago Tribune*, Aug. 9, 1991, section 3, pp. 1, 3; "A World Boom in Mountain Bikes Revives American Manufacturers," *New York Times*, Apr. 1, 1991, pp. A1, C7.

It is important to recognize, however, that a market-oriented organization is one that takes its lead from the *market*, not necessarily from the *marketing department*. Market-oriented firms acquire an understanding of their customers and competitors, determine which customers and needs fit best with the organization's capabilities and profit goals, and develop their responses to the marketplace in a highly coordinated fashion and with a long-term perspective.

Even in a market-oriented organization, however, it is not a simple matter to implement the marketing concept. Organizations are faced with many alternative markets and customers and with a vast array of alternative policies and programs for meeting customer needs. Organizations cannot pursue *all* possible buyers and cannot take *all* possible marketing actions because human and financial resources are usually limited and do not permit such extravagance.

In order to deal with the problems involved in implementing the marketing concept, we have suggested a planning approach. Conducting a situation analysis and setting objectives before developing strategies and programs improve the chances for choosing the best marketing policies. Further, planning really should take place on two levels. At the middle-management level, planning focuses on an individual product or on a line of related products. At the top-management level, planning focuses on the broad question ("What business should we be in?") and on the total mix of products and product lines.

It is important to recognize that holding a preeminent position in a market is no guarantee of future success. All firms must vigilantly maintain a market orientation and engage in planning for the future. Consider, for example, the experience at Schwinn Bicycle Co.

QUESTIONS AND SITUATIONS FOR DISCUSSION

1. "If firms practiced the marketing concept, all new products would be based on extensive consumer research, and few products would not be successful." Do you agree or disagree? Explain your answer.

2. Of the eight dimensions of quality, which ones would be most important to an organization that primarily sells services (such as banks, hospitals, or airlines) rather than physical goods?

3. "Repair service is more a function of production than marketing, just as the extension of credit is more a function of finance than marketing." Do you agree or disagree with this statement? Explain.

4. How would you answer the business manager of the local symphony who made the following statement? "At times, I've thought about using marketing more in our affairs, but I simply cannot afford the cost of surveys and advertising campaigns. Anyway, people will always come to hear good music. The quality of our programs is the only important consideration."

5. How would you explain the marketing concept to a university official who is interested in applying it to noncredit programs offered in several urban communities?

6. The 3M Company has 50,000 products ranging from Scotch tape to heart-lung machines. How would formal marketing planning differ in 3M from a company having only a few products?

7. Consider the following statement: "When a firm selects the customers it desires to serve, it also selects its competitors." How does this statement relate to the concept of market orientation?

8. Develop a list of possible top-management issues that might be considered by the McDonald's Corporation. What middle-management issues would this firm likely deal with?

9. Would marketing planning be more difficult for the Ford Motor Company or for Steelcase (a leading manufacturer of office furniture)? Why? For which company would marketing planning be more important? Taking both answers into consideration, what generalization would you make about the usefulness of planning?

10. In 1917, the DeVries Brothers formed a chemical manufacturing company located in Holland, Michigan. This company grew over the years to become a major producer and manufacturer of fertilizers and chemicals. In many of the product lines, DeVries held the leading market share. Chemicals were sold under their own brand names and were added to various feeds to protect against diseases and to stimulate growth. Then the leading competitor (Chase Chemical) improved production facilities by installing modern processing equipment that was faster than that of DeVries. As a result, Chase Chemical was able to meet customer specifications so quickly that they soon replaced DeVries as the industry leader.

DeVries responded to the competitive change in several ways. Historically, they used the crystalline method of manufacturing their chemicals. Quickly they added new tablet, liquid, and powdered forms. They also ordered new process equipment to increase the speed of their production runs. At about the same time they brought in all their salespeople from the six regions to a general sales meeting. At this meeting several things were covered. Among the major points were: (1) briefing on new forms of products, (2) briefing on new process machinery purchases, (3) review of new products and emphasis on the importance of increasing sales, (4) price lists and future advertising support for new product forms, and (5) motivation to restore DeVries to its leading position in the industry.

Initial (second-quarter) sales of the new forms were poor. Company officials had been optimistic that sales would be much higher and asked district managers to account for such low sales. District managers reported that potential buyers and purchasing agents asked highly technical questions about the new product forms that salespeople were unprepared to answer. To rectify this situation, technical people were assigned to assist salespeople when encountering such problems. Management felt this would correct the problem and anticipated a much higher level of sales for the third quarter of the year.

When sales figures were reviewed, results were disappointing. A 3 percent increase over the previous quarter was evidence to the national sales manager that new salespeople whose principal job would be to sell the product forms were necessary. This, combined with a series of advertisements emphasizing the greater effectiveness of the new product forms, as opposed to the crystalline products, was viewed as the solution to the poor reception by the market.

Fourth-quarter results indicated a 5 percent sales increase over the second quarter. Management felt that it was time to coordinate all marketing activities in the sale of their products and created a new position of marketing manager. Although they would have preferred to promote from within the company, they felt that no one had a broad marketing viewpoint and sought someone from outside. After a short search, Warren Brown was hired for the position.

Brown had previously worked in chemical sales with a leading industrial chemical firm. He had held a variety of staff positions with this same company, including marketing development and sales research and analysis, and had been involved in the development and marketing of several new products as a member of a new product group. In reviewing the DeVries difficulties, he felt that it was necessary to undertake a study of actual sales as well as sales potential for the industry. This study was completed by a member of the staff and forwarded to Brown for his review.

Brown, after his review, concluded that DeVries should not have anticipated increased sales as a result of the new product variations as there had been inadequate identification of the appropriate target markets for these products. In addition, in reviewing production schedules, he found that scheduling these new variations had resulted in slowing down the production of the crystalline forms. Sales analyses showed that customers purchasing the new product variations were smaller operators and these products were a negligible portion of their operation. This resulted in higher costs for order processing and, in many cases, these orders appeared to be unprofitable.

Brown felt that it was necessary to concentrate on the original product line and phase out the new variations. In preparing his recommendation, he also felt it was necessary to establish procedures to avoid such a situation in the future.

a. What do you think of DeVries's planning process?
b. What do you think the proper approach should have been?
c. Do you feel that the sales force's lack of technical expertise contributed to the lackluster performance and should this have been anticipated?

SUGGESTED ADDITIONAL READINGS

Bonoma, Thomas V., "Marketing Subversies," *Harvard Business Review*, November–December 1986, pp. 113–118.

Gilliatt, Neal, and Pamela Cuming, "The Chief Marketing Officer: A Maverick Whose Time Has Come," *Business Horizons*, January–February 1986, pp. 41–48.

Houston, Franklin S., "The Marketing Concept: What It Is Not," *Journal of Marketing*, April 1986, pp. 81–87.

Jackson, Barbara Bund, "Build Customer Relationships That Last," *Harvard Business Review*, November–December 1985, pp. 120–128.

Kohli, Ajay, and Bernard Jaworski, "Market Orientation: The Construct, Research Propositions, and Managerial Implications," *Journal of Marketing*, April 1990, pp. 1–18.

Levitt, Theodore, "Marketing When Things Change," *Harvard Business Review*, November–December 1977, pp. 107–113.

Payne, Adrian, "Developing a Marketing-Oriented Organization," *Business Horizons*, May–June 1988, pp. 46–53.

Shapiro, Benson, "What the Hell Is 'Market Oriented'?" *Harvard Business Review*, November–December 1988, pp. 119–125.

Stasch, Stanley F., and Patricia Lanktree, "Can Your Marketing Planning Procedures Be Improved?" *Journal of Marketing*, Summer 1980, pp. 79–90.

Walker, Orville, and Robert Ruekert, "Marketing's Role in the Implementation of Business Strategies: A Critical Review and Conceptual Framework," *Journal of Marketing*, July 1987, pp. 15–33.

CHAPTER 2

CORPORATE MARKETING PLANNING

OVERVIEW

We saw in Chapter 1 that an organization's success ultimately depends on its ability to satisfy its customers profitably. We also noted that, while middle managers are primarily responsible for the design and implementation of specific programs for the various products, top management is responsible for establishing the firm's broader, long-term direction and goals.

Corporate marketing planning is the process by which an organization sets its long-term priorities regarding products and markets in order to enhance the value of the overall company. Two kinds of top-management decisions are involved in corporate marketing planning—*corporate strategy* and *product mix strategy* (see Figure 2-1). In corporate strategy, management identifies the businesses in which the company will be involved in the future by specifying

- The range of markets to be served, and
- The kinds of products to be offered.[1]

In making corporate strategy decisions, the critical question to be answered is "In what markets will our particular resources be most effective in implementing the marketing concept?"

Once a corporate strategy has been chosen, management must develop a product mix strategy to identify the role each product is expected to play in building the value of the business. In particular, this strategy will usually specify

- The relative share of the firm's resources to be devoted to each product or product line, and
- The kind of contribution (such as rapid sales growth or high profitability) that each product or product line is expected to make toward building the company's value.

[1] For a more detailed examination of these issues, see George Day, *Analysis for Strategic Market Decisions*, West Publishing, St. Paul, Minn., 1986.

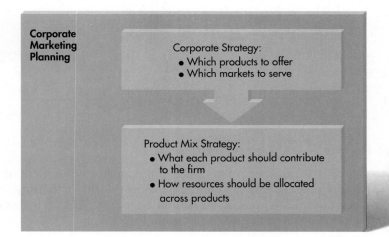

FIGURE 2-1
Elements of corporate marketing planning.

The product mix strategy provides guidance to middle managers about top management's expectations. As we discuss throughout this book, knowing the role the product is expected to play in the overall corporate picture is essential to the development of marketing strategies and programs.

The purpose of this chapter is to identify the various corporate strategies and product mix strategies available to top management and to present procedures and tools for developing a corporate marketing plan. We will also consider the relationship between corporate-level decisions and the marketing planning process at the middle-management level.

CORPORATE STRATEGY

As we indicated at the start of this chapter, corporate strategies are long-range plans designed to select the various businesses a company should be in. They identify the markets to be served (defining them in terms of needs or customers or both) and the product lines and services to be produced on the basis of an assessment of the company's environment, resources, and objectives.

As portrayed in Figure 2-2, corporate strategies should be derived from the analysis of three elements: environmental problems and opportunities, organizational resources and competencies, and corporate mission and objectives. A corporate strategy should be consistent with a company's objectives and achievable with existing (or anticipated) resources. Further, it should take into account prospective problems and opportunities in the environment.

FIGURE 2-2
Factors influencing
corporate strategy.

Environmental Problems and Opportunities

Every organization operates in a dynamic environment that can create a variety of problems or opportunities in the firm's existing or potential markets. Specifically, managers should be aware of the possible impact on their markets of six major environmental forces.

1. *Demographics*, such as the age distribution of the population, birthrates, population growth, regional population shifts, and the percentage of two-worker households
2. *Social and cultural values*, such as attitudes toward health and nutrition, the need for self-expression, materialism, ecological concerns, and product safety
3. *Economic factors*, including inflation and unemployment rates, economic growth, raw material scarcities, energy costs, interest rates, import duties, and excise taxes
4. *Technology*, particularly developing and anticipated changes that affect the kinds of products available in a market and the kinds of processes (such as automation or the use of synthetic materials) used to produce these products
5. *Legal and regulatory actions*, including regulations on the type of advertising available to a product, product labeling and testing requirements, limitations regarding product contents, pollution control, and restrictions or incentives with respect to imports or exports
6. *Competition*, which to a large extent is a function of the other environmental forces. Specifically, both the *identity* of competitors and the *type of focus* (for example, price-oriented versus technology-oriented) of competition may change because of

   ■ The entry of new firms (especially foreign firms),
   ■ The acquisition of a small competitor by a large, well-financed organization,
   ■ Deregulation, changing economic conditions, or new production processes that foster increased price competition, and
   ■ Changing social and cultural values or new technology that causes buyers to purchase products or services previously considered noncompetitive (such as the renewed popularity of cloth diapers).

Examining these forces is essential to develop corporate strategies because these factors will shape the attractiveness of various businesses. Often such factors will create new opportunities or lead to the rejuvenation of mature markets.

The modern organization must develop global assessments of the environment, as trends and developments on these six dimensions are likely to vary around the globe. For example, while the population of the United States is aging, in most of Asia young people dominate the population, resulting in huge opportunities for companies such as McDonald's and Coca-Cola on that continent.

Resources and Competencies

Because environmental changes result in changing *opportunities* and changing *threats*, they are fundamental considerations in the development of corporate strategies. However, not all firms are equal in terms of their ability to take advantage of an opportunity or to avoid a threatening situation. A second fundamental consideration in selecting a corporate strategy is whether the firm possesses the resources and competencies required to take advantage of opportunities and to avoid damaging situations.

In developing a corporate strategy, top management should also analyze the resources that will be available to the organization. In the broadest sense, these include

- Financial resources, such as cash reserves,
- Labor and managerial skills, such as the expertise to produce high-technology products or to manage large advertising budgets,
- Production capacity and efficient equipment,
- Research and development skills and patents,
- Control over key raw materials, as in the ownership of energy resources, and
- Size and expertise of the sales force or distribution system.

Too often firms limit their evaluation of resources to the more tangible ones, such as cash and facilities. Yet management and marketing capabilities are often more important. For example, Frito-Lay's success in the snack business is due primarily to effective advertising management and its extensive sales force, which rotates and replenishes the stock in the retail stores. These competencies enhance the company's ability to continue to bring successful new products to the marketplace—a necessity in a market where product variety is important to the buyer.

Relying on a firm's strongest resources is generally referred to as using a *distinctive competency*, and in selecting among potential corporate strategies, a firm should usually rely on its distinctive competencies or on competencies it can acquire. Table 2-1 suggests some ways a firm can effectively employ various distinctive competencies.

TABLE 2-1	USING DISTINCTIVE COMPETENCIES		
COMPETENCY	POTENTIAL USE	EXAMPLE	
R&D capability	Emphasize high technology in product development	Minnesota Mining & Manufacturing extends imaging technology into medical equipment products	
Financial resources	Acquiring other businesses	RJR tobacco acquires Nabisco	
Company reputation for quality	Select markets where reputation is known	Motorola emphasizes markets familiar with its success in electronics	
Strong sales force	Select new products that can be sold by same sales force	Frito-Lay division of PepsiCo frequently brings out new snacks	
Control over materials and other supplies	Emphasize products that require these resources; compete as low-cost producer	Gallo controls its supply of grapes, glass bottles, and trucking so it can use price to penetrate markets	

Corporate Mission and Objectives

In most organizations, strategic decisions are guided by statements of corporate mission and/or corporate objectives. A corporate mission describes the broad purposes the organization serves and provides general criteria for assessing *long-run* organizational effectiveness.

Corporate objectives reflect management's specific expectations regarding organizational performance. Table 2-2 lists some of the more common types of corporate objectives that might be established. Remember that an organization may have more than one objective at a given time. However, there is usually only one primary goal toward which the corporate strategy can be directed.

As the environment changes, organizations often modify their missions and objectives. For example, the elimination of many regulations in the banking industry and an increase in the types of financial investment products (such as Money Market Accounts) have led many firms to broaden their missions. Thus, many banks now view themselves as "financial institutions." Similarly, changes in technology or the natural extension of existing technology can create an opportunity for broadening the definition of a business. The regional telephone companies (the so-called Baby Bells) created from American Telephone and Telegraph Corporation's (AT&T's) old telephone monopoly are no longer "telephone companies" but telecommunications firms, doing business in office automation, data systems, and a host of other goods and services with related technological bases.

TABLE 2-2	**COMMON TYPES OF CORPORATE OBJECTIVES**

PROFITABILITY

- Net profit as a percent of sales
- Net profit as a percent of total investment
- Net profit per share of common stock

VOLUME

- Market share
- Percentage growth in sales
- Sales rank in the market
- Production capacity utilization

STABILITY

- Variance in annual sales volume
- Variance in seasonal sales volume
- Variance in profitability

NONFINANCIAL

- Maintenance of family control
- Improved corporate image
- Enhancement of technology or quality of life

It is important to recognize that there may be built-in conflict when a firm tries to achieve more than one objective. For example, a small business that sets sales growth as a primary goal may find that it must increase working capital and production facilities dramatically to meet rising demand. To acquire the investment funds to support this expansion, the firm may be forced to take on new investors—an action that could conflict with an objective of maintaining family control.

Moreover, a long-range goal of profitability or increased sales may only be achieved if short-run sacrifices are made. For example, Greyhound Corporation sold its Armour Food subsidiary (which accounted for nearly one-half of its sales) in order to improve its return on investment and to generate funds for investing in businesses that promised higher long-range sales growth.

In sum, the process of developing a corporate strategy is based on

- Examining environmental problems and opportunities,
- Selecting corporate objectives that are consistent with these problems and opportunities, and
- Examining the resources and distinctive competencies that can be used in implementing the strategy.

Figure 2-2 portrays the relationship among these factors.

Although this process appears rather simple, any number of corporate strategies are available to top management. Only by understanding the different types of strategies available can managers effectively select the ones most appropriate for a particular firm's situation.

Types of Corporate Strategy

Organizations have two fundamental directions in which to proceed when selecting a corporate strategy: growth or consolidation. Traditionally, organizations have pursued *growth strategies*, even when sales growth was not the primary corporate objective. Essentially, a growth strategy is one in which sales growth (usually from new products and markets) becomes a vehicle for achieving stability or enhanced profitability.

In recent years, however, both large and small organizations have begun to realize that unbridled and random growth can create as many problems as it solves. *Consolidation strategies*, in which firms seek to achieve current goals (especially enhanced profits) through nongrowth means, have, accordingly, become increasingly popular.

Table 2-3 summarizes the basic types of corporate strategy and shows the specific kinds of strategies in each category.

Growth Strategies for Current Markets

A firm that finds many opportunities and few problems in its present markets is likely to select some form of current-market strategy. Even when problems such as a scarcity of raw materials, new competition, or technological change

TABLE 2-3	BASIC TYPES OF CORPORATE STRATEGY

GROWTH STRATEGIES

FOR CURRENT MARKETS:
- Market penetration
- Product development
- Vertical integration

FOR NEW MARKETS:
- Market development
- Market expansion
- Diversification
- Strategic alliances

CONSOLIDATION STRATEGIES

- Retrenchment
- Pruning
- Divestment

are encountered, if the current markets are attractive in sales growth, sales stability, or profitability, the corporate strategy may still focus on the current market.

The three strategies that focus on current markets are:

■ Market penetration,
■ Product development, and
■ Vertical integration.

MARKET PENETRATION

The term *market penetration* refers to a strategy aimed at increasing sales of existing products in the current markets. Typically, market penetration is achieved by increasing the level of marketing effort (as by increasing advertising or distribution) or by lowering prices.

Indeed, the sales potential of many products goes unrealized because the company is too small to initiate such efforts. As a result, large firms often acquire such products and then engage in the proper market-penetration efforts. For example, sales of Gatorade increased dramatically after Quaker Oats acquired the brand in 1983 and sharply expanded advertising and distribution.

Because market penetration requires no change in a firm's products or markets, it is essentially a *status quo* strategy. As long as current performance is sound, and as long as the environment supports growth and provides profit opportunities, a firm may want to stick with its basic business.

Additionally, market penetration may not be feasible when a brand reaches a practical ceiling of sales. WD-40, the leading spray lubricant, is stocked in 70 percent of all homes in the United States. Realistically, the chances of increasing domestic sales are slim, so the firm has turned its attention to overseas markets.[2]

PRODUCT DEVELOPMENT

Product-development strategies involve the development of new products for existing markets in order to

■ Meet changing customer needs and wants,
■ Match new competitive offerings,
■ Take advantage of new technology, and
■ Meet the needs of specific market segments.

[2] David Kiley, "Safe at Home, WD-40 Tackles Europe," *Adweek's Marketing Week*, Nov. 26, 1990, p. 21.

Typically, this strategy involves replacing or reformulating existing products or expanding the product line. Usually, product development is appropriate when changing needs and tastes result in the emergence of new segments or when competitive and technological changes motivate firms to modify their product lines.

For example, Toyota and Nissan introduced their Lexus and Infiniti models in large part due to an increase in the relative demand for luxury sedans at the expense of compact cars. Similarly, Gillette introduced Sensor to meet increased demand for high-quality shaving systems. The new razor relied on advanced injection molding technology to offer the benefit of two blades that could move independently.[3]

Additionally, forces in the environment are prompting many product-development strategies. Here are just two examples.

Varta, a German battery maker, introduced a new line of batteries which contained no mercury or cadmium. Those chemicals can be hard to dispose of and are toxic in large quantities. Because of this introduction, Varta's share of the $120 million British supermarket business increased from 5 percent to 15 percent. Approximately at the same time, Swedish pulp and paper maker Svenske Cellulosa introduced Britain's first diapers made from pulp that is bleached without using toxic chlorine gas. The product quickly increased their market share from 10 percent to 13 percent of the British $500 million dollar market. Both of these decisions were responses to the "Green" Consumer Movement in Europe toward ecologically safe consumer products.[4]

VERTICAL INTEGRATION

To make a firm more efficient in serving existing markets, vertical integration strategies can be selected. Such integration is often accomplished when a firm becomes its own supplier (in *backward integration*) or intermediary (in *forward integration*). As a general rule, these strategies will be most appropriate when the ultimate markets have high growth potential, because integrating requires extensive resources. Some specific types and purposes of vertical integration strategies can be seen in the following examples.

The forward integration strategy of Quaker State Corp. (a motor oil company) in acquiring the chain of stations owned by McQuik's Oilube Inc. assures the company of a high-volume outlet for its product.

IBM continues to manufacture its own semiconductors, which are vital components of computers, to ensure that it does not become dependent on Japanese producers with respect to prices or access to the latest technology.

Humana is known as one of the nation's largest operators of hospitals. But the company actually derives most of its operating income from its health insurance

---

[3] Richard Coletti, "Leading Edge," *Financial World*, Jan. 8, 1991, pp. 48–49.
[4] Shawn Tully, "What the Greens Mean for Business," *Fortune International*, Oct. 23, 1989, pp. 46–52.

business. As an insurer, Humana essentially pays itself when Humana-insured patients select a Humana hospital.[5]

In practice, vertical integration is not nearly as simple as other current-market strategies. For example, the managerial and marketing skills required for forward integration into retailing clothing are far different from those involved in manufacturing clothing. Similarly, backward integration may backfire if a firm cannot produce its own supplies efficiently.

Growth Strategies for New Markets

In examining environmental forces and sales trends, top management may conclude that the sales growth, sales stability, or profitability of current markets will be unsatisfactory in the future. Such a conclusion will lead these firms to seek out new markets that will present better opportunities.

In entering new markets, four kinds of corporate strategies can be used:

- Market development
- Market expansion
- Diversification
- Strategic alliances

MARKET DEVELOPMENT

The market-development strategy represents an effort to bring current products to new markets. Typically, management will employ this strategy when existing markets are stagnant and when market-share increases are difficult to achieve because market shares are already very high or because competitors are very powerful. This strategy can be implemented by identifying new uses or new users, as the following examples show.

> Arm & Hammer has long held a dominant market share of the baking soda market. However, this market had been growing very slowly until the company began to promote additional uses of its product (most of which were suggested by regular customers), such as cleaning toilets or deodorizing refrigerators.
>
> VISA has led a movement among credit card firms to expand card usage. The company has initiated a promotional campaign directed at doctors and dentists in an effort to broaden the numbers of medical practices that accept the card. At the same time, to gain wider acceptance by supermarkets, VISA-member banks reduced the fees they charge to supermarkets.

[5] Zachary Schiller, "Humana May Be Wearing Too Many Hats," *Business Week*, June 8, 1992, p. 31.

MARKET EXPANSION

A market expansion strategy involves moving into a new geographic market area. Many firms originate as regional competitors and later move into other areas of the country. For example, Coors beer was sold only in the western part of the nation for many years, and Borden's has recently taken its Cream-ette's line of pasta products from a Midwestern base to nearly national distribution.

In today's business world, companies are likely to expand their markets internationally, and frequently this is the growth strategy most likely to achieve large sales and profit growth.

Although Whirlpool's U.S. appliance sales grew steadily in the 1980s, the company's main thrust for the 1990s has been on global expansion. In part the shift in emphasis is explained by the intensive price competition that has evolved in the American market resulting in reduced earnings in spite of strong sales growth. Additionally, appliance sales growth prospects are greater overseas, especially in Europe where Whirlpool has acquired the assets of Philips—one of Europe's market leaders.[6]

International market expansion can be pursued at three levels: regional strategy, multinational strategy, or global strategy.[7]

A *regional* strategy implies that a company will concentrate its resources and efforts in one or two areas. Thus, Fiat of Italy has historically competed primarily in Europe and Latin America. This strategy generally is employed when a firm intends to rely primarily on its home base for business.

Multinational strategies involve a commitment to a broad range of national markets including those in Europe, Asia, and the Americas. Such firms organize their businesses around nations or regions so that separate marketing strategies (including decisions on the range of products to offer) are largely left to the local subsidiary. IBM, Nestle, and Royal Dutch-Shell are among the firms that are considered multinationals.

A *global* strategy is employed when an organization operates in a broad set of markets but with a common set of strategic principles. Put another way, this strategy views the world market as a whole rather than as a series of national markets. Country strategies are thus subordinated to a global framework. Global strategies are most appropriate when a firm's competitors or customers are globalized. For example, Caterpillar competes with Komatsu for earth-moving equipment in virtually every market, and financial institutions like Morgan Guaranty Trust Company work with corporate clients who are themselves global or multinational.

---

[6] David Woodruff and Fred Kapor, "Whirlpool Goes Off on a World Tour," *Business Week*, June 3, 1991, pp. 99–100.

[7] This discussion is based in part on Jean-Pierre Jeannet and Hubert D. Hennessey, *International Marketing Management*, Houghton Mifflin, Boston, 1988, pp. 252–260.

DIVERSIFICATION

A strategy that involves both new products and new markets is termed diversification. This strategy is likely to be chosen when one or more of the following conditions exist:

- No other growth opportunities can be established with existing products or markets.
- The firm has unstable sales or profits because it operates in markets that are characterized by unstable environments.
- The firm wishes to capitalize on a distinctive competence.

Between 1960 and 1970, Minebea grew from being Japan's leading manufacturer of miniature ball bearings to the world's biggest producer with 70% of the market. Unfortunately, this market was relatively small and had a modest growth outlook. Because of Minebea's dominant market share, market penetration was not a viable strategy. While Minebea could have expanded the product line into larger bearings, these products were purchased by firms in completely different industries from those Minebea supplied with miniature bearings. The company finally decided to leverage its skills in precision machining and in the electronics of controlling delicate techniques for manufacturing small components by diversifying into markets such as computer keyboards, gauges, loudspeakers, and fasteners.[8]

When the markets for many of its most successful hardware products (such as drills and chain saws) began to level off, Black & Decker turned its attention to the development of housewares products. Relying on its expertise in cordless-appliance technology, the company achieved success with its Dustbuster vacuum, Spotlighter (a rechargeable flashlight), and the cordless screwdriver. Based on these successes and its ability to manufacture products at low cost, Black & Decker continued its diversification into housewares products by purchasing General Electric's small-appliance business. Within three years, Black & Decker had become the market leader in irons.

STRATEGIC ALLIANCES

Often a firm can successfully move into a new market only if it can acquire new resources or competencies. In such cases, the firm's strategy may be to form a strategic alliance with another firm. A strategic alliance is more than a joint venture. In the case of a joint venture, two firms essentially create a third entity that develops on its own. In a true strategic alliance, two firms collaborate in a far more complete way by *exchanging* some key resources (although new entities may also be formed) to enable both parties to enhance their performance. Typically, alliances involve exchanges of one or more of the resources listed below.

---

[8] "The Nonconformist," *The Economist*, Aug. 22, 1992, pp. 61–62.

- Access to sales and distribution networks
- New product technology
- Production technology and capacity[9]

PepsiCo and General Mills have created a snack-food joint venture in Europe, where General Mills had snack sales of about $325 million. While General Mills had made inroads to northern Europe, PepsiCo had previously focused most of its attention in southern Europe, notably Spain. By providing a broader product line, the firms expect to have more clout with retailers as well as achieve better geographical coverage.[10]

In the world of pharmaceuticals, new products are essential to success, but the expansion of biotechnology has made it costly for firms to stay on top of all new developments. Because of the extraordinary costs required for R&D, few firms have the funds available to expand geographically through their own efforts. As a result, many have followed the pattern developed by the British company Glaxo, which trades proprietary drug products with Japanese firms to broaden its product line and generate greater sales volume from its established European sales and distribution network.

Carnival Cruise Lines formed a European cruise joint venture with Club Mediterranee, the French chain of vacation villages. The alliance combines Club Med's sales force and its expertise in European vacation-travel marketing with Carnival's ships and its expertise in designing and mass-marketing cruises to middle-income households.[11]

Consolidation Strategies

A major strategic development (observable beginning in the mid-1980s) is the increased emphasis on consolidation. Led by large conglomerates, more and more firms are undoing some of their recent growth strategies. Basically, there are three types of consolidation strategies:

- Retrenchment
- Pruning
- Divestment

RETRENCHMENT

Retrenchment is essentially the opposite of market development: A firm reduces its commitment to its existing products by withdrawing from weaker markets. Generally, this strategy is pursued when a firm has experienced uneven performance in different markets. For example, many retail firms

---

[9] See Kenichi Ohmae, "The Global Logic of Strategic Alliances," *Harvard Business Review*, March–April 1989, pp. 143–149, for a thorough discussion of international strategic alliances.
[10] Michael McCarthy and Richard Gibson, "General Mills, PepsiCo Plan Venture Abroad," *The Wall Street Journal*, May 13, 1992, pp. B1, B9.
[11] Michael McCarthy, "Carnival Plans Europe Venture with Club Med," *The Wall Street Journal*, May 19, 1992, p. B1.

have decided to concentrate their marketing efforts in a few regions of the country.

> Because of slowing growth in consumer electronics, Michigan-based Highland Superstores closed 22 stores in Texas and 10 in New England to concentrate on its stronger mid-Western markets. Similarly, Exxon withdrew from the Los Angeles market where its market share had declined to 4%, less than half the share generally considered necessary for a reasonable return on advertising costs.[12]

PRUNING

Pruning occurs when a firm reduces the number of products offered in a market. In effect, pruning is the opposite of product development and occurs when a firm decides that some market segments are too small or too costly to continue to serve.

> Although Black & Decker enjoyed immense success with product development in recent years, its core business—power tools—has had some profitability problems. In large part, these stemmed from an extraordinarily long product line. By the mid-1980s, the company produced over 100 different motor sizes in 25 plants. So from 1984 to 1987, the company began to streamline the product line, eliminating six plants and hundreds of product variations in the process. As a result, the utilization of individual production facilities was greatly improved.[13]

DIVESTMENT

Divestment occurs when a firm sells off a part of its business to another organization. Because this usually means that a firm is taking itself out of a product line and out of a particular market, divestment is essentially the opposite of diversification.

A firm typically pursues divestment strategies when management becomes aware that a particular business is not meeting the organization's objectives for it. Often, divestment occurs after an organization realizes that a diversification strategy has failed. This is more likely to occur when the business does not fit the organization's competencies and when top management fails to appreciate the kinds of skills central to success in that market.

> Adolph Coors elected to spinoff its non-beer businesses (including ceramic computer boards, vitamins for animal feed, and auto parts). In explaining the logic of this decision, chairman Peter Coors said, "The brewery is a consumer operation and all the others are business to business. The mentality and philosophy are quite different."[14]

---

[12] Marianne Taylor, "Highland Closes 32 Stores in Texas, New England," *Chicago Tribune*, June 5, 1991, p. C1, and Caleb Solomon, "Exxon to Pull Out of Gasoline Business in Los Angeles," *The Wall Street Journal*, May 14, 1992, p. A4.
[13] Christopher Eklund, "How Black & Decker Got Back in the Black," *Business Week*, July 13, 1987, pp. 86–90.
[14] Ronald Grover, "Coors Is Thinking Suds 'R Us," *Business Week*, June 8, 1992, p. 34, and George Lozarus, "Coors Eyes Spinoff of Non-Beer Units," *Chicago Tribune*, May 15, 1992, p. 3:4.

In other cases, companies divest to make better use of resources.

Shell decided to sell its coal mining unit to concentrate on its oil and natural gas holdings. One reason for the divestment was that coal requires huge investments (to develop mines and buy equipment), and company officials felt that such funds could be better used elsewhere.[15]

PRODUCT MIX STRATEGY

A corporate strategy provides an organization with a basic direction by establishing the general product and market scope to be pursued. Given this scope, a firm usually elects to divest or prune businesses and products that do not fit the strategy and to commit resources to those products and businesses that do fit this strategic scope. However, in most organizations a number of products and businesses are likely to remain within the product market scope, and management must have some basis for establishing priorities among those products and businesses that will remain.

A product mix strategy helps management solve the problem of establishing priorities. Specifically, a product mix strategy is a plan that specifies

■ How various products or businesses will be prioritized for the purpose of allocating scarce resources, and
■ What objectives will be established for each product or business to ensure that corporate objectives will be met.

Top management can rely on two useful concepts in developing a product mix strategy: the *product life cycle* and *product portfolio models*.

The Product Life Cycle

The product life cycle (PLC) concept plays an important part in the development of a product mix strategy. It helps managers to identify the significance of sales trends and to assess the changing nature of competition, costs, and market opportunities over time.[16]

---

[15] James Hirsch, "Shell Oil Co. Plans to Leave Coal Business," *The Wall Street Journal*, June 22, 1992, p. A2.

[16] Alternative perspectives on the product life cycle are available in: Theodore Levitt, "Exploit the Product Life Cycle," *Harvard Business Review*, November–December 1965, pp. 81–94; Hans B. Thorelli and Stephen Burnett, "The Nature of Product Life Cycles for Industrial Goals Businesses," *Journal of Marketing*, Fall 1981, pp. 97–108; David Rink and John Swan, "Product Life Cycle Research: A Literature Review," *Journal of Business Research*, September 1979, pp. 219–242; George Day, "The Product Life Cycle: Analysis and Applications Issues," *Journal of Marketing*, Fall 1981, pp. 60–67.

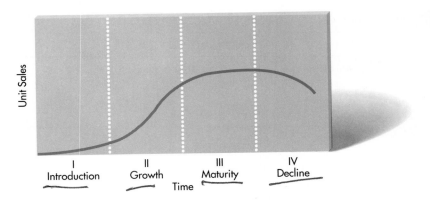

FIGURE 2-3
Stages of the
product life cycle.

The product life cycle represents a pattern of sales over time, with the pattern typically broken into four stages (see Figure 2-3). The four stages are usually defined as follows.

CH#2 7

Primary Demand
Prestige
Vs
Penetration

selective demand

1. *Introduction*. The product is new to the market. Since there are therefore no direct competitors, buyers must be educated about what the product does, how it is used, who it is for, and where to buy it.
2. *Growth*. The product is now more widely known, and sales grow rapidly because new buyers enter the market and perhaps because buyers find more ways to use the product. Sales growth stimulates many competitors to enter the market, and the major marketing task becomes to build market share.
3. *Maturity*. Sales growth levels off as nearly all potential buyers have entered the market. Consumers are now knowledgeable about the alternatives, repeat purchasers dominate sales, and product innovations are restricted to minor improvements. As a result, only the strongest competitors survive: It is very difficult for the weaker firms to obtain distribution and to increase market share.
4. *Decline*. Sales slowly decline because of changing buyer needs or because of the introduction of new products that are sufficiently different to have their own life cycles.

It is important to note that managers could select from more than one portrayal of a life cycle for a given product. As Table 2-4 indicates, for example, an executive at a company that makes tea could consider three different levels of the market in which that product competes when measuring unit sales: (1) beverages, (2) tea, or (3) a specific form of tea such as herbal tea. The decision involved in selecting a level is known as determining the relevant market and is treated in detail in Chapter 3. For our present purposes, however, it is important to recognize that one could arrive at a very different

TABLE 2-4	DIFFERENT DEFINITIONS OF THE RELEVANT MARKET

LEVEL	ILLUSTRATIVE MEASURE(S)
Product form	Sales of regular tea or decaffeinated tea or herbal tea
Product class	Sales of tea
Generic need	Sales of all beverages

interpretation of the product life cycle depending on how the relevant market is defined.

Sales of herbal tea are growing much more rapidly than sales of tea, and sales of tea are growing somewhat more rapidly than sales of all beverages taken as a group. Most important, however, herbal tea is in the growth stage of the life cycle, while tea itself is essentially in the maturity stage.

Generic-need life cycles are seldom useful for strategy purposes because (by definition) they seldom experience significant changes. But *product-form* and *product-class* life cycles are of substantial value to the process of developing strategies. In Chapters 4 and 7 we will see some of the implications of the product life cycle for the development of competitive marketing strategies for a product or product line. From the viewpoint of corporate marketing planning, however, the product life cycle has two major contributions:

- First, the product-form life cycle stage tells more about the market opportunities than does the current brand growth rate. Low brand-sales growth may occur because the market share is declining in the growth stage or because the market share is stable in a mature market. But knowing which state a product is in enables management to evaluate the opportunities for enhancing brand-sales growth.
- Second, knowing the stage of the product life cycle enables a firm to project future costs and profits. Marketing costs (especially advertising) tend to be greatest in the introduction and early growth stages of the life cycle. In the introduction stage, extensive advertising and selling efforts are required to communicate the basic benefits to be derived from the new form or class. In the early growth stage, high marketing expenses for promotion and minor product modifications are necessary as firms jockey for strong market-share position in order to be strong enough to survive the shakeout of competitors that often comes at maturity.

The product life cycle concept is not without its limitations.[17] For example, it doesn't take into account the specific competencies and resources of the

---

[17] These arguments are discussed in depth in Mary Lambkin and George Day, "Evolutionary Processes in Competitive Markets: Beyond the Product Life Cycle," *Journal of Marketing*, July 1989, pp. 4–20.

various competitors in a given market. Thus, if competitors have extensive financial resources, the level of marketing expenditure necessary at various stages may be greater than the model suggests. Additionally, competitors that are financially strong due to sales of other products may survive into market maturity even with small market shares. Another limitation is that competitors may mistake a leveling of growth as an indicator of maturity when the true cause is a lack of industry promotional effort or prices that are too high. The result, often, is a self-fulfilling prophecy: Firms reduce marketing expenditures, which in turn retards sales growth. (The degree to which competitors in a market can actually influence the sales curve is discussed in more depth in Chapter 5.)

Despite these concerns, the product life cycle concept can be a valuable tool in corporate marketing planning because it enables the manager to understand the growth and profit opportunities facing each product or business. As discussed later in this chapter, this information is useful in developing the growth and profit expectations for a product and for assessing the resource needs of various products. As such, the product life cycle is a useful adjunct to the widely used product portfolio models.

Product Portfolio Models

Serious investors usually have a *portfolio* of different kinds of financial investments, each with special characteristics regarding risk, rate of return, and appreciation. Likewise, organizations have a range of products with varying characteristics. Just as an investor attempts to balance the growth, risk, and yields of the various instruments in an investment portfolio, top management should strive to find a desirable balance among alternative products. In seeking this long-run balance, managers must recognize that some products will generate large amounts of cash over and above what is required for operating expenses or for additional investment in production facilities and inventory. However, other products will, at least in the short run, generate far less cash than is needed for operating expenses (including marketing efforts and research and development) and for additional investment.

Portfolio models are methods that managers can use to classify products in order to determine the future cash contributions each can be expected to make and the future cash requirements each product will have. Thus, in using a portfolio model, managers usually must examine the competitive position of a product (or product line) and the opportunities presented by the market.

To illustrate how portfolio models work, we shall examine two of the most widely known: the BCG Growth-Share Matrix and the Directional Policy Matrix.

THE BCG GROWTH-SHARE MATRIX

The Boston Consulting Group (BCG) model assumes that cash flow and profitability will be closely related to sales volume. Accordingly, products are classified in terms of the product's market-share dominance and in terms of

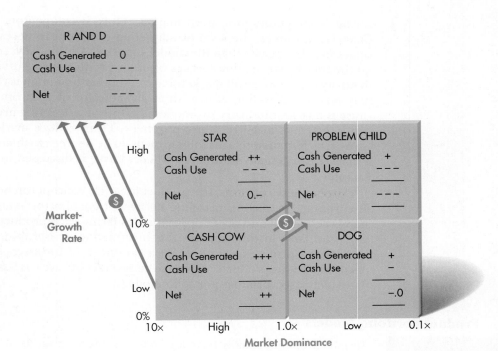

FIGURE 2-4
The Boston Consulting Group Growth-Share Matrix portfolio model. (*Source: George Day, Analysis for Strategic Market Decisions, West Publishing, St. Paul, Minn., 1986, p. 174.*)

the rate of growth in that market. As Figure 2-4 indicates, a firm's relative market share is the ratio of its share to that of the largest competitor (X). If our share equals that of the largest competitor, our relative market share would be 1.0X. Additionally, the rate of growth of the market can be interpreted as reflecting the stage in the PLC—high growth reflecting the first two stages and low growth reflecting maturity or decline.[18] The BCG model enables a manager to classify a firm's products into four basic types: stars, cash cows, dogs, and problem children.

Stars are products that hold a major market share in a high-growth market. Because such products can be expected to enjoy rapidly growing sales and profits, they will likely generate a large cash flow. However, high-growth markets are attractive to competitors. Consequently, stars must receive continuing cash resources to provide a level of marketing support that will enable middle-level managers to protect the market-share position. Moreover, because sales will grow rapidly, additional investment in production facilities and inventories may be needed. As a result, most of the cash flow generated by stars must be reinvested in these same products.

[18] Boston Consulting Group, *The Product Portfolio* pamphlet no. 66, Boston, 1970; see also George S. Day, "Diagnosing the Product Portfolio," *Journal of Marketing*, April 1977, pp. 29–38.

Cash cows are also market leaders, and so the sales volume from these products is usually large enough to generate substantial profits and cash flow. However, because cash cows are in low-growth markets, the cash generated will not typically have to be reinvested in additional marketing expenses or in expanded facilities. Consequently, these products are a firm's primary source of cash flow.

Dogs are low market-share products in low-growth markets and consequently are likely to be weak cash providers. If such products have loyal core markets, they may yield consistent profits and cash. However, because the future contribution of these products is not likely to be very large, they normally should receive a relatively small share of the firm's scarce cash resources for marketing purposes.

Problem children are so named because they have great potential (being in high-growth markets) but require a good deal of attention (in order to build market share). To put it another way, a problem-child product may ultimately be a good cash provider if the firm can successfully build its market share. However, problem children will often be heavy users of cash because large dollar commitments for product reformulation, advertising, improved distribution, or other marketing activities will be necessary in order to achieve a profitable market-share level.

In practice, the BCG matrix is generally viewed as far too simplistic for managing the resource allocation process. Some of the reasons for this view are discussed in the following sections of this chapter. However, this matrix was an important contribution to management thought because it was the first systematic model for managing a large set of businesses in a modern, diversified corporation. Additionally, it introduced terms for important types of products (such as cash cows and problem children) that remain widely used in business strategy discussions.

DIRECTIONAL POLICY MATRIX

The BCG model suggests that market share and industry growth are the best predictors of profitability. However, strict reliance on only these two dimensions may not be appropriate for several reasons. First, some products will be borderline cases since they cannot clearly be classified as high or low on at least one of the dimensions. Second, current market share says very little about the feasibility of increasing or maintaining that share. Third, some high-growth markets may not be attractive because of their size or stability or because of other factors.

To overcome these limitations, managers will usually want to examine other competitive strengths (besides market share) and other dimensions of market attractiveness (besides industry growth). Table 2-5 lists some of the questions that managers should consider in evaluating competitive strength and market attractiveness. These dimensions can be used to supplement market-share and industry sales-growth information in implementing the

TABLE 2-5	EVALUATING COMPETITIVE STRENGTH AND MARKET ATTRACTIVENESS

COMPETITIVE STRENGTH DIMENSIONS

1. Does our market share suggest that we have a strong customer base?
2. Do we have the managerial skills needed to compete?
3. Are our production facilities modern and efficient?
4. Do we possess the technology required to maintain a competitive rate of innovation and product development?
5. Do customers have a positive image of our products?
6. Does our cost structure enable us to be competitive on price while maintaining profitability?
7. Are our distributors well established and supportive?
8. Do we have an adequate number of qualified sales and customer service personnel?
9. Do we have stable and reliable suppliers?

MARKET ATTRACTIVENESS DIMENSIONS

1. Is the industry sales-growth rate high?
2. Is the market size large enough to sustain many competitors?
3. Are industry sales susceptible to cyclical, seasonal, or other fluctuations?
4. Is the rate of product obsolescence high?
5. Does extensive government regulation constrain actions or pose uncertainties?
6. Is the industry demand very low relative to industry capacity?
7. Is there a risk of raw material or component shortages?
8. Are there a large number of well-financed competitors?
9. Do a small number of buyers account for a disproportionately large percentage of industry sales so that we will be heavily dependent on them?
10. Overall, does the industry present a strong potential for profit?
11. Does this industry have a high degree of fit with our corporate strategy?

BCG model. Alternatively, these dimensions are used in other portfolio models such as the Directional Policy Matrix (DPM).

The DPM uses nine portfolio categories. Typically, managers will rate each business on each dimension, using a scale (perhaps five points ranging from very low to very high). The result will be two composite scores for each business: one on overall market attractiveness, the other on overall competitive strength. The overall rating of market attractiveness allows for a high rating—even if industry sales growth is low—when the overall size, stability, or cost of competing is positive enough to make the market attractive. The overall competitive strength rating reflects the firm's ability to compete successfully in building or maintaining market share. In general, products classified in the "maintain" or "challenge" categories can be viewed as problem children and stars, those on the diagonal will be comparable to cash cows, and the remainder can be considered dogs (with those in the low business strength/ low market attractiveness category being the leading candidates for elimina-

FIGURE 2-5
The Directional Policy Matrix.

tion). Figure 2-5 portrays the DPM and shows some typical views of the role each type of product should play in the organization's portfolio.

Portfolio Models and Product Planning

Portfolio models help managers plan resource allocations and in so doing force managers to articulate the expectations and objectives for each product or product line. The various labels in Figure 2-5 suggest some likely expectations for products or product lines falling into each category.

MAINTAIN LEADERSHIP

Essentially, the goal here is market-share maintenance, a typical objective for stars that hold large shares in growing markets. Because markets are attractive, new competitors are likely to emerge, and existing competitors are likely to provide strong support for their products and brands in order to expand sales. For the dominant firm, a major consideration will be establishing brand or supplier loyalty to fortify its market position.

CHALLENGE LEADER

A market-share growth objective is typically appropriate for problem-child products, especially if markets are in the early stages of the PLC, where growth rates are very high. In such cases, the opportunities for market-share growth are often good since brand or supplier preferences may not yet be firmly established and since much of demand is from new (first-time) buyers of the product.

CASH GENERATOR/MANAGE FOR EARNINGS

The objective here is to generate earnings with modest or minimal reinvestment.

This objective is a common one for so-called cash cow products with large market shares in mature (or even slightly declining) markets. Such markets have stable market shares and few new competitors. Consequently, attention is focused on marketing expenditures that stimulate increases in product usage rates or on modifying price and expense structures so that profit margins can be increased.

NICHING

If markets are attractive but a product lacks the ability to challenge for market share, a reasonable objective is profitable smallness. Essentially, this objective seeks solid profitability with only modest increases in marketing effort by pursuing unique market positions that are not directly competitive with those of market-share leaders. This can often be achieved by focusing on a small segment of the market that has unique needs (that is, by becoming a *product market specialist,* or *market nicher*).

HARVEST/DIVEST

Products such as "dogs" that cannot find profitable enclaves and yet require some valuable resources such as production capacity are candidates for harvesting or elimination. Harvesting reflects a *gradual* withdrawal of marketing resources on the assumption that sales will decline at only a slow rate and profitability will remain positive even at lower volume. In contrast, *divestment* means a firm will immediately exit from the business.

Implications and Limitations

As the preceding discussion has indicated, portfolio models can provide insights into the appropriate allocation of resources and product performance objectives. According to these models, stars and problem-child products should emphasize market-share objectives while cash cows and dogs should be profit-focused.

These implications should be examined with care, however, because the models are founded on assumptions that are not always appropriate. Managers who use portfolio models should be especially aware of the following considerations:

■ Portfolio models implicitly assume that the portfolio must be in cash balance; therefore, there must be a sufficient number of cash cows and dogs to fund stars and problem children. In reality, firms may also generate resources through borrowing, and so it may not be necessary to extract all the cash flow from products in lower-growth, less attractive markets just because of high cash needs in attractive, higher-growth markets.

■ Portfolio models suggest that cash cows can be milked with impunity because of their established market position and because they are in mature markets. In reality, many market-share leaders do experience extensive competitive challenges to their leadership position—especially in large, stable consumer-goods markets. Thus, profitability objectives may have to be subordinated to an objective of market-share maintenance, at least in the short run.

■ Portfolio models indicate that resources should be invested in stars and in problem-child products in order to enhance the market shares of these products. However, there is no assurance that the application of more resources will lead to increases in market share. The ability to maintain or increase market share is dependent not only on having adequate resources but also on the existence of competitive advantage. Thus, managers should invest in high-growth markets only if they can identify a feasible competitive marketing strategy.

■ The BCG model is criticized for relying on only two elements while the Directional Policy Matrix accommodates a large number of factors. However, because each element of market attractiveness and competitive strength has a different degree of importance in each situation, it is impossible to have a standard method for weighing the importance of the various elements.[19] Additionally, the ratings are somewhat subjective, so different managers may not always rate a particular business the same way on every dimension.[20]

Additionally, portfolio models in general have been attacked for the view that the only interdependencies among the products or businesses in a portfolio are the cash flows. Harvard's Michael Porter points out that this perspective is part of the reason for the lack of success of so many diversification strategies. In successful diversifications, either the new business should be stronger by virtue of being associated with the parent firm or it should benefit the firm's other businesses by bringing some competitive strength to them (such as new technology or access to broader distribution channels).[21] The term *synergy* is generally applied to such relationships. Synergy means that the whole is worth more than the sum of its parts, that two or more product lines operating in the same firm will be more successful than if they operated in separate organizations because of some commonality in resources employed. Thus, in assessing the role each product line plays in the organization, managers should be careful to identify important synergistic relationships.

[19] Patrick McNamee, "Competitive Analysis Using Matrix Displays," *Long Range Planning*, June 1984, pp. 110–113.

[20] David Hussey, "Portfolio Analysis: Practical Experience with the Directional Policy Matrix," *Long Range Planning*, January 1978, pp. 2–8.

[21] Michael Porter, "From Competitive Advantage to Corporate Strategy," *Harvard Business Review*, May–June 1987, pp. 43–59.

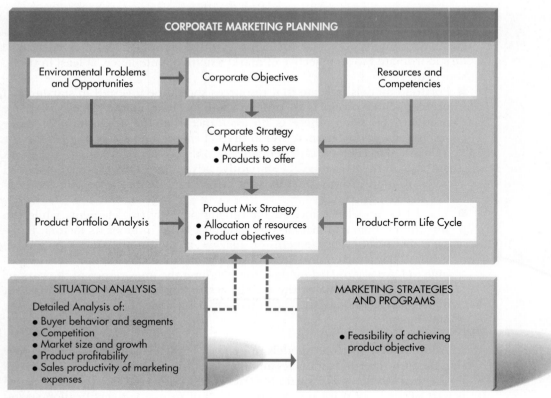

FIGURE 2-6

Relationship between corporate marketing planning and middle-management activities.

THE CORPORATE PLAN AND MIDDLE MANAGEMENT

The corporate marketing plan is important to marketing managers in two respects. First, in most organizations, marketing plays a major role in influencing corporate and product mix strategy. Second, all marketing personnel are responsible in one way or another for developing and implementing the marketing strategies and programs necessary for achieving corporate objectives and product objectives.

Figure 2-6 summarizes the major elements in the corporate marketing planning process and indicates that middle managers can provide two basic kinds of inputs to this process. First, middle managers can provide the most detailed information on each individual product regarding the size of the market, the profitability of the product, and the likely sales results of increasing the marketing expenditures on a product. Second, middle managers must identify the kinds of marketing strategies and programs that can be used to achieve the product objective. In identifying these strategies and programs, it frequently will become apparent that the cost of achieving a product objective will be excessive or that there is no feasible way to achieve the objective because of a lack of resources or because of competitors' strengths or other factors. Consequently, corporate marketing plans may need to be revised once feasibility has been assessed.

Chapters 3 to 13 examine the analytical tools and procedures for performing the situation analysis and for selecting strategies and programs. As we shall see, the starting point for these analyses and decisions must always be an examination of the needs of the marketplace. Accordingly, we will focus on this topic in Chapter 3.

CONCLUSION

Corporate strategies provide the blueprint for the long-term development of a viable, profitable organization by establishing the markets to be served and the products and services to be offered. In this chapter a variety of types of corporate strategies were presented, and the reasons for selecting each type of strategy were established. In general, corporate strategies are selected on the basis of an analysis of environmental factors (especially market growth), corporate resources, and long-run objectives. Further, in deciding which corporate strategy to select, it is important to identify a firm's distinctive competencies. That is, an organization must have the specific resources required to be successful in the specific product and market arenas in which it will compete.

Product mix strategy is an essential element in corporate marketing planning because it forms the bridge between corporate strategy and the development of marketing strategies and programs on a product-by-product basis. The foundation for this bridge is the development of product objectives, which indicate the role each product is expected to play in meeting the firm's future growth and profitability requirements. Further, the product objectives provide a general format for allocating resources among products. In selecting these objectives, portfolio models and the product life cycle are useful tools. In general, product objectives should be determined on the basis of a firm's competitive strength in the market and on the attractiveness of the market as measured by opportunities for growth and profitability.

In order to appreciate more clearly the scope and significance of corporate marketing planning, consider some of the recent developments at Siemens.

SIEMENS: MULTINATIONAL CORPORATE MARKETING PLANNING*

Siemens Aktiengesellschaft, with world headquarters in Munich, Germany, was founded in 1847. By 1991 sales had risen to $45.6 billion. However, profits for that year were a mere 2.5 percent of sales in spite of Siemens' strong positions in many of its 300 business units.

Heinrich von Pierer was named to become Siemens' chief executive, effective in September 1992. It was expected that von Pierer would largely continue the strategic thrust established by his predecessor, who invested billions in acquisitions and new technologies.

Most industry observers view Siemens' main areas of strength as telecommunications, medical equipment, and industrial automation. Siemens' telecommunications businesses included both public communications, which generated $7.1 billion in sales in 1991, and private communications (such as private branch exchange systems for businesses), where it became the world sales leader ($3.2 billion) following its acquisition of United States-based Rolm from IBM. In medical engineering ($4.6 billion), Siemens and General Electric are the two world leaders but face price-cutting challenges from Japanese firms. Although Siemens is the European leader in factory automation ($3.6 billion), it has failed to make a profit in the U.S. market in this area.

Siemens' major trouble spots have been in computers and semiconductors. Siemens became Europe's top computer firm (with $7.6 billion in sales) after its acquisition of its German competitor Nixdorf. But only 5 percent of its computer sales came from outside Europe, and the company's product line was geared toward the declining mainframe and minicomputer segments of the business. In semiconductors ($1.3 billion), Siemens ranked only sixteenth in the world but had substantially improved on its technology.

The outlook for many other Siemens businesses was quite positive. In power generation,

Siemens (at $3.1 billion in sales) was third behind the Swiss firm ABB and General Electric, and in 1992 it was about to acquire majority interest in the strong Czech engineering and energy firm Skoda. Industrial and building systems ($5.5 billion) were expected to experience substantial growth with the rebuilding of the infrastructure of eastern Germany and Eastern Europe. And with the acquisition of eight companies in two years, Siemens had become a leading force in the world market for high-speed trains.

In its quest for further sales growth and profits, Siemens had embarked on a number of new initiatives by 1993. For one, it had signed twenty-six joint venture agreements in Eastern Europe involving factory automation and the modernization of telephone communication networks. Siemens also signed joint venture agreements with Sweden's Ericsson (to cooperate in developing cordless telephone technology), with Picture Tel of the United States (to develop full-color, full-motion business telephones), with IBM and Toshiba (to develop new computer chips capable of storing 256 million bits of data), and with United Technologies (to develop new components for a new generation of gas turbines).

Of all the company's businesses, semiconductors appeared to be the one targeted for the greatest growth. In particular, Siemens hoped it would be able to expand sales to non-German firms (which made up only about one-half of

---

* Developed from Gail Schares, Jonathan Levine, and Peter Coy, "The New Generation at Siemens," *Business Week*, Mar. 9, 1992, pp. 46–48; "Siemens Reveals Ambitious Sales Plans for Next Decade," *Newsbytes News Network*, June 2, 1992; Janis Moutafis, "Siemens Rethinks Its Chip Strategy," *Electronic World News*, May 18, 1992, p. 2; "IBM in Chip Deal with Toshiba and Siemens," *New York Times*, July 13, 1992, pp. C1, C2; "VonPierer Named as Siemens' New Chief," *Financial Times*, July 3, 1992, p. 24.

continued

Siemens' semiconductor volume) and develop chips that would allow them to meet the needs of microcomputer manufacturers. However, in striving to be a top-ten semiconductor firm, "in-house" sales were expected to be the strongest source of growth. Although Siemens' other businesses represented 8 percent of all Western European semiconductor demand, the firm's semiconductor division was supplying only 30 percent of the company's needs.

1. Why might Siemens have such low profitability when it is a leader in so many businesses?
2. Suggest a mission statement that might fit Siemens' current set of businesses.
3. What are the various corporate strategies that Siemens is pursuing?
4. Would the BCG Growth-Share Matrix be an effective approach for developing a product mix strategy for Siemens? Why or why not?

QUESTIONS AND SITUATIONS FOR DISCUSSION

1. In the 1980s Federal Express held a 45 percent share of the domestic overnight delivery market. However, Federal's growth had slowed due to increasing competition from UPS and the boom in facsimile machines. Additionally, price competition had squeezed domestic profits, and the company was actually losing millions on its international business. One response to these events was to acquire Tiger International, the world's largest heavy cargo airline, well known for its Flying Tiger Line airfreight service. Federal Express had not yet cracked the heavy freight business. Additionally, the company looked forward to using Flying Tiger planes for overseas package delivery, reducing the need to subcontract its deliveries to other carriers as they had previously had to do in many countries.

What corporate strategies is Federal Express pursuing? What do these strategies suggest about Federal's environment, competencies, and objectives.

2. Dunkin' Donuts shops have to be open between twenty and twenty-four hours a day since part of their appeal is coffee and doughnuts ready whenever they are wanted. However, over 50 percent of sales are between 6 and 10 a.m. If the operating hours cannot be changed, what alternative growth strategies could be pursued.

3. Maytag Company's acquisition of Magic Chef broadened its product line to include brands that serve virtually every segment of the home appliance market. Maytag's refrigerators are now sold under the Magic Chef, Admiral, Norge, Warwick, and Jean Air brands. What type of corporate strategy would Maytag seem to be following? What are the problems and limitations of such a strategy?

4. **a.** For each of the following products, indicate the stage of the product life cycle that best describes where it is located.
   - camcorders
   - ready-to-eat cereals
   - mutual funds
   - telephones

   b. Discuss the difficulties in applying the product life cycle concept to these product categories.

5. Many firms have pursued consolidation strategies in recent years to focus on their core businesses. But many of these core businesses are in the mature stage of the product life cycle. Does this mean that these companies necessarily have low-growth prospects? Explain.

6. Portfolio management theory suggests that management should assemble a collection of businesses in different industries and different states of maturity to diversify risk. What would be some of the reasons that these same managements may later have to follow consolidation strategies?

7. What if, after charting your business on a growth-share matrix, you found you had only cows and dogs? Does a portfolio model tell you where new business should come from?

8. Europe is a growth market for soft drinks. The average European now drinks only 15 gallons of carbonated drinks per year compared to the U.S. consumer's 50 gallons, and European growth is expected to double the rate for the United States in the 1990s. With this growth and the European Economic Community's unified market, Coca-Cola Europe has begun to buy back distribution rights in some countries and form joint ventures with bottlers in others. Previously, Coke had relied upon licensees and independent regional bottling companies for much of its manufacturing and distribution in Europe. By centralizing bottle filling and distribution, Coke feels it can cut costs and lower its prices to increase sales. In order to do this, Coke standardized on "convenience packaging"—the plastic bottles and aluminum cans that are less expensive, lighter, and easier to transport than bottles. In some European countries such as Britain, 90 percent of all soft drinks are now sold in cans or plastic. However, in countries such as Germany and Switzerland, most beverages come in reusable bottles. In Germany there are 1,100 brewers who also produce soft drinks, and local grocery stores collect and return bottles to local plants.

A recent law in Germany discourages the use of plastic beverage containers by putting the equivalent of a 25-cent deposit on each bottle.

Discuss the corporate strategy options facing Coca-Cola Europe.

SUGGESTED ADDITIONAL READINGS

Cravens, David W., "Strategic Forces Affecting Marketing Strategy," *Business Horizons*, September–October 1986, pp. 77–86.

Feldman, Laurence P., and Albert L. Page, "Harvesting: The Misunderstood Market Exit Strategy," *Journal of Business Strategy*, Spring 1985, pp. 79–85.

Gray, Daniel H., "Uses and Misuses of Strategic Planning," *Harvard Business Review*, January–February 1986, pp. 89–97.

Hall, George E., "Reflections on Running a Diversified Company," *Harvard Business Review*, January–February 1987, pp. 84–92.

Hamel, Gary, and C. K. Prahalad, "Strategic Intent," *Harvard Business Review*, May–June 1989, pp. 63–76.

Haspeslagh, Philippe, "Portfolio Planning: Uses and Limits," *Harvard Business Review*, January–February 1982, pp. 58–73.

Lambkin, Mary, and George Day, "Evolutionary Processes in Competitive Markets: Beyond the Product Life Cycle," *Journal of Marketing*, July 1989, pp. 4–20.

Lenz, R. T., "Managing the Evolution of the Strategic Planning Process," *Business Horizons*, January–February 1987, pp. 34–39.

Ohmae, Kenichi, "The Global Logic of Strategic Alliances," *Harvard Business Review*, March–April 1989, pp. 143–149.

Raymond, Mary Anne, and Hiram C. Barksdale, "Corporate Strategic Planning and Corporate Marketing: Toward an Interface?" *Business Horizons*, September–October 1989, pp. 41–48.

Varadarajan, P. Rajan, "Marketing Strategies in Action," *Business*, January–March 1986, pp. 11–23.

PART TWO

SITUATION ANALYSIS

As we demonstrated in Part 1, middle-management decisions should be consistent with the broad decisions that top management makes regarding the long-term purpose and direction of an organization. Specifically, top management is responsible for identifying the role each product or product line should play in achieving an organization's long-run objectives and for effectively communicating what this role is to be through the formulation of a *product objective*.

Essentially, middle managers have the basic task of achieving the product objective. Later on, in Part 3, we will present some fundamental tools and approaches for selecting marketing *strategies* and action *programs* that can be used to achieve the various types of product objectives. However, in order to develop a logical, planned approach to selecting the marketing strategies and programs that are appropriate, managers must not only be aware of the product objective but also understand the specific problems and opportunities confronting a product or a product line.

By performing a *situation analysis*, managers should be able to identify the major problems and opportunities that can be employed to guide the selection of marketing strategies and programs. The chapters in Part 2 are designed to provide the most important and useful analytical procedures and concepts for performing a situation analysis.

Generally, the most significant problems and opportunities are those related to the market for a product. Accordingly, in Chapter 3 we examine the process of market analysis. In particular, we examine the issue of identifying possible target markets, and we present a sequential approach for understanding how buyers (and potential buyers) are likely to respond to different marketing actions.

Because the extent of a market opportunity also depends on competition, managers must assess the current and potential competitive situation in a market. In Chapter 4 we examine ways of identifying the sources of competition, of predicting the nature and intensity of competition over time, and of assessing the relative strengths and weaknesses of competitors attempting to serve the same market.

In Chapter 5, alternative procedures for measuring the size of a market and for forecasting sales are presented. By understanding the uses, assumptions, and limitations of these procedures, managers will be more capable of identifying the size of a market opportunity and the potential problems that are involved in achieving sales growth.

Chapter 6 examines the relationship between sales and profitability. Because marketing activities cost money, middle managers must know how to determine the sales and profit impact of proposed marketing expenditures. Accordingly, in this chapter we present some basic tools for identifying the problems and opportunities associated with budgeting decisions in marketing.

CHAPTER 3

MARKET ANALYSIS

OVERVIEW

In our discussion of the marketing concept in Chapter 1, we noted the central importance to an organization of understanding the customer. The ultimate objective of market analysis is to determine which needs of a buyer the firm hopes to satisfy and how to design and target the offer to satisfy these needs. In order to achieve this objective, managers must develop an understanding of the choices available to potential customers and the processes potential customers use in making buying decisions.

In this chapter we present a five-step approach for analyzing markets, which is useful for managers concerned either with long-term corporate planning or with short-term marketing strategies. Our approach is designed to clarify the different kinds of demand managers must consider in strategic decision making. Additionally, it offers a series of diagnostic questions that are designed to guide managers through the process of analyzing demand and establishing targets for marketing strategies and programs.

1. *Define the relevant market.* Managers cannot analyze a market unless they first define it, and frequently there are a large number of products and services available for satisfying basic needs and wants. A market can be defined narrowly (to include only products that are very similar to one another) or broadly (for example, to include a variety of different types of products). It is important to remember that the way a market is defined will have a major impact on the specific findings we can expect in the subsequent steps.
2. *Analyze primary demand for the relevant market.* In this step managers attempt to understand the common dimensions of the buying process for all brands and products in the relevant market. Specifically, we provide a series of questions to help managers diagnose who the buyers (and nonbuyers) in the relevant market are and why they buy (or don't buy).
3. *Analyze selective demand within the relevant market.* In this step we examine the process by which buyers select specific alternative brands or suppliers within the boundary of the relevant market.
4. *Define market segments.* There are few buying situations in which all customers have similar motivations and undergo similar choice processes. The concept of market segmentation explicitly recognizes this reality. This step

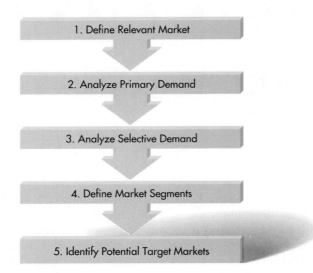

FIGURE 3-1
Steps in market analysis.

in the process presents some alternative ways of separating buyers into segments whose members are similar in their response to marketing programs.

5. *Identify potential target markets.* Ultimately, the goal of market analysis is to identify the best opportunities for creating customers. This final step demonstrates how the information from preceding steps can be used to identify the specific markets (and market segments) that managers should consider as targets when selecting marketing strategies.

DEFINING THE RELEVANT MARKET

The *relevant market* is the set of products and/or services (within the total product market structure) that management considers to be strategically important. As we noted in Chapter 2, a product mix strategy can change substantially depending on how the relevant market is defined. For example, a specialized brand of decaffeinated herbal teas may have a relatively large share of that market but a very small share of the total tea market. Moreover, the total tea market is not growing nearly as rapidly as the herbal tea market. Thus, this product might be viewed as a "star" if the relevant market is herbal tea but a "cash cow" or even a "dog" if the relevant market is tea.

Defining the relevant market usually involves two steps. First, management will attempt to describe the product market structure. Subsequently, the relevant market boundaries within that product market structure will be defined.

Describing the Product Market Structure

A market can only exist when both sellers and buyers are present. Consequently, in order to define a market, managers must identify both the *needs of the buyers* and the *goods and services offered by the sellers* to meet those needs.

A *product market structure* is a representation of the degrees of substitutability that exist among a set of products and/or services that satisfy similar needs. By describing the product market structure, managers can more readily identify the various ways in which the market for a product *might* be defined. Specifically, managers can use the product market structure to identify the types of products and services they must compete with in various need-satisfaction situations.

In Chapter 2 we suggested that managers could classify competing alternatives at three levels:

1. Competing brands (or suppliers) within a product form
2. Competing product forms within a product class
3. Competing product classes serving a generic need

In describing the product market structure, our immediate concern is to classify product forms and classes in order to identify possible ways of defining the market to be analyzed. Because brand or supplier competition can best be analyzed *after* the relevant market is defined, we discuss the classification of brand alternatives in the third step of the market analysis process.

Several methods are available to identify and classify alternative product forms and product classes.[1] Typically, however, classification is based either on the similarity of *characteristics or functions* among alternatives or on the similarity of the *usage situations*.

SIMILARITY OF CHARACTERISTICS OR FUNCTIONS

In this approach, managers classify products as highly similar if they share physical or chemical characteristics or if they function technically in the same way. For example, within the generic-need "breakfast foods," cereals, pastries, and eggs would be considered as distinct product classes based on the differences in their composition and in the processes used to prepare them. Cereals could be subsequently divided into product forms (nutritional cereals, presweetened cereals, and so on) that share some technical characteristics but still exhibit some differences.

---

[1] An extensive review of approaches for describing product market structures is available in George Day, Allan Shocker, and Rajendra Srivastava, "Customer-Oriented Approaches to Identifying Product Markets," *Journal of Marketing*, Fall 1979, pp. 8–19.

SIMILARITY OF USAGE SITUATIONS

Consumers do not always select the most functionally similar alternative when switching product forms or classes. Accordingly, managers may want to obtain customers' judgments of similarity among various product alternatives. However, when asking what products are most substitutable, managers should attempt to account for differences in usage situations. For example, although hot cereal and cold cereal may be more similar to each other than cold cereal and frozen waffles, consumers may elect to substitute frozen waffles (rather than oatmeal) for cold cereal if the usage situation calls for fast preparation.

Defining Broad Relevant Market Boundaries

Generally, top management will be concerned with identifying long-run growth opportunities (especially via product development) and with identifying potential threats to the firm's growth due to a changing environment. For example, soft-drink manufacturers have been increasingly concerned with shifts in beverage preferences toward natural and health-oriented products. Similarly, manufacturers of large computers have been concerned about the way the increasing use of personal computers by business firms has influenced demand for larger machines.

Specifically , it is appropriate that managers (especially at the top-management level) define the relevant market *broadly* when the following conditions occur:

- Regulatory and technological changes are expected to create new alternatives on the seller's side of the market.
- Economic, demographic, and/or social and cultural changes are likely to change the type or frequency of usage on the buyer's side of the market.
- A company's sales gains and losses are coming increasingly from alternative forms and classes (rather than merely from brand competitors).
- Competitors do not exist at the product-form level (often because the product is an innovative form).

Taking a broad view of the market often leads a firm to shift in and out of product categories. For example, General Mills added a line of oatmeal cereals in 1987 when the U.S. consumer was gobbling up increasing quantities of cholesterol-fighting oat cereals. Four years later, with oatmeal sales declining and ready-to-eat cereal demand continuing to grow, new-product development is focused on the cold cereal side of the market.[2]

Defining Narrow Relevant Market Boundaries

Middle managers are more likely to define the relevant market in terms of a product form rather than a product class. This focus is most likely to be

[2] Fara Warner, "Oatmeal Blues," *Adweek's Marketing Week,* June 24, 1991, pp. 18–19.

appropriate to the extent that the planning focus is on short-run decisions and in the following situations:

■ Brand or company competition is far more significant than competition among forms and classes.
■ Major environmental changes are not anticipated or are not expected to lead to major changes in alternative forms or in usage situations. (Although it is often dangerous to assume a no-change situation, the assumption may be reasonable in the short run.)
■ The product form or the product class is used for a unique set of usage situations so that there are no easily substitutable products.

In the automotive industry, for example, product-form competition (compact versus subcompact versus luxury) exists as does product-class competition (public transportation versus motorcycles versus recreational vehicles versus automobiles). However, the environmental changes influencing product-form choice are usually gradual, and the cost and time involved in responding to major product changes are extensive. For middle managers, then, the primary focus is usually on developing marketing strategies and programs for individual brands and models at the product-form level. On the other hand, top management will be more concerned with long-range strategies reflecting the product mix growth potential of various product forms and of the automobile product class.

The major steps involved in selecting a relevant market and the consequences of the choice of broad or narrow boundaries are portrayed in Figure 3-2. As suggested in this figure, managers who are concerned with narrow relevant market boundaries will be focusing their attention on brand or

FIGURE 3-2
Elements and implications of the process of defining the relevant market.

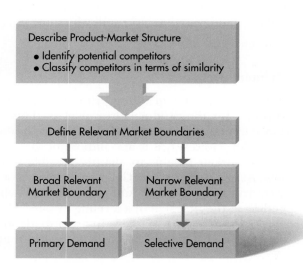

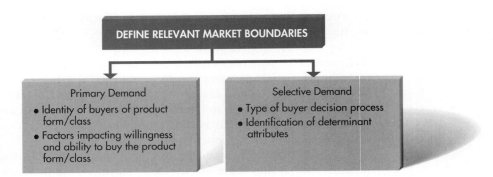

FIGURE 3-3
Analyzing primary and selective demand.

supplier choice, otherwise known as *selective* demand. On the other hand, when management sets broad relevant market boundaries, their primary next concern is the analysis of *primary* demand. Figure 3-3 identifies some of the issues in analyzing these two forms of demand.

ANALYZING PRIMARY DEMAND

By defining the relevant market, a manager will have identified the set of relevant competing products and services within which the buying process should be analyzed.

Primary demand is the demand for the product form or product class that has been defined as the relevant market. By analyzing primary demand, managers can learn why and how customers buy a product form or class and who the buyers are in the relevant market. For example, if we define the relevant market as herbal teas, the analysis of primary demand should reveal who buys herbal teas (and who does not), and why some people buy and some do not.

Key Elements in Analyzing Primary Demand

The most important reason for analyzing primary demand is to identify the growth opportunities for the product form or class. This information is of special importance to managers of new product forms (in the initial stages of the product life cycle). However, it is also important that managers of products in low-growth markets be able to identify possible ways of boosting or revitalizing sales. As we suggested in Chapter 2, there is a danger that the product life cycle will become a self-fulfilling prophecy when firms reduce marketing spending at the first sign of a leveling of sales. In fact, new growth opportunities may exist in mature markets. In order to identify growth opportunities and the actions that should be taken to realize these opportunities, managers should attempt to answer a series of diagnostic questions about the buying process. These questions fall into two categories:

■ Buyer-identification questions
■ Willingness-to-buy and ability-to-buy questions

Buyer Identification

By identifying the existing buyers of a product form or class, managers can obtain insights about the potential growth opportunities in a market and about appropriate means of communicating to the market. Specifically, by identifying the current buyers, managers can learn which types of buyers are likely to have a need for the product form or class. To the extent that these buyers can be described in terms of age, location, and similar characteristics, managers can also project changes in primary demand based on population trends for different groups. Additionally, by identifying the heavier users in a product category, managers can select communications media that are efficient in reaching buyers or can identify individuals the sales force should call on. Table 3-1 lists the major diagnostic questions that might be used in buyer identification.

BUYER OR USER CHARACTERISTICS

The characteristics of customers provide managers with a variety of insights into what communication programs are appropriate. In particular, three kinds of characteristics are useful for describing buyers of a product form or class: location, demographics, and lifestyle.

1. *Location.* Rates of purchase of various product forms may be influenced by climate, population density, cultural traditions, and other factors that vary according to region or urban-suburban-rural distinctions. For example,

TABLE 3-1	DIAGNOSTIC QUESTIONS ON BUYER IDENTIFICATION

1. CHARACTERISTICS OF BUYERS OR USERS

Can buyers of this product category be classified by location, demographics, or lifestyle and psychographics? If so, how?

2. THE BUYING CENTER

Who is involved in the buying process (reference groups; colleagues; family members)?

3. CUSTOMER TURNOVER

Is there a high degree of customer turnover due to mobility or because purchase is tied to age or other demographic factors? If so, why?

weather conditions result in a greater demand for ski equipment in New England and in other Northern and Western states. Accordingly, it may be appropriate for manufacturers of ski equipment to spend a greater share of the advertising budget and to have more retail outlets in those regions.

2. *Demographics.* Age, sex, education, occupation, and family size are among the characteristics that may typify buyers of a product form. Demographics are useful because most advertising media measure these characteristics in describing their audiences and make this information available to prospective advertisers. Consequently, if we know that the majority of buyers are aged 25 to 44, media can be selected to reach these customers efficiently. Similarly, knowing the characteristics of buyers is considered important by many industrial and retail store managers. These managers often believe that buyers will more likely buy from someone who is viewed as similar in age, education, or other demographic traits. Accordingly, they may assign salespeople to accounts partly on the basis of similarity with the buyer.

3. *Lifestyle.* Measures of lifestyle (also called *psychographics* by some marketers) attempt to reflect the way in which products fit into a consumer's normal pattern of living by examining how people spend their time, what things are important to them, and what opinions they have about themselves and the world around them.

In effect, lifestyle measures primarily reflect the influence of social forces on consumption processes. To the extent that lifestyles are related to product-purchase behavior, they may provide clues about why people do or do not use a product regularly. Additionally, the media and advertising setting will be most effective in reaching buyers if it is at least somewhat consistent with customer lifestyles.

One potential problem in relying on buyer characteristics, however, is that this method relies on the past. For example, banks often target men and multiperson households with incomes of $75,000 or more in selling financial services because these kinds of customers have historically dominated demand. But the increasing number of single women in the professions and in management represents a largely ignored market of substantial size.[3]

THE BUYING CENTER

The buying center for a product consists of all the individuals who are involved in the buying decision. In fact, the actual buyer is frequently not the user of a product or service. Accordingly, managers should identify all the individuals who may be involved in the buying process and understand the kind of influence exerted by each one. In the case of some nutritional cereals, for example, advertisements have been directed at parents as well as children, since both are involved in the decision-making process in many homes. Sim-

[3] Laura Zinn, Heather Keets, and James Treece, "Home Alone—With $660 Billion," *Business Week*, July 29, 1991, pp. 76–77.

ilarly, a manufacturer of sophisticated medical diagnostic equipment found that the sales force was paying too much attention to the purchasing agent and not enough to the chief of surgery, the pathologist, the head nurse, and others with an interest in the product and an influence on the purchase decision.

CUSTOMER TURNOVER

This term refers to the rate at which an organization must replace all or a substantial part of the individuals in its market because of a change in some aspect of the buyer's characteristics. For example, the high rate of geographic mobility in the United States means that a large proportion of the customers of local retail institutions (such as banks) will be newcomers. In other cases, age may be a key factor in customer turnover. For example, buyers of disposable diapers are usually in the market for only a short time. In these situations, managers should recognize that a large part of the marketing effort must be directed toward continually identifying and reaching first-time users or patrons. And since these targets will be less knowledgeable about the product, different marketing strategies and programs must often be designed for them.

A number of major ski resorts such as Vail in Colorado and Waterville Valley in New Hampshire have recognized that as skiers get older, they often decrease their skiing activity. Specifically, skiers in their late twenties and thirties are often parents and have less money for ski vacations, and older skiers often drop out altogether for safety reasons. Accordingly, such resorts have begun to revise their advertising and promotional programs, targeting an increasing proportion of their messages to these demographic groups.

As this example demonstrates, the potential market for a product form is often larger than the current level of demand when some potential customers do not buy the product or service or do not buy as frequently as they might. But knowing that a market can be expanded because other potential users exist is not sufficient—even if managers can identify such prospects. In addition, managers must understand the factors influencing the willingness and ability to buy the product form or class.

Willingness and Ability to Buy

Customers cannot be created for a company unless potential buyers are first willing and able to purchase the product form or class. To the extent that managers can identify ways of improving the willingness and ability to buy, primary demand can be increased either because potential buyers become actual buyers or because actual buyers increase their rate of use. Table 3-2 lists the major diagnostic questions that might be used to answer these questions.

WILLINGNESS TO BUY

The main determinant of the willingness to buy a product form or class is the buyer's perception of a product's utility for one or more usage situations. A manager's analysis of the product market structure should identify the usage

TABLE 3-2	DIAGNOSTIC QUESTIONS ON WILLINGNESS AND ABILITY TO BUY

1. WILLINGNESS TO BUY

Would new or improved related products and services increase utilization?
What usage problems exist or are perceived to exist?
Is the product or service compatible with the values and experiences of the buyer?
What types of perceived risks are significant in the purchase of the product form?

2. ABILITY TO BUY

To what extent do purchase prices and other acquisition or maintenance costs inhibit purchase?
Are product size or packaging factors creating space problems for customers?
Is the product available at a time and place that meets customer needs?

situations to which a product form is potentially applicable. However, in order to determine why some potential buyers do not use the product for one or more of these purposes, several specific questions should be raised.

1. *Related products and services.* Usage may be limited because the related products and services that are essential to satisfactory usage are inadequate. Manufacturers of personal computers have found that the lack of programs for applications that are not job-related serves as a barrier to sales growth for in-home computers. In contrast, the market for videocassette recorders was expanded when consumers became able to rent cassettes of a variety of movies rather than having to buy them. Similarly, managers involved in marketing fitness centers are recognizing that related services are important in luring older clients. For example, *NutraSweet Co.* is opening a series of WellBridge Fitness Centers to serve the over-50 market. This market actually needs fitness training more than the young people typically targeted by health clubs. However, WellBridge centers not only focus on exercise programs designed specifically for this group, they also offer nutritional counseling.[4]

2. *Usage problems.* Some products are not perceived as performing equally well under all circumstances. It is important to identify situations in which problems occur and to determine whether the problems lie in the product features or in the user's lack of knowledge about how to use the product correctly. In the first case, new product features may have to be designed; in the second, customer training or technical assistance is necessary to overcome perceived deficiencies. To a large extent, the growth of microwave ovens was due to the efforts of manufacturers and retailers to educate consumers about the correct use of the product so that they could avoid overcooking or undercooking various foods.

[4] Michael Gougis, "NutraSweet Targets Aging Boomers for New Clubs," *Marketing News*, Oct. 14, 1991, p. 15

3. *Value or experience compatibility.* When a new product requires a change in buying or using behavior that conflicts with customers' prior usage experiences or with broader value systems, the rate of adoption will be slower. To overcome this source of resistance, managers should design communications that stress not only the advantages of the product but also the advantages of the change in values or usage experiences that go with the product. For example, although earlier low-calorie beers were market failures, Miller's Lite was extremely successful even though it had essentially the same features. In large part, this success reflected the company's foresight in associating a low-calorie count with the positive advantage of being *less filling* to appeal to the heavy beer drinker. Values are also tied to cultures, so primary demand for some products can vary dramatically across cultures.

The Japanese penchant for saving is legendary and one byproduct of this attitude is a tremendous demand for life insurance. Per capita life insurance premiums in Japan are now in excess of $1,000 per year and growing. By contrast, per capita premiums in France are less than $300 and in Greece and Spain less than $100. While insurance demand is dependent on income, the primary source of these differences is culture.[5]

4. *Perceived risk.* The willingness to buy a product form or product class will also depend on the types of risks perceived by potential buyers. Perceived risks will exist when buyers believe there is a strong likelihood of making a poor decision and that the consequences of a poor decision are significant. Specifically, there are six types of risk that may exist when purchasing a product form or class.

   a. Economic or financial risks—if the purchase price, maintenance costs, or operating costs are high
   b. Time or convenience risks—if there is the potential for using up a large amount of time in purchasing or using a product
   c. Performance risks—if there is concern about how well the product performs its basic function
   d. Physical risks—if there is a threat to the health or appearance of the buyer
   e. Social risks—if the purchase or use of the product may affect the attitudes of reference groups toward the buyer
   f. Psychological risks—if the purchase or use of the product may influence the buyer's self-image or self-esteem

   By knowing the types of risk perceived by buyers, managers will be able to design marketing programs to reduce these risks and thus enhance the willingness to buy. For example, bottled-water suppliers offer home deliv-

---

[5] Resa King, Larry Armstrong, Steven J. Dryden, and Jonathan Kapstein, "Who's That Knocking on Foreign Doors? U.S. Insurance Salesmen," *Business Week*, Mar. 6, 1989, pp. 84–85.

ery to reduce the convenience risk that a consumer may not want to bring home large, heavy jugs of water. Similarly, some firms offer special trial sizes or money-back guarantees to reduce economic risks. Social risks may be reduced if products or services are advertised in a way that emphasizes that they are socially acceptable.

ABILITY TO BUY

The ability to buy a product may be limited by a number of factors, many of which are not under the direct control of managers.

1. *Cost factors*. If a product is a discretionary item, or if less expensive product-form alternatives exist, the price and/or associated buyer costs (operating cost, credit cost, installation cost, maintenance cost) are likely to inhibit primary demand. For example, the demand for solar collectors to heat homes has been limited by the large initial investment required of a homeowner even though solar energy is often very price-competitive viewed in the long run. Similarly, high interest rates on home mortgage loans and automobile loans were partly responsible for declines in new home and automotive sales during the late 1970s and early 1980s.

2. *Packaging and size factors*. Product-form sales may be limited by virtue of space and size requirements. Some potential buyers of home computers, big screen televisions, and similar products simply have a space problem in accommodating these items. Similarly, space limitations may inhibit the purchase of a product in large volumes.

3. *Spatial availability*. The cost of acquiring a product may be a function of locational factors. For example, people in very rural communities have less access to health care and, consequently, visit physicians less frequently. Similarly, the rate of purchase of low-value, postponable purchases can be enhanced by improved access. Consider, for example, the impact on soft-drink sales if vending machines were not available.

Although our discussion of the willingness and ability to buy has focused on the implications for assessing opportunities for building primary demand, these forces can often be important in analyzing selective demand as well. Certainly a firm that gains an advantage on cost or location or that does a better job of reducing perceived risk or offering related services will enhance its ability to acquire customers. Indeed, by developing a thorough analysis of primary demand, managers will usually be in a better position to understand the processes determining brand or supplier choice.

ANALYZING SELECTIVE DEMAND

While primary demand is the demand for a product form or class (such as tea, herbal tea, or instant tea), selective demand is the demand for a specific brand or supplier within the relevant market. So if instant tea is chosen as the relevant market, selective demand is the demand for Lipton Instant Tea or Nestea Instant Tea or any other individual brand.

In analyzing selective demand, managers are primarily interested in understanding how buyers make choices from the alternative brands or suppliers within the relevant market. However, not all buyers are alike in their choices. Rather, choice is a function of buyers' needs (desired benefits) and buyers' perceptions of alternatives in the context of the specific usage situation.

In this section we present an approach for examining selective demand. The first step in this approach is to identify the type of decision-making process likely to be used. The second step is to identify the determinant attributes. Table 3-3 summarizes the diagnostic questions used in analyzing selective demand.

Identifying the Types of Decision Processes

Buying decisions are typically categorized in terms of three types: (1) extensive problem solving, (2) limited problem solving, (3) routinized response behavior.[6]

Extensive problem solving occurs when buyers have no prior experience (or at least no recent prior experience) in purchasing a product or service and when the product or service carries a high degree of perceived risk. Because of these conditions, such buying decisions involve extensive information search and deliberation. Buyers must develop an understanding of what the alternatives are and what the important considerations in making a choice should be. The purchase of a house by a consumer or a corporate jet by an organization involves extensive problem solving.

Limited problem solving characterizes situations in which the buyer has a generally sound knowledge of the product category and is familiar with the important considerations in making a choice, but still takes time to compare

---

[6] See William Wilkie, *Consumer Behavior,* 2nd ed., Wiley, New York, 1990, chap. 18, for a detailed treatment of the topics in this section.

TABLE 3-3   **DIAGNOSTIC QUESTIONS ON SELECTIVE DEMAND**

1. DECISION PROCESSES

How extensive is the search for information?
Do buyers use personal or impersonal sources of information?
Do buyers seek information about brand or supplier characteristics?

2. DETERMINANT ATTRIBUTES

What are the benefits buyers hope to obtain from usage or ownership of the product?
What product attributes (characteristics) are viewed as providing these benefits?
What is the relative importance of the various benefits desired?
How much variation is perceived among the alternatives on each of the important attributes?

and evaluate alternatives. This form of problem solving usually occurs for products with which the buyer has some experience but where the alternatives may change over time or where buyers change their preferences for different attributes. For example, the set of alternatives may change owing to the market introduction of new brands of suppliers, modifications to existing products, or price changes. Preferences may change because of changes in buyers' financial circumstances, changes in product usage, or simply because the buyer is seeking variety. Thus, a buyer may purchase different wines or shirts on different purchase occasions because of changes on the supply side of the market and/or because of changes in the buyer's needs.

Finally, *routinized response behavior* occurs when the decision deals with frequently purchased items. In such cases, buyers have experience with the brands in the product category and perceive no need to search among the alternatives. In some cases of routinized behavior, strong brand loyalty exists so brand choice decisions are reached almost immediately.

Traditionally, these three types of decision processes have been used to describe decisions made by consumers. For organizational buyers, a parallel set of processes (see Figure 3-4) can be identified. The *new task* is a situation in which extensive problem solving will occur because the product is being purchased for the first time. The *modified rebuy* is the term used for limited problem solving in organizational purchases. *Straight rebuys* are essentially routinized response behaviors in that little active search will take place (although for many products in the straight rebuy category, some buyers divide their orders among two or more established suppliers).

There are two reasons why the distinction among types of decision processes is important. First, an understanding of the type of decision process involved in the purchase of a product enables managers to understand buyer search behavior. The more extensive the problem solving required, the greater the amount of search and the more likely customers will be to rely on personal sources of information (including family members, friends, and salespeople). At the other extreme, routinized decision making leads to lim-

FIGURE 3-4
Types of decision processes.

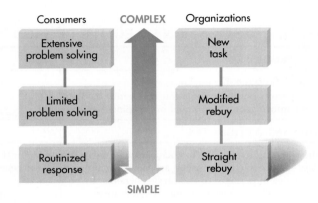

ited (even perhaps zero) search, with impersonal sources of information likely to play a stronger role than personal sources.

Second, the kind of information required by buyers will vary according to the type of decision process. In routinized decision making, additional information may not even be needed: Buyers may simply respond to those brands or suppliers that have the greatest levels of buyer awareness. In limited problem solving, the key information sought is that which relates to brand or supplier characteristics (attributes). In extensive problem solving, it is necessary not only to acquire information on brand or supplier characteristics but to learn what the important considerations should be in making a choice. Stated differently, in extensive problem solving, buyers must learn the determinant attributes.

Identifying Determinant Attributes

A basic assumption of choice behavior is that buyers will choose the brand or supplier that best fits the buyer's needs. However, because needs represent internal drives and motives, they are difficult to observe and measure. Instead of needs and drives, therefore, marketers use the concept of *benefits sought*. The functional and psychological benefits that buyers hope to receive are generally considered to reflect these underlying needs. Frequently, marketers use the term *attributes* interchangeably with benefits. Attributes represent the specific features or physical characteristics that are designed into a good or service. Benefits are the results the customer receives from using or owning the product. For example, the size and gasoline mileage rating of an automobile are attributes that buyers can use to evaluate the *economy of operation* benefit.

Managers should be aware that, often, the attributes governing choice are not attributes of the physical product but, rather, are those of the broader offering. For example, quick, reliable delivery of raw materials is a critically important attribute to many industrial firms. Convenience is generally the most important factor in determining where people have their checking accounts.

Additionally, the attributes governing choice may change as technology makes new attribute combinations feasible. Consider, for example, the success of Lever 2000.

Lever 2000 captured 8.4% of the United States bar soap market within 6 months of introduction. The critical factor in consumer acceptance was a patented process that allowed Lever to combine moisturizing and deodorizing properties. Previously, consumers were forced to choose between moisturizing bars (such as Dove) which don't deodorize or deodorants (such as Dial) that left skin dry.[7]

[7] Christopher Power, "Everyone Is Bellying Up to This Bar," *Business Week*, Jan. 27, 1992, p. 84.

Frequently, several products are similar in a large number of attributes. In such cases, it is important to distinguish one or more of the determinant attributes—that is, attributes that are most likely to determine the buyer's choice.[8] The preferred supplier or brand will generally be the one that enjoys the buyer's best overall rating on the determinant attributes. Two dimensions help make an attribute a determinant attribute: importance and uniqueness. An attribute will be considered important if it provides desirable benefits; however, if all competing alternatives have the same feature, then that attribute will not determine brand choice.

To gain a better understanding of the determinant attribute concept, consider Figure 3-5. Basically, a buyer could evaluate any individual attribute as falling into one of the four categories portrayed in this figure. For example, someone considering alternative brands of lawn mowers would probably consider "easy to start" important. But if most or all competing mowers are equally easy to start, then this becomes a *defensive* attribute—something that is necessary to avoid being eliminated from consideration but not something that will cause people to choose a product. On the other hand, some attributes may make a product different but are not (currently) considered to be very important. Such attributes are "bells and whistles" or *optional* attributes (such as a lawn mower steering wheel that can be tilted at different angles). Of course, optional attributes have the potential to become determinant attributes if they become important. In states with restrictions on the dumping of grass clippings, the first lawn mowers with mulching blades held a temporary competitive advantage because this attribute moved from optional to determinant. Once many competitors offered the mulching blade, this attribute moved from determinant to defensive.

It is especially necessary to consider both dimensions of attribute determinance in the process of new-product development, as the following example demonstrates.

[8] The concept of determinant attributes was first introduced in James H. Myers and Mark Alpert, "Determinant Buying Attitudes: Meaning and Measurement," *Journal of Marketing*, October 1968, pp. 13–20.

FIGURE 3-5
A framework for assessing if an attribute is determinant.

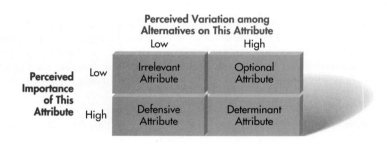

Procter & Gamble developed a scallop-shaped soap called Monchel with a special fragrance and package to complement its unusual shape. When consumers used the product in blind tests (where the brand was not identified) they indicated a preference for it over other brands. But when the product went to market it flopped. P&G found that they had created a product that was distinctive, but on dimensions that were essentially unimportant to consumers; the product failed to perform better on the attributes that really counted. So when the time came for consumers to spend money, the novelty effects wore off.[9]

The most difficult problem marketers have in assessing determinant attributes is that not everyone is alike. Indeed, in most product categories, a broad array of brands of suppliers offering different benefit combinations is available. The ability of all these alternatives to exist is testimony that different attributes are determinant for different buyers. In effect, the relevant market is segmented.

DEFINING MARKET SEGMENTS

The answers to the diagnostic questions relating to primary and selective demand usually reveal that not all buyers or potential buyers are alike. In terms of primary demand, we know that some potential customers buy heavily in a product category while others (lacking either the ability or willingness to buy) do not currently purchase the product form or class. Similarly, that most product categories consist of a variety of brands or suppliers offering differing attributes indicates variation among buyers in terms of selective demand.

Market segmentation is the process of identifying groups of customers with highly similar buying needs and motives within the relevant market. Since these groups (or segments) are similar, managers may elect to refine the firm's market offerings to meet the needs of one or more target segments more precisely. This refinement should result in enhanced customer satisfaction. More specifically, in analyzing *primary* demand, market segmentation can allow managers to target the marketing effort toward heavy users or to develop new product offerings to be targeted toward segments lacking the ability or willingness to buy. In analyzing *selective* demand, market segmentation can enable managers to design different products, delivery systems, or promotional appeals targeted toward groups using different choice criteria.

There are, however, practical limits to the usefulness of market segmentation. The more products a firm produces and the more promotional campaigns used, the greater the firm's costs. Additionally, firms may find some segments more attractive than others because of variations in segment size, growth potential, or competition.

[9] Zachary Schiller, "Ready, Aim, Market: Combat Training at P&G College," *Business Week*, Feb. 3, 1992, p. 56.

In the remainder of this section, we offer a framework for helping managers identify those market segments that might serve as potential target markets. This framework has two components:

■ Selecting the basis for forming segments
■ Describing segment membership and behavior

Bases for Segmenting Markets

Because buyers and potential buyers can differ on virtually any of the diagnostic questions discussed earlier in this chapter, the range of possible ways of segmenting the market is broad. However, most of the time the purpose of segmentation is either: (1) to determine the best attributes and benefits to offer (and promote) to each segment, or (2) to allocate marketing resources (especially advertising and promotional expenditures). In the first case, the most useful bases for segmenting markets will be those that are related most directly to buyers' choice criteria. In the second case, emphasis is given to segmentation bases that are related to primary demand.

PRIMARY DEMAND SEGMENTATION

As noted above, the analysis of primary demand segments is generally geared to isolating segments with different rates of demand for a product form or class. As discussed in the section on buyer identification, buyer characteristics can help predict categories. Thus, segmentation on buyer characteristics can be an effective way to identify the segments that should receive the highest allocations of promotional spending.

If management's segmentation goal is to target low-volume or nonbuying segments in the market, then buyer characteristics can be helpful, but only if the lack of ability to buy or the lack of willingness to buy is derived from motives that are highly correlated with these characteristics. For example, the low rate of sales of bicycles to older adults reflects factors that are correlated with old age: Older adults face more serious consequences of injuries caused by falling down, and they have a lower degree of acceptance of uncomfortable seats. The task, then, is to find a solution to the nonbuyer's underlying problem.

For years, large banks marketed their "private banking" concept to people in their 60s who had inherited wealth, usually were not working full time, and lacked either an interest or expertise in money management. This product (which involves highly personalized, one-stop shopping for all financial needs including access to hefty loans and professional investment management) is now being targeted toward new potential buyers. One such group is corporate officers in small or mid-sized firms. Banks such as Bank of Boston and Chemical Bank now try to get busy corporate clients to consider doing their personal financial business with the same bank. Such individuals are appealed to on the basis that they are extremely busy and lack the time to effectively manage their own money.[10]

The private banking example shows that buyers who differ demographically can have different motives for buying the same product form. Private banking eliminates the performance risk of financial self-management for one target market and the time risk for the second target market. Thus, by learning how answers to the diagnostic questions differ across segments, it is often possible to build primary demand though reaching new target markets.

SELECTIVE DEMAND SEGMENTATION

We can usually anticipate that there will be differences across buyers in the attributes that are used to make choices among brand or supplier alternatives. Because of the direct link between determinant attributes and choice, managers concerned with selective demand generally attempt to segment the market on the basis of the attributes (or benefits) sought. Thus, to return to our private banking example, managers at Bank of Boston would want to know how potential customers make choices among the different private banking plans available. Are some motivated by service charges, others by the qualifications of the banker they worked with, and others by the availability of tax assistance? Generally, such information must be gathered by surveys of potential customers within a firm's market. While collecting it is often time consuming and costly, this may be the most useful set of marketing data a firm can have.

It is also important to remember that differences in benefits or attributes desired are often caused by differences in the product usage situation.[11] As we suggested earlier, most products can be used in a variety of situations. (Orange juice may be drunk with breakfast or after exercise, or it may be mixed in a cocktail. A large computer may be used to perform research, to control a production process, or to process an organization's payroll records.) Accordingly, alternative brands or suppliers within a relevant market may be used in different situations, and as the situation differs, the specific needs (benefits) that buyers hope to satisfy from buying or using a product may also differ.

Of course, differences in benefits or usage may be closely associated with differences in other buying-process variables (such as demographics or lifestyle). While it will be useful for managers to know that such relationships exist (for communications purposes), it is often dangerous to infer buying motives from demographics. Buyer characteristics may be useful for predict-

---

[10] Peter Pae, "Private Bankers Court Merely Affluent," *The Wall Street Journal*, May 12, 1992, pp. B1, B7.
[11] Peter Dickson, "Person-Situation: Segmentation's Missing Link," *Journal of Marketing*, Fall 1982, pp. 56–64.

ing who will purchase a product form or product class but are generally much less useful in predicting brand choice.

An exception to this principle must be noted, however. Often, product benefits are difficult for a consumer to evaluate objectively—at least prior to purchase. (Consider toothpastes and perfumes for examples.) In such cases, marketers often promote a product by characterizing the kind of person who would desire that stated benefit. To the extent the characterization is successful, a strong correlation between a benefit and a demographic group may develop (such as mothers of children being concerned about tooth decay).

Additionally, for some homogenous demographic groups, an attribute that is optional for most buyers may become determinant for that group. For example:

> Ariel is a famous Procter & Gamble detergent brand in Latin America and has been brought into Southern California from Mexico for years. Recognizing the familiarity and popularity of this brand among West Coast Hispanics, P&G decided to create Ariel Ultra, a super concentrated version (with bilingual packaging) specifically for the Hispanic community.[12]

Describing Segment Membership and Behavior

By defining market segments in terms of buyers' ideal combinations of determinant attributes, managers can isolate the key choice criteria used in different segments in order to design market offerings. However, managers are also interested in knowing what potential sales opportunities are presented by each segment and how the members in each segment can best be targeted in attempting to influence their choice. Table 3-4 lists some of the types of questions managers should try to answer in assessing sales opportunities and targeting options.

POTENTIAL SALES OPPORTUNITIES

Not every segment of the market will present the same potential sales opportunity and, because organizations operate with limited resources, the relative importance of different segments should be considered in determining how resources will be allocated. For example, managers in industrial firms must determine how to allocate the time and effort of the sales force to different segments and among specific accounts within each segment. Similarly, decisions regarding whether to design specific features or special advertising programs for a given segment should only be made after the sales opportunity is known.

For example, many banks have directed special efforts toward "upscale" customers who are able to maintain large account balances and who use a variety of bank services. These special efforts have included new products

---

[12] Dan Koeppel, "P&G Tests Foreign Brands in L.A.," *Adweek's Marketing Week*, June 24, 1991, p. 4.

TABLE 3-4	DIAGNOSTIC QUESTIONS FOR DESCRIBING SEGMENTS

1. ASSESSING POTENTIAL SALES OPPORTUNITIES

How many buyers are there in each segment?
How frequently does the usage situation occur?
In the case of durable goods, how frequently is the product replaced?
In what volumes or quantities do segment members buy?
What is the potential for selling related products and services to these customers?

2. TARGETING SEGMENT MEMBERS

What are their demographic/lifestyle characteristics?
Who are the key decision makers in the family or organization?
What media are they exposed to?
Where do they shop?

(such as special checking-type accounts that earn high rates of interest if large minimum deposit levels are maintained) and special services (such as "personal bankers"—individual bank personnel who are assigned to work on all the needs of selected high-balance customers). Similarly, most industrial firms offer quantity discounts to large-volume buyers, and many have established *national account* programs in which selected personnel are assigned to provide special technical assistance and/or service to all offices or facilities of large customers who operate in a variety of locations.

TARGETING SEGMENT MEMBERS

In order to make the most effective use of the segmentation concept, it is useful to determine if segments differ in terms of the identity of the buyers and/or in terms of the search processes they use. If, in fact, the members of a segment are similar in terms of characteristics or search processes, managers can use this information in several ways:

- To select appropriate advertising media
- To identify the individuals to be called on by the sales force
- To develop special methods for presenting a sales message
- To determine the types of retail outlets through which to sell

Specifically, managers should attempt to identify similarities among the members of each segment by answering the questions listed in Table 3-4. In considering this information, managers must recognize that the purpose is to examine similarities within benefit or attribute segments. That is, demographics may well give clues to the buyer's determinant attributes, but seldom do all individuals with a given set of demographic characteristics have the same determinant attributes.

For example, if we were to find that the low-caffeine segment of the cola market is heavily composed of adults over 50 years of age, this is useful in deciding how to select media for marketing a low-caffeine cola. But this information does not mean that all (or even most) adults over 50 years of age prefer caffeine-free colas. There may be other segments of the cola market that actually have more buyers in the over-50 age group. The key point is that within a relevant market, demographics are generally more useful for *describing* a benefit segment than for *defining* a target market segment because specific benefits sought usually vary among people with similar traits.

IDENTIFYING POTENTIAL TARGET MARKETS

The process of market analysis is the first step in designing a marketing strategy for a product or a line of related products. Specifically, a market analysis enables managers to identify potential target markets toward which the marketing effort might be focused.

Note that a target market could consist of either: (1) the total market for a product form or product class, or (2) one or more market segments *within* a product form or product class market.

If the market analysis indicates there is an opportunity to substantially increase the willingness or ability to purchase a product form or class, then a firm could consider the total product-class or product-form market as a potential target market. If the market analysis indicates there are one or more market segments where the firm could offer the benefits desired and could effectively target the members of such segments, these segments would constitute potential target markets.

The diagnostic questions presented in this chapter enable managers to acquire the kinds of information needed to assess the needs of any target market or target segment. However, not all potential market needs can be profitably met by every competitor. The success of a marketing strategy ultimately depends not just on its ability to meet a need revealed by market analysis but also on other factors that influence the market opportunity and the ability to meet the requirements for success in that target market.

Figure 3-6 portrays the relationship between market analysis and the other sources and types of information that will influence the final selection of a target market and marketing strategy. As this figure suggests, managers must also consider the other elements of the situation analyses in order to obtain answers to questions like these:

- What are competitors' capabilities, and how do consumers evaluate our offerings versus those of competitors?
- What is the size of and what are the growth prospects for this market?
- What costs are involved in meeting market needs and in targeting our offer, and are these reasonable relative to the expected sales payoff?

Answers to these questions can be obtained from the analyses discussed in Chapters 4, 5, and 6. Additionally, as we discussed in the preceding chapter,

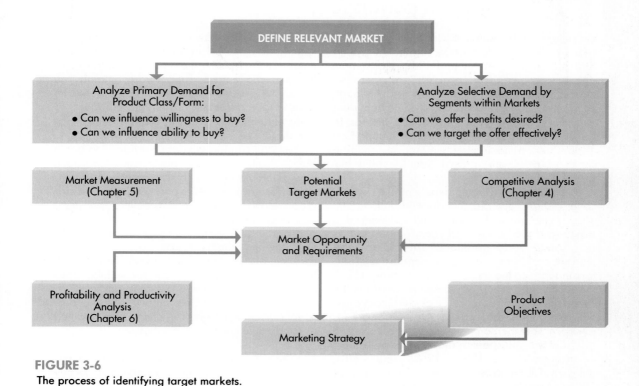

FIGURE 3-6
The process of identifying target markets.

the final decision on a marketing strategy will also be consistent with the product objective.

CONCLUSION

If an organization is to achieve customer satisfaction, it must first and foremost understand its market. In this chapter we have presented an approach for analyzing markets that is useful for managers concerned with long-term corporate planning and for those concerned with short-term marketing strategies. Specifically, we examined the process of defining the relevant market—the primary competitive arena of concern to a manager. Subsequently, we presented diagnostic questions and concepts that managers can employ to analyze primary and selective demand within the relevant market and to define market segments. Finally, we discussed how the information from these various analyses could be used to identify potential target markets and to define the kinds of market offerings needed to achieve customer satisfaction in these target markets.

Each of these steps is important to the selection of a marketing strategy. However, market analyses should not only be performed when entering a new

TUPPERWARE: CONFRONTING CHANGING DEMAND CONDITIONS*

As refrigerators replaced iceboxes as the primary method of cold food storage in the United States during the 1920s and 1930s, consumers encountered a new problem—refrigeration caused food to wilt and lose its flavor. Although paper packaging and wrapping could help deal with this problem, paper could leak or tear. In the 1940s, a Massachusetts inventor named Earl Tupper began making lightweight, unbreakable plastic bowls with airtight lids to solve this problem.

Although the product was unique, housewives did not immediately adopt this innovation. They were wary of plastic (still considered a mysterious substance) and saw Tupperware as an expensive, nontraditional solution to food storage problems. Finally, Tupperware distributors thought up the device of home parties to sell the product. A group of women gathered in the home of a friend for lunch or dessert, conversation and games, and a demonstration by a Tupperware salesperson. The hostess received a gift, and the salesperson made some sales.

Throughout the 1950s, 1960s, and 1970s, sales of Tupperware (by then a subsidiary of Dart Industries) grew rapidly—fast enough to entice Rubbermaid to enter the market using the same basic sales approach. But by 1980 there was a noticeable decline in married couples with children, there were fewer children per family, and labor-force participation by women with children was growing rapidly. Although working women have more money to spend, they have less time for parties and are often less concerned about storing leftovers.

Recognizing the significance of this trend, Rubbermaid dropped the home party approach in favor of distribution through grocery stores. Additionally, a number of smaller rivals entered the market, selling low-quality, low-priced bowls through drugstores and other retail outlets. By 1992, Tupperware's unit market share had declined from 60 percent to about 40 to 45 percent while Rubbermaid's share had risen to an estimated 30 to 40 percent. Rubbermaid had been very innovative during this period. For ex-

ample, in 1983 they designed a seven-piece space-saving set of bowls designed for use in microwave ovens. In the meantime, other competitors challenged Tupperware, mainly on price. As industry observers have noted, it doesn't take a tremendous amount of quality to keep leftover peas fresh in the refrigerator for five days.

By 1992, Tupperware was preparing to battle back. Insisting that the party sales approach would remain central to its strategy, the company was nevertheless experimenting with a catalog selling approach. Moreover, the party approach had been expanded to include office and parking lot locations to better serve working women. Finally, Tupperware unveiled its own line of "TupperWave" microwavable plastic that is stackable to allow for simultaneous cooking of three dishes. The company also offers a microwave recipe service plus the personal advice of its sales force that is now trained in microwave cooking techniques.

1. Which diagnostic questions on buyer identification and on willingness and ability to buy are useful in analyzing primary demand in this market?
2. Describe the decision process that you would use in buying plastic storage bowls. Would others use a different process?
3. Which attributes are *determinant* in the purchase of plastic storage bowls? Which attributes might be characterized as *defensive* and which as *optional "bells and whistles"*?
4. What is Tupperware's current target market segment? What are some possible reasons why the company chose that target?

---

* Based on Laurie Grossman, "Going Stale: Families Have Changed but Tupperware Keeps Holding Parties," *The Wall Street Journal*, July 21, 1992, pp. 1, 4; "After the Party: Tupperware Burps Out Array of New Products," *Adweek*, Sept. 23, 1991, p. 1; "Tupperware to Explore Catalog Sales," *Crain's Chicago Business*, May 31, 1992, p. 78; Bart Greer, "New Tupperware Cookware Resembles Rubbermaid Line," *Plastic News*, Sept. 3, 1990, p. 5.

market. Rather, the diagnostic questions should be examined continuously in order to keep up with changing conditions, a situation confronted by Tupperware.

QUESTIONS AND SITUATIONS FOR DISCUSSION

1. What factors would have influenced the willingness and ability of consumers to use or buy each of the following?

- Microwave ovens
- Automatic bank tellers
- Videocassette recorders

2. Sub-Zero manufactures expensive, custom-finished refrigerators built into fancy kitchens. Sub-Zero's best-seller is a 30.5-cubic-foot side-by-side refrigerator-freezer, which costs $2000 more than the top-of-the-line unit made by Amana. Is the relevant market for Sub-Zero the same as that for Amana? How would you explain why a buyer would select either the Sub-Zero or the Amana brand?

3. The athletic director at your university has asked you to help identify ways of improving attendance at home baseball games. Discuss the diagnostic questions you would try to answer, and illustrate how the answers you might obtain would lead to the development of specific marketing strategies and programs.

4. Psychographics reveal BMW automobile owners to be (or want to be) aggressive, athletic, high-achieving types who buy high-risk stocks and graphite tennis rackets. In addition, they have fewer children than owners of Saab and Mercedes Benz cars. How would information such as this be useful to the manufacturers of BMWs and to the local BMW dealer?

5. As a rule, most firms that sell to organizational buyers would prefer to be able to segment their markets on a basis of product usage rather than on benefits. Why do you think this is the case?

6. Indicate some ways of segmenting the market for printers used with personal computers. How would these various potential target markets differ from the viewpoint of marketing strategy?

7. After purchasing European appliance-maker Philips Electronics, the Whirlpool Corporation set out to learn more about European consumers. It has always been suggested that country-by-country differences made it necessary to offer different models for each country. But Whirlpool's findings suggest that these differences do not reflect preferences. For example, most French households have narrow, top-loading washing machines because that is what French washing machine makers produced. But Whirlpool's research showed that consumers across Europe want a system that gets clothes clean, that is easy to use, that is energy efficient, and that has trouble-free service.

How does Whirlpool's research help identify the possible determinant attributes for washing machines? Which attributes would be defensive, and which would be optional? Would you expect the determinant attributes to vary across countries? Why or why not?

8. American Express introduced its Optima card as an addition to its existing line of green, gold, and platinum credit cards. Optima was designed to serve those who wanted revolving credit like that offered by VISA and MasterCard rather than to serve those who pay off their balances each month. Moreover, Optima was made available only to people holding another American Express card.

  a. Discuss the different ways in which American Express might have defined the relevant market.

  b. What are the likely reasons behind the selection of the target market for the Optima card?

SUGGESTED ADDITIONAL READINGS

Davidow, William, and Bro Uttal, "Service Companies: Focus or Falter," *Harvard Business Review*, July–August 1989, pp. 77–85.

Day, George S., Allan Shocker, and Rajendra Srivastava, "Customer-Oriented Approaches to Identifying Product Markets," *Journal of Marketing*, Fall 1979, pp. 8–19.

Dickson, Peter, "Person-Situation: Segmentation's Missing Link," *Journal of Marketing*, Fall 1982, pp. 56–64.

Green, Paul E., Abba M. Krieger, and Catherine M. Schaffer, "Quick and Simple Benefit Segmentation," *Journal of Advertising Research*, June–July 1985, pp. 9–17.

Holak, Susan, and Donald Lehman, "Purchase Intentions and the Dimensions of Innovation," *Journal of Product Innovation Management*, March 1990, pp. 59–73.

Laughlin, Jay L., Charles L. Laughlin, and Charles R. Taylor, "An Approach to Industrial Market Segmentation," *Industrial Marketing Management*, May 1991, pp. 127–136.

Morden, A. R., "Market Segmentation and Practical Policy Formulation," *Quarterly Review of Marketing*, January 1985, pp. 1–12.

Novak, Thomas P., and Bruce MacEvoy, "On Comparing Alternative Segmentation Schemes: The List of Values (LOV) and Values and Lifestyles (VALS)," *Journal of Consumer Research*, June 1990, pp. 105–109.

Segal, Madhav, "Implications of Single vs. Multiple Buying Sources," *Industrial Marketing Management*, August 1989, pp. 163–178.

Stanley, Thomas, "Targeting the Affluent Consumer," *Journal of Business Strategy*, September–October 1988, pp. 17–20.

Wells, William, "Psychographics: A Critical Review," *Journal of Marketing Research*, May 1975, pp. 196–213.

CHAPTER 4

COMPETITIVE ANALYSIS

OVERVIEW

In Chapter 3 we discussed the forces that influence primary and selective demand and presented a five-step approach for analyzing a market. The final step in that approach was the identification of potential target markets. As we suggested in that discussion, achieving success in a target market involves more than just the ability to satisfy customer needs: Consideration must also be given to the competitive situation in a market.

In this chapter we present a four-step approach for performing a competitive analysis. The steps in this approach are portrayed in Figure 4-1.

1. *Define the target market.* This step is the result of the market analysis discussed in Chapter 3. Recall that by performing this step we establish the product-market boundaries of interest and identify any specific target segments within those boundaries.
2. *Identify direct competitors.* Direct competitors are those who are most likely to take customers away from us (or to be sources of new customers) because they serve the same target market.
3. *Examine competitive market forces.* The nature and intensity of competition and the dynamics of competition are influenced by market forces.
4. *Assess competitive advantage.* Ultimately, managers must have a sense for what advantages each competitor possesses. This entails examining both the *positions of advantage* achieved (from the customer's perspective) and the skills and resources that constitute the *sources of advantage.*

DEFINING THE TARGET MARKET

As we discussed in Chapter 3, the relevant market is defined by the product-market boundaries that management considers to be strategically important. Additionally, we noted that the relevant market could be defined at various levels:

1. Competing brands (or suppliers) within a product form
2. Competing product forms within a product class
3. Competing product classes within a generic need

FIGURE 4-1
Steps in
competitive
analysis.

A target market is the relevant market or the portion of the relevant market that a firm is most interested in serving. The target market might be defined in terms of the demand for a generic need (recreation), a product class (bicycles), a specific product form (ten-speed, touring bikes), or a target customer segment for one of those markets (safety and price-oriented buyers between 21 and 40 years of age).

The determination of the target market should help management identify the current direct competitors—those perceived as presently serving the target market.

IDENTIFYING DIRECT COMPETITORS

We define direct competitors as firms who are likely to gain or lose a substantial share of customers from each other over time because they serve the same customers and offer similar benefits. A consequence of this definition is that the delineation of direct competitors should be made by customers in the target market. That is, two firms are direct competitors if customers (or potential customers) say they are.

Consider, for example, Figures 4-2 and 4-3. Figure 4-2 portrays the product-market structure of the product class cookies, indicating some of the various product forms and subforms in this category. If a firm were to identify the "moist and chewy" cookie market (which represents about 15 percent of total packaged cookie industry sales) as the target market, the five most direct competitors can be identified by management based on the technical characteristics "moist" and "chewy."

But do consumers view all these cookies as equal competitors? Because there may be a large number of brands in a category and because many

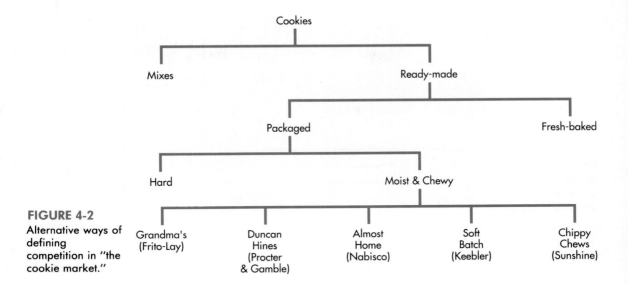

FIGURE 4-2
Alternative ways of
defining
competition in "the
cookie market."

products have highly subjective characteristics, managers usually rely on some *perceptual mapping* techniques. This class of techniques is designed to portray the way consumers perceive the various potential competitors in a market.

Perceptual Mapping Techniques

Figure 4-3 is an example of a perceptual map generated by a technique called *multidimensional scaling*. In this technique, consumers are asked to rate each pair of products in terms of their degree of similarity, using a scale such as that in Figure 4-4. These similarity judgments are then analyzed by statistical programs that determine the relative closeness of the brands from the perspective of the target market customers as a whole. Because traditional multidimensional scaling approaches map only the similarity judgments, the

FIGURE 4-3
A perceptual map
of the moist and
chewy cookie
market using
multidimensional
scaling.

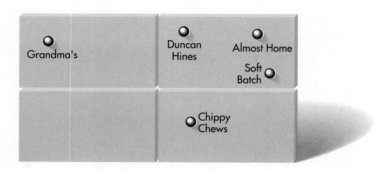

	Very Similar 1	2	3	4	Very Different 5
Grandma's/Duncan Hines	—	—	—	—	—
Grandma's/Almost Home	—	—	—	—	—
Grandma's/Soft Batch	—	—	—	—	—
Grandma's/Chippy Chews	—	—	—	—	—
Duncan Hines/Almost Home	—	—	—	—	—
•					
•					
•					
•					
Soft Batch/Chippy Chews	—	—	—	—	—

FIGURE 4-4
Measuring perceived similarity.

reasons why some pairs of brands are more similar than other pairs must be inferred. So, the axis in Figure 4-3 will normally have to be labeled based on the researcher's judgment.

A second basic approach to perceptual mapping is *factor analysis based.* Rather than using similarity judgments, buyers are asked to rate each competitor on each of the determinant attributes, using a scale such as the one in Figure 4-5. These ratings are then subjected to a statistical factor analysis that examines the correlations among the ratings. Based on this examination, the procedure usually finds that the various attributes can be reduced to a very small number of underlying "factors" (for example, economy, stays fresh in the box, appeals to the whole family, and so forth) that are used to evaluate alternatives.

FIGURE 4-5
Rating alternatives on attributes for a factor analysis.

Attribute no. 1

____________ cookies stay fresh in the package

	Strongly Agree 1	2	3	4	Strongly Disagree 5
Grandma's	—	—	—	—	—
Duncan Hines	—	—	—	—	—
Almost Home	—	—	—	—	—
Soft Batch	—	—	—	—	—
Chippy Chews	—	—	—	—	—

Attribute no. 2

You get your money's worth with ____________ cookies.

•
•
•

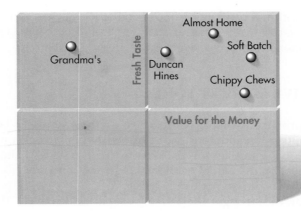

FIGURE 4-6

A perceptual map of the moist and chewy cookie market using factor analysis.

Figure 4-6 is a hypothetical perceptual map developed from a factor analysis. As we can see, the factor analysis method not only portrays which brands are closest competitors (based on their nearness to one another) but also gives some clues as to *why* some brands are close to each other and others are not. Table 4-1 summarizes some advantages and disadvantages of the two alternative methods.

Perceptual mapping techniques are readily available and can be performed on most current personal computers. Because they enable managers to obtain the consumer's perception of the market, they can be of tremendous help in understanding the competition. It is also important, however, to recognize a key assumption underlying these techniques: uniformity of perceptions. To the extent that members of the target market are familiar with all these brands or suppliers (at least through advertising), they are more likely to share similar perceptions. However, when buyers vary widely in their awareness of alterna-

TABLE 4-1

COMPARING PERCEPTUAL MAPPING TECHNIQUES

FACTOR ANALYSIS	MULTIDIMENSIONAL SCALING
INPUT	
Consumer's ratings of brands on attributes	Consumer's direct judgments of similarity
ADVANTAGES	
Can understand why brands are perceived as similar	Does not require list of benefits
DISADVANTAGES	
Requires that all benefits and attributes are known	Reasons for similarity must be inferred
Some subjective benefits are hard to measure	Maps often change if we add or delete brands from process

Source: Adapted from Glen L. Urban, John R. Hauser, and Nikhilesh Dholakia, *Essentials of New Product Management*, Prentice-Hall, Englewood Cliffs, N.J., 1987, p. 117.

tive brands within a product form or product class, their perceptions will also vary. In the latter case, separate analyses should be conducted to determine how perceptions vary across segments.

EXAMINING COMPETITIVE MARKET FORCES

While the primary focus of competitive analysis tends to be on the direct competitors, the overall intensity of competition in a market is a function of a web of underlying market forces. Harvard University's Michael Porter developed the "five forces" model (shown in Figure 4-7) to describe these underlying determinants of competitive intensity.[1]

In general, the stronger these five forces are collectively, the more intense the competition and the less the profit potential for those competing in that market. Consequently, the five forces model can be helpful in assessing market attractiveness when a manager is analyzing a product portfolio. Additionally, assessing the forces individually will enable managers to understand better the kinds of competitive advantages and strategies that will be most important over time in a market.

[1] Michael Porter, "How Competitive Forces Shape Strategy," *Harvard Business Review*, March–April 1979, pp. 137–145.

FIGURE 4-7
Forces governing competition in an industry. (Source: Michael Porter, "How Competitive Forces Shape Strategy," *Harvard Business Review*, March–April 1979, pp. 137–145.)

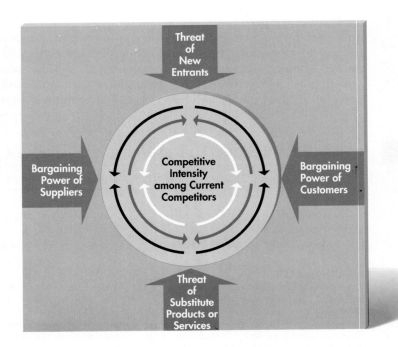

Threat of New Entrants

While recognizing current direct competitors is important, it is equally essential to be able to identify likely future competitors. However, in many cases the identities of all potential competitors may not be immediately obvious. Sometimes consumer usage patterns will change, creating different industry and market boundaries. Consider, for example, the following:

> The publisher for the trade journal *Confectioner* recently noted that "Candy isn't an industry in itself anymore." Indeed, the lines between candy, ice cream bars, and other snacks are becoming less distinct. When consumers want something sweet, they consider a whole range of choices.[2]

As market boundaries change, firms find themselves competing with different product forms and classes and with different organizations. Often these organizations produce a variety of different products and may compete on several fronts. For example, Mars Inc. now markets Snickers candy bars and Dove Bar ice cream products. Nestlé Foods competes with Mars in both markets. However, when Nestlé and Mars entered the ice cream business, they also began competing with a variety of non-candy-producing firms. New competition can also arise from firms with which a company does business.

> Kroy Inc. sold a patented machine that puts letters onto transparent tape. The tape can then be applied to folders or drawings or other items. In 1982, Kroy opened direct sales centers, bypassing its independent dealers. Two former Kroy employees then decided to organize a competing firm, Varitronic, found someone to develop a competing machine and capitalized on the disenchantment of Kroy's dealers to gain an effective entry into the market.[3]

Table 4-2 lists some of the most likely directions from which new competitors may come.

[2] "Candy May Be Dandy but Confectioners Want a Sweeter Bottom Line," *Business Week*, Oct. 6, 1986, p. 66.
[3] Alyssa Lappen, "How to "Exploit Someone Else's Mistake," *Forbes*, Nov. 14, 1988, pp. 164–168.

TABLE 4-2

IDENTIFYING COMPETITORS: LIKELY SOURCES OF NEW COMPETITORS

SOURCE	EXAMPLE
1. Competitor in segment we don't serve	Regional airline goes national
2. Indirect (product form or product class) competitors	Chocolate granola bar is developed to compete with ice cream bars
3. Customers	Brewer decides to produce own cans
4. Suppliers	Manufacturer of contact lenses opens optical products stores

TABLE 4-3	TYPICAL BARRIERS TO ENTRY

1. Economies of scale in production, delivery, advertising, selling
2. Initial financial investment requires extensive resources
3. Lack of access to sources of production (raw materials, technology, labor skills)
4. Limited access to distribution channels
5. Government regulation
6. Customer loyalty to existing sellers

BARRIERS TO ENTRY

The probability that potential competitors will actually enter the relevant market is a function of the *barriers to entry* to that market. Such barriers are the conditions that make it difficult to become a significant competitor in a new market. Table 4-3 lists some of the more typical barriers to entry.

An economies of scale barrier exists when a very high volume of production is necessary to be cost competitive. As we discuss in detail in Chapter 6, a high volume of production allows a firm to spread fixed costs (such as advertising and production overhead costs) across a greater number of units. Thus, when fixed costs are very high (as in the case in the beer industry, for example), existing firms with large market shares will have a strong cost advantage over new entrants.

Additionally, the initial financial investment involved in facilities, equipment, or initial marketing expenses may constitute barriers to entry. For example, to bring its brand new Saturn line of automobiles to the market, General Motors originally budgeted $5 billion, a sum far beyond the reach of most business organizations.

In other markets, entry may be thwarted even if investment and production barriers are low. It is difficult to enter the detergent market successfully because retailers are not likely to be easily persuaded to carry yet another brand. In other markets consumer loyalty may be well established, and so the marketing costs required in acquiring competitors' customers are prohibitive.

INTERNATIONAL ENTRY BARRIERS

Table 4-4 lists some barriers that can be troublesome when attempting to enter new international markets. These barriers may increase the costs of doing business, make a firm's product more costly to the consumer, or encourage favoritism on behalf of locally owned competitors.

While tariff barriers have declined in importance in recent years, nontariff barriers appear to be gaining in prominence and can be very costly. Ford, for example, claimed that the price of its Escort was 50 percent higher in Japan than in the United States because of licenses and other nontariff barriers.[4]

---

[4] Sak Onkvisit and John Shaw, "Marketing Barriers in International Trade," *Business Horizons*, May–June 1988, pp. 64–74.

TABLE 4-4	INTERNATIONAL ENTRY BARRIERS

1. Tariffs and duties paid as fees to import a product
2. Quotas (voluntary or involuntary) on the amount or type of products that can be imported
3. Product requirements regarding health and safety, product standards and testing, packaging and labeling
4. Customs and entry procedures including inspection and licensing
5. Government participation through subsidies, procurement policies favoring domestic firms, level of intervention in competition
6. National attitudes toward domestic versus foreign products
7. Access to distribution channels limited by preference for established local suppliers, shortages of space for new products

SIGNIFICANCE OF NEW ENTRY

In assessing changes in the identity of competitors, managers must determine whether new entrants will have a significant impact on competition. Of particular concern is the new entrant who threatens to create a major disruption by creating improved *price performance trade-offs*, by bringing *new skills* to the industry, or by virtue of *cross-subsidization*.

A classic example of an improved price performance trade-off occurred in the domestic airline industry during the early 1980s. Several new airlines (such as People Express) were successful in disrupting the industry pricing structure because of cost advantages associated with their newness: their flight crews were younger and thus lower-paid, their aircraft were often newer and more efficient, and they were not encumbered by the need to continue serving low-profit routes.[5]

Philip Morris is a classic example of the impact of bringing new skills to an industry. The firm acquired Miller Brewing and a small, regional, "low-calorie" beer and employed its skill at segmenting markets and managing large advertising budgets to make Miller Lite a market leader.

Cross-subsidization occurs when a competitor uses the profits from a dominant position in one market to support an entry into a new market. For example, Procter & Gamble spent tens of millions of dollars to enter the cookie market with its Duncan Hines brand. This entry was financed by its profits from a strong position in other snack-food segments. The potential for cross-subsidization is important to recognize because firms who have such opportunities are likely to be persistent and significant competitors. The existence of potential competitors who bring improved price or performance or cross-subsidization is an important consideration in understanding the intensity of competitive rivalry and in analyzing competitive strengths and weaknesses.

[5] George S. Yip, *Barriers to Entry*, Lexington Books, Lexington, Mass., 1982, p. 26.

Threat of Substitution

As we discussed in Chapter 3, alternative product classes can be substituted for each other, especially if changes in the relative importance of various attributes occur for one or more market segments. For example, part of the decline in sales of steel in the past decade is attributable to the increased use of aluminum in automobiles. This shift was stimulated by the need to reduce vehicle weights in order to meet emerging fuel economy regulations.

Another source of substitution is technological advancement that results in a *technological discontinuity*. Ultimately, most product life cycles end—often abruptly—because of a technological innovation. Thus, if the future competitive structure of a market is to be understood, managers should attempt to determine the potential for a technological discontinuity.

A technological discontinuity results when a major enhancement of a consumer benefit occurs due to new technology. In effect, the new product form totally eliminates the life cycle of an existing product. For example, the share of total automotive tire sales held by glass-belted radial tires dropped by 40 points in 18 months when steel-belted radials were introduced. Similarly, sales of electromechanical cash registers slid from 90 percent of the market in 1972 to 10 percent in 1976.[6]

Predicting the decline and fall of a product life cycle due to changing technology is not always easy. However, there is a greater motivation for competitors and potential competitors to pursue an innovative technology when the current technology (the foundation for the current product line) is close to its limits. Based on studies conducted by McKinsey & Co. consultants, there appear to be several warning signs that a technology is approaching obsolescence.

- Greater efforts are needed to produce even small improvements in performance.
- R&D shifts more toward process improvement and away from product improvement.
- Sales growth comes primarily from minor product modifications that serve new segments rather than from quality improvements that improve penetration across all segments.
- There are wide differences in R&D spending among competitors with apparently minor differences in market-share effects.
- Some market leaders begin to lose share to smaller rivals in selected market segments, a possible indicator that the small firms have a new technology enabling them to be more productive with their dollars.[7]

[6] Richard N. Foster, *Innovation: The Attacker's Advantage*, Summit Books, New York, 1986, p. 162.
[7] Ibid., pp. 215–217.

Powerful Buyers and Powerful Suppliers

If the firm's *buyers* have a large amount of bargaining power, they can place extra demands on competitors for lower prices, special product options, or more service. For example, the major U.S. automobile manufacturers have systematically pressured their component suppliers to reduce prices while increasing product quality in recent years.

In general, buyers will be powerful if:

- They are large in volume but few in number (so that sales are heavily concentrated among a few customers);
- The products are highly standardized so that one vendor is easily substituted for another;
- The product being purchased is not likely to have a noticeable or major impact on the buyer's product or business (for example, paper clips); and
- Buyers have the potential to integrate backward to make the product themselves.

If a firm's *suppliers* have a large amount of bargaining power, they can raise prices or reduce services, making it more difficult for the firm to control its marketing offering. For example, carpet mills are dependent on chemical firms like Du Pont and Monsanto, who control the price and quality of the basic fiber materials.

A supplier is likely to be powerful in a given industry if:

- There are few alternative suppliers;
- The supplier has successfully differentiated its product through distinctive quality, features, or services;
- The industry is not an important part of a supplier's business;
- The supplier threatens to vertically integrate forward; and
- The firm would find it very costly to select another supplier because (for example) the firm has unique specifications that some suppliers can't or won't adhere to or because of the time required to learn a new supplier's equipment.

Competitive Intensity among Current Competitors

Competition is a matter of degree in business as well as in games: Competition in some markets is simply more intense (and thus more costly) than in other markets. The importance of assessing competitive intensity is twofold: to determine the likely cost of meeting competition and to recognize the bases and types of competition that are likely to be most important.

Several basic conditions foster intense competition:

■ Competitors are numerous or are roughly equal in size and power.
■ Industry growth is slow, leaving market-share gains as the only avenue to growth.
■ Products and services are essentially undifferentiated.
■ The cost to buyers of switching from one supplier to another is low because sellers have not developed a way to tie their customers into long-term relationships.
■ Economies of scale are significant or the product is perishable, creating the temptation to cut prices to build volume.
■ The industry is characterized by frequent periods of overcapacity.
■ Companies remain in the market in spite of low profits because of management's loyalty to a business or because the business involves specialized assets that are difficult to sell.[8]

Fundamentally, it is important to assess competitive intensity in order to understand the degree to which price competition will be a factor. To the extent that most of the foregoing conditions exist, price competition will be severe, as we've seen in industries such as airline travel, steel, basic chemicals, and paper plates.

A second purpose of this analysis, however, is to identify the factors that cause competitive intensity in a given industry. By recognizing which conditions apply in a given instance, firms can often develop strategies to change those conditions or to respond to them. For example, a firm might try selling off part of its excess capacity and focusing on making specialty products for small market niches, as many steel manufacturers did in the 1980s. In the airline industry, competitors have attempted to tie their customers into long-term relationships through frequent-flyer programs.

As these examples suggest, an understanding of the forces shaping competitive intensity can help identify the company's capabilities necessary for success. Usually, however, a firm needs to develop a thorough assessment of competitive strengths and weaknesses in order to determine where a competitive advantage lies.

ASSESSING COMPETITIVE ADVANTAGE

The ultimate purpose of performing a competitive analysis is to identify possible avenues for attaining a sustainable advantage over competitors to achieve the objectives set for a product or product line. Specifically, managers

[8] Michael Porter, "How Competitive Forces Shape Strategy," *Harvard Business Review*, March–April 1979, pp. 137–145.

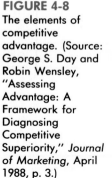

FIGURE 4-8
The elements of competitive advantage. (Source: George S. Day and Robin Wensley, "Assessing Advantage: A Framework for Diagnosing Competitive Superiority," *Journal of Marketing*, April 1988, p. 3.)

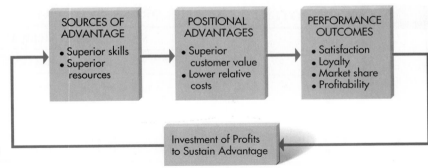

are concerned with achieving certain performance outcomes such as repeat-purchase loyalty, market-share growth, and profitability.

Market success depends in large part on the firm's ability to deliver the benefits desired by customers more effectively or at lower cost than the competition. Consequently, the first step in assessing competitive advantage is to identify the *positions* and *sources* of advantage that lead to desired market performance outcomes as shown in Figure 4-8.

Positional Advantages

As Figure 4-8 suggests, positional advantages are the immediate causes of performance outcomes. These positional advantages can include any of the following:

- Lowest delivered price
- Superior product benefits
- Superior customer services
- Established brand name or company reputation for quality
- Innovative features or options
- Better spatial availability to the buyer (due to delivery policies or distributor locations)

Importantly, it is the customer's perception of these advantages that counts. We may have built a better product, but only the *customer's* judgment about our relative position is important in terms of the performance results. This underscores the importance of perceptual mapping as a vehicle for understanding positional advantages.

PIONEERING ADVANTAGE

In many cases a positional advantage results from the market advantages of being the innovator (or "pioneer") in a market.

TABLE 4-5

SHARE POTENTIAL VERSUS ORDER OF ENTRY

NUMBER OF BRANDS IN MARKET	MARKET SHARE HELD BY					
	1st	2d	3d	4th	5th	6th
1	100	—	—	—	—	—
2	58.5	41.5	—	—	—	—
3	43.6	31.0	25.4	—	—	—
4	35.7	25.4	20.8	18.1	—	—
5	30.8	21.9	17.9	15.5	13.9	—
6	27.3	19.4	15.9	13.8	12.4	11.2

Source: Adapted from G. L. Urban, T. Carter, S. Gaskin, and Z. Mucha, "Market Share Rewards to Pioneering Brands: An Empirical Analysis and Strategic Implications," *Management Science*, June 1986, p. 654.

Table 4-5 provides a very strong picture of the advantages of pioneering. This table shows that the average market share attained by a consumer product depends substantially on when it enters a market. (The study was designed to hold product performance and advertising effects equal for all competitors.) For example, if a market contained five brands, on average, the first brand to enter (that is, the *pioneer*) held a 30.8 percent share, while the fifth brand held a 13.9 percent share.

Why do pioneers hold such an advantage? There appear to be several factors involved.

1. Because they are the *prototypes* for all products that follow, the pioneer influences judgments about which attributes are important.[9]
2. The first brand has more of an opportunity to build loyalty through repeat purchasing.
3. Later entrants will have more difficulty in getting distribution and consumer awareness and trial. Unless the late entrant has some clearly unique attribute, there will be little incentive for distributors to stock it or for consumers to try it.

The pioneer's advantage depends heavily on the rate of trial for the product category, however. Thus, while Apple was really the pioneer in personal computing, IBM was able to catch up and take the lead because the rate of adoption was modest in the introductory stage of the life cycle.

[9] See Gregory Carpenter and Kent Nakamoto, "Consumer Preference Formation and Pioneering Advantage," *Journal of Marketing Research*, August 1989, pp. 285–298, for a detailed discussion of this point.

Additionally, other research has shown that the pioneering advantage is not automatically maintained into maturity. A pioneer's ability to maintain the leadership position depends on;

- Maintaining a high level of quality relative to price;
- Offering a breadth of product-line options to meet the needs of different segments;
- Maintaining superior distribution; and
- Not having to make many seasonal or periodic model changes to meet competition.[10]

Indeed, many firms choose to be followers instead of pioneers. Although they are mindful of the pioneering advantage, they also recognize that there are three advantages from being a follower.

1. Followers usually incur fewer initial marketing costs because the pioneer has performed the task of educating the market about the product class or form. For example, Kimberly Clark allowed Procter & Gamble to spend millions pioneering the concept of disposable diapers before entering the market.
2. Followers can learn from competitors' actions regarding the selection of distribution channels, pricing, demand estimates, or user problems. IBM's success as a follower in the personal computer market was aided by the company's observation of the importance of developing a strong network of retail dealers.
3. Followers can apply the latest in technology. Sony was the pioneer in videocassette recorders, but eventually was overtaken by followers who employed the newer VHS technology instead of the beta technology.

Sources of Advantage

Three basic sources of advantage can be identified: the *superior skills* of people within the organization, the *systems or arrangements* that have been developed for responding to the market, and the organization's *resources*. All positional advantages derive from one or more of these sources.

Superior skills exist when one competitor has the ability to perform a function more effectively than its competitors. Among the most important of these skills (and some firms known for each one) are the following:

---

[10] William T. Robinson and Claes Fornell, "Sources of Market Pioneer Advantages in Consumer Goods Industries," *Journal of Marketing Research*, August 1985, pp. 305–317.

- The ability to generate innovative new products (3M Company)
- Precision manufacturing to assure quality (Gillette)
- Ability to manage large advertising budgets (Philip Morris)
- Obtaining dealer cooperation in display and retail promotion (Frito-Lay)

Systems or arrangements are often developed that enhance company skills. Usually such arrangements result in enhanced positions of advantage by virtue of strengthening a company's ties with a customer. Among the kinds of systems or arrangements most important to a competitive analysis are

- Long-term contractual arrangements whereby customers receive special prices or services in exchange for buying in specified quantities,
- Complementary products and services (including software or systems) that enhance the value or utilization of the main product, and
- Customized product specifications or customized, on-line computer ordering systems that simplify customer reordering.

One of the most effective systems for developing a strong customer-supplier relationship was developed by Baxter Healthcare Corp. Baxter, which resulted from a merger between Baxter Laboratories and American Hospital Supply, offers a huge variety of healthcare equipment and supplies to hospitals. Not only do they offer a wide range of complementary products, but the company was a pioneer in offering computer-linked systems to speed reordering of routine supplies. Additionally, Baxter often signs agreements with hospitals and hospital chains offering price discounts and technical services that help control costs in exchange for large guaranteed sales volumes.

Three major types of *resources* are relevant: intellectual property rights, brand equity, and tangible resources. Such resources can enable a firm to be more price competitive or to offer better performance than the competition (or even unique performance).

Intellectual property rights can confer a strong technological advantage on a company, especially in industries such as pharmaceuticals or electronics, and indeed are necessary to justify much of the huge research and development expenditures in such industries. Products such as Crest toothpaste and Polaroid's instant camera succeeded in large part because a patent helped preserve their pioneering advantage. In contrast, IBM's inability to patent the technology of its original personal computer allowed many competitors to develop lower-priced "clones."[11] However, even though patents have a 17-year life, much of that time can elapse before a patent results in a commercial

---

[11] Paula Dwyer, Laura Jereski, Zackary Schiller, and Dinah Lee, "The Battle Raging Over Intellectual Property," *Business Week*, May 22, 1989, pp. 78–90.

product. For example, Monsanto's patent on aspartame (which is marketed under the trademark NutraSweet) expired in 1992 but did not receive approval from the Food and Drug Administration until 1981, a delay that reduced its commercial life by one-third.

Brand equity is the added value that a brand name brings to a product beyond its functional qualities. Typically, strong brand names (such as Kraft, Jell-O, IBM, and American Express) are characterized by

- High levels of brand loyalty,
- Widespread brand name awareness,
- A high level of perceived quality, and
- Strong associations with other specific attributes.[12]

For example, research has demonstrated that the Dole brand is strongly associated with "freshness" and "sunshine."[13]

It appears as though a strong brand equity results from three elements: the delivery of superior performance, the building of strong associations between a brand name and the product category (for example, the link between Sunkist and orange products), and the development of a consistent image through spokespersons (such as Bill Cosby for Jell-O) or characters (such as the Jolly Green Giant).[14] From a resource point of view, having a strong brand equity enables firms to

- More readily resist competitive challenges,
- Launch new products using the same brand name with lower marketing costs,
- Charge premium prices, or
- Obtain stronger support from wholesale or retail distributors.

Indeed, today a good deal of effort is usually expended in trying to set a value on brand names because brand equity is considered to be such an important element of the value of a business.[15]

Tangible resources include the physical assets of the firm, financial resources, and marketing resources such as the number of salespeople and distributors available to cover the marketplace. Such resources influence the amount of effort that can be exerted to support positional advantages. Consequently, an understanding of competitors' resources should help management

[12] David Aaker, *Managing Brand Equity*, The Free Press, New York, 1991, pp. 15–16.
[13] Dan Koeppel, "Dole Wants the Whole Product Aisle," *Adweek's Marketing Week*, Oct. 22, 1990, pp. 20–26.
[14] Peter Farquhar, "Managing Brand Equity," *Marketing Research*, September 1989, pp. 24–29.
[15] Aaker, pp. 17–28.

predict the kinds of competitive advantage that firm will have. For example, a commercial bank's ability to generate deposits will be greatly enhanced if it has more branches, more automatic tellers, more human tellers, and a larger advertising budget.

Additionally, understanding a competitor's resource base enables a manager to better predict how that competitor will react to a major change in strategy. Knowing the potential resources available to competitors and being able to estimate their reaction is especially important when contemplating a challenge to a market leader. Some scholars have likened such a marketing strategy to the military strategy of a frontal assault, where the rule of thumb is that the attacker needs a 3-to-1 advantage in firepower to be successful.[16] Accordingly, managers must have some idea of the ability and motivation of competitors to build resources for retaining or acquiring customers.

In general, managers should expect a competitor to support a product or brand aggressively through price cutting or by expanding marketing expenditures when the competitor has

- A distinct cost advantage because of higher sales volume and economies of scale, modern or automated production facilities, lower labor costs, ownership of its sources of components or raw materials, or superior production processes;
- A large number of profitable products in other markets, which can serve as cash cows to provide funding for this product;
- The reputation of being a single-industry competitor and thus highly committed to maintaining a strong presence in this market;
- Recently made major investments in research and development in this market; or
- A financial position enabling it to generate extensive additional funding through borrowed funds as needed.

To illustrate, in the domestic wine industry, Gallo has a substantial resource advantage. Gallo grows its own grapes and owns a glass bottle plant, an aluminum cap business, and a large fleet of trucks, all of which enable it to be cost competitive. Additionally, in those states where it is permitted, Gallo's own distributors call on retail stores, helping to assure it a positional advantage in terms of retailer service and availability.

But price is not the only positional advantage a firm can derive from abundant resources because not all markets are highly price-sensitive. Where competitive reactions to a new entrant or a new strategic initiative are concerned, the positional advantage that will be sought will be that which a firm

[16] Philip Kotler and Ravi Singh Achrol, "Basic Military Strategy for Winning Your Marketing War," *Journal of Business Strategy*, Winter 1981, pp. 30–41.

Assets and Skills	Weakness							Strength
Product quality	W V		B	A G		L	M	
Market share/share economies	V B W		A		G		M	L
Parent in related business	B W			V		G	A M	L
Package		W	B V L	G		A	M	
Low-calorie position	V G		M	B		A L W		
Sales-force/distribution	V B		W		G		A M	L
Advertising/promotion	V B	G		W		A M		L
Ethnic position	W A	L	M				G	V B

L   Stouffer's Lean Cuisine (Nestle's-also makes Stouffer "Red Box" line)
M   Le Menu (Campbell's Soup–also makes Swanson's, Mrs. Paul's)
W   Weight Watchers (Heinz)
A   Armour Dinner Classic/Classic Lite (Con Agra-also makes Banquet)
V   Van deKamp Mexican Classic and other ethnic lines
B   Benihana
G   Green Giant Stir Fry Entrees (Pillsbury)

FIGURE 4-9
A competitor strength grid. (Source: David Aaker, *Strategic Market Management*, 2d ed., Wiley, New York, 1988, p. 86.)

views as most effective. If a firm believes that advertising is its most effective weapon, that is how it is likely to respond to a competitive threat.[17]

Implementing a Competitive Analysis

One way to summarize the results of a competitive analysis is through a competitor strength grid. Figure 4-9 presents a competitor strength grid for the gourmet frozen-foods market. The relevant skills and resources in the grid are listed in approximate order of importance. Then the major competitors are positioned on each dimension. Based on this grid, Stouffer's Lean Cuisine would appear to hold the greatest overall position of strength.[18]

An important issue in developing and using competitive grids is the relative importance of each dimension. In some cases, managers may want to assign weights to different dimensions to reflect their differential importance, rather than just rank ordering them. In any event, it is critical to recognize that there is little to be gained by being best on unimportant factors.

While the idea of a competitive grid has great appeal, the grid is only as useful as it is accurate. Thus, consumer perceptions should be obtained when making judgments on dimensions like quality. These can then be combined with other sources of competitive intelligence.

[17] Hubert Gatignon, Erin Anderson, and Kristiaan Helsen, "Competitive Reactions to Market Entry: Explaining Interfirm Differences," *Journal of Marketing Research*, February 1989, pp. 44–55.
[18] David Aaker, *Strategic Market Management*, 2d ed., Wiley, New York, 1988, pp. 85–86.

OBTAINING COMPETITIVE INTELLIGENCE

Information on many dimensions of a strengths-and-weaknesses analysis can be readily obtained by simple observation. However, more and more organizations are establishing formal processes for collecting competitive intelligence. The procedures rely on sources that fall into three basic categories.

Published Material and Documents

Electronic data bases such as those published by Business Research Corporation and Economic Information Systems can be accessed by personal computer and provide information such as the production volume of competitors' industrial facilities and research reports on competitors compiled by investment bankers. Simpler, but often more useful, sources include labor contracts negotiated by competitors (which yield clues as to competitors' labor costs), speeches given by company officers, and press releases. There is even a company that monitors help-wanted ads, which can be used to track expansion plans or new engineering directions. Some important specific sources of information that can be used to assess the competition are also general market measurement sources. These are discussed in the next chapter, and many are summarized in the Appendix to this book.

Competitors' Employees, Suppliers, or Customers

Firms flirt with ethical questions (and sometimes legal questions) in using these sources. While "picking a competitor's brain" about general industry problems is a legitimate way to project competitors' thinking, hiring competitors' key employees can be construed as illegal if it can be proved that the sole purpose in making the hire was to acquire trade secrets. Less obvious, but sometimes questionable, are techniques designed to use competitors' suppliers and customers to provide information about competitors' new-product development activities, forthcoming promotions, or sales levels.

Direct Observation

It is often said that the first ten buyers of any new product are competitors' salespeople. The technique of *reverse engineering* involves taking apart a new competitive product to analyze the product's attributes, to determine the cost of production, and, sometimes, even to copy the technology. To the trained observer, even simple plant tours can yield useful insights regarding plant capacity and costs.

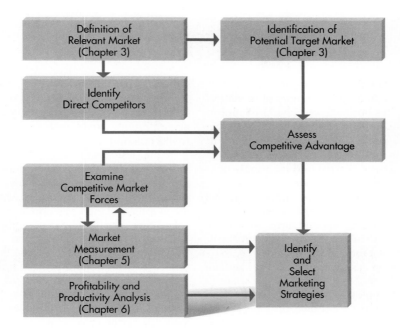

FIGURE 4-10
Steps in
competitive
analysis and their
relationship to
other aspects of
the situation
analysis.

CONCLUSION

Both for-profit and not-for-profit organizations operate in a complex environment in which there is competition for the attention, patronage, and financial resources of customers and clients. Accordingly, it is essential to have a clear understanding of the alternatives from which potential customers can choose and of potential customers' assessments of those alternatives. As summarized in Figure 4-10, organizations must assess the competitive environment in which they will operate and the competitive advantages (and disadvantages) they will have in a potential target market. (Note the bidirectional arrow in Figure 4-10 between competitive market forces and market measurement. This reflects the fact that industry sales are influenced by these forces and, at the same time, competitive intensity is influenced by the market potential and the growth in industry sales.)

Clearly, the process of competitive analysis is a critical prerequisite to the selection of a marketing strategy, as the situation at MCI Communications suggests.

MCI COMMUNICATIONS
AND THE LONG-DISTANCE INDUSTRY*

Long-distance telephone service today is a market worth about $65 billion in annual revenues. For decades, this business was a virtual monopoly under AT&T, which also owned most local telephone companies. With the deregulation of this industry in the 1980s, AT&T gave up ownership of local phone service and monopoly control of the long-distance market.

Over the past decade, competition in this market has been characterized by heavy advertising and promotional expenditures. MCI spent $100 million to introduce its "Friends and Family" promotional plan, which provided 20 percent discounts on customers' calls to a fixed set of twelve other MCI customers. In 1992, Sprint countered with a plan called "The Most," which provided 20 percent discounts on calls to the one number a person called most often in a month. AT&T responded with advertising designed to reinforce its historical image for reliability and quality, relying on the tag line, "It's just not AT&T," to characterize the firm's competitors. Additionally, $50 checks were offered in 1992 to any customer willing to switch to AT&T.

The "Friends and Family" program turned out to be a very successful short-run strategy for MCI. Within a year, the company signed up 7.5 million households for this plan, two-thirds of them new customers. As a result, MCI's share rose to 16 percent versus 68 percent for AT&T and 9 percent for Sprint. (The remainder was divided among a group of smaller companies.) In part, the success of this program was due to a short-term technological advantage. MCI had developed some complex new technology to keep track of discount billing. Competitors could emulate this technology, but not immediately. Additionally, unlike MCI, AT&T relied on local companies to calculate residential bills. This meant its information system for recording telephone call patterns was too cumbersome to emulate the MCI plan cost effectively. Moreover, with its dominant market share, AT&T knew most

customers for an AT&T plan comparable to "Friends and Family" would be existing AT&T customers. Thus, the lost revenues from 20 percent discounts would likely be too costly relative to the potential gains.

In the business market, a major development in the past decade has been the evolution of a set of long-distance brokers and resellers. Resellers buy long-distance services from the three large long-distance companies at the cheapest rates, then use their own telephone switching systems to resell to small and medium-sized businesses (at rates below those that would otherwise be available to smaller firms). Many resellers (like LDB International of Minneapolis) also offer sophisticated billing systems allowing careful tracking of long-distance use and high levels of customer service.

By the early 1990s the competitors were witnessing another major development in this market. Revenues in the cellular telephone market were growing at a rate of 30 to 40 percent annually, making the potential for long-distance wireless service greater. Although Sprint was planning a merger with cellular telephone giant Centel, the company also owned many local telephone companies that would be bypassed under wireless long-distance. For MCI and AT&T, however, the ability to bypass local phone companies meant eliminating the charges paid to such companies for delivering calls to

---

*Developed from Mary Lu Carnevale, "Long Distance Phone Companies Gird for Wireless War," The Wall Street Journal, Aug. 5, 1992, p. B4; Mark Lewyn, "MCI's Winning Pitch," Business Week, Mar. 23, 1992, p. 36; Kate Fitzgerald, "Cash Offers, Tie-ins Fuel Phone War," Advertising Age, July 13, 1992, p. 4; Jon Van, "MCI Discount Plan Enlists Friends, Family," Chicago Tribune, Mar. 19, 1992, section 3, p. 1; Robin Goreiss, "Sprint Goes for 'The Most' to Rival MCI Calling Plan," Communications Week, June 15, 1992, p. 15; Betsy Weinberger, "Low Long Distance Prices Aren't Enough These Days," Minneapolis-St. Paul City Business, Aug. 5, 1992, p. 17.

continued

residences from the long-distance networks. These so-called "access charges" are the single largest cost for this industry, so even a small percentage drop would allow AT&T and MCI to increase profits or reduce prices substantially.

Of course, the cost of entering this market will be enormous because billions of dollars will need to be invested in digital technology and large macrocells for transmission. Certainly the existing cellular phone companies are interested in this market. The Federal Communications Commission must ultimately decide whether and how to grant licenses and frequencies for long-distance transmission.

1. Discuss the various forces governing competition in the long-distance telephone industry. Which ones are most influential?
2. Is competition intensive in this industry? Explain.
3. Does AT&T have a pioneering advantage? Does it have superior brand equity? Explain.
4. What competitive advantages might MCI have in this market?

QUESTIONS AND SITUATIONS FOR DISCUSSION

1. In 1989, Toyota and Nissan introduced their Lexus and Infiniti luxury automobiles. A major element in both introductory strategies was the decision to establish separate dealerships for these cars rather than marketing them through existing Toyota and Nissan dealers. Which steps in competitive analysis could have been used by Toyota and Nissan that would have led to this decision?

2. If you were working for a manufacturer of consumer electronics, what types of information about competitors would you expect to obtain from each of the following sources: consumers, distributors, trade shows?

3. Discuss some difficulties that a firm operating only in the United States would have in developing a competitive analysis as it prepares to expand into the Far East.

4. Many firms have begun their overseas operations by developing joint ventures with a local firm (for example, Toyota and General Motors developed a joint venture called NUMMI to produce Corollas and Novas in California). What special resources would you look for in a joint-venture partner to help be more competitive overseas? Would your answer differ if you were selling industrial versus consumer goods?

5. How important would the United States dollar's strength (measured against foreign currencies) be in a competitive analysis undertaken by:
    a. A manufacturer of personal computers?
    b. A travel agency selling "see America" tour packages in Western Europe?
    c. A manufacturer of Portland cement?

6. The sun can burn the cornea of the eye as it does skin, and long-term

exposure to sunlight can cause cataracts. Your company has recently developed clear eyedrops that will block 98 percent of ultraviolet rays for up to 4 hours. How would you proceed to develop a competitive analysis for this product? What are the major difficulties you would anticipate in analyzing the competitive situation for this new product?

7. In 1990, the ready-to-eat cereal market was expected to be worth over $6.5 billion. After many years of very slow growth, this market has been propelled at a double-digit growth rate in recent years, primarily due to the growth of adult cereals. By the end of the 1980s, adult cereals accounted for 40 percent of the ready-to-eat market.

In the late 1980s, industry leader Kellogg dominated the adult cereal business with over a dozen brands. During the early 1980s, Kellogg doubled spending on research and development and on advertising. This resulted in a string of successful new products such as Nutri-Grain (Kellogg's first cereal with whole grain, no sugar, and no preservatives), Mueslix (an upscale version of granola with a European heritage), Nutrific (combining barley, bran, almonds, and raisins), and Pro-Grain (another multigrain cereal). Along with traditional mainstays like Raisin Bran, Product 19, and All-Bran, Kellogg's seemed to have the adult cereal business blanketed—especially in the bran/fiber varieties. Six firms competed in the cereal market. Of these only Kellogg's and General Mills relied on this business for a dominant share of earnings and sales. In 1986, Kellogg was estimated to have 48 percent of the fiber and adult nutritional cereal market compared to General Foods Post division's 29 percent share. General Mills, Nabisco, Quaker, and Ralston-Purina trailed with 16, 3, 2, and 2 percent, respectively. Overall, Kellogg's total share of the cereal market was around 41 percent. However, Kellogg's share declined to 39 percent over the ensuing three years, as General Mills expanded its adult lines with an especially heavy emphasis on oat bran, a substance that had been the subject of numerous positive health claims recently.[19]

a. What are the key positional advantages and sources of advantage in this industry?

b. What problems must be overcome if perceptual mapping is to be a useful analytical tool in this market?

c. How strong is the pioneering advantage in this market?

d. Is intensive price competition likely to surface in this industry?

e. As market leader, does Kellogg's fit the profile of an aggressive defender/reactor?

---

[19] Developed from Julie Erickson, "Kellogg Pours Out More Cereals," *Advertising Age*, July 25, 1988, pp. 2 and 66; Rebecca Fannin, "Crunching the Competition," *Marketing and Media Decisions*, March 1980, pp. 70–74; Paula Schnorbus, "Brantastic," *Marketing & Media Decisions*, April 1987, pp. 93–96; Julie Franz, "Cereals Growing Up," *Advertising Age*, Feb. 9, 1987, p. 3; and Janet Key, "Kellogg Wises Up to Health Ads," *Chicago Tribune*, Aug. 31, 1989, pp. B1, B4.

SUGGESTED ADDITIONAL READINGS

Cecil, John, and Eugene Hall, "When It Really Matters to Business Strategy," *The McKinsey Quarterly*, Autumn 1988, pp. 2–26.

Day, George S., and Robin Wensley, "Assessing Advantage: A Framework for Diagnosing Competitive Superiority," *Journal of Marketing*, April 1988, pp. 1–20.

Devine, Hugh, and John Morton, "How Does the Market Really See Your Product?" *Business Marketing*, July 1984, pp. 70–79, 131.

Farquhar, Peter, "Managing Brand Equity," *Marketing Research*, September 1989, pp. 24–33.

Gatignon, Hubert, Erin Anderson, and Kristiann Helsen, "Competitive Reactions to Market Entry Explaining Interfirm Differences," *Journal of Marketing Research*, February 1989, pp. 44–55.

Henderson, Bruce, "The Anatomy of Competition," *Journal of Marketing*, Spring 1983, pp. 7–11.

Karakaya, Fahri, and Michael J. Stahl, "Barriers to Entry and Market Entry Decisions in Consumer and Industrial Goods Markets," *Journal of Marketing*, April 1989, pp. 80–91.

Porter, Michael, "How Competitive Forces Shape Strategy," *Harvard Business Review*, March–April 1979, pp. 137–145.

Robinson, William, "Marketing Mix Reactions to Entry," *Marketing Science*, Fall 1988, pp. 368–385.

Schnaars, Steven, "When Entering Growth Markets, Are Pioneers Better Than Poachers?" *Business Horizons*, March–April 1986, pp. 27–36.

CHAPTER 5

MARKET MEASUREMENT

OVERVIEW

In Chapters 3 and 4, we discussed some fundamental steps managers should take in analyzing buyers and competitors within markets in order to understand the underlying processes influencing primary and selective demand. Chapter 5 also focuses on primary and selective demand. However, in this chapter our concern is with measuring the amount of primary or selective demand in a market in order to determine the size of various sales opportunities within it.

Market measurements are critically important in a number of management decisions. Top management must be aware of the size and rate of growth of various markets in order to select corporate strategies. Middle-management decisions regarding marketing strategies, programs, and budgets for individual products cannot be made effectively without some estimate of the expected levels of industry and company sales. Additionally, in order to evaluate the performance of a company, a product, a sales territory, or a distributor, some benchmark (such as a sales goal or quota) must be established. And both top management and middle managers will use benchmarks that are based on some estimate of market demand.

Managers need to understand market measurement procedures for several reasons. In some cases, managers may have to do their own measurement because the firm does not have qualified staff researchers. However, even if managers are only the users of market information, an understanding of these procedures is important. In order to specify the information they will need, managers must be aware of the kinds of measures that are available. Further, before using the information, managers should be familiar with the limitations of these measurements and the potential sources of error or bias inherent in them. Market measurements are estimates, and few are so reliable that managers can simply accept a single number as perfectly accurate. By understanding the assumptions used to develop any measure, managers can better evaluate by how much such measures are optimistic or pessimistic and how much such measures should be relied on.

The purposes of this chapter are to demonstrate the uses of the various types of market measurements and to point out the assumptions and limitations of the most widely used techniques for developing these measurements.

Basic Types of Market Measurements

Before examining the basic approaches to market measurement, it is important to define the major kinds of measures that are useful to managers.

1. *Actual sales* represent either the past or current levels of demand actually achieved. Those realized by a firm come under the category of *company and product sales*, and those of a group of sellers are known as *industry sales*.
2. *Sales forecasts* are estimates of future levels of demand. Industry sales forecasts indicate the level of demand that is expected to be achieved by all firms selling to a defined market in a defined period of time. A statement such as "Automobile sales in the United States between the years 1995 and 2000 are expected to be 100 million units" is an industry sales forecast. Similarly, company (or product-line or brand) sales forecasts indicate the expected level of demand that will be met by an individual supplier.
3. *Market potential* represents the upper limit of demand in a defined period of time. That is, market potential is either the maximum sales opportunity that can be achieved by all sellers at the present time (called *current market potential*) or the one that can be achieved during some future period of time (*future market potential*).

Figure 5-1 portrays the relationship among company sales, industry sales, and market potential measurements. As the figure suggests, company sales will generally be lower than industry sales. (The only exception to this rule is the case of a monopoly. If a firm has no competitors, company sales will equal industry sales.) The ratio of company sales to industry sales is the firm's market share. Additionally, as Figure 5-1 suggests, industry sales will usually be below market potential.

FIGURE 5-1
Basic kinds
of market
measurements.

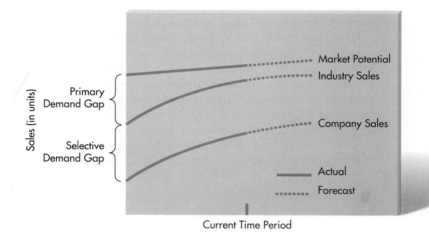

In developing the three types of measurements, managers should normally be concerned with the forecasted rate of growth in the measurements over time and the size of the *strategic gaps* among the measurements. More specifically, market potential may increase because the number of potential buyers or the rate of purchase may increase over time. Industry sales may increase over time for several reasons:

- Prices may decrease, improving potential customers' ability to buy.
- Industry marketing efforts (regarding product quality, advertising and selling expenditures, and extent of distribution) may become more extensive so that a greater number of potential customers fully perceive or obtain the product's benefits.
- Environmental factors (such as economic conditions or changing social values) may stimulate the willingness or ability to buy the product.

Pharmaceutical manufacturer Eli Lilly manufactures Prozac, the world's leading anti-depressant drug. When competitors Pfizer and Smith Kline Beecham launched similar so-called "serotonin" anti-depressant drugs, industry experts predicted total industry sales of serotonin drugs would rise. These expectations were based largely on the beliefs about the impact of having three firms aggressively marketing these products. Specifically, it was expected that the efforts of the firms' sales representatives would make more physicians aware of the symptoms of depression (thus decreasing the number of undiagnosed cases) as well as getting more physicians to prescribe serotonin-based treatment. Further, as competition heated up, prices were expected to decline, thus making serotonin drugs more price competitive with traditional anti-depressants.[1]

Company sales may increase over time for one of two reasons. First, the sales of all firms competing in a given industry may increase because of an overall increase in industry sales. Second, some firms may gain sales at the expense of competitors by offering and communicating superior combinations of benefits and thus increasing market share.

The most important strategic implications of these three measures can be isolated by comparing market potential to industry sales and by comparing industry sales to company sales. If a large difference exists between market potential and industry sales, then a large *primary demand gap* exists. This means that managers should examine the factors influencing primary demand (discussed in Chapter 3) to determine how industry sales may be increased. If a large difference exists between industry sales and company sales, then a *selective demand gap* exists. In such situations, managers should examine buyers' choice processes to identify opportunities for increasing market share.

---

[1] Thomas Burton, "Lilly's Controversial Prozac May Benefit from Marketing of Two New Competitors," *The Wall Street Journal*, July 17, 1992, pp. B1–2.

Defining What to Measure

Managers must clearly identify the market to be measured in order to measure industry sales and market potential accurately. That is, the relevant market must be defined (in terms of product form, product class, or generic needs). Further, if only certain segments of the relevant market (such as geographic areas or age groups) will be served, this should be stated as well. (For example, a cereal manufacturer may be interested in determining industry sales of cereals among single-person households in New England.) Additionally, the time frame must be established. For some kinds of decisions, our concern is with current levels of sales or potential. In other cases, estimates of sales or potential at some specific future time may be required.

In the remainder of this chapter, we will examine four basic kinds of market measurements: absolute market potential, relative market potential, industry sales forecasts, and company sales forecasts. Our discussion of each measure will begin by indicating how each measure can be used in decision making.

ABSOLUTE MARKET POTENTIAL

Absolute potential is an estimate of maximum potential demand, usually based on two factors: the number of potential users and the rate of purchase. For a given market, absolute potential indicates the total dollar or unit volume that could be sold by all suppliers. There are three kinds of decisions that generally require an estimate of absolute market potential:

1. *Evaluating market opportunities.* In order to decide what market opportunities to pursue in the future, a firm will want to assess the market potential. This is particularly true in the case of new-product-form or new-product-class markets. Consider, for example, the large resource commitments made by companies entering the market for products such as videotape recorders, personal computers, and industrial robots. These commitments could not have been economically justified if the companies had not been able to identify a large potential demand. In the case of existing products, market opportunities can be more easily examined if the market potential can be measured and compared with industry sales. If the market potential is significantly larger than industry sales, then all suppliers have an opportunity to increase sales volume by pursuing policies (such as lower prices) to close the primary demand gap. However, if industry sales are already close to market potential, then a firm will know that the only avenue for company sales growth is to improve market share. Consequently, in the latter case, the market opportunity is generally smaller (unless, of course, a firm believes it has some unique advantage that can be used to build market share).

2. *Determining sales quotas and objectives.* Market potential must usually be considered in order to establish reasonable objectives for the sales force and for distributors. Potential demand in some sales territories may be growing so rapidly that sharp yearly increases in sales objectives are appropriate. However, other territories may be stagnant in the number of potential buyers and purchase rates. Consequently, a fair evaluation of sales-force and distributor performance should be based on the potential for sales.

3. *Determining the number of retail outlets.* Firms that sell through retailers generally will have a desired number of retail distributors for a market of a given size. For instance, an automobile manufacturer may want to have one dealer for every 2000 units per month of market potential in order to assure adequate coverage of the market. Accordingly, the potential in a given retail market area will be a major input into these decisions.

Measuring Absolute Market Potential

There are essentially two components of market potential: the *number of possible users* and the *maximum rate of purchase* that can reasonably be expected. Frequently, managers can obtain estimates of market potential (often broken down by geographic area, industry type, or household type) from trade associations or commercial research firms specializing in such estimates. More typically, managers themselves must estimate at least one of these two components of market potential.

ESTIMATING POTENTIAL IN CONSUMER MARKETS

When the characteristics of all potential buyers are known and readily measurable, the easiest way of estimating the number of buyers is to use already published data. If potential buyers for consumer goods can be described in terms of basic demographic or locational factors (such as age, county, home ownership, or income), both government and private industry data sources can be employed. For example, the annual *Survey of Buying Power* (published by *Sales and Marketing Management* magazine) provides data on the size and the distribution of the population by age group and income category for each county and for metropolitan areas within each county.

Managers often use data obtained from trade associations, from government, or from commercial publications in estimating purchasing rates. Particularly in cases where they are estimating current market potential, managers may use the existing ratios of sales per household or sales per person. These kinds of ratios can often be obtained directly from secondary sources. For example, the Conference Board, a New York-based, industry-supported organization, publishes a distribution of household expenditures on various product categories. Alternatively, if data on total industry sales are available, average demand per household (or per person) may be calculated by dividing total sales by the number of households.

Although a wide variety of sources of data are used in estimating market potential, the following example is typical of the approach used in estimating potential for consumer markets.

Southco Sport Sales is a company that serves as a manufacturer's representative for a variety of sports equipment and sports apparel firms in the Southeast. Recently, the company was asked to represent a golf shoe firm in the state of Florida, so the company's vice president for sales decided to estimate the market potential for golf shoes.

Based on industry data, the manager knew that 2.2 percent of the adult population bought golf shoes in the previous year. Given that Florida's adult population was about 10,482,000, the market potential could have been estimated as 2.2% × 10,482,000, or 230,604 pairs.

As with most consumer products, however, golf shoes are not bought at the same rate by all population segments. Examining data on golfing and golf shoe purchase rates leads to the calculations given in Table 5-1. This estimate (243,130) is higher and likely to be more accurate because Florida's population profile is older than that of the United States on average and because golf shoe sales are higher among golfers who are older.

As the previous example suggests, if different buyer types are likely to differ extensively in their purchase rates, total market potential should be measured by summing the potentials for each group of customer types. In addition to improving accuracy, this allows the manager to account more readily for the effects of projected demographic changes on future market potential levels.

This example is typical of many market potential estimates in that the current average rate of purchase is a good approximation for the maximum rate of purchase. Although this assumption will be valid in many cases, managers should examine the diagnostic questions on willingness and ability

TABLE 5-1

ESTIMATING MARKET POTENTIAL FOR GOLF SHOES IN FLORIDA (in thousands)

AGE GROUP	PERCENT OF ADULTS BUYING GOLF SHOES IN YEAR	×	FLORIDA ADULT POPULATION*	=	POTENTIAL SHOE SALES
18–24	1.5%		1227		18.41
25–34	1.2%		2131		25.57
35–49	2.3%		2712		62.38
50+	3.1%		4412		136.77
Total			10482		243.13

*Source: *1992 Sales Management Survey of Buying Power*, Aug. 24, 1992, p. C47.

to buy (discussed in Chapter 3) to determine if the current rate of purchase could be increased. For example, across markets, the actual rate of golf shoe purchases may vary because of the relative popularity of golf. If secondary data were available on a statewide basis to adjust the national estimates, then the estimate of potential could be refined. Additionally, it may be possible to increase golf shoe purchases if manufacturers offer lower prices, broader styles, or innovative features. Thus, to the extent that the maximum rate of purchase can be realistically increased, managers should modify this rate to reflect more accurately the gap between actual usage rates and potential usage rates.

ESTIMATING POTENTIAL IN ORGANIZATIONAL MARKETS

Secondary data sources such as the U.S. Department of Commerce's *County Business Patterns* and the *Annual Survey of Industrial Buying Power* are useful in projecting market potential for organizational markets. Each of these two sources is especially useful in identifying the number of buying organizations.

But secondary sources of data are usually less useful in measuring purchase rates in organizational markets than in consumer markets. There are two major reasons for this. First, many manufacturers sell highly specialized product lines, but industry sales data are usually available only for broad product categories. For example, a manufacturer of envelopes will not be able to measure industry envelope sales per customer because industry sales will be available only for the broader category "paper products." Second, buyer purchase rates usually vary substantially according to the size of the organization and from one buying industry to another. This is a point of particular concern if market potential is being estimated for a limited geographic area. That is, in a local market a small number of buyers of widely varying sizes and purchase rates may exist. Some of these firms may buy much more than the national average sales per customer and some may buy much less than the average simply because of the size of the organization.

Because of the first problem—lack of specific industry sales data— estimates of purchase rates must often be made through primary marketing research. Because of the problem caused by the widely varying sizes of organizational buyers, managers usually attempt to *weight* the potential of each prospective buyer in order to account for differences in size.

Two measures that are widely used to account for size differences are the *number of employees* and the *value of shipments*, a measure of the value of the production output of a specific industrial plant or facility. The value of shipments and the number of employees usually are closely correlated with the rate of purchase (at least within a given industry). Additionally, these measures are reported annually and are reported for different industries, classified through the Standard Industrial Classification code (SIC code). The SIC code, established by the U.S. Department of Commerce, is a method for classifying individual business establishments (such as stores or manufacturing plants) in each county into industry categories. Data on the number of em-

| TABLE 5-2 | SOME SIC CODES FOR APPAREL AND TEXTILE PRODUCTS MANUFACTURING |

CODE			INDUSTRY
23			Apparel and textile products
	231		Men's and boys' suits, coats
	232		Men's and boys' furnishings
		2321	Men's and boys' shirts
	233		Women's and misses' outerwear
		2335	Dresses
		2337	Coats and suits
	234		Women's and children's undergarments

ployees and the value of shipments are then aggregated at the county level for each industry code. Government publications (such as *Census of Retailing, Census of Manufacturing, County Business Patterns,* and *U.S. Industrial Outlook*) and commercial publications rely on SIC codes to report such data along various geographic lines. Data are aggregated at what are called two-digit, three-digit, and four-digit levels, as indicated in Table 5-2.

In order to understand how this type of data can be used in estimating potential in organizational markets, consider the following example.

Rockmorton Chemical Corporation is a manufacturer of various inks that are used in many types of printing operations. In planning to establish sales quotas for his district, the Midwest sales manager wanted to first determine the market potential for his product line. His five salespeople were located in Pennsylvania, Ohio, Michigan, Indiana, and Illinois. Upon reviewing sales history for the company, he felt the primary ink-using industries were SIC 2711 (newspapers), SIC 2721 (periodicals), SIC 2732 (book printing), and SIC 2751 (letterpress commercial printing). Close inspection of his sales records combined with his knowledge of the industry led him to conclude that the cost of printing ink comprises about 0.1 percent of the value of shipments for the ink-using industries. Basing his estimates on data from the Commerce Department, he calculated the value of shipments in each SIC group for each state as indicated in Table 5-3.

Many of the uses of market-potential information require management to obtain estimates to cover a number of future years. Estimating the *number of potential users* is not generally difficult in the case of consumer goods, because projections regarding the number of households, age-group populations, and many other demographic factors are readily available from secondary sources.

In the case of industrial goods, the number of customers may change rather slowly. However, some buying industries may grow more rapidly than others. Further, geographic movements (such as the recent trend in some industries to shift facilities to the Sunbelt) may change the distribution of potential

TABLE 5-3

ROCKMORTON CHEMICAL CORPORATION: ESTIMATING MARKET POTENTIAL

SIC	VALUE OF SHIPMENTS, MILLIONS OF DOLLARS				
	ILLINOIS	INDIANA	MICHIGAN	OHIO	PENNSYLVANIA
2711	$ 810.8	$121.5	$397.6	$606.2	$ 262.4
2721	1638.5	0	0	264.1	689.3
2732	0	358.0	71.3	0	0
2751	1031.7	0	45.1	36.0	53.3
Total	$3481.0	$479.5	$514.0	$906.3	$1005.0
× .001 Estimated potential	$3.481	$0.479	$0.514	$0.906	$ 1.005

For the five-state area, the total value of all shipments was $6385.8 million. When this total was multiplied by 0.1 percent, the estimated potential was calculated at $6,385,800.

among sales territories. Government publications (such as *Current Industrial Reports* and *U.S. Industrial Outlook*), trade association data, and commercial publications (such as *Predicasts*) are easily obtained and are generally sufficient for projecting buying industry growth patterns in output and employment.

More difficult is the problem of estimating changes in purchase rates. As a practical matter, management generally assumes that these rates will remain stable. However, managers often project rate changes judgmentally—on the basis of sales-force opinions or of recent trends in usage rates.

In the case of durable goods (such as appliances or industrial machines) the future market potential will also depend on the rate at which owners scrap a product because of wear or obsolescence. Managers can estimate scrappage rates either by examining the technical service life of a product or the historical long-term rate of voluntary scrappage. That is, some products must be scrapped on account of technical failure. However, the time until scrappage (or resale) is often a function of economic conditions. For example, new-car lending rates, other economic conditions, or changes in automotive product design (leading to new features, greater efficiency, or improved capability) may influence the voluntary rate of replacement of a durable item. If historical data on scrappage rates can be calculated from a sample of users, managers can use actuarial methods to estimate the replacement potential for products of different ages.

To see how replacement potential for videocassette recorders might be estimated, for example, consider the data in Tables 5-4 and 5-5. Assume that a VCR manufacturer is attempting to estimate replacement market potential for 1994 and is armed with past industry sales data plus data from a consumer survey of VCR owners who purchased their products between 1983 and 1993.

Table 5-4 shows the scrappage rates of VCRs purchased between 1983 and 1989. (Because none of the units bought between 1990 and 1993 had been

TABLE 5-4

CALCULATING SURVIVAL RATES

YEAR PRODUCT WAS PURCHASED	AGE OF PRODUCT	PERCENT OF UNITS SCRAPPED IN 1993	ANNUAL SURVIVAL RATE	PERCENT OF UNITS REMAINING AT END OF 1993
1989	4	1	99	99
1988	5	5	95	94
1987	6	10	90	85
1986	7	25	75	63
1985	8	50	50	32
1984	9	80	20	6
1983	10	100	0	0

scrapped as of the end of 1993, none of the data for those years is relevant to the calculations in Table 5-4.) The table indicates that 1 percent of those who purchased VCRs in 1989 scrapped their 4-year-old VCRs during 1993. This means that 99 percent of the VCRs purchased in 1989 survived to the end of 1993. Of the VCRs purchased in 1988, 5 percent were scrapped in 1993. If we assume that the scrappage rate for 4-year-old VCRs remained the same, 1 percent of the VCRs purchased in 1988 would have been scrapped during 1992. So, of the original units sold in 1988, the percent surviving to the end of 1993 would be calculated as follows:

Percent of units remaining after 4 years	.99
× survival rate during 5th year	× .95
Percent of units remaining after 5 years	.94

TABLE 5-5

ESTIMATING REPLACEMENT POTENTIAL

YEAR PRODUCT WAS SOLD	INDUSTRY SALES (IN THOUSANDS)	PERCENT LEFT AT START OF 1994	NUMBER LEFT AT START OF 1994	ANNUAL SCRAPPING RATE	1994 REPLACEMENT POTENTIAL
1990	10,300	100	10,300	1	103
1989	10,100	99	9,999	5	500
1988	9,800	94	9,212	10	921
1987	10,700	85	9,095	25	2,274
1986	11,700	63	7,371	50	3,686
1985	13,500	32	4,320	80	3,456
1984	12,000	6	720	100	720
					11,660

Once the scrappage and survival rates are calculated, future replacement potential can be estimated as long as prior industry sales data are available. Table 5-5 demonstrates how this estimate could be developed for 1994. Given that no units are scrapped until the fourth year, we would begin with 1990 sales data. From Table 5-4 we know that 1 percent of units that are 4 years old will be scrapped. So of the units sold 4 years ago (in 1990), 1 percent will be scrapped during 1994. The VCRs sold in 1989 will be 5 years old in 1994. One percent of these were scrapped in 1993, and 5 percent of the remaining 9,999,000 units are expected to be scrapped in 1994. Total 1994 replacement potential (11,660,000) is calculated by adding the number of units expected to be scrapped from each age group.

RELATIVE MARKET POTENTIAL

Relative market potential is simply the percentage distribution of market potential among different portions of a market (such as geographic areas or customer groups). Typically, measures of relative potential are used to help management allocate certain resources efficiently. In particular, there are three major uses of relative market potential:

1. *Allocating promotion expenditures.* A national marketer will generally want to allocate the sales promotion and advertising budget among different markets on the basis of the relative importance of each market. For instance, the rate of purchase of room air conditioners or snow tires will vary dramatically among television markets of equal population. By knowing the percentage distribution of market potential between different television markets, management can allocate advertising expenditures in proportion to actual demand.
2. *Allocating salespeople among territories.* A manufacturer or wholesaler will want to assign salespeople in the most efficient manner. Accordingly, if one territory has twice the sales potential of another, it should probably receive twice as many salespeople (assuming each member of the sales force is about equal to every other member in effectiveness).
3. *Locating facilities.* In order to minimize transportation costs and to maximize the ability to deliver products quickly, most organizations will attempt to locate facilities closer to markets of larger potential than to markets of lesser potential. Thus, in locating warehouses, production facilities, and district sales offices, the relative potential of the market being served is often a major input.

Measuring Relative Market Potential

When estimating relative potential, managers begin by identifying factors that are measurable and that are likely to be correlated with market potential. These measures, called *corollary factors*, can be used to represent market potential.

SINGLE-COROLLARY FACTOR APPROACHES

A manager in an industrial goods firm may know that market potential is directly related to a single, easily measured factor such as the number of production workers in the industries to which it sells or the total production value of shipments made by such industries.

For example, Pitney Bowes' Business Systems Division makes mail-handling equipment, such as postage meters, for industrial and commercial customers. In seeking a method for determining the size of the sales force needed in each geographic area, the company found that a single factor—employment growth in the area—seemed to correlate well with sales. Employment growth results from new businesses being formed and from existing businesses being expanded, and these were the two factors that drove the need for new or additional mail-handling equipment. Additionally, employment statistics are frequently reported and easily available.

For a consumer-goods firm, typical corollary factors include the number of housing units (for appliances), the number of single-family dwelling units (for home-repair items), disposable-income levels, the number of people in an age group, and several other buyer characteristics.

MULTIPLE-COROLLARY FACTOR INDEXES

Managers can use more than one corollary factor in estimating relative market potential. In those cases, indexes will be developed to reflect the relative importance of the different factors.

For many frequently purchased consumer goods, a useful index is the Buying Power Index (BPI) provided by Sales and Marketing Management's *Survey of Industrial Buying Power*. A BPI is computed for each county to reflect the percentage of total United States buying power in that county. The index is compiled by weighing three individual factors (each of which is reported separately in the survey) as follows:

$$\text{BPI} = .5 \times \text{percent of effective buying income}$$
$$+ .3 \times \text{percent of U.S. retail sales}$$
$$+ .2 \times \text{percent of U.S. population}$$

To illustrate one use of the BPI, consider the following example.

In 1992, a regional chain of department stores emphasizing middle-quality clothing and other "soft goods" began to look at several alternative new markets with an eye toward expanding the number of stores. Company officials knew that competition would have to be examined in each potential market, but before doing that, they wanted to know which markets had the greatest potential in the five-state market area the company currently served. On the basis of their knowledge of the size of the areas from which their stores drew, potential markets were defined in terms of the counties that would be included, and data were obtained from the *Survey of Buying Power* for each market. Results from four of the markets in the state of Iowa are portrayed in Table 5-6.

TABLE 5-6	USING THE BUYING POWER INDEX TO MEASURE RELATIVE MARKET POTENTIAL

METRO AREA	POPULATION	MEDIAN BUYING INCOME PER HOUSEHOLD	RETAIL SALES PER CAPITA	BPI
Cedar Rapids	170,500	$35,801	$8,783	.0745
Dubuque	86,000	31,311	8,440	.0339
Iowa City	98,100	32,628	7,397	.0401
Sioux City	115,700	29,298	7,867	.0446

"1992 Survey of Buying Power," *Sales & Marketing Management*, Aug. 24, 1992, C69-C72.

On the basis of the BPI data, Cedar Rapids was clearly the highest-potential market. Given these comparisons, the company was then able to concentrate its efforts on seeking out specific sites in those markets with the greater relative potential.

In practice, of course, management would also want to project population and buying power changes expected in the future in order to assess the long-run potential of each market.

Targeting High Potential Markets

In many cases, industry and company sales will vary quite sharply across geographic territories. In some territories, per capita purchases of a product (such as powdered lemonade mix) may be very high compared to those in other territories. This suggests that the primary demand gap is somewhat larger in the area with low per capita sales. Similarly, brand share differences often vary substantially across markets. Country Time lemonade may have a much larger selective demand gap in New Jersey than in Texas, for example.

Marketers frequently construct special indexes to portray these regionally based gaps. A *category development index* (or CDI) is a measure that helps identify territories in which primary demand gaps are relatively large or small. A *brand development index* (or BDI) is a measure that can be used to assess selective demand gaps across territories.[2] The process of developing these indices is demonstrated in Table 5-7.

As Table 5-7 suggests, the same basic procedure is used to calculate a CDI or a BDI. Specifically for a CDI, within each territory the total sales for a product category (such as powdered lemonade) is divided by the number of households in that market. A BDI for Country Time would be calculated by dividing Country Time sales in that same market by the number of households.

[2] F. Beaven Ennis, *Marketing Norms for Product Managers*, Association of National Advertisers, New York, 1985, pp. 26–31.

TABLE 5-7

CALCULATING A DEVELOPMENT INDEX

AREA	ANNUAL CASE SALES (CATEGORY OR BRAND)	÷	THOUSANDS OF HOUSEHOLDS	=	SALES PER 1000 HOUSEHOLDS	INDEX
Total	1,600,000		80,000		20	100
A	22,500		900		25	125
B	13,500		750		18	90
C	52,800		2,400		22	110

Total index = 100. Index for each territory is calculated as:

$$\text{Index} = \frac{\text{sales per 1000 households in territory}}{\text{sales per 1000 households total}} \times 100$$

Category and brand development indexes are useful as diagnostic tools to help managers identify the markets in which the largest primary demand or selective demand gap exists. For example, the hypothetical indexes in Table 5-8 would enable managers to spot four kinds of variations from average market performance:

■ High CDI/high BDI (Boston): In these markets, both brand and category consumption are very high. There is little need for additional development activity.

TABLE 5-8

TYPICAL CATEGORY/BRAND DEVELOPMENT INDEXES

	CDI	BDI
Total U.S.	100	100
Eastern region		
Boston	144	239
New York	94	137
Baltimore	127	213
Southern region		
Atlanta	87	71
Memphis	74	58
Dallas	92	84
Central region		
Minneapolis	114	101
St. Louis	108	95
Denver	79	139
Western region		
Seattle	118	57
San Francisco	83	84
Los Angeles	73	70

Adapted from F. Beaven Ennis, *Marketing Norms for Product Managers*, Association of National Advertisers, New York, 1985, p. 27.

■ High CDI/low BDI (Seattle): The brand needs support if it is to grow. Distribution and promotional support are probably inadequate.

■ Low CDI/high BDI (Denver): Opportunities appear to exist to expand primary demand if management can identify why some people are not using the product.

■ Low CDI/low BDI (Memphis): Neither the brand nor the category has widespread acceptance in this market.

ZIP CODE-BASED INDEXES

In recent years, marketers have gained access to new data bases for gaining a better understanding of relative potential and relative performance while at the same time enhancing their ability to target advertising and promotions. The best-known system for accomplishing this is PRIZM—Potential Rating Index by Zip Markets. This index is based on the observation that demographically similar neighborhoods share the same consumer patterns regardless of the region of the country they are in. PRIZM assigns each U.S. ZIP Code into one of forty "ZIP quality" clusters, each of which is internally similar on demographic and lifestyle grounds. Because so much consumer data is available on a ZIP Code basis (for example, magazine subscription lists, warranty cards, auto ownership, and many consuming buying polls), PRIZM provides an array of useful data on media and purchasing patterns by which ZIP Codes can be compared.[3]

Table 5-9 illustrates the kind of information available on PRIZM for two of the forty ZIP quality clusters. Note that these two clusters share common age ranges, but their consumption habits and media patterns are substantially different. Clearly, marketers interested in selling canned stews or foreign tour packages would not want to target their promotion efforts toward both clusters.

INTERNAL DATA BASES

In many industries, especially those characterized by intensive competition, market leaders are often most concerned with targeting high-potential opportunities within the existing customer base. Specifically, such firms are concerned with focusing marketing efforts on those customers who are likely to purchase in larger volumes or who are likely candidates to purchase additional products from the firm. Internal data bases consist of information about the behavior of customers that has been systematically gathered during the course of prior business transactions. Table 5-10 provides a list of some typical data elements that might appear on a marketer's internal data base.

Few industries have internal data bases that are more useful than that of the financial services industry. Such firms not only have precise transaction histories, but they also obtain extensive additional information when customers

[3] Michael J. Weiss, *The Clustering of America*, Harper & Row, New York, 1989, pp. 12–16.

TABLE 5-9

A COMPARISON OF TWO ZIP QUALITY CLUSTERS

ZQ 8: YOUNG SUBURBIA		ZQ 16: BLUE-COLLAR NURSERY	
5.3% of U.S. households		2.2% of U.S. households	
Primary age range:	25–44	Primary age range:	25–44
Median household income:	$35,582	Median household income:	$30,007
Median home value:	$93,281	Median home value:	$67,281

THUMBNAIL DEMOGRAPHICS   **THUMBNAIL DEMOGRAPHICS**

Upper-middle-class outlying suburbs	Middle-class child-rearing towns
Single-unit housing	Single-unit housing
Predominantly white families	Predominantly white families
College educations	High school educations
White-collar jobs	Blue-collar jobs

POLITICS   **POLITICS**

Predominant ideology:	conservative	Predominant ideology:	conservative
1984 presidential vote:	Reagan (76%)	1984 presidential vote:	Reagan (74%)
Key issues: fiscal conservatism, trade protection		Key issues: fiscal conservatism, nuclear arms	

SAMPLE NEIGHBORHOODS   **SAMPLE NEIGHBORHOODS**

Eagan, Minnesota (55124)	West Jordan, Utah (84084)
Dale City, Virginia (22193)	Maryville, South Carolina (29440)
Pleasanton, California (94566)	Princeton, Texas (75044)
Smithtown, New York (11787)	Richmond, Michigan (48062)
Ypsilanti, Michigan (48197)	Haysville, Kansas (67060)
Lilburn, Georgia (30247)	Magnolia, Houston, Texas (77355)

LIFESTYLE   **LIFESTYLE**

High usage	Index	Low usage	Index	High usage	Index	Low usage	Index
$75,000 + life insurance	229	Theater	83	Campers	222	Downhill skiing	64
Swimming pools	228	Laxatives	81	Unions	192	Watch tennis	45
Health clubs	217	Convertibles	80	Watch pro wrestling	186	Foreign tour packages	45
Ice skating	213	Malt liquor	78	Toy-sized dogs	175	Malt liquor	43
Lawn furniture	184	Civic clubs	65	Bowling	172	Money-market funds	41
Racquetball	179	Soul records/ tapes	63	Hunting	171	Environmentalist organizations	38
Home computers	178	Watch pro wrestling	38	1960s rock records/ tapes	164	Travel by railroad	21
Foreign tour packages	158	Snuff	29	Tupperware	141	Slide projectors	16

TABLE 5-9

A COMPARISON OF TWO ZIP QUALITY CLUSTERS (continued)

ZQ 8: YOUNG SUBURBIA | **ZQ 16: BLUE-COLLAR NURSERY**

MAGAZINES/NEWSPAPERS | MAGAZINES/NEWSPAPERS

High usage	Index	Low usage	Index	High usage	Index	Low usage	Index
World Tennis	255	*National Enquirer*	76	*Lakeland Boating*	287	*Forum*	37
Business Week	190	*Esquire*	75	*Mother Earth News*	202	*Fortune*	35
Skiing	187	*True Story*	47	*Outdoor Life*	166	*Rolling Stone*	34
Golf	177	*Jet*	33	*American Photographer*	165	*Atlantic Monthly*	12

CARS | CARS

High usage	Index	Low usage	Index	High usage	Index	Low usage	Index
Mitsubishi Galants	263	Plymouth Gran Furys	98	Ford EXPs	232	Jaguars	29
Ford EXPs	215	Chevrolet Impalas	97	Chevrolet Chevettes	208	BMWs	28
Toyota vans	209	Dodge Diplomats	97	Plymouth Turismos	196	Mitsubishi Galants	18
Nissan 300ZXs	208	Rolls Royce	39	Ford Escorts	188	Ferraris	18
				Chevrolet Cavaliers	184	Alfa Romeos	4

FOOD | FOOD

High usage	Index	Low usage	Index	High usage	Index	Low usage	Index
Cheese spreads	138	Whole-wheat bread	95	Canned stews	141	Whole-wheat bread	85
Pretzels	134	TV dinners	94	Pretzels	119	Canned corned-beef hash	78
Frozen waffles	133	Canned stews	87	Children's vitamins	116	Canned orange juice	65
Children's vitamins	126	Powdered fruit drinks	76	Baked beans	115	Frozen corn-on-the-cob	56

TELEVISION | TELEVISION

High usage	Index	Low usage	Index	High usage	Index	Low usage	Index
Cheers	130	*Knots Landing*	78	*Newhart*	132	*Miami Vice*	92
Night Court	123	*Highway to Heaven*	78	*Night Court*	127	*NBC Sports World*	80
Newhart	116	*The Young and the Restless*	62	*Love Connection*	124	*Sunday morning interview program*	64
Family Ties	115	*Friday Night Videos*	61	*Highway to Heaven*	117	*American Bandstand*	53

Source: Michael J. Weiss, *The Clustering of America*, HarperCollins Publishers, New York, 1988, pp. 292–293 and 316–317. An index of 100 would indicate usage at the national average.

TABLE 5-10	SOME TYPICAL DATA ELEMENTS IN INTERNAL DATA BASES

- Customer identification
- Name and address
- Telephone number
- Dates of promotions to prospect/customer
- Responses to those promotions
- Date of first purchase, of subsequent purchases, of last purchase
- Frequency of purchases
- Item(s) purchased by product ID, category, or department
- Product usage information obtained from records of customer transactions
- Purchase amounts and average purchase amount
- Method of payment (check, cash, type of credit card, etc.)
- Personal information generated by transactions with the company (such as age, income, home value, marital status, ages of children, occupation, and automobile ownership)
- Product and/or purchase information (including reasons for purchase, competitive products considered or owned, intended use of product) obtained from questionnaires packaged with products, which buyers complete and return

Developed from Jack Bickert, *Adventures in Relevance Marketing*, 2d ed., Briefcase Books, Denver, 1990; Ernest Schell, "Lifetime Value of a Customer," *Marketing Insights*, Fall 1991, pp. 85–89; Stan Rapp and Thomas Collins, "The Great Turnaround: Selling to the Individual," *Adweek's Marketing Week*, Aug. 27, 1990, pp. 20–26.

apply for credit cards, loans, and so on. Armed with such data, banks could identify, for example, high-income customers who have only a checking account (and thus are good potential customers for certificates of deposits and other investment products). Additionally, the efficiency with which such firms can use marketing resources is improved by using data bases to identify high-potential targets: Whereas most direct mail solicitations generate only 1 to 2 percent responses, bank marketers generally cite response rates that are five times larger, thanks to effectively targeting promotional messages on special certificate of deposit or home equity loan products.[4]

SALES FORECASTING

Market-potential measures can be of significant value to managers, as the examples in this chapter have indicated. However, because market potential is related to industry and company sales, the usefulness of the market-potential estimates can be enhanced by comparisons with sales forecasts.

Sales forecasts are estimates of future levels of demand. These market measurements can have a tremendous impact on all functional areas of an organization because they are used in making a number of different decisions. There are, however, important differences in the types of sales forecasts and in the methods of sales forecasting, which are discussed in the remainder of this chapter.

[4] Jon Berry, "The Rich and the Worthy," *Adweek's Marketing Week*, May 11, 1992, pp. 21–23.

Basic Types of Sales Forecasts

The two major types of sales forecasts are industry sales forecasts and company sales forecasts. However, within these two classes, forecasts can be made at different levels of aggregation of sales.

INDUSTRY SALES FORECASTS

Managers may use an industry sales forecast to estimate the total sales that will be achieved by all suppliers in the relevant market. Depending on how the firm has defined the relevant market, industry sales can be measured for a product form, for a product class, or for all competing classes satisfying the same generic need. Indeed, a manager may develop industry sales forecasts for more than one of these levels of aggregation, depending on how the forecast will be used.

There are four basic uses of industry sales forecasts. First, industry sales forecasts indicate the expected rates of growth of alternative markets. Therefore, they are useful elements in corporate marketing planning (as discussed in Chapter 2). Further, to the extent that industry sales forecasts indicate different rates of growth for various product forms or various product classes, decisions on the appropriate relevant market can be made. For example, if one product form (such as nutritional cereals) is growing faster than a competing form (such as presweetened cereals), then top management will probably provide greater marketing support to brands in the product-form market with higher growth. Alternatively, if sales forecasts show that industry sales for either a product form or for a product class (such as cereals) are growing at a low rate, then strategies for stimulating sales of the product form or class may be examined.

Second, as we discussed in Chapter 4, the rate of industry sales growth is a major influence on competitive intensity. If management's forecast indicates a dramatic decline in the rate of industry sales growth, they will know that future company sales gains must come from increases in market share, a condition that often fosters heavy price and promotion competition.

Third, industry sales forecasts are also important to middle management. Knowing the future level of industry sales enables a firm to calculate the market share required to reach its sales goals. For example, given a sales objective for a product of one million units and an industry sales forecast of five million units, the managers can judge whether or not it is feasible to attain a 20 percent market share based on the company's planned level of marketing effort and on the product's current market-share position. The relationship between industry sales forecasts and marketing budgets is discussed in detail in Chapter 6.

Finally, the rate of industry growth generally has a major influence on company sales growth. Accordingly, an industry sales forecast is often an important input to the company sales forecast.

COMPANY SALES FORECASTS

Just as the industry sales forecast can be developed at any of three levels of aggregation, company sales forecasts can also be developed at more than one level. That is, a firm may wish to forecast company sales of a specific item (such as regular-size Tide), a brand (Tide), a product line (Procter & Gamble detergents), or total company sales (all Procter & Gamble sales).

Forecasts at the *item* level are generally most useful for decisions related to production scheduling and to the transportation of goods to distributors. Forecasts at the highest level of aggregation, *company sales*, are most useful for overall company financial planning. From a marketing strategy and planning perspective, the most important forecasts are those that focus on *brand sales* or *product-line sales* because marketing decisions are most often designed to influence sales at these levels of aggregation. However, not all forecasting approaches are equally useful for marketing decision making. That is, even when brand or product-line sales are being forecasted, the managerial usefulness of the forecast will depend on the type of approach used to develop the forecast. When our concern is simply to get the best estimate of expected sales (which is usually the major concern of production and finance managers), time-series methods are generally used. However, causal forecasts are appropriate if we are concerned with understanding how our price and marketing budget might *influence* future sales.

Basic Forecasting Approaches

Although an extensive array of forecasting approaches exists, there are really three basic types of approaches: time-series models, causal models, and judgmental approaches. Any of these approaches can be employed in forecasting either industry or company sales.[5]

TIME-SERIES MODELS

The basic assumption underlying time-series models is that sales can be forecast with acceptable accuracy by examining historical sales patterns. These models are relatively easy to use because the only data needed are past sales and because they can be implemented by means of easy-to-obtain "canned" computer programs. A further advantage of these models is that the probable range of the deviation of actual sales from forecasted sales (called the *forecasting error*) can be estimated statistically.

As a general rule, time-series models are most useful when market forces are relatively stable within the forecasting horizon. That is, if sales trends are

---

[5] See, for example, Spyros, Makridakis and Steven Wheelwright, "Forecasting: Issues and Challenges for Marketing Management," *Journal of Marketing*, October 1977, pp. 24–38; and David M. Georgoff and Robert G. Murdick, "Manager's Guide to Forecasting," *Harvard Business Review*, January–February 1986, pp. 110–120.

not likely to change because of economic changes, marketing actions, or technology, these models are likely to be reasonably accurate. These conditions are often found when short-run forecast horizons (less than 1 year) are required. They may also be found over longer forecast periods in the case of markets that are technologically mature, are not very susceptible to the effects of economic fluctuations, and are expected to witness few major changes in marketing effort.

Even in the most stable markets, however, seasonal variations, changes in trends, and random fluctuations do occur. Accordingly, a variety of procedures have been developed for "smoothing out" random fluctuations by averaging recent sales levels, for giving weights to monthly sales levels to adjust for seasonality, and for increasing the importance of more recent sales data to reflect trends.

In cases where pronounced trends exist, where random fluctuations are not severe, and where managers wish to forecast several periods into the future, direct curve-fitting approaches are often employed to identify the sales time series. In this approach, a computer program is used to determine the equation of the "best-fitting" curve—the line or curve that most closely approximates the historical trend. This equation is then used to forecast future sales by projecting that same line or curve into the future.

Consider, for example, Figure 5-2. The dots in this figure portray annual sales for the Tootsie Roll company from 1966 to 1983. As we can see, there is clearly an upward sales trend with modest fluctuations. The dashed line is the straight line that, according to a simple regression analysis between sales and time, best portrays the past trend. Sales forecasts for the subsequent years (1984 through 1986) were made by simply extending the trend line.

FIGURE 5-2
A time-series forecast for Tootsie Roll Inc. (Developed from data presented in W. R. Dillon, T. J. Madden, and N. H. Firtle, *Marketing Research in a Marketing Environment*, Times Mirror, Mosby, St. Louis, 1987, pp. 705–706.)

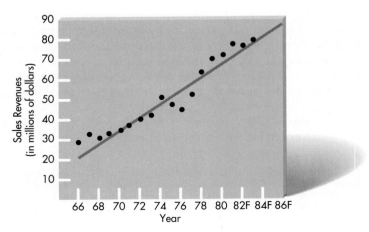

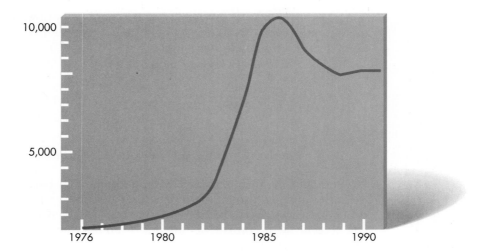

FIGURE 5-3
VCR sales history
(in thousands).

TIME-SERIES DIFFUSION MODELS

One special class of time-series models of particular interest to marketers is diffusion models, which are used to portray first-purchase, sales-growth patterns for new durable products or services. An example of this sales-growth pattern can be seen in Figure 5-3, which portrays the unit sales history of videocassette recorders in the United States. Sales growth was slow at first as buyers waited to hear about the experiences of other households before buying. As word of the product's benefits spread and prices declined in the mid-1980s, sales took off dramatically. By 1986 about 42 million VCRs had been sold. With fewer nonowners remaining in the market and because the product typically had a long life, sales began to decline in 1987.

This type of pattern creates a special challenge to management. It is important to be able to distinguish the long-term sales opportunity from the one-time sales peak in order to determine the appropriate level of production capacity and marketing budgets. Accordingly, a special class of forecasting models has been developed following the lead of Frank Bass, who developed a model to predict the sales peak for color television sets.[6]

Basically, the model requires the manager to be able to make three estimates:

1. m, the number of potential buyers in the market
2. p, the coefficient of innovation (initial trial rate)
3. q, the coefficient of imitation (diffusion rate)

[6] See Frank Bass, "A New Product Growth Model for Consumer Durables," *Management Science*, January 1969, pp. 215–227.

In this, p represents the probability of purchase (adoption) by individuals who are not influenced by other owners, and q represents the effect of each adopter on each nonadopter.

The specific formula for this model is

$$S_t = pm + (q - p)Y_t - \frac{q}{m} Y_t^2$$

where S_t = number of sales during time period t
Y_t = cumulative number of previous sales up to time t

Essentially, the formula states that sales in the time period being studied (S_t) are determined by three factors. The first (pm in the equation) is the number of buyers who will try the new product on their own when it is introduced. The second factor represents buying by those who rely on word-of-mouth information from those who have already purchased. At any point in time, the number of these imitators will, of course, depend on the number of people or firms who have already bought (Y_t). The final factor reflects the fact that, ultimately, first-time sales will decline. As the number of previous buyers (Y_t) increases, the number of people left in the market who have never tried the product declines. At the start of the process there were m potential buyers. But at time t there are only $m - Y_t$ people or firms who have yet to buy.

There are basically two complementary approaches to using this model. In the early stages of a product's life, p, q, and m will be set judgmentally with the aid of marketing research and the experience of similar products. For example, p is typically around .02 (slightly higher for consumer durables than for industrial products) and q is typically .4 to .5 (slightly higher for industrial innovations). Additionally, market research that explains or demonstrates the product and then asks for customers to state their likelihood of purchasing it can help managers gauge p and m. Later on, when actual sales data begin to come in, p and q may be estimated through statistical methods. But while statistical estimates can be developed that fit the historical data quite well, they may still fail to predict the future accurately.[7]

Before using time-series forecasts, managers should answer the questions posed in Table 5-11. Specifically, managers should have a substantial number of data points if they expect a trend to be reliable. Additionally, time-series models represent only the past. Such projections may be too optimistic if industry sales are approaching market potential (and thus likely to have a substantially reduced growth rate). Finally, major changes in future sales often occur due to changes in the demographic or economic environment, in the

---

[7] Additional discussions on the typical values of p and q for different products and on the uses and limitations of such model are available in Fareena Sultan, John Farley, and Donald Lehman, "A Meta-Analysis of Diffusion Models," *Journal of Marketing Research*, February 1990, pp. 70–77.

TABLE 5-11	QUESTIONS FOR EVALUATING THE RELIABILITY OF TIME-SERIES FORECASTS

1. Do we have a long enough history of sales data to construct a reliable trend?
2. Can we expect industry growth trends to level off because industry sales are approaching market potential?
3. Is it likely that industry sales will shift because of economic, demographic, or technological factors?
4. Can new competition (including competition from other product forms or classes) be anticipated that will influence industry or company sales?
5. Can we expect major changes in the marketing activity of competitors?
6. Does the industry (company) have the production capacity to fulfill industry (company) sales forecasts?
7. Does our company plan any major changes in its marketing programs?

firm's marketing effort, or in competitive activity, and the potential effects of such changes can only be captured through the use of causal models.

CAUSAL MODELS

When environmental changes can be expected to create a shift in the historical pattern of sales, then time-series models are likely to prove unsatisfactory. In such situations, managers are more likely to seek to use forecasting techniques that link sales to one or more factors that are thought to cause or influence sales.

The simplest type of causal model is the leading indicator forecast. Leading indicators are often used to forecast industry sales over a fairly short time horizon—usually 6 months or less. Specifically, some fairly broad economic changes in sales of business forms usually trail changes in sales of the nation's Gross National Product by 6 months, and the monthly consumer confidence index published by the Conference Board (a New York-based research group) predicts outboard motor sales with a lead time of 6 months.

Multiple-regression models are used when a number of factors have an impact on sales. These factors will include leading indicators, especially in *industry* sales forecasts. Additionally, however, multiple-regression forecasts also allow managers to incorporate the expected effects of any *controllable* marketing variables that are likely to be significant when forecasting *company* sales. That is, if historical data on price, advertising expenditures, or other marketing variables are available, managers can attempt to predict the different levels of sales that will occur for varying levels of price or advertising expenditures. Therefore, assuming that the relationship between sales and these controllable marketing variables can be clearly established, multiple regression provides a forecasting approach that can serve as a planning tool.

(In contrast, time-series sales forecasts do not permit managers to examine the effects of changes in controllable marketing variables.)

Multiple-regression models, like time-series models, rely on historical data and are easily implemented through canned computer programs. However, they attempt to define equations that give the best historical statistical fit between sales (industry or company) and one or more causal (or *predictor*) variables.

For example, a company in the home-furnishings industry developed the following multiple-regression equation to forecast company sales.[8]

$$\begin{aligned}
\text{Annual sales (\$ millions)} = {} & -33.51 \\
& + \quad .373 \text{ (previous year's sales)} \\
& + \quad .033 \text{ (previous year's housing starts,} \\
& \qquad\qquad \text{thousands)} \\
& + \quad .672 \text{ (disposable personal income, \$ billions)} \\
& - 11.03 \quad \text{(time from beginning of data, } yr)
\end{aligned}$$

Although it did not incorporate all the possible factors influencing sales, this equation explained 95 percent of the year-to-year variation in company sales over the previous 20 years. Additionally, as in any statistical forecast, the company was able to determine the standard error of the forecast—in this case $9.7 million. That is, there is always some imprecision in a statistical forecast. The standard error indicates the size of this imprecision in terms of past sales and past forecasts. Two-thirds of the time, the forecast estimate of sales will be within one standard error (in this case $9.7 million) of actual sales; 95 percent of the time, forecasted sales will be within two standard errors (in this case $19.4 million) of the actual sales.

While multiple-regression models do overcome many of the disadvantages of time-series models, they are never perfectly reliable. Several assumptions are made in the construction of regression models. Accordingly, managers should answer a number of important questions in order to assess the reliability of regression forecasts. The most important of these questions are presented in Table 5-12. If the answer to any of these questions is unfavorable, then the accuracy of the forecast result will be limited. More specifically:

- If important causal factors have been left out, sales may fluctuate for reasons not explained by the model. If these factors can have a major impact on sales, then the regression sales forecast should be adjusted judgmentally (if possible) to account for the other factors.
- If some causal factors cannot be accurately projected into the future, then management should develop a series of forecasts, each based on different

[8] George C. Parker and Edilberto L. Segura, "How to Get a Better Forecast," *Harvard Business Review*, March–April 1971, pp. 99–102.

| TABLE 5-12 | QUESTIONS FOR EVALUATING THE RELIABILITY OF MULTIPLE-REGRESSION FORECASTS |

1. Have any important factors that influence sales been ignored in testing the various equations?
2. Can the predictor variables that cause or influence sales be predicted or controlled?
3. Will some of the predictors change so dramatically in the future that their impact on sales will change?
4. Are the various predictor variables independent of one another, or do two or more of those variables really measure the same thing?

assumptions about the future levels of these factors. For example, if average industry prices or competitors' prices are important but hard-to-predict factors, managers can make different estimates about future prices and see how each estimate changes the forecasted level of sales.

■ If some of the predictors are expected to change dramatically, the historical relationship with sales may not hold up. For example, a dramatic rise in prices may increase buyers' sensitivity to price. If this happens, the relative importance of price in influencing sales will become greater than the regression equation suggests.

■ If two predictors are highly correlated (for example, population and total household income), then the proportion of historical variation in sales explained by the equation will not be accurate. That is, our measures of the statistical error of the forecast will not be reliable.

While the last problem can be resolved by redefining the equation to eliminate one of the correlated predictors, the first three problems can be resolved only by the application of management judgment.

JUDGMENTAL APPROACHES

Frequently it will not be possible to rely heavily on statistical approaches to forecasting. Time-series methods may be inappropriate because of wide fluctuations in sales or because of anticipated changes in trends. Regression methods may not be feasible because of a lack of historical data or because of management's inability to predict (or even identify) causal factors. The judgmental approach will be management's only possible avenue for forecasting in these situations.

Even where statistical estimates are available, managers may need to use judgment to supplement these approaches because even the most sophisticated statistical models cannot anticipate all the potential external factors that can influence sales (such as strikes at customers' facilities or major competitive innovations).

Moreover, statistical forecasts are less reliable when forecasting demand by sales territory or customer segment. Managers must rely on the judgment-based estimates of field sales personnel to develop such detailed forecasts. Similarly, if a few customers dominate sales, sales-force judgment is essential. For example:

> Royal Appliance experienced a sudden downturn in sales of its Dirt Devil vacuum cleaner in 1992, and its Vice President for Finance admitted that the company had not foreseen the decline. A major difficulty in making forecasts was that Wal-Mart and K-Mart represented 45 percent of Dirt Devil sales, so sharp changes in monthly orders from either of these powerful retailers would have a drastic impact on total sales. Industry observers suggested that Royal was guilty of not having its sales force performing audits of the various retail stores on a regular basis to track product movement. This prevented corrective action in the way of marketing expenditures from being taken.[9]

The sales force and distributors are usually the most expert at monitoring and assessing buying patterns and local competitive conditions. However, other management personnel may also be involved in the forecasting process. Particularly in the case of regression sales forecasting, the judgments of marketing and advertising research personnel or brand managers may be employed to estimate the impact of a change in marketing budgets or strategies on sales.

Interpreting the Forecast

In evaluating the managerial implications of a sales forecast, managers should be fully aware of both the *sensitivity* of forecast results to slight changes in forecast assumptions or techniques and the *costs* of forecasting errors.

SENSITIVITY ANALYSIS

If several techniques give essentially the same results, the reliability of a forecast should be greater. Accordingly, some firms develop parallel forecasts based on alternative techniques. Similarly, several regression forecasts may be developed, each one based on different assumptions regarding causal factors. Knowing how different techniques or assumptions lead to alternative demand estimates enables a manager to determine how sensitive the forecast result is to a change in these factors. When forecasts are highly sensitive, managers should expect greater imprecision and should closely monitor the environment to find out which model and which assumptions most closely approximate reality.

---

[9] Valerie Reitman, "Royal Appliance Slips After Flooding Its Market," *The Wall Street Journal*, July 30, 1992, p. B3.

| TABLE 5-13 | POSSIBLE RESULTS OF COMPANY SALES FORECAST ERRORS |

RESULTS OF OVERESTIMATION

Excess capacity leading to layoffs, loss of skilled labor
Price cuts or additional marketing expenses to move product
Distributor ill will because of excess distributor inventories
Inventory costs:
   Cash flow problems and cost of capital tied up in finished goods, components, raw materials
   Technical obsolescence or damage
   Storage or warehousing costs

RESULTS OF UNDERESTIMATION

Lost sales or customer goodwill
Overtime costs
Costs of expediting shipments
Reduced quality control due to reduced maintenance of machinery at full production capacity
Production bottlenecks due to lack of materials and parts

THE COSTS OF FORECAST ERRORS

If a sales forecast has a large standard error (a wide range of possible values), managers should consider the costs of overestimating and underestimating demand. To illustrate this point, assume that a manager has been given a company sales forecast of 200,000 units with a standard error of 10,000 units. In using this information, the manager may choose to plan around a level somewhat lower or higher than 200,000 depending on the firm's cost and competitive structure. A manager planning production and marketing budgets on the basis of exactly 200,000 units implicitly assumes that the costs of overestimation and underestimation are equal, but in most firms these costs are not equal.

As Table 5-13 indicates, there are different kinds of consequences associated with overestimating and underestimating *company sales*. For some firms, the cost of holding excess inventory may be extremely high (perhaps because the product is perishable) while the amount of sales lost because of delayed shipments is very low (perhaps because the company has loyal customers). Accordingly, if a firm is in that situation, management will be more willing to risk underestimation than overestimation. This is because the cost of excess inventory resulting from excess production will outweigh the lost revenue from an inadequate level of production. Because the costs of overestimation are greater for that firm, managers will probably want to base decisions on a forecast that is more conservative than 200,000 units. For example, statistical theory tells us that there is a 95 percent chance that the actual level of sales will be within two standard errors. Thus, with a standard error of 10,000, there is a 95 percent chance that sales will be within the range of 180,000 to 220,000 units. Further there is a $2^1/_2$ percent chance that sales will be less than 180,000 and a $2^1/_2$ percent chance that sales will exceed 220,000. However, managers operating in very dynamic and uncertain markets usually face substantial costs from *underestimation*, as the following situation shows:

> The enthusiastic market response to nicotine patches (designed to help people quit smoking) was not accurately forecasted by any of the leading pharmaceutical firms that introduced these products in 1991. However, Marion Merrell Dow, the maker of Nicoderm, was impacted the most. Because it subcontracted its production to a small California firm, it was slow to respond when industry sales exploded. Between February and April of 1992, Nicoderm's market share slipped from 42 percent to 27 percent as retail stockouts sent customers racing to competing brands. Because the market was young (so brand images were undeveloped), the products were virtually identical, and the Food and Drug Administration tightly restricted product claims, the potential cost of lost future sales was substantial.[10]

Additionally, errors in industry sales forecasts can create problems for managers. The most significant of these problems is that a forecast error may lead to misclassifying a product in a firm's product mix plan. For example, if industry sales are *overestimated*, management may treat a cash cow as though it were a star; the result would be excessive marketing expenditures and lower profitability. On the other hand, if industry sales are *underestimated*, management may make the mistake of prematurely reducing marketing support in the belief that the market has matured and that less spending is necessary to maintain market share; the result in this case may well be a loss in market share because of inadequate spending relative to the competition.

In sum, managers must recognize that sales forecasts are only estimates and are based on certain assumptions. By being aware of these assumptions and the nature of the risks associated with forecast errors, managers should be able to make better judgments on how to use the forecast.

CONCLUSION

Market measurement is an activity of critical importance for a wide range of decisions. Market-potential estimates and industry and company sales forecasts are essential for the development of corporate marketing strategies and product objectives. Middle-management decisions regarding the size and allocation of marketing expenditures depend heavily on sales forecasts and on the relationship between forecasts and the factors to be considered in the next chapter.

[10] Suein L. Hwang and Lourdes Lee Valeriano, "Marketers and Consumers Get the Jitters After Severe Shortage of Nicotine Patches," *The Wall Street Journal*, May 22, 1992, p. B1.

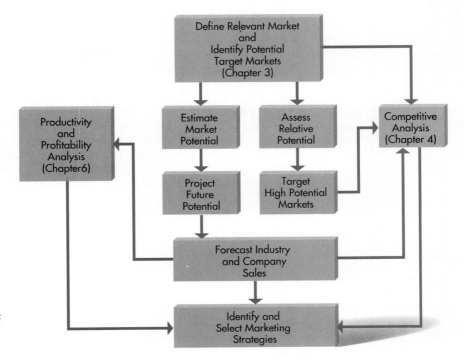

FIGURE 5-4
Steps in market measurement and their relationship to other aspects of the situation analysis.

In this chapter, we have examined the different kinds of market measurements, their uses, and the various ways in which they can be developed. By understanding the purpose and assumptions behind a given market measurement, it will be easier for a manager to specify the kind of information needed in a given situation and to understand the degree of reliability that should be placed on a given market-measurement estimate.

Additionally, managers should be aware of the available data sources that can be used for developing market-measurement estimates. Some of these sources were mentioned in this chapter. However, a more complete listing and description of prominent sources of market information is contained in the Appendix.

The various steps in market measurement and the relationships among these steps are portrayed in Figure 5-4. To gain a better understanding of some of these relationships, and to become more aware of the challenges involved in market measurement, consider NBC's experience with the 1992 Olympics Triple Cast.

NATIONAL BROADCASTING CORPORATION: PROJECTING DEMAND FOR PAY-PER-VIEW OF THE OLYMPICS TRIPLE CAST*

In 1989, the National Broadcasting Corporation (NBC) paid $401 million for television broadcast rights to the 1992 summer Olympic games in Barcelona, Spain. In addition to the rights fee, the costs of production, promotion, and satellite time were expected to reach $350 million. The sale of network advertising time was expected to provide NBC with $500 million in revenue. But to come close to breaking even, the network was counting on revenue from a source not previously used in the Olympics—pay-per-view television.

In concert with cable television operators around the country, NBC planned to offer live round-the-clock coverage of the Olympics on three cable channels, in addition to the free evening network coverage, for $125. NBC was to receive about 55 percent of the pay-per-view sales revenue, with the rest going to cable operators. The cost of production and promotion to NBC and its cable operator partners was $100 million. Included in this cost was the purchase of enough electronics to equip 10 percent of all households with cable systems that could provide pay-per-view coverage. (This equipment could be used for future pay-per-view events.) At the time of their bid for the Olympics, NBC anticipated that 40 million of the 60 million cable-subscribing households would be able to purchase pay-per-view by 1992.

Prior to 1992, the most notable uses of pay-per-view were in boxing, with the 1991 match between George Foreman and Evander Holyfield pulling the largest pay-per-view audience ever, about 1.4 million households. Industry experts noted that, typically, 90 percent of pay-per-view orders were placed in the final week prior to an event. However, NBC began promoting the Triple Cast in December of 1991.

In January of 1992, NBC appeared to be optimistic about Triple Cast. A sales target of 3.5 million was set, based on the assumption that 35.9 million households would be able to buy pay-per-view and that (relying on some research) 10 percent actually would buy. The optimism of the NBC projection was not shared by industry observers, who noted that the buy percentage for the Foreman-Holyfield fight had been 7.8 percent of a much smaller base.

In March, *Television Digest* reported that a survey of intentions made by the marketing researchers at Strategic Media Research yielded the estimate that 2 percent of cable subscribers planned to buy. Among those who indicated a reason for not buying, 28 percent were not interested in the Olympics, 27 percent cited the high price, and 18 percent said the networks would offer adequate free coverage.

By July it was apparent that the Triple Cast was in trouble financially. But only 20 million households were able to order pay-per-view on demand and thus able to make an "impulse buy" at the last minute (as opposed to having special attachments brought in). Thus, even the final promotional blitz was of limited help. In the end, only 250,000 households bought the Triple Cast.

1. What was the best way to estimate the market potential for Triple Cast?
2. Why was NBC's forecast so far off the mark? How would you have gone about developing a sales forecast for Triple Cast?
3. Could the demand for Triple Cast have been analyzed as a diffusion of innovation forecast? Explain.
4. What were the costs of overestimation and underestimation to NBC? Which cost do you think was more important to avoid?

---

* Developed from Mark Robichaux, "Pay-Per-View Games: Down but Not Out," *The Wall Street Journal*, Aug. 7, 1992, p. B1; Mark Lewyn and Mark Landler, "NBC's Triple Cast Never Made a Run at the Gold," *Business Week*, Aug. 17, 1992, pp. 34–35; "NBC Olympic Loss Low?" *Television Digest*, July 20, 1992; "Triple Cast Success Lies in Unknowns," *Electronic Media*, July 13, 1992, p. 23; "Financial Evaluation of the 1992 Summer Olympics Pay-Per-View Triplecast Buy," *Mediaweek*, Mar. 16, 1992, p. 26; "Summer Olympics Pay-Per-View," *Television Digest*, Mar. 2, 1992; "NBC High on Triple Cast," *Television Digest*, Jan. 13, 1992, p. 1.

QUESTIONS AND SITUATIONS FOR DISCUSSION

1. Your company markets a line of clothing products for both secondary and university/college students. Your sweatshirts and T-shirts are embossed with the school's name and appropriate identifying symbols. How would you measure market potential to determine the different geographic territories you would assign to your salespersons? Would you measure potential differently if this was a new line for your company?

2. You have been given the assignment of determining relative market potential for each of the 50 states for (a) Morton salt, (b) Rolex watches, (c) Motown compact discs. In each case, what are the most effective ways to complete this assignment?

3. Which of the following represent estimates of company potential and which represent estimates of market potential? Explain.

    a. Potential demand for cellular phones facing a firm with a franchise to sell a specific brand in the state of Nebraska

    b. Potential demand for graduation photographs of high school seniors within a single school district

    c. Potential demand for a computer software sales forecasting package that runs only on color monitors and only on Apple computers

4. The U.S. Hispanic population has recently been increasing at four times the rate of the overall population growth. As a bottler of sugared colas, you know that the Hispanic market consumes 65 percent more colas per capita than the general population. How would this information be useful to you in determining the market potential for soft drinks? Would it affect your decision to use either time series or multiple regression in your sales forecast? Why?

5. Which of the following would linear trend extrapolation be more accurate for? (a) annual population for the twelve nations comprising the European Common Market, or (b) annual sales of cars produced in the common market by Fiat. Why?

6. If an industry sales forecast is needed for each of the following products, for which product will a time-series approach be the most appropriate?

    a. Automobiles

    b. Laundry detergent

    c. Baby food

7. General Foods quit advertising its Maxwell House coffee brand for 9 months. During this period, Maxwell House lost several points of market share. Would this affect the basic approach(es) Maxwell House could use in forecasting sales?

8. In each of the following situations, would you tend to avoid overestimation or underestimation?

    a. Your product has a large market share with loyal customers.

    b. You compete in a market where technology changes and design changes are frequent.

    c. You are a new competitor trying to build market share.

    d. In order to maintain good employee relationships, your company wants to avoid layoffs.

    e. Your product is not greatly differentiated from competitive products.

    9. ATRA (Algarve Tourism Research Associates) performs market studies for a variety of tourism-related businesses and public agencies in the Algarve province of Portugal. Early in 1989, ATRA was asked to forecast the number of hotel guest arrivals to the province for the four quarters of the coming year. ATRA had the historical data on guest arrivals between 1979 and 1988 shown in Table 5-14.

    Using a trend forecasting model, ATRA's researchers developed the following forecast of guest arrivals:

1989	First quarter	165,652
1989	Second quarter	327,955
1989	Third quarter	441,596
1989	Fourth quarter	208,410

TABLE 5-14 **GUEST ARRIVALS TO HOTELS AND SIMILAR ESTABLISHMENTS***

YEAR	QUARTER	IN 1000s	YEAR	QUARTER	IN 1000s
1979	1	65	1984	1	100
	2	158		2	223
	3	225		3	307
	4	96		4	149
1980	1	70	1985	1	150
	2	178		2	290
	3	245		3	360
	4	100		4	171
1981	1	69	1986	1	161
	2	177		2	306
	3	214		3	388
	4	104		4	181
1982	1	88	1987	1	132
	2	204		2	318
	3	244		3	412
	4	119		4	175
1983	1	101	1988	1	149
	2	209		2	312
	3	263		3	426
	4	119		4	193

*Includes self-catering villas and apartments.
Source: National Institute of Statistics (Portugal).

a. For the first quarter of 1989, the standard error of the forecast is 17,080. If the users of this forecast want to take no more than a 2½ percent chance of underestimating guest arrivals for the first quarter of 1989, what level of demand should they plan around?

b. Do you think that users of these forecasts (such as hotels or car-rental companies) should be more concerned about avoiding overestimation or underestimation? Explain.

c. How would you go about attempting to estimate market potential for the Algarve region? What factors determine the size of the gap between market potential and industry sales in this case?

SUGGESTED ADDITIONAL READINGS

Bishop, William S., John L. Graham, and Michael H. Jones, "Volatility of Derived Demand in Industrial Markets and Its Management Implications," *Journal of Marketing*, Fall 1984, pp. 95–103.

Dalrymple, Douglas, William Strahle, and Douglas Bock, "How Many Observations Should Be Used in Trend Regression in Forecasts," *Journal of Business Forecasting*, Spring 1989, pp. 7–10.

Frisbie, Gilbert, and Vincent A. Mabert, "Crystal Ball vs. System: The Forecasting Dilemma," *Business Horizons*, September–October 1981, pp. 72–76.

Georgoff, David M., and Robert G. Murdick, "Manager's Guide to Forecasting," *Harvard Business Review*, January–February 1986, pp. 110–119.

Mahajan, Vijay, Eitan Muller, and Frank Bass, "New Product Diffusion Models in Marketing: A Review and Directions for Research," *Journal of Marketing*, January 1990, pp. 1–26.

Proctor, R. A., "A Different Approach to Sales Forecasting: Using a Spreadsheet," *European Management Journal*, Fall 1989, pp. 358–365.

Schnaars, Steven P., "Situational Factors Affecting Forecast Accuracy," *Journal of Marketing Research*, August 1984, pp. 290–297.

Sobek, Robert, "A Manager's Primer on Forecasting," *Harvard Business Review*, May–June 1973, pp. 6–15.

CHAPTER 6

PROFITABILITY AND PRODUCTIVITY ANALYSIS

OVERVIEW

In Chapters 3 and 4, we examined the importance of understanding buyers and competitors when framing marketing decisions. Additionally, in Chapter 5, we considered the relationships among market potential, industry sales, and company sales in the process of market measurement. As a result of performing the analyses in those chapters, managers should be in a position to identify market opportunities and strategies for taking advantage of such opportunities. Before embarking on a marketing strategy, however, middle managers will generally have to do a detailed analysis of what it will cost to implement a strategy and what the expected sales and profit consequences will be.

Productivity analysis is the assessment of the sales or market-share consequences of a marketing strategy. Specifically, a productivity analysis involves the estimation of relationships between price or one or more marketing expenditures (such as advertising budgets) and the sales volume or market share of a particular product or product line. As we show in this chapter, these estimates are generally developed based on insights obtained from market and competitive analyses and from market measurements.

Profitability analysis is the assessment of the impact of various marketing strategies and programs on the profit contribution that can be expected from a product or product line. In considering the role played by profitability analysis, managers should be aware that this analysis is important regardless of the kind of product objective that has been established. Certainly a manager would seldom significantly increase the marketing budget for a cash cow if the increase would not improve profitability. But even when the primary product objective is sales or market-share growth (rather than profitability), it is still important for a manager to know how much profitability must be sacrificed to achieve a given sales or market-share target.

For an overview of the concepts, tools, and approaches involved in analyzing the impact of marketing expenditures, consider the following situation. Linkster Inc. manufactures a variety of golf umbrellas, golf sweaters, and lightweight water-repellant caps and jackets for golfers. The line is advertised in selected golf magazines and sold by company salespeople (who are paid a

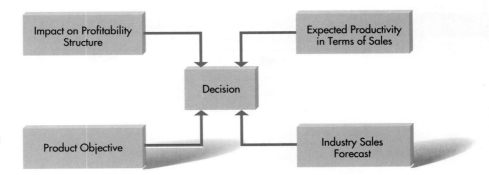

FIGURE 6-1

Factors to be considered in making marketing expenditure decisions.

salary and commission) to selected pro shops at golf courses and sporting goods stores.

Linkster is presently reviewing its results for the year just ended. In preparing the budget for the coming year, the firm's marketing manager is considering an increase in the advertising budget for jackets. Specifically, an increase of $100,000 is under consideration.

As Figure 6-1 indicates, Linkster's management must consider four factors in making this decision:

1. The relative importance of market share and profitability as *product objectives* for jackets
2. The *industry sales forecast* for jackets
3. The anticipated *productivity* (that is, the effectiveness) of the increased advertising in increasing jacket sales
4. The various types and levels of cost that determine the *profitability structure* of jackets

In this chapter, we present procedures for measuring product profitability and for estimating the productivity of marketing expenditures. In addition, we illustrate how product objectives, sales forecasts, profitability, and productivity are related to marketing budgeting decisions, using the specific example of Linkster.

MEASURING PRODUCT PROFITABILITY

As most managers know, the income (profit-and-loss) statement is generally inadequate for analyzing product profitability. Consider the profit-and-loss statement for Linkster given in Table 6-1.

If Linkster were a single-product organization, the conventional profit-and-loss statement would provide a reasonably useful measure of product prof-

TABLE 6-1

LINKSTER INC.: PROFIT AND LOSS STATEMENT
(in thousands of dollars)

Sales		$4640
Less cost of goods sold		2300
Gross profit margin		$2340
Operating expenses:		
Advertising	$600	
Sales salaries	500	
Sales commissions	220	
Designers' salaries	400	
Other (general and administrative costs)	600	
Total operating expense		2320
Net operating profit (loss) before taxes		$ 20

itability. However, because the firm is a multiproduct organization, management will also be interested in the profitability of each of the various products. Moreover, the conventional profit-and-loss statement provides few clues to how profitability would be influenced by changes in those costs (such as advertising) that lead to changes in sales volume.

In order to examine these issues, we need to make two kinds of distinctions in types of costs. First, the distinction must be made between *fixed* and *variable* costs. Second, fixed costs should be separated into those that are *direct* or *traceable* to individual products and those that are *indirect* or *nontraceable*.

Variable versus Fixed Costs

Variable costs are costs that vary with sales volume. Sales commissions, material, labor, and packaging are typically variable costs because they go up proportionately with sales. That is, each of these costs is incurred every time a product is produced and sold.

Nearly all other costs are *fixed*; that is, they remain essentially the same regardless of volume levels—at least as long as increases in the size of a production facility or in administrative and clerical staff are not required. Although some of these costs can be *changed* by management (such as advertising budgets and sales-force salaries), they do not vary *automatically* as sales change. For a manufacturer, the cost of goods sold (in the income statement) usually includes both fixed and variable elements. That is, each unit sold is assigned a share of the fixed costs to be added to its variable cost. For a retailer or wholesaler who only resells products made by other firms, the cost of goods sold is only a variable cost because it simply reflects the purchase price of items being resold.

For Linkster, the fixed costs of production (such as supervisory salaries) are considered part of cost of goods sold (shown in Table 6-1) but not in the

TABLE 6-2	**LINKSTER INC.: CONTRIBUTION MARGIN STATEMENT** (in thousands of dollars)

Sales...		$4640
Less variable cost of goods sold (labor, materials, packaging)		1620
Gross profit margin		$3020
Less other variable selling costs (sales commissions).....................		220
Variable contribution margin..		$2800
Fixed costs:		
Advertising	$600	
Sales salaries...	500	
Fixed production costs...	680	
Designers' salaries..	400	
General and administrative overhead...............................	600	
Total operating expense		2780
Net operating profit before taxes		$ 20

variable cost of goods sold (shown in Table 6-2). Conversely, Linkster's sales-people earn commissions on each unit sold to their retailers. These costs are variable costs (as seen in Table 6-2) but are not included in the cost of goods sold in Table 6-1.

By separating fixed costs from variable costs (as we have done in Table 6-2), the portion of cost that is sensitive to volume is identified. Out of $4,640,000 in sales, $1,840,000 (that is, $1,620,000 plus $220,000 in commissions) is spent on variable costs. The remaining $2,800,000 is the amount that is contributed to cover all fixed costs and profit after variable costs have been subtracted.

With costs separated in this way, managers can calculate a very useful measure: the *percentage-variable-contribution margin* (PVCM). This measure indicates the percentage of each additional sales dollar that will be available to help the firm cover its fixed costs and increase profits. The percentage-variable-contribution margin can be calculated in either of two ways:

$$\text{PVCM} = \frac{\text{variable contribution margin}}{\text{dollar sales}}$$

or

$$\text{PVCM} = \frac{\text{unit price} - \text{unit variable cost}}{\text{unit price}}$$

In the case of Linkster Inc. then,

$$\text{PVCM} = \frac{\$2,800,000}{\$4,640,000} = 60.3\%$$

In order to appreciate fully the usefulness of this measure to a marketing manager, it is necessary to understand the distinction between direct fixed costs and indirect fixed costs.

Types of Fixed Costs

When fixed costs are incurred in a multiproduct firm, they are incurred either on behalf of the business as a whole or on behalf of one or more specific products. For example, organizations may design advertisements to communicate a message about a particular product or product line, or they may use *institutional* advertising, which presents a message about the company as a whole and may not even mention the specific products or services sold. Costs such as product-specific advertising that are incurred on behalf of a specific product or service are known as *direct fixed* costs. Costs such as institutional advertising that are incurred to support the total business are *indirect fixed* costs.

In practice, firms recognize that there are really two categories of indirect cost: traceable and nontraceable. *Traceable* costs are indirect costs that can be allocated to various products on some nonarbitrary basis. For example, if a common sales force is used to sell two or more products, the total selling cost is usually allocated between the two products on the basis of some factor such as the percentage of selling time devoted to each one.

The purpose of distinguishing the various types of fixed costs is to provide a basis for evaluating the contributions made by different products or services to the overall profitability of the firm. Thus, firms assign direct and traceable indirect costs to products in order to gauge the costs of supporting each product. But nontraceable indirect costs are not assigned.

Table 6-3 illustrates how the profitability of individual products and services can be measured once management has separated the fixed costs. The bottom line for the individual products and services is no longer net operating profit but *total contribution*. The total contribution is the amount that an individual product or service "contributes" to the coverage of nontraceable indirect costs and to profit. (From a portfolio perspective, large contributions would be expected from cash cows and small or even negative contributions would be expected from problem-child products.)

By examining Table 6-4, we can see that umbrellas and jackets generated total contributions that were nearly as large as the total contribution from sweaters even though the sales volume from sweaters is much larger. This results from the higher share of direct, traceable fixed costs going to sweaters (sweater sales are twice jacket sales, but the direct costs of design, sales, and advertising are more than twice as high for sweaters).

Additionally, jackets are slightly more profitable than sweaters in terms of the percentage-variable-contribution margin. Table 6-4 summarizes unit price

| TABLE 6-3 | **LINKSTER INC.: CONTRIBUTION BY PRODUCT LINE**
(in thousands of dollars) |

	COMPANY TOTAL	UMBRELLAS	SWEATERS	JACKETS	CAPS
Sales	$4640	$840	$2400	$1200	$200
Variable cost of goods sold	1620	400	800	380	40
Gross profit margin	$3020	$440	$1600	$ 820	$160
Other variable costs	220	40	120	60	0
Variable contribution margin	$2800	$400	$1480	$ 760	$160
Direct, traceable fixed costs:					
Sales salaries	$ 500	$ 20	$ 360	$ 120	$ 0
Designers' salaries	400	0	300	100	0
Fixed production costs	680	100	340	230	10
Advertising of specific product lines	300	40	200	60	0
Total	$1880	$160	$1200	$ 510	$ 10
Total contribution	$ 920	$240	$ 280	$ 250	$150
Indirect, nontraceable fixed costs:					
Institutional advertising	$ 300				
General and administrative overhead	$ 600				
Total	$ 900				
Net operating profit	$ 20				

| TABLE 6-4 | **LINKSTER INC.: PERCENTAGE-VARIABLE-CONTRIBUTION MARGINS** |

	UMBRELLAS	SWEATERS	JACKETS	CAPS
Number of customers	28,000	40,000	20,000	50,000
Average price paid	$30	$60	$60	$4
Variable cost per unit	$15.71	$23.00	$22.00	$0.80
Variable contribution margin per unit (Average price − variable cost per unit)	$14.29	$37.00	$38.00	$3.20
PVCM $\dfrac{(\text{Price} - \text{VC})}{\text{Price}}$	47.6%	61.6%	63.3%	80%

and cost data for the various lines and shows the PVCM calculations. For each $1000 in additional sales of jackets, Linkster will retain about $633 after variable costs are subtracted. For sweaters, $616 would be retained if sales rose by $1000.

IMPLICATIONS OF PROFITABILITY ANALYSIS

By identifying the fixed and variable components of cost and by distinguishing between direct and indirect costs, managers will be able to examine some of the profitability implications of pricing and marketing expenditure decisions. Specifically, by understanding the profitability structure for a product, managers can identify *cost-volume-profit relationships* and *implications for marketing budgets*.

Cost-Volume-Profit Relationships

In many organizations, a large portion of the total operating cost is essentially fixed. In these situations, managers generally will pursue policies that take advantage of *economies of scale*. These economies will exist when a large increase in volume leads to a significant reduction in the average cost of a product.

Consider, for example, Table 6-5. As sales volume doubles (from 40,000 to 80,000 units), total costs increase by a smaller percentage amount because a high proportion of total costs are fixed. Consequently, the average cost per unit is reduced from $53 to $38.

The existence of strong cost-volume-profit relationships means that managers should be more willing to increase marketing expenses or cut prices if these actions will lead to significant increases in volume. Returning to Table 6-5, we can see that at a price of $53 per unit, the firm will just cover its average costs at a volume of 40,000 units. However, the product could be profitable at a lower price (such as $39) if volume could be doubled as the result of that lower price.

The advantages of employing economies of scale to be price competitive are fundamental to the strategies of low-cost champions such as Heinz, Briggs & Stratton (small motors), and Kellogg.[1] Additionally, fixed costs are often extremely high in high technology businesses where expenditures on research and development are very large (such as pharmaceuticals) and where manufacturing has become heavily automated. Particularly among global marketers, labor and material costs have declined relative to fixed costs. As a result, firms like Saab have been forced to deal with the issue of economies of scale.

[1] Bill Saparito, "Heinz Pushes to Be the Low Cost Producer," *Fortune*, June 24, 1985, pp. 44–54.

TABLE 6-5	ECONOMIES OF SCALE FOR SWEATERS	

	ANNUAL SALES VOLUME	
	40,000 UNITS	80,000 UNITS
Unit variable cost	$ 23	$ 23
Multiplied by volume	40,000	80,000
Total variable cost	$ 920,000	$1,840,000
Plus Total direct or traceable fixed cost	$1,200,000	$1,200,000
Total direct cost	$2,120,000	$3,040,000
Divided by volume	40,000	80,000
Average unit cost	$ 53	$ 38

In 1990, General Motors purchased a fifty percent interest in Sweden-based Saab which had lost $300 million the previous year. It quickly became apparent to General Motors' managers that Saab could not remain competitive with its existing cost structure because Saab was a low volume producer in an industry with substantial economies of scale. Accordingly, fixed costs were slashed and labor productivity improved and by 1992 Saab could cover all of its fixed costs at an annual sales volume of 100,000 cars (compared to the 200,000 needed in 1992).[2]

Managers not only must be aware of the opportunities associated with economies of scale, they also need to recognize the potential difficulties they create. As we saw in Chapter 4, when fixed costs are high and industry sales growth is low, intensive competition usually results. This can pose real difficulties for firms that lack established market positions as the following demonstrates:

IBP Inc. is one of the few meatpacking firms to regularly experience profitability in recent years. Many industry experts attribute this to IBP's aggressive expansion strategy in an industry plagued by excess capacity. Because fixed costs are very high and contribution margins are slim, firms must operate at a high capacity level. By paying top prices for cattle, IBP has been able to ensure that it operates with the best economies of scale in the industry. Essentially, its higher variable costs are offset by economies of scale enabling it to be a price leader in this highly competitive market.[3]

In order to compete with firms that possess such size advantages many firms use strategies that require minimal fixed costs. Specifically, some firms

[2] John Templemann, "Saab: Halfway through a U-Turn," *Business Week*, Apr. 27, 1992, p. 121.
[3] Scott Kilman, "IBP Gobbles Up Weak Rivals in Meatpacking Industry," *The Wall Street Journal*, Aug. 31, 1992, p. B3.

operate in market segments where the high fixed costs associated with advertising, selling, or high development costs are very low. Consider, for example, Rhino Records.

> Rhino Records is a very small competitor in the U.S. record industry, with less than 1% of total industry dollar sales in 1989. But the company has been quite profitable, focusing its efforts on repackaging 1960s rock and roll albums. For example, the firm produced "best of" collections by Roy Orbison, the Turtles, and the Monkees, among others, and released one album containing ten renditions of "Louie, Louie" from artists ranging from the Kingsmen to the Rice University Marching Owl Band.
>
> Rhino has no fixed artists' salaries or recording costs for developing an album: All songs are licensed from their owners for about $.10 to $.15 per album. With variable distributor commissions and minimal marketing, Rhino's total fixed costs may be as low as $30,000 per album. At a $8.98 retail price, unit variable contribution is around $3. As a result, all fixed costs are recovered once sales volume hits 10,000 records.[4]

Some firms have also found that variable costs may decline as volume increases. This phenomenon, known as the *experience-curve* effect, has been observed in companies such as Texas Instruments (consumer electronics), Black & Decker (power tools), and Du Pont (chemicals). Generally, these cost reductions occur as a firm becomes more experienced in producing a product for one or more of the following reasons:

- The firm may design more efficient production equipment or processes.
- The firm may improve its ability to obtain discounts or to control inventories, leading to reduced costs for materials and components.
- Production workers may become more efficient (especially in assembly operations) as they become more familiar with the production process.[5]

In sum, when average costs can be dramatically reduced because of economies of scale or experience curves, managers generally have a greater incentive to use competitive pricing or increased marketing expenditures in order to stimulate sales volume.

Semifixed Costs

Semifixed costs (also known as step-variable costs) represent a potential limitation to economies of scale. Essentially, semifixed costs are costs that do not vary automatically on a per unit basis (as variable costs do) but may change if substantial increases in volume occur. For example, a firm may need to set up an additional delivery route, rent or build new facilities for production or inventory, or hire more salaried supervisory workers or customer service

[4] Fleming Meeks, "The Gold in Oldies," *Forbes*, May 1, 1989, pp. 68–72.
[5] See George S. Day and David Montgomery, "Diagnosing the Experience Curve," *Journal of Marketing*, Spring 1983, pp. 44–58, for a thorough discussion.

TABLE 6-6	EFFECT OF SEMIFIXED COSTS		
	ANNUAL SALES VOLUME UMBRELLAS		
	28,000	35,000	40,000
Unit variable cost	$15.71	$15.71	$15.71
Multiplied by volume	28,000	35,000	40,000
Total variable cost	$439,880	$549,850	$628,400
Total direct or traceable fixed/semifixed cost	160,000	160,000	240,000
Plus total variable cost	439,880	549,850	628,400
Total direct cost	$599,880	$709,850	$868,400
Divided by volume	28,000	35,000	40,000
Average unit cost	$21.42	$20.28	$21.71

personnel if production output increases dramatically. As Table 6-6 shows, a step-up in certain fixed costs will offset the effects of economies of scale. While fixed costs for umbrellas stay the same as sales volume grows through 35,000 units, average costs decline. But once capacity is reached, large increases in fixed costs will be incurred. In Table 6-6, we see that certain previously fixed costs must be increased from $160,000 to $240,000 in response to the higher sales levels. As a consequence, average costs will edge upward, at least temporarily.

An example of the negative consequences of increased demand is the experience of Arkansas Freightways.

> Arkansas Freightways hauls goods across ten states from Texas to Illinois, and in 1991 had sales of about $200 million. In July of 1991, the company's major competitor, Jones Truck Lines, filed for bankruptcy and ceased operations. Arkansas Freightways immediately signed up a number of Jones' customers, and sales volume rose 20% in 24 hours. But the increased volume proved to be very costly, as the company had misjudged its capacity. Employees labored overtime, and five hundred trailers had to be rented to meet demand. While existing trucks were now carrying more goods, packing more into a truck increased loading and unloading time. Finally, greater utilization pushed up maintenance costs. As a consequence of these problems, net income actually fell during the last quarter of 1991.[6]

Special Profitability Issues for Retailers

In addition to evaluating the impact of margins and direct fixed costs on profitability, retailers must assess the amount of space (physical assets) or inventory investment (financial assets) that is appropriate for a given product, product line, or department. That is, since space and inventory dollars are

---

[6] Michael Selz, "Benefiting from a Rival's Failure May Take Restraint," *The Wall Street Journal*, May 19, 1992, p. B2.

really the most critical resources for most retailers, managers involved with retail decision making should also assess profitability in terms of these assets.

Whether measuring profitability on a product, product-line, or departmental basis, retailers typically use four basic measures:

■ Inventory turnover
■ Sales per square foot
■ Gross-margin return on inventory investment
■ Gross-margin return per square foot

Inventory turnover is the ratio of a product's sales to the average dollar value of the inventory held for that product.

Sales per square foot is the ratio of a product's sales to the amount of selling space (measured in square feet) used for the product.

Gross-margin return on inventory investment measures the profit return rather than the sales return on inventory investment. This measure is calculated by multiplying inventory turnover by the percentage gross profit margin.

Gross-margin return per square foot is equivalent to sales per square foot multiplied by percentage gross profit margin.

Table 6-7 summarizes these four measures. In choosing one of them, managers should consider two issues. First, retailers may differ over whether inventory or space is the more critical resource. Some firms have adequate space but limited financial resources for purchasing inventory. Accordingly, these firms should use inventory turnover or gross-margin return on inventory investment, because the most critical decisions will revolve around inventory allocation. However, if space is the scarcer resource, then sales per square foot or gross-margin return per square foot should be used.

A second consideration is whether to use sales or gross margin as a measure of return. Many retailers continue to use sales rather than gross margin

---

TABLE 6-7   MEASURES OF PRODUCT PROFITABILITY FOR RETAILERS AND WHOLESALERS

Inventory turnover	$=$	$\dfrac{\text{sales}}{\text{average value of inventory}}$
Sales per square foot	$=$	$\dfrac{\text{sales}}{\text{square feet of selling space}}$
Gross-margin return on inventory investment	$=$	$\dfrac{\text{gross margin}}{\text{price}} \times \text{inventory turnover}$
Gross-margin return per square foot	$=$	$\dfrac{\text{gross margin}}{\text{price}} \times \text{sales per square foot}$

because it is simpler to measure sales when product-line or departmental profitability is being measured. If departments or product lines vary significantly in gross margins, however, using sales as a measure of profitability will definitely be inadequate for comparing profitability.

Implications for Marketing Budgets

As we suggested at the beginning of the chapter, managers should have an understanding of the product objectives and an industry sales forecast in order to develop a budget. Further, managers must have some estimate of the productivity of a proposed price and marketing expenditure level in generating company sales (after taking the industry sales forecast into account). We will examine some procedures for developing these productivity estimates later in this chapter. However, assuming that management has developed these estimates of productivity, the budgeting process can proceed in either of two ways: the *direct* approach or the *indirect* approach.

THE DIRECT APPROACH

In this approach, managers must make specific estimates of the sales that will result from a given price and marketing budget. (The steps in this approach are summarized in Table 6-8.) If data are available for developing industry sales forecasts, managers can obtain an estimate of company sales by estimating the market share they expect to obtain for a given price and marketing budget and then multiplying this market share by the industry sales forecast.

To illustrate, recall that Linkster is considering a $100,000 increase in the advertising budget for jackets. Assuming that no changes occur in price or in other costs, the only elements in the profitability structure that will change are the advertising budget (which also leads to a change in total direct, traceable fixed costs) and variable costs. That is, if the increase in advertising results in increases in sales volume, then *by definition* total variable costs will increase as well.

TABLE 6-8   **STEPS IN THE DIRECT APPROACH TO MARKETING BUDGETING**

1. Develop an industry sales forecast (where feasible).
2. Estimate the market share that will result from a given price and marketing expenditure level. (If no industry sales are available, directly estimate company sales instead of market share.)
3. Calculate the expected company sales (market share × industry sales forecast).
4. Calculate variable contribution (company sales × PVCM).
5. Calculate total contribution (variable contribution margin less direct and traceable fixed costs included in proposed budget).
6. Determine whether the sales, market share, and total contribution levels are acceptable, given the product objectives.

If total jacket sales in Linkster's market are expected to be 250,000 units, and if Linkster's marketing manager predicts the company's market share to be 10 percent, then projected company sales would be 25,000 units. Assuming the average selling price remains at $60, dollar sales would be $1,500,000. Recalling from Table 6-4 that PVCM for jackets is 63.33 percent of sales, Linkster's variable contribution margin will increase by $38 (63.33 percent × $60 selling price) for each additional jacket sold. Table 6-9 summarizes the calculation of the projected profitability of jackets for the proposed budget.

The calculations suggest that the sales increase of $300,000 will result in an increase of $190,000 in the variable contribution margin (the remainder going to variable costs). Further breakdown of the $190,000 increase in variable contribution margin shows that $100,000 will be spent on the increase in advertising, leaving a net gain in total contribution of $90,000. The new total contribution of $340,000 must be evaluated (along with the projected market share) against the product objectives. If the projected share and total contribution are high enough to meet top-management expectations, the new advertising budget would be considered adequate. If not, then the manager must consider other possible budget levels.

The foregoing example is a rather simple illustration in that we have assumed only one change in projected expenditures. In a more typical case, managers would find that other changes would occur. Sales-force salaries might be increased, variable costs may change, or prices may rise or fall. If such changes are expected to occur, they should be incorporated in the profitability projections. (Note that a change in price or variable cost will require a change in the PVCM and in the variable contribution margin per unit.)

TABLE 6-9	**LINKSTER INC.: PROJECTED PROFITABILITY FOR JACKETS** **(in thousands of dollars)**			
			CURRENT YEAR	PROJECTED
Sales			$ 1200	$ 1500
× PVCM			.6333	.6333
Variable contribution margin			$ 760	$ 950
Direct, traceable fixed costs				
Sales salaries	$120		$120	
Advertising	60		160	
Design	100		100	
Fixed production	230		230	
Total direct, traceable		510		610
Total contribution			$ 250	$ 340

Further, some degree of uncertainty usually exists in projecting sales and costs. Accordingly, managers who use the direct approach often must calculate several different estimates of total contribution to determine how much the total contribution figures would change if sales or various cost elements turned out somewhat higher or lower. Fortunately, nearly all marketing managers have access to one or more computer spreadsheet programs that allow them to go through the many calculations required by this process very rapidly.

In most cases, the highest degree of uncertainty will rest with the productivity estimates. When managers are very uncertain about these estimates (a situation that is typical of relatively new products), it is often useful to employ the *indirect* approach.

THE INDIRECT APPROACH

In the indirect approach (summarized in Table 6-10), an estimate of the sales productivity of a given price or budget is not required. Rather, managers are required to estimate only whether a benchmark level of sales can be achieved.

Specifically, managers who use this approach must first calculate the level of sales required to achieve the minimum acceptable target contribution for a given budget. This calculation requires three pieces of profitability information:

■ The percentage-variable-contribution margin (or the variable contribution margin per unit) based on the expected prices and variable costs
■ The total direct and traceable fixed costs to be incurred (including any expected changes in the marketing budget)
■ The minimum target contribution that will be acceptable to top management

TABLE 6-10	STEPS IN THE INDIRECT APPROACH TO MARKETING BUDGETING

1. Establish the target level of total contribution.
2. Calculate the level of sales required to achieve target total contribution for a given price and marketing expenditure level: [(Proposed total direct and traceable fixed costs plus target total contribution) divided by PVCM].
3. Calculate the required market share: (Required level of sales divided by industry sales forecast).
4. Based on estimated productivity of the proposed price and marketing expenditures, determine whether the required sales and market share can be achieved.
5. Determine whether the required market share and required sales will be acceptable for the given product objectives. If not, determine whether the sales or market-share objectives can be reached with the proposed budget.

Given this information, the *required level of sales* can be calculated using the following formulas.

$$\text{Total dollar sales required} = \frac{\text{(target total contribution)} + \text{(total direct or traceable fixed costs)}}{\text{PVCM}}$$

or

$$\text{Total unit sales required} = \frac{\text{(target total contribution)} + \text{(total direct or traceable fixed costs)}}{\text{PVCM per unit}}$$

In the case of Linkster, recall from Table 6-4 that the PVCM on jackets is 63.33 percent and that the variable contribution margin per unit is $38. Given the proposed $100,000 increase in advertising, direct and traceable fixed costs will increase to $610,000 (as was shown in Table 6-9). If the owner is satisfied with the *current* total contribution of $250,000, then:

$$\text{Total dollar sales required} = \frac{(\$250,000) + (\$610,000)}{.6333}$$
$$= \$1,357,966$$

$$\text{Total unit sales required} = \frac{(\$250,000) + (\$610,000)}{\$38}$$
$$= 22,632 \text{ jackets}$$

Note that if any changes in the target total contribution are made or if prices, variable costs, or other direct or traceable fixed costs are also changed, then the total sales required will change. For example, if Linkster were to reduce prices so that the average price paid was reduced from $60 to $50, the PVCM would be reduced to 56 percent. That is, PVCM would be calculated as: ($50 − $22)/$50. Combining the proposed $100,000 increase in advertising with the reduction in price would result in the following calculations:

$$\text{Total dollar sales required} = \frac{(\$250,000) + (\$610,000)}{.56}$$
$$= \$1,535,714$$

$$\text{Total unit sales required} = \frac{(\$250,000) + (\$610,000)}{\$28}$$
$$= 30,714 \text{ jackets}$$

The immediate task now facing the owner is to determine the market share that will be required. As suggested in the previous section, it is assumed that industry sales will climb to 250,000 units in the coming year. Based on the proposal of a $100,000 increase in advertising and a target total contribution of $250,000, the required level of sales was 22,632 units. Therefore,

$$\text{Required market share} = \frac{\text{required level of sales}}{\text{industry sales forecast}} = \frac{22,632}{250,000} = 9\%$$

By determining the required market share, a manager develops a benchmark for evaluating the budget. That is, the manager can now evaluate the proposed budget by addressing the question, "Will a $100,000 increase in advertising allow us to attain a 9 percent market share?" Although this question is not necessarily an easy one to answer, it is usually easier than developing a direct, specific estimate of the sales productivity of the marketing budget.

It should be noted, however, that the required market share calculated through the indirect approach gives only the minimum share needed in order to meet profitability requirements. In some cases, the product objective may call for market-share levels substantially higher than the share required to meet the target total contribution. In such cases, managers will also have to address the question of whether the proposed budget will be sufficiently productive to achieve the market-share objective.

PRODUCTIVITY ANALYSIS

Productivity analysis is the process of estimating the impact on sales of a change in price or in marketing expenditures. That is, the change in sales resulting from a given change in a marketing program indicates how productive that marketing program is. Frequently, the term *sales-response functions* is used to represent relationships between price or a marketing expenditure and sales.

Traditional Methods of Productivity Analysis

Most firms attempt to estimate productivity using one or more of the following approaches.

ANALYSIS OF HISTORICAL RELATIONSHIPS

Frequently, managers look to historical experience in estimating the responsiveness of sales to various expenditures. For instance, internal data may be available to estimate

- The average sales per retail outlet (when an organization is attempting to expand its market coverage);
- The sales increases that have resulted from increases in past advertising budgets;
- The sales per sales call on new-prospect accounts;
- Historical price elasticity.

To the extent that these relationships are applicable to the current situation, they may provide some clues to the impact of proposed expenditures on sales. While management should not rely too heavily on such observed relationships unless they are supported by extensive sales data, more and more firms are developing computerized data bases tracking the purchases of customers. If data are also available on the prices buyers paid or on special promotions buyers took advantage of, firms can begin to gauge the effectiveness of these tools. For example, American Express could examine customer account records to determine historically the sales response to direct mail promotions of a luggage product at various prices.

COMPETITIVE PARITY ANALYSIS

This approach also relies on historical experience but is designed to consider relative marketing effort explicitly. For example, when competing products are highly similar in quality, a manager may find a very high correlation between a product's market share and

- Its share of industry advertising expenses.
- The number of sales calls made relative to competitors' sales calls.
- The relative number of retail accounts that carry the product.
- The price of the product relative to the average industry price.

To the extent that competitors' actions can be predicted, a competitive parity approach can provide clues to the likely impact of increased expenditures on market share. For example, it has been shown that successful new products maintain an advertising spending level over 2 years such that the brand's share of advertising is about *twice* the target share of market.[7]

MARKET EXPERIMENTS

In a market experiment, managers test a proposed policy (such as a price change, a sales-call policy, or an advertising theme) on some portion of the market and then observe the sales response. Often, marketers will attempt to test the effectiveness of a change in advertising or of a sales promotion plan by employing the plan in a designated market area. The observed sales will then be compared with the sales that would be expected in the absence of the change in marketing effort. In other cases, management may set different prices or different advertising weights (that is, different levels of spending) in two or more metropolitan areas and compare the sales results. Additionally, the syndicated marketing research firms A. C. Nielsen and Information Resources Inc. offer *electronic test markets*, which work as follows:

---

[7] See J. O. Peckham, *The Wheel of Marketing*, A. C. Nielsen, Northbrook, Ill., 1975; and Simon Broadbent, *The Advertiser's Handbook for Budget Determination*, Lexington Books, Lexington, Mass., 1988, pp. 131–132.

- Different sales promotions (such as coupons) are targeted (via mail) or different advertising levels (in terms of number of advertisements) are targeted (via cable television) to distinct groups of households within a market.
- Each household has a special card, which is scanned along with the household's purchases at supermarket checkout counters.
- Comparisons are made among the groups receiving each ad level or each type of direct mail promotion.

As a result of using electronic test markets, many consumer-goods firms have modified their marketing programs. For example, Nestlé found that sales of Quik chocolate drink responded very sharply to increases in newspaper ads that were combined with store displays.[8]

Single-Source Data

Each of the firms that offer electronic test market services has gradually been developing comprehensive systems of services to provide what has been termed *single-source data*. While their use is likely to be limited to manufacturers and retail firms marketing nondurable products, these systems promise to have a major impact on the ability to do productivity analyses.

Specifically, single-source systems will record each marketing signal (each price, each advertising message, each promotional action) that has an impact on a household either directly (at home) or indirectly via the retailer. The systems will trace each signal and link the content of each signal (for example, each price level) to household purchase behavior.[9]

While a firm's own sales data will be the starting point for single-source systems, such data will be integrated with the single-source systems such as those offered by A. C. Nielsen and Information Resources Inc. Electronic scanners in selected cities provide data on store-level sales and household-level purchases of each product. In-home meters monitor television viewing in panel households, with each service also auditing magazine and newspaper advertising in panel cities.

In effect, single-source data provide a broad experimental capability while at the same time permitting the analysis of competitive parity (via price and *share of voice* advertising audits) and establishing a data base for conducting analyses of historical relationships.

Judgment-Based Productivity Estimates

Although traditional and single-source estimates can be useful, in many industries the data bases and syndication services necessary for effective use of these techniques may be absent. Additionally, experimentation is difficult (if not

---

[8] Zachary Schiller, "Thanks to the Checkout Scanner Marketing Is Losing Some Mystery," *Business Week*, Aug. 28, 1989, p. 57.
[9] David Curry, "Single Source Systems: Retail Management Present and Future, *Journal of Retailing*, Spring 1989, pp. 1–19.

impossible) when a firm has a limited market and produces a very expensive product, such as aircraft or mainframe computers. Finally, whether or not a firm uses some quantitative data obtained by these methods, it is not always certain that the observed relationship will hold up in the future. Specifically, managers must recognize several potential limitations when applying observed sales-response functions.

INTERACTION EFFECTS

Historical relationships may not be valid when two or more major changes take place simultaneously. For example, a firm may have a good understanding of the historical relationship between advertising expenditures and sales. However, if that firm combines a change in advertising with a sharp change in price, the historical advertising-sales relationship may not continue. Unless a firm has an extensive history of combining advertising and price changes, it will be difficult to establish historical relationships among price, advertising, and sales.

COMPETITION

When competitors modify their marketing policies as a reaction to competitive changes, the effectiveness of a given policy is often diminished. For example, a large increase in the advertising budget may lead competitors to respond by matching the increase, thus preventing any relative advantage from being gained.

MARKETING EFFECTIVENESS AND EFFICIENCY

The effectiveness of marketing programs may improve over time and the efficiency with which expenditures are made and allocated may change. In both cases, improvements will mean that the same dollars will yield a larger sales payoff. Thus, advertisements that do a better job of communicating a product's benefits will be more productive on a per dollar basis than less effective advertisements. Similarly, improved selection of media may allow a firm to reach more potential buyers at the same cost. So to the extent that improvements in effectiveness and efficiency are forthcoming, a given marketing expenditure may be even more productive than would be projected from historical data.

NONLINEARITY

Many marketing phenomena have a changing response function over time or over levels. For instance, promotional efforts may have a pattern of sales effects similar to that presented in Figure 6-2. As this illustration demonstrates, the rate of sales response to an increase in marketing expenditures often changes over time, and thus the relationship is curvilinear. As the figure suggests, sales respond only minimally to low levels of advertising, but after a threshold level is reached, sales increase more rapidly with increases in advertising. Conceivably, at very high levels of advertising, a supersaturation point

FIGURE 6-2
Hypothesized
relationship
between
advertising
expenditures and
sales. (Reprinted
by permission from
R. L. Ackoff and
J. R. Emshoff,
"Advertising
Research at
Anheuser-Busch,"
*Sloan
Management
Review,* Winter
1975, p. 4.)

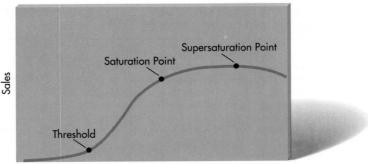

could be reached. Beyond this point, sales might actually decline if advertising expenditures were to increase further.

In judgment-based productivity estimation, managers use their knowledge of the factors influencing demand, competitors, potential environmental changes, and planned changes in marketing strategies and programs (that is, how marketing dollars will be spent) as supplements to (or even as substitutes for) the other three methods.

One of the most widely publicized approaches to judgment-based estimation is that developed by John D. C. Little. In Little's approach, managers attempt to quantify their judgments about the relationship between each marketing variable and market share by answering four questions.

1. What level of expenditure is needed to maintain the current market share through the next budget period? (That is, what is the maintenance level of expenditures?)
2. What minimum level of market share will result in the next period if expenditures are reduced to zero?
3. What level of market share will result in the next period if expenditures are increased by 50 percent over the maintenance level?
4. What is the maximum market share that could be obtained in the next period if expenditures were unlimited?[10]

In answering these questions, managers can use any information they might obtain from examining historical ratios, experiments, or competitive parity analysis. However, managers will also consider factors (such as those listed in Table 6-11) that are likely to influence the impact of changes in marketing expenditures or price on market share in the next period.

[10] See John D. C. Little, "Models and Managers: The Concept of a Decision Calculus," *Management Science,* April 1970, pp. B-466–B-485. An extended version of the model can be found in John D. C. Little, "Brandaid: A Marketing Mix Model," *Operations Research,* July–August 1975, pp. 628–673.

TABLE 6-11	FACTORS TO CONSIDER WHEN MAKING JUDGMENTAL ESTIMATES OF PRODUCTIVITY

1. Stage in product-form life cycle
2. Anticipated prices and expenditures by competitors
3. Likelihood of competitive retaliation if a major increase in expenditures or decrease in prices is made
4. Extent of distribution availability of the product
5. Major improvements in the efficiency with which dollars are spent
6. Major improvements in the effectiveness of strategies and programs that are expected to result in more favorable perceptions on determinant attributes
7. Extent of customer turnover
8. Degrees of customer awareness and preference for our product versus competing products or brands

Given these four estimates, managers can develop a pictorial representation (that is, a *model*) of their productivity judgments. Consider, for example, a situation in which a manager is concerned with examining the impact of a change in advertising expenditures on market share. Depending on the answers to Little's four questions, the manager might portray the advertising-market-share relationship in a number of ways. One possible portrayal is presented in Figure 6-3. (This figure was developed by plotting the market shares at the zero, maintenance, and plus-fifty advertising levels, by identifying the maximum share, and by connecting these points with an approximately S-shaped curve to reflect the assumption that the relationship is nonlinear.)

In Figure 6-3, the estimates suggest that an increase in advertising from $1.5 to $2.0 million will be needed simply to maintain market share and that sharp increases or decreases in market share will result from major changes in the budget. These estimates might reflect judgments on several of the factors listed in Table 6-11. That is, market share may be highly sensitive to advertising expenditures if the brand is competing in the early stages of the product life cycle where neither brand awareness nor brand preferences have been strongly established, or if the market is characterized by a high degree of customer turnover so that few previous buyers of a brand are still in the market.

Once a manager has developed a model of the productivity relationship, the effect of a proposed expenditure level can be incorporated into the budgeting process. Managers can use this model either to establish direct estimates of market share or, if the indirect method is being used, to determine the likelihood of achieving a required level of market share.[11]

[11] John D. C. Little provides a method for determining the equation for this curve based on four estimates. With this equation, a manager can identify the market share that would result from any level of expenditure (assuming of course that the judgmental estimates are reliable). In order to determine the equation, managers must also estimate the long-run share that the brand will achieve with zero advertising.

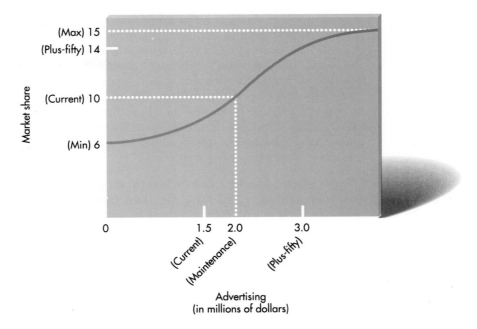

FIGURE 6-3

Cross-Elasticity Effects

Earlier we discussed the concept of indirect costs, indicating that these costs reflect the interdependencies in a multiproduct firm. However, products may also be interdependent in demand. Cross-elasticity effects reflect the interdependencies in demand across a set of products. These effects can be of two types: substitution effects and complementary effects.

Substitution effects take place when two or more products or services are used to perform the same generic function. Thus, eyeglasses and contact lenses are substitutes, and substitution effects will occur when one product receives a relative increase in marketing support: Increases in advertising for contact lenses are likely to have some negative impact on demand for eyeglasses.

Complementary products are those products (or services) that experience a sales increase when related products experience an increase in support. This relationship can occur for a number of reasons:

- *Related use.* When two products are naturally used in conjunction with one another (as are men's suits and ties, or mainframe computers and high-speed printers), the purchase of one product may lead to the purchase of the second. Consequently, many firms offer related products to satisfy customer usage needs more completely.
- *Enhanced value.* One product may enhance the value or increase the utiliza-

tion of another. For example, a new attachment may make a camera easier or more interesting to use.

■ *Quality supplements.* Products designed for repair, maintenance, or operating assistance may enable a customer to obtain or maintain a high level of quality performance. For this reason, many industrial and consumer firms today find that service contracts sold with electronics products and other durable goods are often very much in demand.

■ *Convenience.* Products that may be totally unrelated in use may be complementary if they are bought from the same source because using a common source reduces buyers' search costs.[12]

Thus, when Linkster's jackets are promoted, not only do jacket sales increase, but sales of related-use caps and umbrellas also increase. However, promoting jackets will likely also lead to a decrease in sweater sales.

To the extent that managers can predict the cross-elasticity relationships among products and services, budgets should be adjusted to account for these effects. Consider, for example, the data in Table 6-12. This table is a simple extension of Table 6-9, which presented a hypothetical projected budget for jackets assuming that a $100,000 increase in advertising resulted in a $300,000 increase in sales.

[12] For a more detailed treatment, see Alfred Oxenfeldt, "Product Line Pricing," *Harvard Business Review*, July–August 1966, pp. 137–144.

TABLE 6-12   **LINKSTER INC.: PROJECTED BUDGET WITH CROSS-ELASTICITY EFFECTS**

	EFFECT OF NEW BUDGET	
	PROJECTED TOTAL	PROJECTED CHANGE
Unit sales	25,000	+ 5,000
Dollar sales	$1,500,000	+$300,000
Total contribution	$ 340,000	+$ 90,000
Plus complementary effects:		
Cap sales		
(5000 × 10% × $4)	$ 2,000	
× PVCM	80%	+$ 1,600
Umbrella sales		
(5000 × 30% × $30)	$45,000	
× PVCM	47.6%	+$ 21,420
Minus substitution effects:		
Sweater sales		
(5000 × 10% × $60)	$30,000	
× PVCM	61.6%	−$ 18,480
Net change in total contribution from budget change		+$ 94,540

Given the average price of $60 per jacket, the expected increase is 5000 units. Assume that Linkster knows from its sales records that:

- Ten percent of jacket buyers also purchase a cap and 30 percent purchase matching umbrellas when the jacket purchase is made.
- Ten percent of jacket buyers would have purchased a Linkster sweater if they did not purchase the jacket.

Given these cross-elasticity estimates and the knowledge of percentage-variable-contribution margins (from Table 6-4), the owner can estimate the net profitability impact of the budget change following the procedure presented in Table 6-12.

CONCLUSION

An understanding of the profitability structure of any product is essential in order to find ways of increasing or maintaining profitability. As we have seen in this chapter, marketing does cost money. In order to examine the desirability of maintaining, increasing, or decreasing the level of marketing expenses, the variable-contribution margin and other elements of the profitability structure for a product must be known. Moreover, some understanding of

FIGURE 6-4
Steps in productivity and profitability analysis and their relationship to other aspects of the situation analysis.

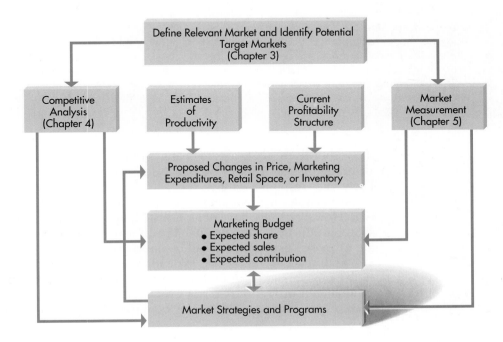

LINKSTER INC.: DEVELOPING A BUDGET

After reviewing Linkster performance for the past year (as presented in Tables 6-1 through 6-4), the company's chief marketing executive began developing the budget for the coming year. Because the sweater business had been so important in the company's short history, she believed it was important to maintain sales growth for that product. Additionally, competition was more extensive in the sweater business than in the umbrella and jacket businesses. Eight different manufacturers were designing sweaters specifically for the golf market, with Linkster holding an estimated 8 percent share of the market.

Industry sales forecasts were usually made by estimating changes in the number of rounds of golf expected to be played in the coming year, which in turn depended on demographic and economic trends. For the coming year, industry sales of golf sweaters were expected to grow 10 percent to 550,000 units.

Linkster's marketing manager had estimated competitors' total advertising expenditures at $3,100,000 for the most recent year. She also knew that the Linkster line was receiving substantially better acceptance among pro shop owners than most competitors because of the product's quality and up-to-date designs.

The marketing manager wanted to build market share for the sweater line without sacrificing profitability. Before she finalized the budget, however, she wanted to examine the market share and profit consequences of various budget levels. To do this in a thorough manner, she built a judgment-based model, establishing the following parameters for golf sweaters:

Maintenance advertising = $220,000
Maximum share   = 11.5%
Plus-fifty share   = 10%
Minimum share   = 4%

1. Discuss some of the specific factors the marketing manager would likely have used in making these estimates.
2. Based on these estimates, develop a graph portraying the relationship between Linkster sweater advertising and Linkster sweater market share.
3. Using this graph, estimate the market share that would result and calculate the profit consequences (using the *direct* approach) if the advertising budget is set:
   ■ At $275,000
   ■ At $330,000
4. How would the market share and profit estimates in Question 3 change if the industry sales forecast were changed:
   ■ To 520,000 units?
   ■ To 580,000 units?

the responsiveness of sales to changes in marketing budgets is essential in the planning process. Productivity analysis is the process of determining what the likely sales response will be.

This chapter has examined the difficulties involved in productivity estimation. However, as we have demonstrated, by combining sales-forecast, market-share, productivity, and profitability information, a manager's ability to evaluate proposed expenditures will be improved.

The impact of marketing expenditures on sales and profitability cannot fully be examined by using the analytical tools presented in this chapter and summarized in Figure 6-4, however. Because they have some strategic purpose, expenditures must also be examined in the context of the marketing strategies and programs that managers design for a product. That is, these expenditures are more likely to achieve target sales and market-share levels if they are spent to support well-chosen strategies and programs.

The process of designing effective marketing strategies and programs is the subject of Part Three of this book. Before continuing on to Part Three, however, consider once again the budgeting issue facing Linkster Inc.

QUESTIONS AND SITUATIONS FOR DISCUSSION

1. In what situations would the indirect approach be more useful than the direct approach for evaluating a proposed change in marketing expenditures?

2. a. Explain the importance of an accurate industry sales forecast to the budgeting process.

   b. Can you think of any situations in which the industry sales forecast may change as a result of changes in the marketing budget? Explain your answer.

3. For which of the following companies would experience-curve effects likely be strongest? For which would economies of scale be greatest?

   a. An aluminum can manufacturer

   b. A garbage collection business

   c. A firm that assembles VCRs

4. The Hudson Chemical Company manufactures and sells a complete line of insecticides and pesticides that are sold to homeowners and gardeners. As an addition to the product line, they began the manufacture of garden sprayers in the 1960s. The first sprayers were stainless steel, but since that time plastic containers have increased in importance. There has been little growth in the garden sprayer industry in the last few years because of the slowdown in new housing construction and the shift to multifamily and condominium living arrangements. Industry sales are expected to remain at the current level of 3 million units for 1992. Hudson has seen its market share decline to 10 percent and was considering a $200,000 increase in its advertising budget for 1992. Hudson sprayers were sold to wholesalers at an average price of $10 per unit. Wholesalers in turn sold the product to retailers for $12 per unit, and retailers priced the units at an average of $20 to consumers. The variable production costs were $5, and direct fixed costs for marketing, including advertising and sales, were about $1 million annually.

   a. Calculate Hudson's current total contribution.

   b. What level of market share will be required if Hudson is to maintain the product's current total contribution to indirect costs and profit?

   c. What are some of the ways the marketing manager can determine if the market share is attainable?

5. The AM General Division of LTV Corporation created the Hummer, a four-wheel drive vehicle that could drive in a variety of terrains, for the U.S. military, and the product received many accolades for its performance in the

Gulf War. In 1992, the company began producing a commercial version, which they expected would be popular among individuals in construction, ranching, or forestry, or just as an unusual off-road recreation vehicle. Capacity at the Mishawaka, Indiana, plant was 260 units per day—a number far above the requirements of AM General's military business. Assume that at production of 40 units per day (or 10,000 per year), the average cost of producing a vehicle is $30,000, with half of that cost going to variable costs and half to direct fixed costs, and that there are no changes in variable cost required for the new model.

a. Calculate the average cost of the military version at volumes of 80 and 120 units per day.

b. How would average costs change (from Question **a.**) if new semifixed costs of $20 million per year were added at a total volume of 80 units?

c. If the variable costs for the commercial version are $10,000 higher than for the military version, how do the answers to **a.** and **b.** change?

6. Midwest Electronics was examining the profitability of two of its cellular phone products. Given below are the cost and revenue figures for 1990.

	AUTO DELUXE	MICRO TALK
Selling price	$550	$800
Unit sales	30,000	10,000
Total variable cost	$250	$300
Traceable promotion expenses	$1,500,000	$1,500,000

Assume that all other costs are indirect.

a. Compare the current profitability of the two products.

b. Given *only* the profitability data, if you had additional funds for promotion, which product should receive those funds?

c. If the price of the Auto Deluxe were reduced by $50, what level of sales would be required to maintain the current level of total contribution?

7. For a standard new compact disc record album, the variable cost of manufacturing and packaging a blank disc is $1.30. A typical royalty to the singer is $1.00 per unit, and the costs of producing the recording session, the video, and the final product could easily run $2 million.

a. If the manufacturer's price to distributors is $10.70 per unit, what is the variable contribution margin?

b. At what level of sales will the record break even in terms of profit? (That is, at what sales level will the total contribution be zero?)

c. At what level of sales will the record break even if we add $200,000 for advertising?

d. Assume that Prince is the artist and his contract calls for him to receive a $10 million advance instead of a royalty. At what level of sales will the album break even?

8. For each hypothetical situation given below, indicate what you think the best way of doing productivity analysis would be, and discuss the major problems a manager would face in doing an analysis in that situation.

  a. McDonald's wants to determine the best price for a new barbecue sandwich.

  b. IBM is considering whether to double advertising for its line of notebook personal computers.

  c. The brand manager for Wisk must decide on next year's advertising budget. Wisk has been on the market much longer than its major direct competitor, Liquid Tide. However, Liquid Tide has a larger budget and has taken over from Wisk as the sales volume leader. In recent years, sales promotion has become increasingly important in this industry.

SUGGESTED ADDITIONAL READINGS

Alberts, William, "The Experience Curve Doctrine Revisited," *Journal of Marketing*, July 1989, pp. 36–49.

Ames, B. Charles, and James D. Hlavacek, "Vital Truths about Managing Your Costs," *Harvard Business Review*, January–February 1990, pp. 140–147.

Cook, Victor J., "The Net Present Value of Market Share," *Journal of Marketing*, Summer 1985, pp. 49–63.

Curry, David, "Single Source Systems: Retail Management Present and Future," *Journal of Retailing*, Spring 1989, pp. 1–19.

Hise, Richard T., Patrick J. Kelly, Myron Gable, and James B. McDonald, "Factors Affecting the Performance of Individual Chain Store Units: An Empirical Analysis," *Journal of Retailing*, Summer 1983, pp. 22–39.

Jones, John Philip, "Ad Spending: Maintaining Market Share," *Harvard Business Review*, January–February 1990, pp. 38–43.

Little, John D. C., "Decision Support Systems for Marketing Managers," *Journal of Marketing*, Summer 1979, pp. 9–27.

Piercy, Nigel, "The Marketing Budgeting Process: Marketing Management Implications," *Journal of Marketing*, October 1987, pp. 45–59.

Schroer, James, "Ad Spending: Growing Market Share," *Harvard Business Review*, January–February 1990, pp. 44–48.

PART THREE

MARKETING STRATEGIES AND PROGRAMS

The primary responsibilities of middle-level marketing managers are to develop and implement marketing strategies and programs for individual products or product lines. In Part 3, we examine concepts and procedures for selecting specific strategies and programs.

It is important to recognize that the concepts and procedures presented in the forthcoming chapters are not independent of those that we presented in previous chapters. Indeed, managers will not be able to make sound decisions on marketing strategies and programs without first having an understanding of:

- The product objectives to be achieved
- The factors that will influence the responsiveness of primary and selective demand to the marketing offer
- The potential market segments that might be served
- The extent, type, and sources of competition
- The size of various market opportunities, as indicated by market potential, industry sales, and company sales trends
- The profitability and productivity implications of making changes in prices or in marketing expenditures

Marketing programs are specific decisions and actions that are the responsibility of middle managers. In Chapters 8 to 13, we examine the decision-making concepts, tools, and procedures for product development, pricing, advertising, sales promotion, and sales and distribution programs. In particular, we will underscore the importance of developing specific program objectives. These objectives can greatly simplify the process of selecting and designing the specific elements of the program. Additionally, we present procedures for understanding the specific budgetary consequences of each of these programs.

Although the development of effective programs is critical to success, different managers are often responsible for designing and executing different programs. Accordingly, some mechanism is necessary for assuring that the various programs are consistent and work in harmony to achieve the product objective. A *marketing strategy* can provide consistency of direction among programs by identifying the kind of total impact on demand that the overall marketing effort is designed to achieve. In Chapter 7, we will discuss the types of marketing strategies that can be employed, the relationship between strategies and programs, and considerations involved in selecting a marketing strategy for a product or for a line of products.

CHAPTER 7

MARKETING STRATEGIES

As we discussed in Chapter 1, middle managers are generally responsible for designing and implementing marketing actions in areas such as advertising, sales promotion, personal selling, customer service, and new-product development. We call these actions *marketing programs*.

Typically, a firm will use two or more types of marketing programs simultaneously, because each type of program has a somewhat different impact on demand. Accordingly, there must be some mechanism for coordinating these programs so that they work together and not at cross-purposes. We call the mechanism for coordinating these programs a *marketing strategy*.

More precisely, marketing strategies are plans that specify the impact that a firm hopes to achieve on demand for a product or a product line in a given target market. The marketing strategy should be designed to fulfill top management's expectations for the product or product line as outlined in the firm's product mix strategy (which we discussed in Chapter 2). The role of marketing programs is to implement the marketing strategy.

To illustrate the distinction between a *strategy* and a *program*, consider the possible reasons a manager might have for reducing the price of a product. Essentially there are four potential reasons for such actions. First, the manager may believe the lower price will lead some potential buyers to buy a product they otherwise would not. (Consider, for example, the tremendous increase in the sales of compact disk players as prices declined.) Second, the manager may believe the price decrease will result in increased rates of purchase of a product. (For example, a decline in soft-drink prices may permit some buyers to consume greater amounts of the product.) Third, prices may be cut to avoid losing existing customers to competitors offering lower prices. Finally, the price cut may be an attempt to lure customers from higher-priced competitors.

Note that price is used to influence demand in each of these four cases, but in decidedly different ways. That is, each pricing program is designed to have a different *type* of impact on demand. In other words, in each case, price is being used to implement a different type of marketing strategy, and consistent with our pricing example, *marketing strategies* can be divided into *four* basic types.

1. Stimulating primary demand by increasing the number of users
2. Stimulating primary demand by increasing the rate of purchase
3. Stimulating selective demand by retaining existing customers
4. Stimulating selective demand by acquiring new customers

In addition, because many firms offer arrays of related products, it is important to consider two types of *product-line* marketing strategy. These are strategies that will have one or more of the four types of impact on demand but do so by virtue of relationships among products. For example, a lower price on a top-of-the-line washing machine model may also increase sales of dryers, or it may cause some buyers to buy a more expensive model than they had originally contemplated. The types of product-line marketing strategy are:

1. Stimulating demand for substitutes
2. Stimulating demand for complements

Further, managers must direct their strategy toward specific *target markets*. In selecting target markets, managers have two fundamental options. First, they can attempt to market the product(s) to *all users* in the *relevant market* (usually all potential users of the product form or class being sold). Second, they can focus on one or a *limited number of market segments* where they believe a

FIGURE 7-1
Basic elements of a marketing strategy.

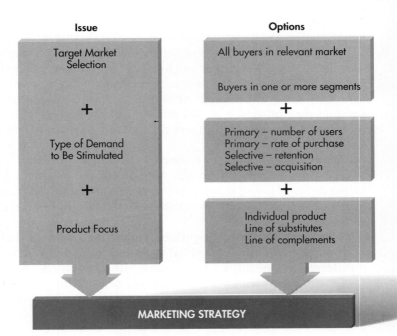

unique competitive position or a higher degree of profitability can be developed. For instance, a firm often attempts to stimulate demand only in high-volume segments or in those segments in which it will have a competitive advantage. Figure 7-1 portrays the basic elements involved in a marketing strategy.

In essence, a marketing strategy is the bridge between corporate strategy and the situation analysis on the one hand and the action-oriented marketing programs on the other. Marketing programs should flow from and be consistent with the marketing strategy. In turn, the selection of a marketing strategy should be based on the results of the earlier steps in the planning process.

In the remainder of this chapter, we examine the various *types* of marketing strategies that can be chosen, we present a *process* for selecting a marketing strategy, and we discuss some important *dynamic* aspects of marketing strategy.

PRIMARY-DEMAND STRATEGIES

Primary-demand strategies are designed to increase the level of demand for a product form or class by current nonusers or by current users. Products in the introductory stage of the product-form life cycle (those having little or no competition) and products with large market shares are both likely to benefit from strategies designed to increase the number of product-form users. Similarly, a firm that attempts to increase the rate of sales to existing product-form buyers is employing a primary-demand strategy. There are, therefore, two fundamental strategic approaches for stimulating primary demand: increasing the number of users and increasing the rate of purchase.[1]

Strategies for Increasing the Number of Users

To increase the number of users, the firm must increase customers' willingness to buy or their ability to buy the product or service, or both.

INCREASING THE WILLINGNESS TO BUY

The willingness to buy may be stimulated by one of three approaches:

- Demonstrating the benefits already offered by a product form
- Developing new products with benefits that will be more appealing to certain segments
- Demonstrating or promoting new benefits from existing products

A focus on demonstrating the basic product-form benefits is often necessary when a new product form is being marketed. For instance, Procter &

---

[1] Another perspective for assessing primary-demand growth opportunities is contained in John A. Weber, *Growth Opportunity Analysis*, Reston Publishing, Reston, Va., 1976, pp. 57–179.

Gamble had to demonstrate the convenience and performance of Pampers disposable diapers to a market in which washing cloth diapers was a time-honored behavior. Similarly, the popular Miller Lite beer advertisements successfully built the willingness of beer drinkers to try a new product form (light beer) by emphasizing the "tastes great, less filling" attributes. When new products yield significant additions to the benefits offered by existing product forms, the needs of some potential customers are more likely to be met.

For example, Carnival Cruise Lines has been leading renewed growth in the cruise business, largely by stimulating primary demand.

> Carnival's success can be traced to the day management stopped selling ocean voyages and began selling fun and entertainment to middle-income people. Recent industry surveys indicate there are 35 million first-cruise candidates, a group which represents Carnival's main target market. (Barely 5% of American vacationers have taken a cruise.) To attract this group, Carnival turned its ships into floating resorts, offering a dazzling array of shows, sports activities, and games designed to offset potential customer's fears of boredom and confinement.[2]
>
> Similarly, M&M Mars introduced a new product, Milky Way II, to capture more demand from calorie-sensitive potential buyers. The new bar has fifty percent fewer calories from fat than Milky Way.[3]

The importance of this strategy type is paramount when a new product form or class is introduced, because new products seldom sell themselves. Additionally, this strategy may not be important in advanced economies if a product is well established, but can be critical in bringing a product to a new market in a different culture. Thus, in the United States, Procter & Gamble must focus its marketing strategy for Pampers on acquiring potential customers from competitors, but in developing countries it will still be emphasizing the basic advantages of disposable diapers in order to stimulate primary demand.

INCREASING THE ABILITY TO BUY

The ability to buy can be improved by offering lower prices or credit or by providing greater availability (through having more distributors, more frequent delivery, or fewer stockouts). For example, reduced prices brought the cellular phone market rapid sales increases in the late 1980s.

Similarly, innovative financing plans can often help stimulate primary demand, as the following example demonstrates.

> The Artege Association of Dallas was founded by two entrepreneurs who were interested in art collecting but found it difficult to buy fine art. Their association offers a specialized credit card with credit limits of up to $5 million for the purchase of art, antiques, and jewelry from any of more than 1000 galleries. The major

---

[2] Mike Clary, "Carnival's Victory at Sea," *Adweek's Marketing Week*, July 17, 1989, pp. 18–25.
[3] George Lazarus, "Hershey Counters in Low-Calorie War," *Chicago Tribune*, Sept. 9, 1992, p. 3:4.

benefit of the card is its comparatively low 10.8% annual interest rate, which makes purchasing art more affordable.[4]

Strategies for Increasing Rates of Purchase

When managers are concerned with gaining more rapid growth in a sluggish but mature market, the marketing strategy may be geared toward increasing the willingness to buy *more often* or in *more volume*, using one of the following approaches.

BROADENING USAGE

Buyers may expand usage if the variety of uses or use occasions can be expanded. In recent years, a number of advertising campaigns have been conducted to suggest broadened uses for products or services. For example, A1 Sauce has been promoted for use on hamburgers, not just on steak, and Kraft has begun promoting Cheez Whiz for use as a cheese sauce for nachos.

Examples of attempts to broaden usage occasions include Coca-Cola's advertising campaign suggesting "Coke in the morning," American Express' obtaining acceptance of its credit card in Exxon gas stations, and Pizza Hut's increased emphasis on developing its lunchtime business by promising speedy service.

INCREASING PRODUCT CONSUMPTION LEVELS

Lower prices or special-volume packaging may lead to higher average volumes and possibly to more rapid consumption for products such as soft drinks and snacks. Or, consumption levels may be stimulated if buyers' perceptions of the benefits of a product or service change. This reasoning underlies the efforts of the pork industry to stimulate consumption. A recent industry advertising campaign emphasized pork's similarity to chicken in terms of the health benefits received and in terms of being a white meat. Similarly, American Express expanded the benefits of its card to include automatic insurance of products that are purchased using the card.

ENCOURAGING REPLACEMENT

Product redesign may be thought of as a selective-demand strategy. It is, however, largely a primary-demand strategy in the fashion industry and in other durable-goods industries. Although a refrigerator may well last 20 years, many replacement sales will be made earlier if product convenience, space utilization, and operating cost can be improved.

In sum, primary-demand strategies may be implemented in a number of ways, as shown in Table 7-1. Although these strategies are generally less widely used than selective-demand strategies, they can be extremely useful if

[4] Marc Meyers, "A Credit Card That Will Cover Picasso," *Adweek's Marketing Week*, Oct. 16, 1989, p. 23.

TABLE 7-1   PRIMARY-DEMAND MARKETING STRATEGIES

HOW DEMAND IS IMPACTED	BASIC STRATEGIES FOR INFLUENCING DEMAND
1. Increase the number of users	Increase willingness to buy
	Increase ability to buy
2. Increase the rate of purchase	Broadening usage occasions for the product
	Increase level of consumption
	Increase rate of replacement

market measurements show large gaps between market potential and industry sales. Further, the analysis of the buying process may have identified the factors limiting the ability or willingness to buy or to adopt a product class or form. If so, managers should have some insights into the kinds of programs that can be used to stimulate primary demand.

SELECTIVE-DEMAND STRATEGIES

Selective-demand strategies are designed to improve the competitive position of a product, service, or business. The fundamental focus of these strategies is on market share, because sales gains are expected to come at the expense of product-form or product-class competitors. As suggested in Table 7-2, selective-demand strategies can be accomplished either by retaining existing customers or by acquiring new customers. In particular, if industry sales are growing slowly and yet are close to market potential, managers who want to build sales can only do so by acquiring competitors' customers. However, when the industry growth rate is high, sales and market share can also be

TABLE 7-2   SELECTIVE-DEMAND MARKETING STRATEGIES

HOW DEMAND IS IMPACTED	BASIC STRATEGIES FOR INFLUENCING DEMAND
1. Acquire new customers	Head-to-head positioning
	a. Superior quality
	b. Price/cost leadership
	Differentiated positioning
	a. Benefit/attribute positioning
	b. Customer-based positioning
2. Retain current customers	Maintain satisfaction
	Meeting competition
	Relationship marketing

increased by acquiring customers who have the ability and willingness to buy but who are just entering the market. For example, new mothers and persons moving into a new location may be new buyers for a diaper-rash product and a local bank, respectively.

Retention strategies, on the other hand, are more likely to be used by firms with a dominant share of the market and by small-market-share firms with entrenched positions in particular segments. Moreover, both retention and acquisition can be segment-specific. Managers may decide to focus the marketing effort on one or on a limited number of target segments, even when a firm currently operates in several segments.

Acquisition Strategies

A firm cannot acquire competitors' customers or new customers unless it is perceived by buyers as more effective in meeting customer needs. As we pointed out in Chapter 3, the choice process centers on a buyer's assessment of which brand or supplier has the best offer on the determinant attributes: Because choices will largely be based on these perceptions, customer acquisition strategies will essentially be based on how the product is to be positioned in the market. That is, a product's *position* represents how it is perceived relative to the competition on the determinant attributes desired by each segment. From a managerial perspective, a firm has two basic strategic options: head-to-head positioning or differentiated positioning.

HEAD-TO-HEAD POSITIONING

With this strategy, a firm offers basically the same benefits as the competition but tries to *outdo* the competition either by *superior quality* or by *price-cost leadership*. For example, IBM recently entered the notebook category of the personal computer market with a color screen that is larger and clearer than competing notebook PCs.[5] Other ways of conducting a head-to-head positioning strategy include outspending the competition on advertising (so your brand has better awareness) or offering wider availability or faster delivery.

Alternatively, firms may compete primarily on a price basis by offering comparable quality at a lower price. As we discussed in Chapter 4, if an industry is characterized by intensive competition (as is the case in the airline industry and long-distance phone service), direct price competition can be expected. Importantly, although leading firms often have economies of scale that yield cost advantages (as illustrated in Chapter 6), small firms can sometimes succeed on price leadership.

EMC Corp. has made significant inroads into IBM's mainframe computer data storage business in recent years. Whereas IBM sells large, complex, single-disk

[5] Lawrence Hooper, "IBM Introduces Its Revamped PC Line Featuring Reasonably Priced Notebook," *The Wall Street Journal*, Oct. 6, 1992, p. B3.

drives, EMC sells dozens of smaller, faster drives, which can be mass produced cheaply and then linked together by special software to provide reliable data storage. The result is a system which reduces customers' storage costs.[6]

Although it's not always possible, marketing managers should avoid head-to-head competition, for if the similarity among competitors' marketing strategies is very strong, several common marketing problems can result. First, if several brands have a common market offering, they are collectively more vulnerable to aggressive new entrants who offer a different benefit of equal value. Second, these commonly positioned brands usually must spend more than unique or niche products to gain support from retailers or other distributors. Finally, because of the difficulty consumers may have in distinguishing such brands, increasing the advertising spending level seldom produces a comparable increase in sales.[7]

DIFFERENTIATED POSITIONING

In differentiated positioning, a firm is trying to distinguish itself either by offering distinctive attributes (or benefits) by catering to a specific customer type.

BENEFIT/ATTRIBUTE POSITIONING

In benefit/attribute positioning, firms emphasize unique attributes (such as Norelco's rotating electric shaver blades), unique packaging advantages (Lipton Cup-A-Soup), or unique benefits (Gatorade replaces key minerals to the body after exercise). Often, a product does not offer a unique attribute but a unique *combination* of attributes. Lever 2000 bar soap was successful because it combined a deodorant benefit with a moisturizing benefit.

In some cases differentiation can result in the establishment of entirely new categories.

Glen Ellen Winery was successfully producing high quality wines in small volumes when the Benziger family that owns the company noticed a huge gap between the market for $3 per bottle "jug" wines and premium wines retailing for $8 and up. The Benzigers had been blending other vintners' surplus chardonnays and decided to create a new line called Glen Ellen Proprietor's Reserve, priced at $4 to $7 a bottle, and created what is now called the "fighting varietal" category.[8]

CUSTOMER-ORIENTED POSITIONING

In customer-oriented positioning (also known as niching), a firm tries to separate itself from major competitors by serving one or a limited number of special segments in a market. Often, niches are defined in terms of particular buyer characteristics. For example, Zenith first entered the personal computer

---

[6] John Wilke, "Little EMC Challenges Leader IBM in Data Storage," *The Wall Street Journal*, July 9, 1992, p. B4.
[7] Beaven Ennis, "Marketing Norms for Product Managers," *Association of National Advertisers*, New York, 1985, p. 41.
[8] Katherine Wiseman, "Mike Benziger's Fighting Varietals," *Forbes*, Feb. 19, 1990, pp. 134–135.

market by focusing solely on government agencies and universities. However, niches can also reflect specialized buyer needs: Shouldice Hospital near Toronto, Canada, accepts only one type of patient—people with hernias. Finally, niching can be based on the development of a unique product usage situation. For example, Nyquil was the first cold medicine designed for night-time use.

Increasingly, firms in complex industries with a wide variety of products have engaged in customer-oriented positioning. Many such firms are in the entertainment industries. Today, for instance, many movies are niche products.

> Warner Bros. 1990 release, *Memphis Belle*, was set in World War II and featured the pilots of B-17 bombers. A main element in Warner Bros. strategy for marketing this film was to reach people with an interest in the movie's time frame. Since Warner is a division of Time Warner, management accessed the mail-order list of households who purchased books or videos on aviation or on World War II, and mailed out 700,000 postcards offering $1 discounts on evening performances.[9]

Retention Strategies

Increasingly, managers have begun to recognize that it can be more profitable to retain existing customers than to search for new ones. The Customer Service Institute, for example, estimates that it costs five times as much to acquire a new customer as it costs to service an existing one.[10] Indeed, some firms (such as the mail-order giant Spiegel) have developed ways of calculating the "lifetime value" of each customer based on the first mail-order purchase.[11]

In order to influence a customer to stay with a brand or supplier, marketers have three basic strategic options:

- Maintain a high level of customer satisfaction.
- Meet competitors' offerings.
- Establish a strong economic or interpersonal relationship with the customer.[12]

MAINTAIN SATISFACTION

Many well-established brands with dominant market shares focus their strategies and programs on maintaining customer beliefs regarding the superior quality of the product. Thus, managers of consumer brands such as Heinz, Budweiser, and Crest design advertisements that reassure customers of con-

---

[9] Laura Landro, "Warner Tries Target Marketing to Sell Film Lacking Typical Box Office Appeal," *The Wall Street Journal*, Oct. 3, 1990, pp. B1, 10.
[10] Joan Szabo, "Service = Survival," *Nation's Business*, March 1989, p. 17.
[11] Ernest Schell, "Lifetime Value of a Customer," *Marketing Insights*, Fall 1992, p. 87.
[12] For a detailed examination of marketing programs for implementing these strategies, see Stanley Stasch and John Ward, "Defending Market Leadership: Characteristics of Competitive Behavior," *Proceeding of the 1992 Fall Educators Conference*, Chicago: American Marketing Association, 1992, pp. 466–472.

tinued high quality. When successful, these efforts result in a positive psychological relationship between the consumer and the seller based on confidence in the brand. Satisfaction with product performance can also be enhanced if a firm provides additional information or services that will lead to proper and effective use of the product. Industrial marketers frequently offer maintenance, repair, and operating (MRO) services to enhance satisfaction, and many consumer-goods firms offer similar programs. For instance, music store retailers frequently offer a limited number of free piano lessons to new owners in the expectation that greater use may ultimately lead to the purchase of more expensive models.

The importance of product satisfaction has been argued as one of the reasons for the long-term market leadership of many brands (as displayed in Table 7-3). Research conducted by the Boston Consulting Group and *Advertising Age* magazine suggests that the loyalty achieved from *value-based* consumer brands is the most enduring of all competitive barriers.

TABLE 7-3	THE LEADING BRANDS: 1925 AND 1985

PRODUCT	LEADING BRAND 1925	CURRENT POSITION 1985
Bacon	Swift	Leader
Batteries	Eveready	Leader
Biscuits	Nabisco	Leader
Breakfast cereal	Kellogg	Leader
Cameras	Kodak	Leader
Canned fruit	Del Monte	Leader
Chewing gum	Wrigley	Leader
Chocolates	Hershey	No. 2
Flour	Gold Medal	Leader
Mint candies	Life Savers	Leader
Paint	Sherwin-Williams	Leader
Pipe tobacco	Prince Albert	Leader
Razors	Gillette	Leader
Sewing machines	Singer	Leader
Shirts	Manhattan	No. 5
Shortening	Crisco	Leader
Soap	Ivory	Leader
Soft drinks	Coca-Cola	Leader
Soup	Campbell's	Leader
Tea	Lipton	Leader
Tires	Goodyear	Leader
Toothpaste	Colgate	No. 2

Source: Reprinted from *The Value Side of Productivity*, American Association of Advertising Agencies, New York, 1989, p. 18. This table was developed from *Advertising Age* and Boston Consulting Group analyses.

MEETING COMPETITION

While maintaining satisfaction is always an important goal, competitors often are able to provide satisfactory products and services. And they may offer more options and features, lower prices, and advertise heavily. Based on research conducted in several industries, the best defensive strategy to a competitive attack on product quality, price, or heavy advertising is to meet (or even surpass) the competition.

Additionally, some firms often find they must match competitors in terms of the number of product-line options offered. This issue is discussed later in this chapter under product-line marketing strategies.

RELATIONSHIP MARKETING

A relationship marketing strategy is designed to enhance the chances of repeat business by developing formal interpersonal ties with the buyer. Long-term relationships are often established through contractual or membership arrangements with customers or distributors. Typically these arrangements are only successful because of some discount or an economic incentive associated with the cost of purchasing. For example, consumers who buy season tickets for a philharmonic orchestra series are essentially engaged in a membership relationship. Similarly, annual fees charged by health spas ensure at least a 1-year relationship. In industrial marketing, simplification programs such as long-term protection against price increases or inventory management assistance frequently are so desirable to buyers or to distributors that they will commit themselves to use one supplier as the sole source of supply for a period of time. Another recent development involves the placement of computer terminals (and often, associated software) in customers' offices. These terminals are then hooked into the sellers' terminals, enabling customers to order products instantly (and thus better manage their inventories), check on the progress of deliveries, and obtain technical assistance. In recent years, firms that have experienced success with these systems include Cigna Corp. (assistance on industrial customers' insurance problems), Inland Steel (ordering and checking on order delivery), and Benjamin Moore (analyzing color samples provided by paint stores to provide pigment prescriptions).

In recent years, there has been an enormous increase in the use of relationship marketing strategies due to the effective use of customer data bases (first discussed in Chapter 5) and direct marketing techniques.

> Land's End, the Wisconsin catalogue firm, uses selective binding technology allowing it to customize each household's catalogue based on past purchases. If a household regularly buys crew-neck sweaters, that household will receive a catalogue with more displays of those products.[13]

---

[13] Nancy Ryan, "Marketers on Cutting Edge of Slice of Life," *Chicago Tribune*, Dec. 23, 1991, pp. 4:1–4.

In France, Nestlé maintains a file of customers who buy its baby foods. Each product's package carries a phone number that allows customers to readily call a Nestlé dietician. The information received from such calls is stored for analysis, and Nestlé uses the data base to send information on nutrition and Mother's Day cards to customers.[14]

PRODUCT-LINE MARKETING STRATEGIES

Most firms offer a line of products that are closely related because they serve similar needs, are used together, or are purchased together. Products that serve the same basic need are functional substitutes for one another. Thus, the various investment vehicles offered by a bank (savings accounts, money market accounts, certificates of deposit) are substitutes. Products that are used together or purchased together and serve related needs are complements. For a bank, checking accounts, savings accounts, and credit cards are all complementary.

Increasingly, firms are developing strategies that take these relationships into account. Developing a marketing strategy for each individual product without considering the impact of that strategy on substitutes or complements can lead to undesirable results. Table 7-4 lists the major kinds of product-line marketing strategies.

Strategies for Substitutes

Increasingly, firms that offer a line of substitute products attempt to focus on the entire line. This practice, sometimes known as *category management*, is expected to result in a more effective use of resources across products in the line. Two important strategic issues in category management are: (1) the setting of product-line prices (which we discuss in Chapter 9) and (2) branding strategy.

[14] Stan Rapp and Thomas Collins, "The Great Turnaround: Selling to the Individual," *Adweek's Marketing Week*, Aug. 27, 1990, p. 25.

TABLE 7-4	PRODUCT-LINE MARKETING STRATEGIES

TYPE OF RELATIONSHIP	BASIC OPTIONS
1. Substitutes	Lines extensions
	Flankers
	Combination branding
2. Complements	Leaders
	Bundling
	Systems selling

Basically, a firm has three kinds of brand strategies to choose from: line extensions, flanker brands, and combination brands.

LINE EXTENSIONS

A line extension is a variation of an existing product that retains the brand name while offering modestly new or different features. For example, Liquid Tide detergent and Hellmann's Light mayonnaise are line extensions. The major advantage of the line extension strategy is that the brand's existing equity is leveraged so it becomes easier to gain market acceptance for the new product. A drawback is that the new product will probably be most appealing to the existing users of the brand, resulting in a greater likelihood of cannibalization. For example, Anheuser-Busch used a line extension strategy when it introduced Bud Dry. But it did so knowing that half of the sales of Bud Dry would come from other Anheuser-Busch products.[15]

FLANKERS

A flanker brand is a new brand designed to serve a new segment of the market. For example, American Express introduced the Optima card as an addition to its green and platinum cards, which carry the American Express logo. Unlike its traditional cards, Optima offers a revolving line of credit, much the way VISA and MasterCard are used. While the use of multiple brands means the company is not taking advantage of the equity it has built up in its brand name, many marketers expect this will reduce the degree to which existing brands are cannibalized. Additionally, a flanker strategy will enable a firm to establish a new position or image that may be necessary to succeed in the new segment.

> Many attribute General Motors' decision to introduce Saturn as a separate division with no direct link to existing GM brands to the need to differentiate Saturn from those brands' images on the quality dimension. While this undoubtedly raised the cost of gaining awareness for Saturn, the effect on GM's other product lines appears to have been minimal. Only 9% of Saturn buyers said Chevrolet was their second choice.[16]

COMBINATION BRANDS

Often firms try to obtain the advantages both of brand leveraging and of new brands by creating a new brand personality within the original brand family. Du Pont Stainmaster carpets, Buick Regal, and Polaroid's Joshua cameras are examples. With combination branding, the core qualities of the family brand equity are retained to reduce the customer's perceived risk, but at the same time, a new personality is developed to underscore the distinctiveness of the new offering. This strategy is likely to be useful if a new segment is being

---

[15] George Lazarus, "Anheuser Pleased with Bud Dry Run," *Chicago Tribune*, Feb. 21, 1990, p. 3:4.
[16] Jim Mateja, "With New Models, Chevrolet Sees Better Days," *Chicago Tribune*, Sept. 24, 1992, p. 3:3.

targeted, a different set of benefits is offered, or a new price quality level is being introduced. For example, the Gillette Sensor needed to be distinguished from Gillette's other shaving products because of its significantly enhanced technology (and higher price). At the same time, Gillette's reputation for quality shaving products clearly enhanced the rate of consumer acceptance.

Strategies for Complements

These strategies are sometimes directed toward retaining customers in support of a relationship marketing strategy. By expanding the number of relationships, the supplier makes switching to an alternative supplier more expensive for the customer. For example, many financial institutions try to get checking account customers to use the institution as a source for their credit cards, loans, and savings accounts. In theory, as consumers concentrate these accounts, they will be less likely to switch suppliers for any one product because it would sharply reduce the convenience of *one-stop* banking. In other cases, these strategies may be designed to leverage a relationship on one product in order to acquire new customers on other goods and services. Three basic complementary strategies can be identified: leaders, bundling, and systems selling.

LEADERS

In a leader strategy, a firm promotes or prices one particular product very aggressively in the expectation that buyers will also purchase complementary goods or services. For example, a low price on a major appliance may result not only in increased sales of that appliance but in more sales of service contracts as well.

BUNDLING

A bundling strategy involves the development of a specific combination of products sold together, usually at a price that is less than the sum of the prices if the products are sold separately. Thus, a bank may offer a credit card at no annual fee to bank customers who maintain large certificate of deposit accounts. This strategy can be effective when buyers have a very strong preference for the product being discounted and a need but no strong brand preference for the product purchased at full price. Additionally, bundling and leader strategies are effective when customers can save time by buying the set of products from a single source.

SYSTEMS SELLING

In systems selling, a firm emphasizes that individual products are designed to be highly compatible with one another. For example, a computer manufacturer may design personal computers that are very technically compatible with its mainframe computers. Thus, mainframe customers who want to purchase PCs that will be able to communicate with the mainframe (to form a system) will be more likely to buy the most compatible equipment.

It is important to recognize that product-line strategies are really special cases of the primary and selective demand strategies discussed earlier. That is, any product-line strategy is directed at influencing either primary or selective demand. However, this class of strategies can be used to increase different types of demand in different situations.

SELECTING A MARKETING STRATEGY

To choose the best marketing strategy, a manager must consider several kinds of information (see Figure 7-2). First, the marketing strategy must be consistent with the *product objective*. Second, the nature and size of the *market opportunity* should be clearly established based on the market analysis and market measurements. Finally, managers must understand what kinds of competitive advantage and marketing expenditure levels will be necessary to achieve *market success*.

FIGURE 7-2
Selecting a
marketing strategy.

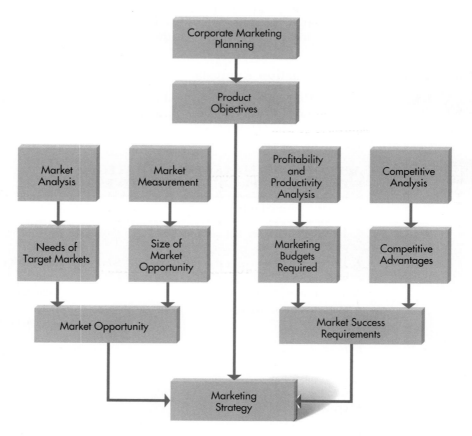

The Role of Product Objectives

Product objectives help determine the necessary basic type of strategy. For example, if market-share objectives are important, managers will employ selective-demand strategies to retain or expand market share. Alternatively, the greater the importance of cash flow and profitability objectives, the more likely a manager will be to select retention strategies and strategies for increasing repurchase rates. That is, these strategies will, in *general*, be less costly than acquisition strategies or strategies aimed at increasing the number of users. (Put simply, it is usually easier to reach and persuade existing brand customers and existing product-form buyers than to convert competitors' customers and nonadopters.)

Table 7-5 summarizes the general types of marketing strategies that managers should typically use to achieve a given product objective. Managers can, however, use more than one strategy simultaneously if adequate resources exist. Of course, in selecting a strategy, managers must also consider any impact the strategy may have on complementary or substitute products.

Additionally, the feasibility of a given strategy depends on the firm's ability to deal with the problems and opportunities identified in the situation analysis. If managers cannot identify a feasible marketing strategy for implementing the product objective, then the objective probably should be modified.

Implications from the Situation Analysis

Each of the issues addressed in the chapters on situation analysis (Part 2) has implications for the selection of marketing strategies and programs.

TABLE 7-5

APPROPRIATE MARKETING STRATEGIES FOR VARIOUS PRODUCT OBJECTIVES

PRODUCT OBJECTIVE	TYPICAL MARKETING STRATEGY
1. To achieve viable level of sales (for new product form or class)	*Primary:* Increase number of users
2. To achieve viable market share (for new brand)	*Selective:* Acquisition of customers
3. Market-share growth	*Selective:* Acquisition of customers
4. Market-share maintenance	*Selective:* Retention of customers, or *Selective:* Acquisition of customers new to the market
5. Cash flow maximization	*Selective:* Retention of customers, or *Primary:* Increase rate of purchase
6. Sustaining profitability	*Selective:* Retention of customers (in limited segments)
7. Harvesting	*Selective:* Retention of customers (with minimum effort)

■ Market analysis provides information on who buys (and who does not buy) the product form, the various situations in which the product is used (or not used), and the factors influencing the willingness and ability to buy. This information can help managers select strategies and programs for increasing either the number of users or the rate of use. By analyzing selective demand, managers should gain insights into the alternative segmentation opportunities that exist and the factors influencing buyer-choice processes.

■ The competitive analysis enables a manager to determine who the competition will be, how intensive the competition will be, and what advantages must be developed in order to compete effectively either against direct brand competitors (in selective-demand strategies) or against indirect product-class competitors (in primary-demand strategies).

■ Market measurements provide information on the size of the *primary-demand gap* between market potential and industry sales. As suggested in Chapter 5, the larger this gap, the greater the opportunity to expand primary demand for a product form or class. Further, the slower the industry sales growth, the more important it will be to find ways of expanding primary demand. Causal company sales forecasts can provide insights into the impact of various marketing programs on sales.

■ By combining productivity estimates with profitability analysis, managers can determine the profit consequences of the strategies and programs required for achieving market-share objectives.

The Globalization Question

Because an increasing proportion of businesses operate across national boundaries, an important question is whether to market a single standardized (and thus globalized) offering or to treat the various nations in the market as segments. If the latter (and more traditional) course of action is taken, the strategy is similar to a product-line flanker strategy. At the opposite extreme, a single brand is marketed with the same marketing programs in all nations.

The principle of selling the same product in essentially the same way everywhere in the world is not new. Exxon has been selling motor oil globally since 1911, and Caterpillar adopted a global approach to its marketing after World War II. Caterpillar organized an international network to sell spare parts and built a few large-scale efficient manufacturing plants in the United States to meet worldwide demand. The product was then assembled by smaller regional plants, which would add those features that were needed for local market conditions. The emergence of global markets has allowed corporations as diverse as Revlon (cosmetics), Sony (televisions), and Black & Decker (power tools) to standardize manufacturing and distribution. Some concessions to cultural differences—such as producing cars with steering columns on the right or left side—are made, but these require only minor modifications, and most other features of the product remain the same.

In the early 1980s, Professor Theodore Levitt of the Harvard Business School declared the global approach to be appropriate for all firms. He argued that advances in communication, transportation, and entertainment technology were bringing about more homogenous world tastes and wants. Companies that failed to adopt a global strategy were seen as vulnerable to global firms that could obtain savings from standardization.[17]

In reality few firms are totally globalized in terms of the full marketing mix. Even the largest multinationals with established worldwide images make some local adjustments. For example, Coca-Cola introduced Diet Coke with a globalized name, concentrate formula, positioning, and advertising but varied the artificial sweetener and packaging across nations.[18] The basic strategic issue is how much customization is necessary and desirable.

Among the factors favoring globalization, four stand out as most significant.

1. *Economies of scale exist.* The greater the economies of scale, the more advantageous a global strategy. The rapid increase in globalization for autos and construction vehicles reflects such economies.
2. *Product usage is stable across cultures.* Some products (particularly those within the home) may not be consumed in comparable ways or rates by people in different cultures. For example, canned soup can be condensed for the North American market but is unacceptable in that form in Europe. In such cases, product or positioning variations are appropriate.
3. *The same competitors exist across markets.* To the extent competitors are global, a firm will likely have to compete in the same way in each market.
4. *Many of the firm's key customers operate globally.* Because so many large firms are multinational, the firms that sell to these multinational customers must offer the same basic strategy in each market. Thus, IBM, Citicorp, and Nippon Steel are likely to be heavily globalized. To the extent that these conditions exist, globalization seems to be an appropriate strategic direction.[19]

Increasingly, it appears that the globalization strategy is driven by a combination of scale economies and the challenge of competing with the same customers across many markets, especially in Europe.

Candymaker Mars Inc. has actually killed off successful European brand names in order to standardize. Its British chocolate bar, Marathon, has been renamed Snickers, and its French candy called Bonitos are now called M&Ms with changes in chocolate formula and coating.

[17] Theodore Levitt, "The Globalization of Markets," *Harvard Business Review*, May–June 1983, pp. 92–96.
[18] John Quelch and Edward Hoff, "Customizing Global Marketing," *Harvard Business Review*, May–June 1986, pp. 59–68.
[19] A more in-depth discussion is contained in Jean-Pierre Jeannet and Huber D. Hennessey, "International Marketing Management," Houghton Mifflin, Boston, 1986, chap. 8.

Unilever also has felt the need to adjust to pan-European marketing in response to archrival Procter & Gamble, which has been introducing single brands across Europe and integrating production. Unilever produces tomato soup using separate recipes for France, Germany, Belgium, and the Netherlands, and produces fabric softeners in eight plants under seven brand names, with different bottles and formulas, leaving the company in a weaker cost position than P&G, which has only one brand, one bottle, and one formula.[20]

DYNAMIC ASPECTS OF MARKETING STRATEGY

A firm must usually change its strategy over time because the situation it faces will change. The product life cycle provides managers with guidance as to how the situation changes over time. These changes (which are summarized in Table 7-6) will have an impact on both the choice of a strategy and the selection of marketing programs for implementing the strategy.

The Product Life Cycle and Strategy Selection

The most obvious impact of the product life cycle is the shift from a primary- to a selective-demand strategy as the life cycle shifts from the introductory stage to the growth and maturity stages. As buyers become more knowledge-

[20] E. S. Browning, "In Pursuit of the Elusive Eurocustomer," *The Wall Street Journal*, April 23, 1992, pp. B1, 3.

TABLE 7-6	HOW THE SITUATION ANALYSIS CHANGES OVER THE PRODUCT LIFE CYCLE

Market analysis
Buyers become more knowledgeable about the product category and the alternatives
Repeat purchases grow and first-time purchases decline
Segmentation increases

Competitive analysis
Innovators stimulate primary demand
Early followers may imitate or leapfrog
Only the strongest survive shakeout

Market measurement
Primary-demand gap declines
Industry growth rate declines
Differences in penetration of geographic markets accelerate

Profitability/productivity
Marketing costs rise, then level out
Production costs decline with experience
Selective-demand response to price and quality increases
Selective-demand response to advertising and distribution decreases

able about the product category and as the primary-demand gap declines, the need for and payoff from primary-demand strategies declines.

A second consideration is that retention strategies should seldom be relied on, even by a market leader, until the life cycle is well into maturity. As long as markets are growing rapidly, acquisition strategies are important.

Third, product-line extensions and flankers should be developed as soon as segmentation opportunities arise. While some marketing consultants have argued that such products should be used to try to reinvigorate life cycles in maturity, the conventional wisdom is now changing. Often line extensions are necessary to move a product through the growth stage because the variation in basic customer needs (for example, personal computers or microwave ovens) is very large. Additionally, market leaders who offer a full product line may preempt competitive opportunities from new entrants or be better able to meet competitive challenges.

> In 1991, Compaq Computer Corp. launched a new line of low-cost computers (the ProLinea line) that could be sold through superstores, mass merchants, and perhaps by mail order. The decision reflected a shift in strategy away from reliance on a strategy of feature-based differentiation. As the PC market matured, the size of the price-oriented segment continued to grow, and Compaq began to see its share eroded by price-oriented competitors like Dell, AST, and Northgate.[21]

The Product Life Cycle and Marketing Programs

As we have suggested, a given type of marketing strategy may be achieved through two or more different marketing programs. For example, acquiring new customers through head-to-head positioning could imply direct competition on price, availability, quality, or brand awareness. However, over the course of the life cycle the productivity of different programs changes. Specifically, as the life cycle moves from introduction toward maturity and decline, the following trends in the response of market share occur.[22]

PRICE The impact of price on primary demand is usually very high during introduction. But the impact of price on market share is relatively low at this stage because of a lack of competitors. As the technology matures so that competing products become more alike and as buyers become aware of more alternatives, market share becomes *increasingly responsive to price*.

PRODUCT QUALITY As buyers gain more information from experience and from word-of-mouth communications, they become more knowledgeable about the relative quality of various products. Thus, market share becomes *increasingly responsive to product quality*.

---

[21] Charles Boisseau, "Compaq Draws Up New Game Plan," *Houston Chronicle*, Nov. 3, 1991, pp. B1, 5; and Kyle Pope, "Compaq Posts Profit in Period as Sales Soar," *The Wall Street Journal*, Oct. 21, 1992, pp. A3, 10.

[22] This discussion is based largely on Gerard J. Tellis, "The Price Elasticity of Selective Demand: A Meta-Analysis of Econometric Models of Sales," *Journal of Marketing Research*, November 1988, pp. 331–341; and Leonard J. Parsons, "The Product Life Cycle and Time Varying Advertising Elasticities," *Journal of Marketing Research*, November 1975, pp. 476–480.

HC - Intro
Low - Decline

ADVERTISING   Over time, awareness of a brand and its attributes will grow with cumulative exposure to advertisements. As discussed in Chapter 6, saturation levels may ultimately be reached. In any event, diminishing returns will ultimately set in, so market share will become *decreasingly responsive to awareness-oriented* (as opposed to *price-oriented*) *advertising*.

DISTRIBUTION   For consumer goods, the sales force usually focuses on obtaining distribution in large-volume stores initially and then on smaller, less important outlets. By maturity, only the marginal outlets are likely to not carry the product. Thus, money spent on additional salespeople, travel expense, or incentives to gain additional distribution will have diminishing returns. Market share will therefore become *decreasingly responsive to distribution expenditures*.

Illustrative of these trends is the situation in the maturing snack foods market.

> While new variations are regularly developed, the basic snack food products are well into maturity. Accordingly, market leader Frito-Lay (a division of PepsiCo Inc.), which holds 40% of the salty snack market, is revising many of its marketing programs. Prices have been reduced to meet discounting competitors like Eagle Snacks. At the same time, because consumers are value conscious, the company plans on increasing spending to improve quality by upgrading raw materials and reducing the number of broken chips. Additionally, while Frito Lay's distribution has been very strong, the fast-growing warehouse clubs are large, important sales opportunities that have recently been targeted.[23]

CONCLUSION

Although marketing strategies indicate the general approaches to be used in achieving product objectives, the implementation of these strategies through marketing programs is the most time-consuming part of marketing management.

Marketing programs (such as product-development programs, advertising and sales promotion programs, and sales and distribution programs) indicate the specific activities that will be necessary to implement a strategy. For instance, if a strategy requires the firm to achieve distributor cooperation, the details of *how* the sales force will achieve cooperation must be worked out in the sales and distribution program. No matter how appropriate a strategy might appear, it will fail if not properly implemented. Consequently, clear statements regarding target markets and marketing strategies are necessary to ensure that the correct programs will be developed.

As we have suggested in this chapter, then, a marketing strategy serves as the major link between corporate marketing planning and the situation analy-

---

[23] Stephanie Anderson Forest and Julia Flynn Siler, "Chipping Away at Frito Lay," *Business Week*, July 22, 1991, p. 26.

FIGURE 7-3
Relationship of marketing strategy to corporate marketing planning, situation analysis, and marketing programs.

sis on the one hand and the development of specific programs on the other. Figure 7-3 portrays this relationship.

Perhaps the most important aspect of this relationship is the fact that marketing strategy should be viewed from a dynamic perspective: As the corporate strategy or the situation analysis changes over time, the marketing strategy should change. Consider, for example, the dynamics involved in marketing strategy at Cumberland Packaging.

CUMBERLAND PACKAGING: MARKETING STRATEGY IN THE TABLETOP ARTIFICIAL SWEETENER MARKET*

Cumberland was founded in New York after World War II by the Eisenstadt family as a sugar packing company and was the first to sell sugar in tiny packets to restaurants. In 1958, the company created the first low-calorie artificial sweetener, Sweet'n Low, using cyclamates. But in 1969, the Food and Drug Administration (FDA) banned cyclamates after research showed they caused cancer in laboratory animals. The Eisenstadts immediately reformulated their product with saccharin.

With the diet movement taking hold in the United States in the late 1960s, Sweet'n Low sales boomed. Then the FDA put warning labels on products made with saccharin, as some evi-

dence began to link this substance with cancer. In spite of the warnings, Sweet'n Low sales continued upward, and by 1980 the distinctive pink Sweet'n Low packets held an 80 percent share of

---

* Developed from Fara Warner, "The Little Brand That Could," *Adweek's Marketing Week*, Aug. 26, 1991, pp. 16–17; Jesus Sanchez, "Sweet'n Lows Profits Still Fat," *Los Angeles Times*, May 17, 1988, p. 6; "Nutra Sweet Offers New Sweetener," *St. Louis Post Dispatch*, Mar. 13, 1992, p. D9; "Court Affirms Blue Packaging for Sweet One," *Food Chemical News*, Nov. 26, 1990; "Other Late News: Cumberland Packaging," *Advertising Age*, May 22, 1989, p. 8; Joe Dwyer, "NutraSweet Develops Strategy to Fend Off Host of Competitors," *St. Louis Business Journal*, July 24, 1989, p. 10A; Carrie Wiener, "Success Is Sung Sweet'n Low," *Newsday*, July 10, 1988, p. 64.

continued

the artificial tabletop sweetener market in restaurants and grocery stores.

In July of 1981, G.D. Searle (now a subsidiary of Monsanto) received FDA approval to market products with a revolutionary new sugar substitute called aspartame. The substance was trademarked as Nutrasweet, and one of Searle's first applications was to create Equal—a sugar substitute. Aspartame was 200 times sweeter than sugar but cost $90 per pound (or 270 times the price of sugar at the time). In contrast, saccharin was only 14 times as expensive as sugar but was 300 times as sweet. (Saccharin was used by Sweet'n Low and by the other leading competitor at the time, Sugar Twin.) The initial advertising spending plans for Equal exceeded the budgets for both major competitors and emphasized Equal's "natural" sugar taste and (secondarily) the absence of saccharin. Because of the cost disparity between aspartame and saccharin, Equal was priced three times higher than its competition.

During the 1980s, Equal gradually developed a strong franchise behind an advertising effort that substantially exceeded Sweet'n Low's. (In 1988, Equal spent $25 million, compared to $5 million for Sweet'n Low.) While Sweet'n Low continued to lead in supermarket unit sales, the higher price of Equal made it the dollar volume leader ($112 million to $66 million). Sweet'n Low continued to dominate sales in the restaurant market during this period. Total sales of all sugar substitutes doubled during these years.

In the 1990s, the pace of competition continued to increase. First, Cumberland launched a new brand, Sweet One, made from a new sweetener developed by Hoescht Celanese Corp. (which marketed a comparable product in Germany), and packaged in blue colors (like Equal). In addition to serving as a beverage sweetener, Sweet One could be used for baking.

When Sweet One was introduced, Nutra Sweet filed suit for trademark infringement on the basis that the product was packaged in pastel blue like Equal. However, the Supreme Court ruled against Nutra Sweet's claim. Meanwhile, Nutra Sweet continued to spend heavily on advertising for the Equal brand and for Nutra Sweet. Its patent on aspartame would expire in December 1992, so new aspartame-based competitors were expected—at least in the nontabletop portion of the artificial sweetener business. Then in 1992, Nutra Sweet unveiled Nutra Sweet Spoonful, which contains aspartame and maltodextrin (a widely used bulking agent) sold in reusable glass containers. A granulated, tabletop sweetener, Nutra Sweet Spoonful was to be targeted toward consumers with active lifestyles who are concerned about what they eat. (While Equal packets were comparable in sweetness to two teaspoons of sugar, one teaspoon of Nutra Sweet Spoonful was equivalent to a teaspoon of sugar. While the new product had only 2 calories per teaspoon—much less than sugar—this was more than an equivalent amount of Equal.)

1. Using the types of marketing strategies discussed in this chapter, indicate the type of strategy that best characterizes:
   ■ Equal's marketing strategy during the 1980s
   ■ Sweet'n Low's marketing strategy before Equal's introduction and after Equal's introduction

2. Describe the product-line branding strategies of Cumberland and Nutra Sweet in the 1990s and explain the likely reasoning underlying these strategies.

3. **a.** Where do you think the tabletop artificial sweetener market is in the product life cycle?
   b. Based on your answer to Question **a.**, how will marketing strategies and programs change in the mid-1990s?

4. If Nutra Sweet wanted to expand sales dramatically to new overseas markets, which of its two tabletop sweeteners should receive priority?

QUESTIONS AND SITUATIONS FOR DISCUSSION

1. Explain how market potential and industry sales measures are important in the selection of a marketing strategy.

2. A leading cereal manufacturer recently mailed coupons to 10 million households. Two hundred fifty different coupon offers were tested depending on what particular brand of cereal shoppers purchased and on how much they bought. The firm's loyal customers received coupons ranging from 20 to 60 cents off the next purchase. Buyers of competing brands received offers ranging from 50 cents off to a free box of cereal. Explain the different offers in terms of underlying marketing strategies.

3. Each of the two leaders in a high-growth industry holds a 20 percent market share. One product has achieved its share by maintaining the lowest prices, the widest distribution, and the largest amount of advertising. The other product has been successful largely because a patented ingredient has enabled it to have a unique additional benefit. Which of the two products is more likely to be successful in acquiring competitors' customers? Explain your answer. What additional information would be useful in selecting a strategy for each product?

4. Neutrogena Corp. is a small, Los Angeles–based business whose majority stockholders are members of the Cotsen family. The company was founded in the 1930s and for years relied on Neutrogena soap for the majority of revenues. Neutrogena soap was effectively positioned as a pure, safe, almost therapeutic product that was well worth its premium price. In the 1980s, this profitable market niche was invaded by Johnson & Johnson's line of Purpose soaps, Noxell's Clarion line, and new lines developed by Vidal Sassoon and Oil of Olay (both owned by Procter & Gamble). What marketing strategies should Neutrogena pursue at this point in time?

5. On June 21, 1989, the National Football League and card maker Pro-Set, Inc., announced the first official card of the NFL. These fourteen-card packs are targeted toward the 8- to 15-year-old consumer. Baseball cards are a $240 million a year market with five card makers, whereas football card sales total $10 million annually with one company selling the large majority of them. Pro-Set and the NFL jointly developed a print and TV ad campaign using the slogan "Collect the Action." Is this a primary- or selective-demand strategy? Why?

6. In 1993, Intel Corp.—a leading manufacturer of computer chips—unveiled the newest generation of microprocessors. Previous microchip lines had been named the Intel 386 and Intel 486. Rather than name its new chip the Intel 586, the company decided to call it the Intel Pentium. What might be the advantages of this branding strategy?

7. Reread the end-of-chapter example on MCI Communication and the Long-Distance Industry in Chapter 4.

   a. What types of marketing strategies are being pursued by these companies?

- AT&T
- MCI
- Sprint

b. How does having a pioneering advantage affect a firm's decisions on marketing strategy?

8. British Bakeries introduced the Hovis bread brand into the market in 1886. Hovis was originally a brown wheatgerm bread and was perceived as healthful and nutritious. However, the brown bread category declined in the 1950s and 1960s to 3 percent of all bread sales.

British Bakeries decided to enter the growing wholemeal bread market in 1981. Because it was felt that Hovis was too closely associated with wheatgerm, a new brand, Windmill, was developed for this market. Windmill was positioned as the health-conscious family's wholemeal, and Hovis was designated as a specialty niche brand. Demand for wholemeal brand increased as a result of the increase in marketing effort, but the advertising effort needed to support two brands proved to be too costly.

An intensive research program was conducted in 1986 on Hovis customers and competitors. Research results showed Hovis to be the best-known name in brown bread. Consumers held a highly favorable opinion of its traditional values and baking skills. As a result, management perceived that the Hovis brand could be a major competitor in the standard wholemeal mass market.

British Bakeries quickly expanded its product line. In successive years Hovis Country Grain, Hovis Granary, Hovis Goldenbran, and Hovis Organic Wholemeal products were introduced. These new products were designed to ensure that the Hovis brand could be extended from wheatgerm. In September of 1989, Hovis Wholemeal was introduced as the ultimate combination—a mass market loaf from the United Kingdom's most famous bread brand.

In entering the wholemeal market, British Bakeries seemed to have fared better with a line extension strategy than with a flanker strategy. Based on the discussion in the text on these product-line marketing strategies, should this have been expected? Explain.

9. In November 1989, Procter & Gamble introduced a new powdered detergent called Cheer with Color Guard into selected U.S. markets. The new product was a superconcentrated detergent that required only a few spoonfuls per washload. Some resistance to the new product was expected because prior research showed that many consumers did not believe that such a small amount would be sufficient to clean the laundry. As a result, the small packages that contained the product looked very expensive.

Some observers suggested that Procter & Gamble's actions resulted from a lesson in Japan. In 1987, Japanese rival Kao introduced a concentrated detergent called Attack, which quickly took 30 percent of the market—largely from P&G's brands. The company was able to regain part of its Japanese share when it responded with a Lemon Cheer superconcentrate in that country.

Superconcentrates have also hit the market in Britain, where, as in Japan, the smaller box is appreciated because the average kitchen is much smaller.

P&G's entry in the British market (where P&G's share is even greater than in the United States) is a brand called Ultra. Additionally, Ultra was marketed in a biodegradable package, which P&G hoped would be well received by the environmentally sensitive Europeans.

a. In marketing Cheer with Color Guard, will P&G need to develop a primary-demand strategy or a selective-demand strategy?

b. Contrast the strategy and programs that would be most appropriate in Japan in 1989 with those that would be most appropriate in Britain.

c. Do you agree with P&G's decision to use a line extension strategy in the U.S. market?

d. Would you advocate a globalized marketing strategy for superconcentrated detergents? Explain.

SUGGESTED ADDITIONAL READINGS

Bloom, Paul, and Philip Kotler, "Strategies for High Market Share Companies," *Harvard Business Review*, November–December 1975, pp. 63–72.

Davidow, W. H., and Bro Uttal, "Service Companies: Focus or Falter," *Harvard Business Review*, July–August 1989, pp. 77–87.

DeBruicker, F. Stewart, and Gregory Summe, "Make Sure Your Customers Keep Coming Back," *Harvard Business Review*, January–February 1985, pp. 92–98.

Dickson, Peter, and James Ginter, "Market Segmentation, Product Differentiation, and Marketing Strategy," *Journal of Marketing*, April 1987, pp. 1–10.

Jain, Subhash, "Standardization of International Marketing Strategy: Some Research Hypotheses," *Journal of Marketing*, January 1989, pp. 70–79.

Kashani, Kamran, "Beware the Pitfalls of Global Marketing," *Harvard Business Review*, September–October 1989, pp. 91–98.

Lambkin, Mary, and George Day, "Evolutionary Processes in Competitive Markets: Beyond the Product Life Cycle," *Journal of Marketing*, July 1989, pp. 4–20.

Levy, Michael, John Webster, and Roger Kerin, "Formulating Push Marketing Strategies: A Method and Application," *Journal of Marketing*, Winter 1983, pp. 25–34.

Shostack, G. Lynn, "Service Positioning through Structural Change," *Journal of Marketing*, January 1987, pp. 34–43.

Woo, Carolyn, and Arnold Cooper, "The Surprising Case for Low Market Share," *Harvard Business Review*, November–December 1982, pp. 106–113.

CHAPTER 8

PRODUCT-DEVELOPMENT PROGRAMS

OVERVIEW

In most industries, firms cannot survive (let alone prosper) without a continuing flow of new products. As we suggested in Chapter 2, the organization needs new "problem child" products to serve as the source of growth and to help maintain a balanced portfolio of products. Additionally, as we saw in Chapter 7, product development is often the critical element in implementing a marketing strategy for a product or a product line.

Because of the significance of product-development efforts, many firms have established explicit sales targets for new products. At Rubbermaid, for example, the firm's goal is to generate 30 percent of total sales from products introduced in the past five years.[1] However, the costs of designing, producing, and marketing new products are increasing: Gillette spent $150 million over 10 years in developing the Sensor razor and $175 million in North America alone in introducing it to the market. At the same time, most new products fail to achieve commercial success.

This chapter covers four critical aspects of product-development program management. First, we classify the different *types of new products* and discuss the implications of the classifications for new-product management. Second, we present a *process for managing product development* that is designed to cope with the time, costs, and risks of development and commercialization. Third, we present several widely used *analytical tools* and concepts that are used in the new-product management process. Finally, we discuss the relative merits of *acquisition and licensing* as alternatives to the internal development of new products.

TYPES OF NEW PRODUCTS

In some industries, product life cycles may be as short as one year, so last year's innovation is no longer new, whereas in other industries the pace of innovation is slower. Additionally, the definition of newness depends on who

---

[1] Jon Berry, "The Art of Rubbermaid," *Adweek's Marketing Week*, Mar. 16, 1992, pp. 21–25.

is making the assessment—the buyer or the seller. In this section we show that the degree to which a new product is new to a buyer or to the firm selling it will have an impact on the amount of risk being taken and should influence the way the new-product development process is managed.

Newness to the Firm

The degree to which a new product is new to the firm depends on its role in corporate and marketing strategy. Table 8-1 summarizes the kinds of new products that would be pursued in implementing each type of corporate strategy.

DIVERSIFICATION

As we discussed in Chapter 2, diversification is a strategy in which the firm enters new markets with products that are functionally different from existing products. Often, diversification is achieved through acquisition. For example, Procter & Gamble entered the pharmaceutical market by acquiring two firms: Norwich-Eaton and Richardson-Vicks. Because diversification involves new products and new markets, it is the product-development avenue that is most "new" to the firm. Thus, the firm is usually less knowledgeable about buyers, distributors, production costs, and processes than for other product categories. This knowledge gap will be somewhat less of a problem if the diversification focuses on products that are complementary to existing products. Thus, Gillette entered the shaving cream market without much difficulty since the buyers and distributors were the same as for their line of razors.

In selecting new markets to enter, firms often try to capitalize on their existing brand equity. As we discussed in Chapter 4, brand equity is an important resource. If it is sufficiently strong, the firm may diversify through a *brand franchise extension*. In this strategy (also known as a "category" extension), a firm uses an established brand name on products that serve markets

TABLE 8-1	TYPES OF NEWNESS TO THE FIRM	
TYPE OF CORPORATE STRATEGY	TYPES OF NEW PRODUCT	TYPICAL EXTENT OF NEWNESS
Diversification	■ Completely new ■ Brand franchise extension	■ New market ■ New technology probable
Market development	■ Technical extension ■ Change in form	■ New use ■ User-related technology
Product development	■ Line extension ■ Flanker	■ New segment ■ New technology possible
Market penetration	■ Product modification (to meet or beat competition)	■ No change in market ■ Small change in technology

that are at least somewhat new to the firm. Some examples of successful franchise extensions include Jell-O Pudding Pops and Bic disposable lighters.

Brand franchise extensions are very popular because they allow a firm to enter a new category at lower costs. Because the brand name is well known, consumers may perceive less risk in trying the new product and are likely to associate many positive aspects of the brand with the extension. In general, brand franchise extensions will be more effective when:

- The products are complementary in usage. (For example, Crest toothbrushes complemented Crest toothpaste.)
- The parent brand and the category extension are perceived as sharing some common benefits or technology. (Sony's reputation for quality electronic gear allowed it to enter a wide range of consumer-goods markets.)
- The firm maintains in the new product the quality standard set by the parent brand so as not to undermine the brand equity.[2]

MARKET DEVELOPMENT

Although there are several routes to market development, a very important one is to use a *technological extension* of an existing product to serve a new usage category and thus stimulate primary demand. For example, Du Pont originally created materials such as rayon, teflon, and nylon for industrial users and subsequently introduced them into consumer products. Although the basic technology for these new products is usually well understood, the company must deal with new users and new distribution channels, which creates a fair amount of uncertainty over market acceptance.

PRODUCT DEVELOPMENT

Basically a corporate product-development strategy is implemented by a product-line marketing strategy of either *flanker brands* or *line extensions* as we discussed in Chapter 7. Because the primary purpose of these strategies is to reach new segments of markets already being served, management should have a fair understanding of the buyer and established distribution channels, and (normally) will rely on known technology and production processes. The basic uncertainty revolves around how well the new product will be accepted compared to competing products and to what extent it will cannibalize sales of other product-line offerings.

MARKET PENETRATION

Minor product modifications are often used as part of a market penetration strategy. Specifically, a "new" or "improved" version or new "options" may be developed to retain customers being lured away by competitors or to increase market share by improving the benefits offered. For example, Procter &

---

[2] This is based, in part, on Edward Tauber, "Brand Franchise Extension: New Product Benefits from Existing Product Names," *Business Horizons*, March–April 1981, pp. 36–41; and Peter Farquhar, "Managing Brand Equity," *Marketing Research*, September 1989, pp. 30–32.

Gamble watched the market share of its Pampers drop from 60 percent in 1980 to 26 percent in 1989. In response, the company introduced a new Pampers with cuffs to block leakage around the leg openings.[3]

It is important to have a clear understanding of the firm's corporate and marketing strategy when examining new-product opportunities for two reasons. First, the purpose of a strategy is to provide direction. Any new product idea should fit the company's primary corporate direction or a current need established by a marketing strategy. Thus, if a company is not immediately interested in diversification but wants to emphasize growth in current markets, new product ideas should focus on product-line marketing strategy or selective-demand marketing strategy.

The second key reason for recognizing the type of newness of a product idea is to have an understanding of the type and extent of risk involved. Clearly, diversifications and technical extensions are higher risk in that less is known about both production and demand than is the case with other types of new products and because major new marketing programs (for promotion and distribution) must be developed.

Newness to the Market

When assessing any new product idea, management must have some sense of how the market will respond to it. Specifically, managers will need to determine buying needs and preferences, the market's size and growth prospects, and the perceptions of the product relative to competitors. All these issues have been discussed in earlier chapters. However, the uncertainty about market response is bound to be greater when a product has yet to reach the market. This uncertainty can create two basic problems. First, uncertainty about the level of demand limits management's ability to determine whether the potential sales volume will be adequate. Second, the design of and costs associated with promotion and distribution programs cannot be determined until market response is assessed.

In general, the degree of uncertainty will depend on the degree of newness of the product from the buyer's perspective. As Table 8-2 suggests, there are four levels of newness that reflect the degree of innovativeness of the new product idea.[4]

DISCONTINUOUS INNOVATIONS

Discontinuous innovations are relatively rare. They represent products that create entire new product classes, usually as the result of technological breakthroughs. Because these products create entirely new demand categories,

---

[3] Alecia Swasy, "P&G Is Altering Pampers to Lift Drooping Sales," *The Wall Street Journal*, Aug. 9, 1989, p. B1.

[4] See Thomas Robertson, "The Process of Innovation and the Diffusion of Innovation," *Journal of Marketing*, January 1967, p. 15, for a discussion of the three nonimitative types of innovation.

TABLE 8-2	TYPES OF NEWNESS TO MARKET	

TYPE OF INNOVATION	TYPE OF NEWNESS	CHANGE REQUIRED OF BUYERS
Discontinuous	New product class	Creates new consumption pattern (computer, radio)
Dynamically continuous	New product form	Changes determinant benefits (personal computer, portable radio)
Continuous	New or improved model	Changes evaluation of brands but not determinant attributes (IBM PS/2-486, Sony Walkman)
Noninnovative	New brand	Changes set of alternatives within a product form (IBM computer clones, other pocket portable radios with earphones)

their ultimate size is very difficult to predict, and the time and cost involved in building primary demand are usually substantial.

DYNAMICALLY CONTINUOUS INNOVATIONS

Dynamically continuous innovations are new products that offer major but evolutionary improvements in the benefits available within a product class. In effect, these are new product forms that offer enhanced or different benefits from the existing forms. Acceptance is less uncertain since the product class already has been accepted. Rather, the concern is for the share of total product-class sales that will go to this form and for the amount of primary-demand stimulation necessary.

CONTINUOUS INNOVATIONS

Continuous innovations are modest enhancements in performance within a product form. Most product-line extensions and product modifications will fall into this category, so the level of brand cannibalization is a matter of concern, as is the impact of the change on the favorableness of buyers' ratings of the brand.

IMITATIONS

Imitations are not innovations at all, but attempts to capitalize on the success of a competing brand by offering a simple, stripped-down, or lower-priced version.

The degree of newness to the buyer has important implications for the steps management will take in the new-product development process. Clearly, more time, effort, and funds will be devoted to develop an understanding of the market for products with higher degrees of newness. Not only is the level of market uncertainty greater for these products, but usually the amount of money at risk is larger because new product forms and classes usually require more marketing expenditures and involve greater investments in technology.

Even for products with a modest degree of newness, however, new products usually fail to meet expectations. A series of studies in several countries has succeeded in identifying nine factors that effectively discriminate between success and failure.

1. *Product superiority/quality.* The competitive advantage the product has by virtue of features, benefits, quality, uniqueness, and so on.
2. *Economic advantage to the user.* The product's value for money for the customer
3. *Overall company/project fit.* The product's synergy with the company—similarity to established marketing skills, managerial skills, and business knowledge
4. *Technological compatibility.* The technological synergy with the company—similarity to established R&D, engineering, and production capabilities
5. *Familiarity to the company.* How familiar the project is to the company (as opposed to entirely new products or projects)
6. *Market need, growth, and size.* The magnitude of the market opportunity
7. *Competitive situation.* How easy the market is to penetrate from a competitive standpoint
8. *Defined opportunity.* Whether the product has a well-defined category and established market (as opposed to a true innovation and new category of products)
9. *Project definition.* How well defined the product and project are[5]

These factors are important to managers involved in product development because they represent issues that should be incorporated into a firm's formal new-product development and evaluation system.

THE NEW-PRODUCT DEVELOPMENT PROCESS

Because of the probability of new-product failure, and since the consequences of new-product failure can be high, most organizations have developed some formalized system or structure for managing the new-product development process. In large companies that make complex products (such as advanced electrical or mechanical goods), this process may involve dozens of specific activities and reviews. In small firms with simple technologies (such as most service organizations), relatively few steps are involved. The *major types* of

[5] See Robert Cooper, "The New Prod System: The Industry Experience," *Journal of Product Innovative Management*, June 1992, pp. 113–127.

FIGURE 8-1
A phased
new-product
development
process.

activities and analyses that are conducted, however, are similar in nearly all situations.

Phased versus Parallel Development

There are two basic kinds of approaches to the process: a *phased* development approach and a *parallel* development approach. These approaches are portrayed in Figures 8-1 and 8-2. In both cases, the activities that are conducted are essentially the same, but the timing and organizational responsibility of the

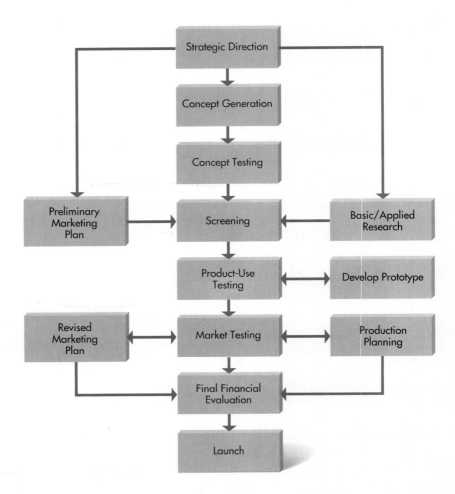

FIGURE 8-2
A parallel
new-product
development
process.

activities will differ. In *phased* development, all activities are conducted in a fixed sequence; the unit performing each step completes its work, then passes the project on to the next phase. In *parallel* development, some activities are conducted simultaneously and, in most cases today, with communication among the units.[6]

PHASED DEVELOPMENT   *Phased* development is more likely to be found in companies that operate in markets where the pace of technological change is slower and more predictable. In such businesses, development speed is less critical and the process is more orderly, with individual managers able to focus on their own areas of expertise (be it manufacturing, R&D, or marketing

[6] This section was developed from Bro Uttal, "Speeding New Ideas to Market," *Fortune*, Mar. 2, 1987, p. 62; Hirotaka Takeuchi and Ikujiro Nonaka, "The New Product Development Game," *Harvard Business Review*, January–February 1986, pp. 137–146; and C. Merle Crawford, *New Products Management*, 2nd ed., Irwin, Homewood, Ill., 1987, chap. 2.

research). The purpose of this process is to permit evaluations of a new idea at several points in time as additional information is developed about demand and costs of the new product. In the phased approach, the least attractive new product ideas can be dropped from further consideration before extensive time and dollar commitments are made. For example, in the phased approach, R&D is less likely to become involved in the process (except in those cases where R&D generates the product concept) before the screening stage.

PARALLEL DEVELOPMENT *Parallel* development has become the more widely accepted approach in high-technology industries such as computers, copiers, consumer electronics, and other product categories where the penalty for being late to market is severe and where new product forms are generated fairly frequently. The enhanced development speed results from improved quality and decreased volume of communications and from the use of new-product teams of eight to twelve members. At 3M, for example, most new products come from someone in a technical area. That individual then forms an action team composed of technical people from other relevant R&D areas, manufacturing, marketing planning, sales, and perhaps finance. The team designs the product, then develops the marketing and production plan.[7] The constant interaction among team members permits R&D, marketing, and manufacturing to proceed in parallel. Additionally, if new technology or marketing opportunities arise during development, adjustments can be accommodated much more quickly.

Regardless of which approach is utilized, the marketing tasks in the new-product development process remain essentially the same. Each of these tasks is discussed below.

Strategic Direction

It is useful for management to begin the development process by signaling a broad goal or strategic direction toward which marketing and research and development could think and work. Essentially, this is accomplished through setting corporate and marketing strategies. For example, if R&D and marketing managers know whether product-line extensions or diversifications are desired, they will be more likely to develop products that fit company needs while still focusing on the market needs and other success criteria discussed above.

Concept Generation

New product ideas can come from a variety of sources. In addition to research and development personnel, useful ideas are often generated from dealers, competitors, salespersons, and other employees. But for most firms, customers remain the best source for new product ideas or for modifications of existing products.

[7] Russell Mitchell, "Masters of Innovation," *Business Week*, Apr. 10, 1989, p. 60.

Often, however, *ideas* are vague and subjective and provide little guidance to the process of actually designing a new product. Consequently, managers really need to generate *concepts*—a more complete specification of the idea that defines the *benefits* that the product will provide and the physical *attributes* or *technology* that will deliver those benefits. Clearly defined concepts will help management test the acceptability of a new product idea as well as improve the chances that the product will be designed correctly to provide the specified benefits. Marketing's primary role in concept generation is to identify the benefits the potential new product should offer. R&D or operations managers will then need to design the physical attributes or technology.

A variety of methods exist for identifying potential new concepts. For industrial products, an effective technique is *lead-user analysis*. Essentially this is an interviewing approach that focuses on identifying the anticipated future requirements of a company's "lead" customers—the customers who have the most to gain from product improvements and who are the technological leaders in an industry. Because lead users tend to be large or technologically advanced, it is expected that they will have the best ideas about the products and attributes that buyers in a given industrial market will need in the future. The effectiveness of lead-user analysis has been shown to be especially useful in technology-driven industrial markets such as computing and scientific instrumentation.[8]

For consumer products, a wider range of concept generation approaches is available. As we discussed in Chapter 4, new product concepts may emerge from analyses of *perceptual maps*. By identifying gaps in a market—combinations of determinant attributes that are not offered by existing products—potential new-product opportunities can be identified. However, mapping techniques are limited in that many consumer usage problems may not be easily revealed simply by looking at perceptual maps. That is, with perceptual mapping we are assuming that the determinant attributes are already known. As a result, mapping techniques usually lead to continuous innovations and product-line extensions.

Problem analysis approaches are more likely to yield product concepts that provide new kinds of benefits because they focus on *usage problems* and *systems*, not just the scanning of existing offerings.[9] In problem analysis, the firm conducts interviews with heavy users in the market for a product category to obtain a list of the problems consumers associate with a category. Users are then asked to rate each problem in terms of its frequency and the degree to which it is bothersome. Problems that are both frequent and bothersome are usually selected as the focus of new-product concept development. For example, Table 8-3 gives the results of a problem analysis conducted in the car wax products industry. Subsequently, managers initiate brainstorming or similar activities that are designed to devise potential solutions. Looking at Table 8-3, we can see why car wax manufacturers would try to make faster, easier-to-

---

[8] Eric von Hippel, *The Sources of Innovation*, Oxford University Press, New York, 1985, chap. 8.
[9] Claes Fornell and Robert D. Menko, "Problem Analysis—A Consumer-Based Methodology for the Discovery of New Ideas," *European Journal of Marketing*, 1981, pp. 61–72.

TABLE 8-3	**MOST FREQUENTLY OCCURRING AND MOST BOTHERSOME PROBLEMS AMONG USERS OF CAR WAXES**

PROBLEMS WITH CAR WAXES	PROBLEM OCCURS FREQUENTLY*		PROBLEM IS BOTHERSOME†	
	%	RANK	%	RANK
Hard to apply	87	2	57	1
Mess up the driveway	35	4	30	4
Uneven shine	12	9	5	9
Gets on clothes	14	8	12	7
Too expensive	23	6	38	2
Too much time	98	1	21	3
Doesn't last	18	7	8	8
Need good weather	31	5	18	5
Doesn't clean tar	40	3	14	6

* The percent who cited the problem as occurring "often" or "sometimes" on a scale that also included "seldom" and "never."
† The percent who said the problem was "extremely" or "very" bothersome on a scale that also included "a little" and "not at all."

apply products. Similar techniques led to new products such as Johnson & Johnson's Band-Aid Sheer Strip.

The most widely used method for identifying problems in the problem-analysis approach and for identifying potential new determinant attributes is the *focus group*. These groups involve eight to ten people (led by trained moderators) in discussions about products, the needs they serve, perceived problems, and ways the product is used. Focus groups can yield major insights or minor product modifications. For example, American Express modified the service provided by its credit card to include extended manufacturer warranties on products purchased with the card as the result of a focus group study.

Finally, direct observation of customers' product usage patterns can be useful in identifying new products or modifications. Braun has modified many of its small kitchen appliances after watching customers use these products and identifying small but annoying problems (such as inconvenient locations of buttons on blenders). Similarly, United States Surgical sales representatives often observe surgeons at work in hospital operating rooms to gain ideas for better products.[10]

Concept Testing

The purpose of concept testing is to develop a more refined estimate of market acceptance for the new product concept or to compare competing concepts to determine the most appealing one (or two). If a product prototype is already available, this step may often be excluded. But when a large number

[10] Jennifer Reese, "Getting Hot Ideas from Customers," *Fortune*, May 18, 1992, pp. 86–87.

of possible concepts exist and the cost of building a prototype is large, concept testing may indicate a number of important aspects of market demand that should be considered before any prototypes are developed.

In particular, concept testing is designed to obtain the reactions of potential buyers to one or more hypothetical product concepts. Product features and benefits are presented in verbal form or explained through visual aids. Potential users are then interviewed to obtain comments about the merits and demerits of each concept or are asked to rate the products in various ways. Table 8-4 indicates some of the specific methods that can be used to help answer the questions management should ask in this step of the product-development process.

Consider, for example, the contents of Table 8-5. After presenting potential buyers with the product concept, the concept was evaluated through a series of questions that would tell management whether the product would likely enjoy a clear competitive advantage, what problems might be encountered in gaining market trial, and whether in general there was a positive reaction to the product. While the probability of trial that is recorded would certainly be a very rough estimate of acceptance, extremely favorable or unfavorable ratings on this question are generally valuable in deciding whether continued research on the concept is warranted.

Additionally, managers are often interested in understanding the buyer's willingness to trade off price for various features because managers often find that there is a practical limit to the amount of quality people will pay for. For example, Clark Equipment introduced a new electric-powered fork lift truck with an unusually durable transaxle and expensive air-cooled brakes following a $25 million investment. But the advanced technology was more than customers needed—very few buyers found the product worth the price.[11] The

[11] Kevin Kelly and Zachary Schiller, "How U.S. Forklift Makers Dropped the Goods," *Business Week*, June 15, 1992, pp. 106–107.

| TABLE 8-4 | QUESTIONS AND TYPICAL METHODS FOR CONCEPT TESTING |

QUESTION	METHOD
1. How desirable is the concept to target customers?	Customers rate the concept on a series of dimensions such as uniqueness, problem-solving potential, believability.
2. What is the probability that the customer would try or use the product?	Customers are asked to rate the product on a scale from "would not try" to "definitely would try."
3. What is the relative utility for various attribute combinations?	a. Customers rank-order their preferences for various combinations of all attributes (full-profile conjoint analysis). b. Customers rank-order their preferences for various pairs of attributes.

TABLE 8-5	EVALUATING A NEW CLEANING PRODUCT CONCEPT

Concept statement

A newly developed, nonabrasive, all-purpose cleaner, which not only cleans but inhibits dirt from adhering to the cleaned surface. By varying the strength of the product, the user can clean windows, vinyl, stainless steel, chrome, aluminum, tires, upholstery, carpet, bathroom fixtures, woodwork, appliances, kitchen cabinets, and counters.

Uniqueness: Which statement best describes this product?

_____ Sounds completely different from any other product now available
_____ Very different from any other product now available
_____ The same as some other product now available

Competition: When people buy a new product, they usually buy it in place of some other product they had been buying. If you were to buy this new product, what item or items would it replace? _____

Need: Does this product solve a problem or need that isn't being satisfied by products now on the market?

_____ Yes   What is the problem or need? _____
_____ No

Merits: What specific features do you find attractive about this new product?_____

Limitations: What specific features do you find questionable about this new product? _____

Believability: Are there any features or claims about this product that you find hard to believe?

Probability of trial: How interested would you be in buying the product described above if it were available at your supermarket?

_____ I would definitely buy
_____ I would probably buy
_____ I might or might not buy
_____ I would probably not buy
_____ I would definitely not buy

highly popular methods of *conjoint analysis* are concept-testing methods that are designed to show:

- How buyers make trade-offs among various attributes (including brand name and price) of a product concept
- The share of preferences each product concept would enjoy when the buyer can choose among existing attribute combinations and the new concept

These techniques assume we know the determinant attributes for a new product concept. If these attributes are independent of one another, if the product is not highly subject to social influence, and if the customer can identify each attribute in a choice situation, the relative utility of each level of each attribute can be assessed through a conjoint analysis. Essentially, this form of concept testing helps managers identify the most preferred combinations of various attribute levels by forcing prospective buyers to rank their preferences for different combinations. Even when the potential combinations are too numerous to permit a rank ordering of the full set, the same result can be obtained by having customers rank a specific subset through a technique known as a fractional factorial design.

Consider, for example, a concept test for a new lightweight printer that would be compatible with any personal computer. Assume that the manufacturer is considering three levels of print quality, three levels of printer speed, and three levels of price. Theoretically, there are twenty-seven possible attribute combinations (that is, 3 speeds × 3 print-quality levels × 3 prices = 27). Potential buyers would have difficulty ranking twenty-seven combinations. But the same information about preferences could be elicited from the reduced array shown in Table 8-6. Now, only nine combinations need to be ranked. (Note that each speed appears once with each letter-quality level and once with each price; all two-way combinations are thus represented in the reduced design.) Specifically, the rankings that result will be adequate to determine how willing buyers are to trade speed for quality, price for quality, and price for speed. The mechanics of the statistical analyses involved are beyond the scope of this book. Additionally, there are a number of variations of this methodology that could be chosen.[12] However, the kind of output that is generated and its potential usefulness in new-product development can be

[12] See Dick R. Wittink and Philippe Cattin, "Commercial Use of Conjoint Analysis: An Update," *Journal of Marketing*, July 1989, pp. 91–96, for a summary of current practices.

TABLE 8-6   **AN EXAMPLE OF A CONJOINT ANALYSIS CONCEPT TEST**

Please rank the nine combinations in order of your preference from 1 (most preferred) to 9 (least preferred).

PRINT QUALITY	PRINTER SPEED (CHARACTERS PER SECOND)		
	180	240	300
Draft copy	$210	$290	$250
Near letter quality	$250	$210	$290
Letter quality	$290	$250	$210

TABLE 8-7	**RESULTS OF A CONJOINT ANALYSIS ON ONE CUSTOMER'S PREFERENCES**

ATTRIBUTE	UTILITY
Print quality	
Draft copy	10
Near letter quality	33
Letter quality	45
Printer speed	
180	14
240	18
300	20
Price	
$210	40
$250	32
$290	18

observed from Table 8-7. Based on the preferences stated by a single customer, the relative utility of each possible attribute combination can be calculated by adding the utilities for each component. For example, this customer's most preferred concept is the combination of letter quality, 300 characters per second speed, and a price of $210. The total utility for that concept is 45 plus 20 plus 40 equals 105. However, the data also show the trade-offs consumers are willing to make. A letter-quality printer and a $250 price are preferred to a near-letter-quality printer at $210. (Add the utilities for these combinations to see why.) By performing the same analysis with other potential buyers, conjoint methods can yield estimated shares of preference for each potential concept within a set of possible competing concepts.

Screening

As the name of this step would suggest, this activity sifts out and eliminates more new product ideas and concepts than any other step in the process. The purpose of this step is to rate the general desirability of the new product concept to the firm. That is, even though the concept may be considered very marketable, it may be viewed as inappropriate for a firm that lacks the specific resources needed to produce and market it successfully. While the concept test provides useful information about potential market acceptance, this information must be interpreted in the context of a given firm and in the context of alternative new-product opportunities.

In evaluating new product ideas at the screening stage, many firms use some type of scoring profile in which each concept is evaluated on the factors thought to be more important to long-term success. Typical of such profiles is Figure 8-3.

FACTORS		SCORE			
	Very poor 1	Poor 2	Average 3	Good 4	Excellent 5
1. Market size	—	—	—	—	—
2. Growth potential	—	—	—	—	—
3. Bought by customer we already know	—	—	—	—	—
4. Product has a competitive advantage	—	—	—	—	—
5. Intensity of competition	—	—	—	—	—
6. Uses existing sales force/channels	—	—	—	—	—
7. Uses existing production capacity	—	—	—	—	—
8. Financial requirements	—	—	—	—	—
9. Within scope of R&D capacity	—	—	—	—	—
10. Can use existing suppliers	—	—	—	—	—
11. Rate of technical change	—	—	—	—	—
12. Likelihood of new competition	—	—	—	—	—
13. Extent of government regulation	—	—	—	—	—
14. Marketing expenditures required	—	—	—	—	—
15. Fit with corporate, marketing strategy	—	—	—	—	—

FIGURE 8-3
A scoring profile for a new product.

In Figure 8-3, we can see that the major dimensions of a screening analysis include market factors, the degree to which the company can use existing resources, environmental constraints, and the strategic fit between this product concept and corporate and marketing strategies. Due to the variety of factors considered, screening must generally be carried out by a multifunctional group or committee so that appropriate inputs from production, finance, R&D, and marketing will be obtained.

Often, there will be disagreement among the evaluators regarding the relative importance of the various factors as well as on the ratings of an idea on each factor. This is part of the management process and should not be viewed as a negative feature of screening. Indeed, a key purpose of screening models is to force a dialogue among managers so that the thinking behind each evaluation is made explicit and managers can identify the specific items of additional information needed in subsequent steps.

Technical Feasibility

As a result of concept testing, only one or a very few concepts will usually be found worth pursuing. However, even those concepts that remain may not be carried to the prototype stage.

Technical-feasibility analysis is the process of determining the technical requirements for designing and producing the concept. The availability of technology and the time and cost required for development of the product will be considered at this point. Essentially, managers must resolve three issues in technical-feasibility analysis:

- Managers must determine if the firm can design a product that actually implements the concept.
- They must estimate the investment that is required for development and production.
- They must estimate the unit cost of production (labor, materials, and packaging costs).

Additionally, technical testing is necessary to assess the performance of a product under different conditions and to develop information vital to the development of selling, advertising, and distribution programs. Specifically, technical testing can provide information on:

- Product shelf life
- Product wear-out rates
- Problems resulting from improper usage or consumption
- Potential defects that will require replacement
- Appropriate maintenance schedules

Each of these kinds of information may have cost consequences for the marketing of the product. Shelf-life estimates will influence the frequency (and cost) of delivery. Significant usage problems will mean additional costs in providing advertising, labeling, or selling information.

Product-Use Testing

Once a prototype of the product has been developed, performance should be assessed from the buyer's perspective. Product-use testing involves any test of the product by the consumer or industrial buyer. These tests may be done "blind" (where the brand or seller's identity is not disclosed).

One purpose of a product-use test is to gauge comparative advantage. To the extent that objective comparisons can be made with existing products on functional features, the significant advantages of the new product can be more effectively used in promotional programs. Comparisons on durability, speed, reliability, and other features are increasingly being employed in promotions by consumer and industrial marketers based on product testing information.

However, buyers' perceptions of the product's performance must also be examined. And these perceptions may be influenced by how each customer uses the product. Consequently, buyer tests of product performance are usually a major part of product testing. These tests can be conducted in several ways. Two prominent approaches are as follows:

1. Consumers are asked to use a product (often unlabeled) in their homes, or industrial buyers are asked to try out a product in their business.
2. Comparison tests are performed. For example, potential buyers are asked to consume or use the test product and one or more competing products and then draw comparisons between them.

TABLE 8-8	QUESTIONS AND TYPICAL METHODS FOR CONSUMER PRODUCT-USE TESTS	
	QUESTION	METHOD
	1. Has the product concept been implemented?	Consumers rate products in terms of the degree to which each attribute in the concept exists in the product.
	2. Is the product used in the manner expected?	Consumers list problems and specific usage situations for which the product works best based on in-home trial.
	3. Based solely on product features and performance, what market share could this product achieve?	Consumers make direct comparisons among alternatives (in-home or in-laboratory setting) and rate brands or rank-order their preferences.
	4. Where will customers for this product come from (nonusers, users of the company's other brands, customers of specific competitors)?	Rank-order preferences and ratings are examined relative to brand currently used.

As Table 8-8 indicates, these tests can be used to answer a variety of questions. Product tests can provide a rough estimate of the achievable market share based solely on product performance. (That is, preferences are usually measured "blind" so that brand name, price, and advertising effects are excluded.) Additionally, the degree to which the new product is likely to acquire new customers rather than simply cannibalize the sales of any existing products can be established. Finally, consumer product testing can provide a check on whether the concept has been implemented. If consumer descriptions of the product do not match the intended concept, then reformulation may be necessary. Alternatively, consumers may not be using the product in the manner expected, causing the performance to differ from the concept. For example, it is often difficult to get all consumers to use detergents in the same way, and different washing techniques and equipment may cause deviations between the benefits buyers receive and the benefits or attributes planned in the concept.

Market Testing

While product-use tests can provide important information regarding the likely acceptance of a new product, they are limited in their usefulness for predicting sales response for two reasons. First, individuals in the sample may state preferences but do not have to make actual choices. Second, sales response is influenced by the firm's promotion, price, and distribution programs in addition to the product-use characteristics—especially in the case of consumer goods. (For this reason, many firms also test consumer reactions to the proposed price and to various advertising campaigns at this stage.)

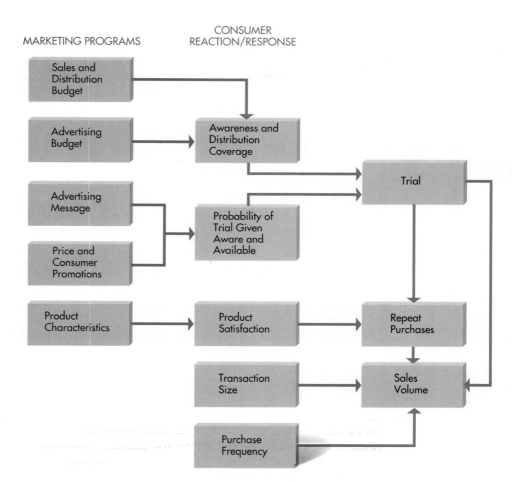

MARKETING PROGRAMS CONSUMER REACTION/RESPONSE

FIGURE 8-4
Determinants and components of first-year sales volume.

Market tests are essentially sales forecasts in which managers attempt to project sales or market-share growth patterns over a period of (typically) 1 year. These projections are made by developing estimates of selected components of sales or share based on observed or judged effects of the marketing programs.[13] Figure 8-4 portrays the relationships among the major elements of the marketing strategy and the components of sales response. Within the figure, the marketing program elements are portrayed along the left side. These programs influence the consumer's awareness and access to the new product, the attractiveness of the product concept (as reflected in probability of trial), and the satisfaction with the product when purchased. The actual

[13] The first major effort at developing such sales forecasting efforts is described in Henry Claycamp and Lucien Liddy, "Prediction of New Product Performance: An Analytical Approach," *Journal of Marketing Research*, November 1969, pp. 414–420. A more recent review that focuses on test-market models is Chakravarthi Narasimhan and Subrata Sen, "New Product Models for Test Market Data," *Journal of Marketing*, Winter 1983, pp. 11–24.

number who will try and repeat and the resulting sales volume are thus a function of how consumers respond to the programs. Typically, early sales are dominated by first-time triers. Then, as the maximum number of potential triers is gradually approached, fewer potential new triers remain, and repeat sales to satisfied customers become the dominant portion of total sales. Figure 8-5 portrays typical growth patterns for sales to first-time and repeat buyers.

Market Testing through Test Markets

Test marketing has traditionally been the most effective way of market testing for consumer products. In test marketing, a firm offers a product for sale in a limited geographic area that is as representative as possible of the total market in which the product will eventually be sold. Test marketing has several distinguishing features relative to other research approaches (see Table 8-9).

- Test marketing lowers the risk of national failure, which could endanger channel relationships, reduce confidence and morale of employees, and have a negative impact upon present customers' images of a firm's other products.
- No special benefits are offered to induce purchasing other than those that would later be available on a national basis.
- The product competes with other competitive products in an authentic sales environment.

In a typical application, a firm selects two to four market areas that are thought to be representative demographically and are sufficiently isolated that local television, radio, and newspapers can be used effectively to reach the market. Arrangements with retailers are made to assure complete distribution (in effect, eliminating lack of distribution as a potential cause of weak sales).

FIGURE 8-5
Typical first-year sales patterns: trial and repeat.

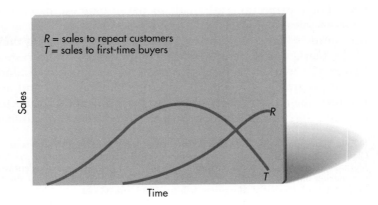

R = sales to repeat customers
T = sales to first-time buyers

Sales

Time

TABLE 8-9	CONSIDERATIONS INVOLVED IN DECIDING WHETHER TO TEST-MARKET

FACTORS FAVORING TEST MARKETING

1. Acceptance of the product concept is very uncertain.
2. Sales potential is difficult to estimate.
3. Cost of developing consumer awareness and trial is difficult to estimate.
4. A major investment is required to produce at full scale (relative to the cost of test marketing).
5. Alternative prices, packages, or promotional appeals are under consideration.

REASONS FOR NOT TEST MARKETING

1. The risk of failure is low relative to test-marketing costs.
2. The product will have a brief life cycle.
3. Beating competition to the market is important because the product is easily imitated.
4. Basic price, package, and promotional appeals are well established.

The firm then applies its planned advertising, promotion, and pricing programs and observes the sales response.

In the context of Figures 8-4 and 8-5, test markets enable the firm to track trial and repeat purchases by monitoring retail sales and using consumer panels (such as the scanner data discussed in Chapter 6) to separate trial from repeat and to identify purchase frequencies and sizes. As we discussed earlier, when single source data are used, the actual links between marketing programs and trial and repeat can also be studied. The importance of being able to do detailed trial and repeat analyses in test markets is exemplified by Ocean Spray's introduction of Mauna La'i Hawaiian Guava Drink.

> Because Guava is different from any other fruit drink in color, taste, and aroma, Ocean Spray's marketing staff was very unsure of the product's ultimate acceptance. Using a BehaviorScan electronic test market (as discussed in Chapter 6), the company tracked trial and repeat rates and the identity of the buyers. Initially, the company was disappointed in the repeat rate. But more detailed analyses showed that while the percent of triers who repeated was below expectations, those who did repeat were purchasing at a much higher frequency than anticipated. Moreover, this niche was largely composed of upscale buyers. By refocusing the advertising media used before the national launch, Ocean Spray was able to enhance trial and repeat substantially within this new segment.[14]

Additionally, because systems like BehaviorScan allow firms to target separate advertisements and promotions to selected panel households within a test market, it is possible for firms to test alternative introductory marketing plans to see which ones are best at stimulating trial.

[14] Leslie Brennan, "Test Marketing Put to the Test," *Sales & Marketing Management*, March 1987, p. 68.

Although the appeal of test marketing is great, most marketers believe it takes at least 10 months to evaluate test-market results, with more conservative companies testing for 1 year or even 2 years. Indeed, test markets for grocery products can easily result in expenditures of millions of dollars. At the same time, test-market results may prove meaningless if competitors disrupt the test by lowering their prices or increasing advertising within these markets. Finally, by test marketing, a firm alerts its competitors about its new products and gives them time to develop matching new products or to design defensive strategies for established products.

Market Testing through Simulated Test Markets

Simulated test markets were designed to be used prior to test marketing but, in practice, are often used in place of test markets. Also called *laboratory test markets* or *pretest market models*, this class of techniques is available from a number of market research service organizations, each of which has developed a variation with its own name. Among the most popular suppliers are Information Resources Inc., A. C. Nielsen, and Yankelovich, Clancy, Shulman.

While each model differs slightly, the general process for these models incorporates the following steps:

1. Interviews (usually intercepting shoppers in a mall) are conducted with roughly 300 consumers who use the product category. Each consumer lists the brands they are aware of, and brand attitudes and preferences are measured.
2. Consumers are then asked to view a series of concept boards or commercials that include ads for the product being tested.
3. Consumers are brought into a mock (laboratory) store, given cash, and offered the opportunity to purchase a product from the product category being studied.
4. People who do not select the test product in Step 3 are given a sample of the test product as a gift.
5. After a period of time sufficient for product trial, telephone interviews are conducted to assess any changes in preference, attitudes toward the new brand, and intentions to repurchase. In some cases, respondents are given repeated options to repurchase the product through phone orders.[15]

Essentially, the research is designed to provide estimates of

- Probability of trial, given awareness and availability (Step 3), and
- Percent of triers who will repeat purchase (Step 5).

---

[15] Allan Shocker and William Hall, "Pretest Market Models: A Critical Evaluation," *Journal of Product Innovation Management*, Fall 1986, pp. 87–88.

Most firms will reduce the trial estimate by some amount, such as 20 percent, because experience shows that this trial measure is probably inflated. Additionally, the models use perceptual mapping and preference analysis techniques to develop parallel estimates of the product's likely market share.

Referring back to Figure 8-4, we can see that trial and repeat are critical elements in projecting first-year sales. Users of the simulated test market also input their judgmental estimates of the percentage of awareness that will be achieved from the proposed advertising budget and the percentage of all outlets that will carry the product based on the sales and distribution program. Combining these estimates with expected purchase size and frequency will yield a sales forecast.

Simulated test markets usually make a number of assumptions, and the effectiveness of these techniques will depend heavily on the realism of the assumptions. Specifically, it is assumed that managers can make good estimates and that the laboratory setting is a reasonable representation of an actual purchase setting. Some experts feel that such market testing efforts are less effective when the new product represents a new product form or class: Buyers can more easily judge the appeal a new product holds for them when there are ready bases for comparison. Additionally, because simulated test markets place a heavy emphasis on the role of advertising in influencing trial, they may not be as reliable in markets where product trial is influenced heavily by sales promotion.

On the other hand, simulated test markets can be conducted for a fraction of the cost of a test market. Moreover, while the overall rate of success of new products in test markets is 40 percent, that percentage doubles among products that have first reached target sales or share levels in simulated test markets.[16] Thus, simulated test markets can serve as a screening device to eliminate questionable new products prior to test market. Additionally, while simulated test markets are far from perfect substitutes for test markets, extremely positive results in a simulated test market may lead a firm to skip the test market, particularly if the costs of failure are low and the risks of competitive imitation are high.

Financial Evaluation

In Chapter 6, the elements involved in product-profitability analysis were examined and the basic criteria for measuring profitability were provided. In the case of new products, the issue of profitability is slightly more complex, for four reasons.

First, sales forecasts are inherently more uncertain for new products. However, the results of product testing can provide rough estimates of the number

---

[16] Glen Urban and Gerald Katz, "Pretest Market Models: Validation and Managerial Implication," *Journal of Marketing Research*, August 1983, pp. 221–234.

of potential buyers for a product, and market tests can further improve the accuracy of sales estimates.

Second, the pattern of sales and costs for a new product will vary by a greater extent over time. New products are seldom adopted immediately, and the cost of marketing will often be very high in the first year because of the need to provide awareness of the product and incentives for product trial. In general, first-year earnings will understate long-term profitability. If a significant additional investment in production facilities is required, projected profitability should be measured over a longer period of time (anywhere from 3 to 10 years, depending on the expected duration of sales and on the life of the facilities).

Third, if the new product will be a potential substitute for existing products or will share production or marketing resources with existing products, only the incremental effect of the new product on profits should be evaluated. That is, if the new item is expected to cannibalize sales, managers should consider the net sales gain in evaluating the profitability of the product. Similarly, management should include only those increases in cost that are directly attributable to the new product. When excess capacity exists, the new product is often charged with a share of indirect costs. But if those indirect costs would be incurred even if the new product were not added, then they would not be incremental costs. By including them, a firm is penalizing a product for helping the firm operate more efficiently.

Finally, new products may require an additional investment in facilities or equipment. Investments are not costs, because they are one-time outlays rather than recurring expenditures. However, because alternative opportunities for capital investment exist and because different products require different amounts of investment, managers must take the size of the initial investment into account in measuring the profitability of new products.

The data presented in Table 8-10 illustrate one kind of analysis that might be used in assessing new-product profitability. In this example, based on market testing, a product-line extension is expected to achieve sales of 500,000 units. However, based on concept tests, of the 500,000 units, 100,000 are expected to result from cannibalization of the existing brand's sales. Thus, the net gain to the firm is 400,000 units. Projected sales and distribution expenses (from the marketing plan) and estimated production expenses (from technical feasibility studies and production planning) provide the data on variable and direct costs. Of these costs, some (such as the new product's allocated share of sales-force costs and a portion of the fixed expenses) are not really incremental. The investment in additional plant and equipment for the new product is $10,000,000, to be depreciated over 10 years.

The analysis shows that the projected first-year return on investment is substantially higher when the project is evaluated on an incremental basis. This kind of assessment is important because most firms will evaluate the new product's financial prospects relative to the return on investment from other new-product opportunities and relative to lower risk investment opportu-

| TABLE 8-10 | FINANCIAL ANALYSIS FOR A NEW PRODUCT |

	NEW PRODUCT PROJECTIONS	INCREMENTAL ANALYSIS
Sales forecast	500,000	400,000
Unit price	$ 22	$ 22
Total revenue	$11,000,000	$8,800,000
Variable expense (30% of sales)	−3,300,000	−2,640,000
Advertising and promotion expense	−1,000,000	−1,000,000
Allocated share of sales-force expense	−1,200,000	0
Other fixed expenses	−1,950,000	−300,000
Depreciation	−1,000,000	−1,000,000
Net profit before tax	$ 2,550,000	$ 3,860,000
Investment	$10,000,000	$10,000,000
Return on investment (ROI)	25.5%	38.6%

nities. Indeed, many firms establish minimum returns in the range of 20 to 30 percent in order to take inflation and risk into account. Additionally, if the firm attempts to project profitability over a number of years, managers will generally calculate the cash flow (which is equal to net profit after taxes plus depreciation) for each future year and then discount these future cash flows to assess their *net present value*.[17]

Launch

Some firms spend so much time and effort in the development of a product that they overlook the planning required to bring the product to market effectively. A number of key decisions are necessary to the development of a launch plan.

First, the timing of the introduction should be carefully evaluated. In particular, it is generally more appropriate to introduce the product during peak periods if demand is highly seasonal. This will permit the firm to obtain a higher level of sales from new-product trial, thus helping to offset large initial advertising and sales promotional expenditures. The introduction should also be timed to ensure distributors will have high levels of inventory by the time the advertising and promotion program kicks off.

Additionally, no attempt at launch should be made until the firm is satisfied that it has done the best job possible in designing the advertising, sales promotion, and sales and distribution programs, and in selecting the best

---

[17] The present value of future cash flow is calculated as follows:

$$\text{Present value of cash inflow in year } i = \frac{\text{cash flow in year } i}{(1 + d)^i}$$

where d = discount rate (desired percentage return)
i = year in the planning-period sequence

price. These programs are examined in detail in subsequent chapters. However, it is important to note that the first few months of a new product's existence are critical to long-term success. Distributors usually have little patience carrying new products that do not show early prospects for success.

ALTERNATIVES TO INTERNAL DEVELOPMENT

Internal product development is only one way to expand the product line. Firms can also expand their product lines by acquiring the products of other companies. Additionally, firms can acquire licenses to market products that are developed and manufactured by other firms. These approaches are more likely to be employed when the product-development objective is diversification or when a lack of time, skills, or financial resources would limit the effectiveness of any internal efforts.

Advantages of Acquisitions and Licensing

There are three major advantages to licensing and acquisitions. First, licensing and acquisitions save a company time. In advanced-technology industries, the time it takes to do the research, as well as the time it takes to build and operate production facilities, often precludes successful market entry. If timeliness is a key factor, licensing or acquisition of the resources of another company may be the only viable alternative.

Second, if a firm is unfamiliar with the management, technology, or production skills needed to enter a market, the chances for success may be improved by acquiring those skills.

Third, acquisitions or licensing may be less costly to the firm than internal expansion. The acquisition of companies by direct purchase or by exchanging securities may appear costly until compared with the future cost of bringing a new production facility on stream during a period of inflation. Further, the cost of building market share may be much greater than the cost of acquiring brands that already enjoy established positions in the market. As we discussed in Chapter 2 this is especially true when high technology or extensive government regulation create long development lead times (as occurs in the pharmaceutical industry).

Establishing Acquisition and Licensing Criteria

In planning for new products through the acquisition or licensing route, management should have clearly established guidelines for evaluating and selecting candidates. Essentially this means that, at a minimum, the steps of establishing strategic direction, screening, and financial evaluation should be followed. Specifically, acquisitions are usually expected to fit the company's corporate strategy and resources and to achieve some target level of return on investment. Other standards that are often established include

- Having a leading position in a market,
- Meeting some minimum sales volume levels, and
- Showing a likelihood of satisfying high-growth-rate goals.

CONCLUSION

With rapid changes in technology and markets, a firm's product mix must be dynamic. New products play an important role in corporate and marketing strategy, and the development of these products should involve all elements of the business. Because of the high rate of failure for new products, it is important that firms develop appropriate product-development objectives to guide the product-development process. Additionally, product-development costs can be high, even for new products that never reach the market. Accordingly, it is imperative that firms develop systematic procedures for identifying and screening new product ideas, for testing concepts and prototypes, and for examining profitability.

In this chapter we have presented a comprehensive approach for guiding the product-development process, and we have examined some specific procedures for projecting the market acceptance and profitability of new products. Clearly, the product-development process will not really be complete until advertising, pricing, and other marketing programs are established. The relationship between product-development programs and other marketing programs is portrayed in Figure 8-6. This figure also illustrates how corporate

FIGURE 8-6

Relationship among corporate marketing planning, marketing strategy, product-development programs, and other marketing programs.

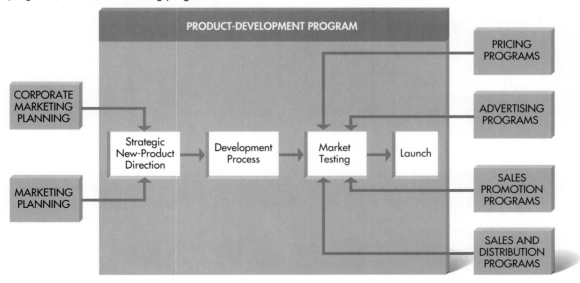

LEVER BROS. INTRODUCES LEVER 2000*

In 1991, Lever Bros., the North American unit of the British-Dutch corporation Unilever, slipped past Procter & Gamble to claim the leadership spot in the $1.6 billion toilet soap market. The product that made this possible was Lever 2000, which was introduced in 1991 and claimed an 8 percent market share in its first year. Including Lever's other bar soaps, Dove, Shield, and Caress, the company's product line achieved a 31.5 percent share (although Dove's share slipped from 18 percent to 16.5 percent with the Lever 2000 introduction).

The Lever 2000 story began back in 1982 when a research group came up with a new soap technology that combined the characteristics of both deodorant and complexion soaps in one product for the first time. David Sharp, senior group product manager for personal washing products, then set up focus groups to test the concept of a soap product that is "mild enough for sensitive skin but leaves a clean, fresh feeling." Following successful concept testing results, the Lever 2000 name was chosen. Management wanted a name that communicated that the soap was a modern product. The firm's willingness to use the Lever name was a reflection of their confidence in the product's success.

In 1987, Lever 2000 was introduced into test markets in Atlanta. Subsequently, in 1990, distribution was expanded to the southeast region of the country, and then in 1991 to other regions as new manufacturing facilities came on stream. Although Lever used extensive couponing and discounting (along with $25 million in advertising) to launch the brand in these markets in 1991, company officials pointed to an estimated repeat rate of 40 percent as evidence that the brand's success would not be short-lived.

1. What marketing strategy does Lever Bros. seem to be following with the development and introduction of Lever 2000?
2. What "type of newness to the market" category (Table 8-2) best describes Lever 2000? Explain.
3. Why would Lever Bros. decide against using an established soap brand name like Dove to market this new soap?
4. Lever used focus groups to test the concept underlying Lever 2000. What specific questions would you most want to address if you were designing this concept test?
5. In the case of this product, it appears that Lever Bros. used a phased development approach with extensive market testing. Why was this appropriate in this situation, and is this always the best approach in this industry?

---

* Developed from "David Sharp: Lever 2000," *Advertising Age*, July 6, 1992, p. S20; "Bar Soap to Rival Lever's Dove," *Brandweek*, July 27, 1992, p. 1; Jennifer Kent and Dick Rowe, "New Lever Bar Soap Challenges P&G," *Cincinnati Post*, Feb. 13, 1992; "Lever Rolls Out New Deodorant Bar," *Adweek's Marketing Week*, Apr.1, 1991, p. 7; Pat Sloan and Bradley Johnson, "P&G Slips on Soap," *Advertising Age*, Sept. 30, 1991, p. 3; "Everyone Is Bellying Up to This Bar," *Business Week*, Jan. 27, 1992, p. 84; "The New Moth of New Brands," *Mediaweek*, Mar.9, 1992.

marketing planning and marketing strategy should influence the selection of a new-product direction. To gain additional insights into these relationships consider Lever Bros.' successful introduction of Lever 2000 bar soap.

QUESTIONS AND SITUATIONS FOR DISCUSSION

1. In 1989, Hershey Foods Co. bought Peter Paul Almond Joy, Mounds, and York Peppermint Patties from Cadbury Schweppes. At about this same time, the CEO of Hershey indicated that new products were Hershey's life-blood and that their objective was to develop at least one new "hot" product a year. What could explain Hershey's decision to acquire these existing brands from Cadbury Schweppes while at the same time developing new products from within the company?

2. Scholastic Inc. was founded in 1920 when the company launched *The Scholastic* newsletter to bring contemporary literature and current affairs into classrooms. In recent years, the company has added a large variety of other educational newsletters and is launching textbooks that involve software, videos, and high-tech teaching aids. Would phased or parallel development be preferable for Scholastic's product-development process? Why?

3. In 1992, Gillette introduced new lines of Gillette Series shaving creams and aftershaves to the market. Like the hot-selling Gillette Sensor razor, the products were premium priced and touted as "The Best a Man Can Get." But many industry experts were skeptical about whether the strategy that worked for Sensor would also work for these lines. How might the company go about testing this strategy without using a test market?

4. Nickelodeon, the cable channel oriented toward children, has become enormously successful with a variety of irreverent contemporary game shows, comic soap operas, and preschool shows like *Eureka's Castle*. For years, the show's creative director was Geoffrey Darby, who relies heavily on focus groups to assess new programming concepts. How (if at all) would you modify the questions in Table 8-5 to assess kids' reactions to new television programs?

5. Timberland Company became immensely successful in the 1970s with the sales of its comfortable, rugged, and water-resistant boots. In the late 1970s and early 1980s, the company added a line of handsewn leather moccasins similar to the popular Topsider "deck shoe." Identify some other possible brand extensions for the Timberland brand name. What specific criteria would be used in selecting brand-extension candidates?

6. Outline the concept testing procedure you would suggest for (a) a car powered by solar energy and (b) a new at-home personal banking and shopping system using a personal computer. Is there any difference in concept testing for products as compared to services?

7. Test marketing and consumer-use testing are two approaches used to assess the potential success of a new product. Based on the strengths and weaknesses of each approach, which method would you suggest for each of the following items?
   a. A new improved detergent
   b. High-definition, flat-screen television

c. A new Nintendo computer children's game

8. An advertising agency conducted a conjoint analysis to determine how consumers traded off among brand name, price, and various features for airline flights. The results indicated that a typical consumer had relative utilities for each attribute as listed below:

Airline	
American	29
Continental	17
Delta	20
TWA	23
United	28
Round-trip fare	
$199	69
$249	45
$299	26
$349	1
Flight plan	
Nonstop	42
One-stop	21
Change planes	2
Smoking	
None	33
Only if flight is over 2 hours	30
Yes	19

Source: Betsy Sharkey, "The People's Choice," *Adweek's Marketing Week*, Nov. 27, 1989 (Special section: Marketer's Report Card 1989, p. 7).

a. What inferences would you draw from such data about brand equity in this industry?

b. If an airline was considering offering a new no-smoking, one-stop flight at a price of $249 to compete in a market with a $299, nonstop flight that permitted smoking because the flight was over 2 hours, what do the conjoint analysis results suggest the typical consumer will do?

SUGGESTED ADDITIONAL READINGS

Aaker, David, and Kevin Keller, "Consumer Evaluations of Brand Extensions," *Journal of Marketing*, January 1990, pp. 27–41.

Cooper, Robert, "The New Prod System: The Industry Experience," *Journal of Product Innovation Management*, June 1992, pp. 113–127.

de Brentani, Ulrike, "Success and Failure in New Industrial Services," *Journal of Product Innovation Management*, December 1989, pp. 239–258.

Gupta, Ashok, S. P. Raj, and David Wilemon, "A Model for Studying R&D Marketing Interface in the Product Innovation Process," *Journal of Marketing*, April 1986, pp. 7–18.

Kerin, Roger A., Michael G. Harvey, and James T. Rothe, "Cannibalism and New Product Development," *Business Horizons*, October 1978, pp. 25–31.

Shocker, Allan, and William Hall, "Pretest Market Models: A Critical Evaluation," *Journal of Product Innovation Management*, Fall 1986, pp. 86–107.

Takeuchi, Hirotaka, and Ikujiro Nonaka, "The New Product Development Game," *Harvard Business Review*, January–February 1986, pp. 137–146.

Von Hippel, Eric, "Get New Products from Customers," *Harvard Business Review*, March–April 1982, pp. 117–122.

Wheelwright, Steven C., and W. Earl Sasser, "The New Product Development Map," *Harvard Business Review*, May–June 1989, pp. 112–127.

CHAPTER 9

PRICING PROGRAMS

OVERVIEW

Most marketing students have taken one or more courses in economics prior to their marketing education. Consequently, they are likely to be familiar with the important role price plays in influencing demand. As we saw in Chapter 7, price can be an integral part of the marketing strategy for a product or product line and can influence demand in a variety of ways.

In this chapter, we present a framework for selecting *pricing programs*, which are the plans a firm develops that indicate what level of price should be charged in order to implement (or at least be consistent with) the marketing strategy. Basically the elements of our framework are as follows:

- Establish the pricing objective.
- Analyze the price-elasticity of demand.
- Identify key factors acting on price competition.
- Estimate the relationship between price changes and volume, cost, and profit changes.
- Based on the analyses of price-elasticity, competition, and cost-volume-profit relationships, establish the basic type of pricing program to use for the product being priced.
- Consider the impact of the planned pricing program on any product-line substitutes or complements.
- Determine if any legal limitations on pricing decisions exist or if any modifications are necessary for international markets.

For firms selling goods or services directly to their final customers, the process outlined above will result in the establishment of a *list* price, which is the basic price the firm normally expects to receive. However, list prices are often modified by sales promotions (such as coupons and cents-off specials) and by sales and distribution arrangements that involve negotiated prices, cash or quantity discounts, or long-term contracts. Although these programs may lead to changes in the actual price paid, they will be discussed in later chapters.

Manufacturing firms selling through wholesalers or retailers will use this process to set the price they receive from their distributor (the manufacturer's selling price) and often to establish a manufacturer's suggested retail price as well. It is important to recognize, however, that once wholesalers and retailers purchase goods from manufacturers, they can set the prices they charge so as to fit their own strategic needs.

PRICING OBJECTIVES

The purpose of any pricing program is to support the marketing strategy that has been developed for the product or product line. Pricing objectives specify how price is expected to help implement the marketing strategy. Table 9-1 lists the major types of marketing strategies discussed in Chapter 7 and some pricing objectives that would typically be associated with each strategy type.

Primary-demand-based objectives are selected if the firm believes price can be used to increase either the number of users or the rate of purchase. Especially in the introductory or growth stages of a product life cycle, lower prices may reduce the buyer's perceived risk of trial. Or, lowering a price may enhance the relative value of one product form versus another. For example, lower prices for notebook computers have not only reduced the risks of trial but have also made the product relatively more attractive compared with conventional personal computers. Alternatively, lower prices could be designed to enhance the rate of purchase either by increasing consumption frequency (as when the prices of high-quality cuts of beef are reduced) or by broadening the number of usage situations to include lower priority uses. For example, lower long-distance telephone rates may lead people to make phone calls to friends they normally would write to.

TABLE 9-1	MARKETING STRATEGIES AND POSSIBLE PRICING OBJECTIVES

MARKETING STRATEGIES	PRICING OBJECTIVES
Primary-demand strategies	
■ Increase number of users	■ Reduce economic risk of trial
	■ Offer better value than competing product forms/classes
■ Increase rate of purchase	■ Enhance frequency of consumption
	■ Enable use in wider range of situations
Selective-demand strategies	
■ Retention	■ Meet competition (establish price parity)
■ Acquisition	■ Undercut competition on price
	■ Use price to signal premium quality
Product-line strategies	
■ Substitutes	■ Get buyers to "trade-up"
	■ Distinguish product-line alternatives on value/features
■ Complements	■ Expand range of products bought by existing customers
	■ Attract new customers on superior value of a system or package of products

Selective-demand-based objectives are those designed to support either a retention strategy or an acquisition strategy. Generally speaking, pricing designed to meet the competition will be used if a firm's primary concern is to retain the existing customer base. When the strategy is acquisition-oriented, the pricing objective may be to become the low-price alternative or to underscore a quality-based differentiation. It should be noted, however, that meeting the competition is not necessarily an inappropriate objective for an acquisition strategy. A firm may want to compete on nonprice factors and thus decide to match competitors' prices in an effort to remove price as a consideration in making a choice.

Finally, product-line-based objectives are those that guide the pricing of a line of substitutes or of a product that has many complements. For substitutes, the objective will be either to encourage some buyers to consider more expensive models within a line (an important issue in pricing a line of automobiles) or to make quality distinctions very clear. For example, most banks offer different prices to distinguish checking account plans that have different balance requirements or check writing limits. For complements, the primary objective may be to expand the range of products purchased by existing customers (as when a bank offers a no-annual-fee credit card to its existing checking account customers). Alternatively, the objective may be to attract new customers through offering superior value on a system or package of new products. Thus, an appliance dealer may offer a free extended warranty on a new television set.

As we shall see later in this chapter, pricing objectives provide substantial guidance for pricing programs. However, managers should recognize that pricing objectives cannot be established simply from knowing the marketing strategy. It may turn out that price will not be useful in implementing a marketing strategy because customers are not sensitive to price, because competitors offset the price programs by the price actions they take in response, or because the profitability consequences of a pricing program are unacceptable.

However, the purpose of setting a pricing objective is to identify the specific kind of impact on demand that management wants to achieve through pricing. After a manager has calculated a price level that will achieve the pricing objective, the profitability consequences can be evaluated by using the procedures we discussed in Chapter 6. That is, the pricing program should result in a price level that will achieve the price objective (and thus help implement the marketing strategy) and at the same time ensure that the product's target contribution will be achieved.

More fundamentally, however, managers cannot establish meaningful pricing objectives unless they believe demand will be responsive to price. That is, managers cannot determine how price may contribute to a marketing strategy unless they have analyzed the price-elasticity of demand.

PRICE-ELASTICITY OF DEMAND

Because the effectiveness of any pricing program depends on the impact of a price change on demand, it is necessary to understand the extent to which unit sales will change in response to a change in price. However, unlike other productivity relationships, a change in price has a twofold effect on a firm's sales revenue: a change in the units sold and a change in revenue per unit. Thus, managers should not be concerned merely with the price-sensitivity of the market; they must also be concerned about the impact of the change on total dollar revenue.

The price-elasticity of demand explicitly takes this into account. That is, price-elasticity is not simply another way of saying price-sensitivity. If a change in price causes a change in *units sold*, we can say demand is somewhat price-sensitive. But when we use the term price-elasticity, we are examining the impact of a price change on *total revenue*.

More specifically, *price-elasticity of demand* is measured by the percentage change in quantity divided by the percentage change in price. Given an initial price P_1 and an initial quantity Q_1, the elasticity of a change in price from P_1 to P_2 is calculated by:

$$e = \frac{Q_2 - Q_1 / \frac{1}{2}(Q_2 + Q_1)}{P_2 - P_1 / \frac{1}{2}(P_2 + P_1)}$$

If the elasticity measure e can be calculated, then management can predict the impact of the price change on revenue, as Table 9-2 indicates.

Note that the important number to keep in mind is -1. If elasticity is -1 or smaller (such as -2 or -3), then demand is very sensitive to price and the change in revenue will be in the opposite direction from the direction (increase or decrease) of the price change. Similarly, if elasticity is greater than -1 (such as $-\frac{1}{2}$ or $+1$), then demand is not very price-sensitive, and an increase (decrease) in price will result in an increase (decrease) in revenue. This point is significant because, in practice, it is difficult for managers to

| TABLE 9-2 | EFFECTS OF DIFFERENT TYPES OF ELASTICITY |

EFFECTS OF DIFFERENT TYPES OF ELASTICITY

VALUE OF e	TYPE OF ELASTICITY	EFFECT ON TOTAL REVENUE OF: PRICE INCREASE	PRICE DECREASE
$e > -1$	Inelastic	Increase	Decrease
$e = -1$	Unitary elastic	No change	No change
$e < -1$	Elastic	Decrease	Increase

develop a precise, reliable estimate of elasticity. But simply being able to determine whether e is greater than -1 or less than -1 will enable managers to understand the general impact of a change in price on revenue.

In making estimates of elasticity, however, managers need to distinguish carefully between elasticity of *market demand* and the elasticity of *company* (or *brand*) *demand* and to recognize that differences in elasticity may exist across segments within a market.

Market, Segment, and Company Elasticity

Market elasticity indicates how total primary demand responds to a change in the average prices of all competitors. Company elasticity indicates the willingness of customers to shift brands or suppliers (or of new customers to choose a supplier) on the basis of price. For a product that offers an example of the significance of this distinction, economists often point to table salt. The market demand for table salt is inelastic, because people cannot consume much more even if all prices are lowered. However, if one producer lowers its price, that producer is likely to gain market share. So although market demand may be inelastic, at the same time company demand can be elastic because buyers may be very sensitive to competitive price differences.

Marketers are not just interested in understanding total market demand, however. Recall from Chapter 3 that, for most products, different buyers have different determinant attributes. So often there are substantial differences in the price-sensitivity of different buyers.

The demand schedules presented in Table 9-3 and portrayed in the demand curves of Figure 9-1 can help to illustrate these points. Assume these data represent demand for flights between Chicago and New York at three price levels. For the total market (which includes all air carriers' sales), as the average price declines, total sales *and* total revenues increase, suggesting that demand is elastic. However, demand in this market is the sum of demand from two basic segments: business travel and nonbusiness (pleasure) travel. Within the business travel segment, while sales increase as prices decline, total

TABLE 9-3

ILLUSTRATION OF MARKET AND MARKET SEGMENT DEMAND SCHEDULES

ROUND TRIP UNDISCOUNTED FARE	WEEKLY MARKET SALES		WEEKLY SALES: BUSINESS FLYERS		WEEKLY SALES: NONBUSINESS FLYERS	
	UNITS	TOTAL REVENUE	UNITS	TOTAL REVENUE	UNITS	TOTAL REVENUE
$350	40,000	$14.0 mill	24,000	$8.4 mill	16,000	$5.6 mill
$325	45,000	$14.625 mill	25,000	$8.125 mill	20,000	$6.5 mill
$300	51,000	$15.3 mill	26,000	$7.8 mill	25,000	$7.5 mill

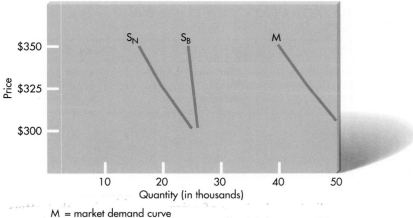

FIGURE 9-1
Illustration of a market demand curve and two market segment demand curves.

M = market demand curve
S_B = demand curve for business travel segment
S_N = demand curve for nonbusiness travel segment

revenue actually declines: demand in this segment is inelastic. (Of course, demand in the nonbusiness segment is very elastic.) Thus, managers who target the business segment need not use aggressive pricing as the basis for a marketing strategy.

Whether a firm's individual pricing strategy is effective, however, will depend on the *company* elasticity of demand. Even if industry prices decline from $350 to $300, a given firm serving even the elastic nonbusiness travel market might conceivably experience inelastic demand if it could clearly differentiate its flights in terms of some other determinant attribute (such as good flight times or special on-board services). If so, that firm could continue to charge prices higher than its competitors' without reducing profitability.

Managers should note that the distinction between market elasticity and company elasticity is directly related to the two major types of marketing strategies discussed in Chapter 7 and to the pricing objectives discussed earlier in this chapter. Specifically, if a manager's pricing objective is to increase rates of purchase for the product form or to increase demand among users (both of which reflect *primary-demand* strategies), then the manager should determine whether *market demand* is inelastic. On the other hand, if the pricing objectives reflect *selective-demand* strategies (such as the retention or acquisition of customers), then managers should be concerned about the elasticity of *company demand*.

However, it is *not* necessary that demand be elastic in order to achieve a pricing objective. Managers may be very committed to retaining customers or to acquiring new customers when the product objective is to maintain share or to increase market share. Often this commitment is so strong that managers will be willing to risk some reduction in total revenue in order to maintain (or in order to establish) a strong position in a market.

TABLE 9-4	ILLUSTRATION OF A COMPANY DEMAND SCHEDULE		
	PRICE	DEMAND	TOTAL REVENUE
	$2.00	500,000	$1,000,000
	$1.50	600,000	$ 900,000
	$1.00	750,000	$ 750,000

To illustrate, consider the company demand schedule in Table 9-4. Demand is inelastic because total revenue declines as the price is reduced from $2.00. However, buyers are still *sensitive* to price: Volume does increase as price declines. Consequently, if the impact of higher volume on total revenue and profitability is acceptable (given the product objective and target total contribution), then a manager may well decide to lower the price, sacrificing some degree of profitability for market share and sales-volume gains.

ESTIMATING PRICE-ELASTICITY

As we have shown in the previous section, managers should have some estimate of the degree of price-elasticity that exists in order to predict the unit sales volume and total revenues that will result at various price levels. In order to develop this estimate, managers can employ several alternative procedures.

Historical Ratios

In Chapter 6, we indicated that historical ratios may exist that will indicate the past effect of changes in a marketing variable (such as price) on sales. Multiple-regression sales forecasting models are often employed to develop the historical relationship between price and sales volume.

When using this approach, managers must have historical data not only on company sales and prices but also on industry sales and competitive prices. That is, to estimate market elasticity, managers need to determine the historical relationship between *industry* sales and some average of *industry* prices. However, both pieces of information are also needed to estimate company elasticity. That is, the effect of a company's price on selective demand will really depend on how much the company's price differs from the prices of direct competitors. (For example, if, in the past, a firm has consistently raised its price without any loss in sales, management cannot necessarily infer that company demand is inelastic because competitors may also have been raising prices.) Further, estimates of company elasticity cannot be made without considering changes in industry sales. That is, an increase in company sales may reflect an increase in market share or an increase in industry sales. (In fact, price cutting frequently leads to increases in both primary and selective demand.) Accordingly, managers should examine the historical relationship between a company's relative price (that is, relative to competitors' prices) and market share when attempting to assess company elasticity.

Managers must also recognize that historical ratios will only reveal price-elasticity levels if no changes in other important marketing or environmental variables have occurred. The relationship between airline prices and sales over time will be difficult to understand if a recession has occurred because such an economic event usually will outweigh the impact of fare levels on demand. Similarly, changes in a firm's advertising or promotional budget may have occurred, the effects of which will be difficult to separate from the effects of pricing.

Experimentation

Field experiments (including the electronic scanner experiments discussed in Chapter 6) in which actual retail prices are manipulated while other factors (advertising, packaging, shelf space) are held constant are often employed by consumer-goods marketers to examine the impact of price changes on sales. This method can be useful but is typically costly and time-consuming. Another disadvantage is that competitors who are aware of the experiment can confuse the findings through the use of short-term sales promotions or other actions in the experimental areas. Finally, distributors are often unwilling to cooperate in such experiments. Since they have legal control over retail prices, distributors may block the experiment effort unless they can see a direct financial benefit to themselves.

Experiments done in a *laboratory setting* can also provide useful information. By simulating a shopping situation and varying prices, it is possible to generate estimates of elasticity. This approach permits control over price, allowing experimenters to manipulate competitors' prices as well as the price of a company's own product. However, the artificial setting reduces the reliability of any precise elasticity estimates derived in this manner.

Survey Methods

When new products are being priced, the historical ratio method cannot be of any real help since no historical data exist. If experimentation is also judged to be impractical, or if managers wish to reduce the number of possible price levels for subsequent experimentation, then various survey methods may be useful. One such method is the *buy-response* survey. In this method, a product is shown or described to a group of potential buyers along with a specific price, and the buyers are asked if they would buy at that price. The process is then repeated with additional buyers using different prices. Because this form of

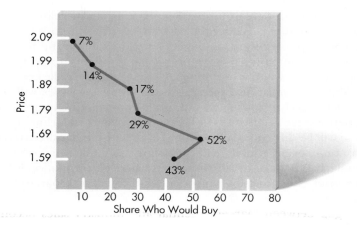

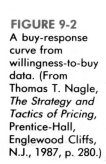

FIGURE 9-2
A buy-response curve from willingness-to-buy data. (From Thomas T. Nagle, *The Strategy and Tactics of Pricing*, Prentice-Hall, Englewood Cliffs, N.J., 1987, p. 280.)

questioning is structured more like an actual purchase decision, responses are thought to be somewhat realistic. Moreover, by aggregating the responses of various consumers, a buy-response curve like that pictured in Figure 9-2 can be generated. The buy-response curve shows the percentage of consumers asked who answered yes at each price. The major use of these data is to identify price levels at which substantial changes in price-sensitivity can be anticipated. For example, in Figure 9-2 consumers seem to be very sensitive to a price increase from $1.69 to $1.79.[1]

Conjoint analysis, a technique we discussed in Chapter 8, is widely considered to be the preferred survey method for identifying the effect of price on demand. Specifically, price can be considered a product feature, and different price levels are therefore like different levels of any other product attribute. Through conjoint analysis, therefore, managers can isolate the differential effect of price on brand preferences given various combinations of product features.

Judgmental Estimates

In Chapter 6, we suggested that some judgmental inputs are usually necessary in estimating productivity, and we illustrated an approach for making judgmental estimates of the productivity of advertising expenditures. Judgmental estimates are also often appropriate for estimating the anticipated productivity (that is, the elasticity) of price changes. (In fact, the same approach discussed in the context of advertising expenditures in Chapter 6 can be employed.)

[1] Thomas T. Nagle, *The Strategy and Tactics of Pricing*, Prentice-Hall, Englewood Cliffs, N.J., 1987, p. 280.

TABLE 9-5	FACTORS SUGGESTING ELASTIC MARKET DEMAND

1. Many alternative product forms or classes exist for which the product can be substituted.
2. Only a small percentage of potential buyers currently purchase or own the product because of the high price and because the product represents a discretionary purchase.
3. The rate of consumption or the rate of replacement can be increased through lower prices.

Managers can gain many insights into the elasticity of market and company demand by examining the diagnostic questions discussed in Chapter 3. For example, Table 9-5 indicates some of the buying-process factors that would suggest market demand is likely to be elastic. To the extent that an industrywide price decline results in an increase in the willingness or ability to buy, the gap between market potential and industry sales becomes smaller. For example, price will have an impact on demand for one product form (aluminum) if competing product forms (such as steel) have similar performance characteristics so that the forms may be substituted for one another on a price basis. Similarly, if the number of potential buyers is far above the number who currently buy the product form, lower prices may be one mechanism to gain new buyers.

Table 9-6 presents some of the buying-process factors that would suggest company or brand demand is elastic. Economic theory suggests that the greater the number of alternatives about which a buyer is informed, the greater the price-elasticity of demand. Additionally, elasticity will be greater if buyers can rely on observation through their search efforts to make comparisons. Thus, airline competition is price-elastic because the primary nonprice determinant attributes (departure times, flight time) are readily observed. Further, if quality differences are perceived to be minimal, demand will be more elastic.

Finally, if the cost involved in searching out alternatives is low, demand will more likely be elastic. For example, the time and effort involved in shifting a person's banking relationship is much greater than the time and effort involved in selecting a different brand of canned peas. Accordingly, a much larger change in price will generally be required to induce customers to switch banks than to switch brands of canned peas.

Additionally, recent research findings are available that provide other useful insights into the judgmental assessment of price-elasticity. These findings result in the following generalizations:

TABLE 9-6	FACTORS SUGGESTING ELASTIC COMPANY DEMAND

1. Buyers are knowledgeable about a large number of alternatives.
2. Quality differences do not exist or are not perceived.
3. The supplier or brand can be changed easily and with minimal efforts or costs.

1. A price change will have no effect on demand unless it is large enough to be noticeable, and (all other things being equal) the higher the price, the larger the price change must be to be noticed.[2]
2. The further a brand's price is from the average price for the product category, the more distinct it is from the competition and the less the price-elasticity is.[3]
3. The lower a brand's market share, the greater the price-elasticity (because a small change in units sold translates into a larger percentage change than is the case for large market-share brands or firms).[4]
4. Market elasticity of demand is generally highest in the early stages of the product life cycle, and company or brand elasticity is generally highest in the later stages of the product life cycle (when technological differences are minimal).[5]

COMPETITIVE FACTORS

Whether a manager is concerned with market or company elasticity, competitors' reactions to a price change must be considered. After all, if the change in price is matched by all competitors, then no change in market share should result. In that event, the price cut will have no effect on selective demand. Accordingly, managers should attempt to determine what competitors' pricing reactions will be.

Usually, it will be useful to examine historical patterns of competitive behavior in projecting price reactions. Some competitors may price their products primarily on the basis of costs. These firms often do not shift their pricing policies over time; instead, they either price very competitively (if they are trying to take advantage of experience curves or economies of scale) or attempt to maintain consistent contribution margins and thus avoid direct price competition. Additionally, by analyzing competitors' historical pricing behavior, managers may obtain insights into the likely customer reaction to a price change. Specifically, if an industry has historically been characterized by extensive price cutting, buyers will more likely be price-sensitive because they will have come to expect price differences.

Managers can also use their knowledge of competitive strengths and weaknesses and of the degree of competitive intensity in an industry (as discussed in Chapter 4) in predicting competitors' responses. However, even when price is the decision issue at hand, managers should assess nonprice reactions as well as direct price reactions in a market because competitors' nonprice actions

---

[2] See Kent B. Monroe, *Pricing: Making Profitable Decisions*, McGraw-Hill, New York, 1978, pp. 40–49, for a discussion of these research findings.
[3] William T. Moran, "Insights from Pricing Research," in E. L. Bailey (ed.), *Pricing Practices and Strategies*, The Conference Board Inc., New York, 1978, p. 9.
[4] Nagle, op. cit., p. 79.
[5] Gerard Tellis, "The Price Elasticity of Selective Demand: A Meta-Analysis of Econometric Models of Sales," *Journal of Marketing Research*, November 1988, pp. 339–340.

may influence price-elasticity. Consider, for example, the relationship between advertising expenditures and price-elasticity.[6] One theory about this relationship contends that advertising reduces brand or company price-elasticity by building brand loyalty. An alternative view is that advertising broadens the number of alternatives about which consumers are informed, which should increase brand or company price-elasticity. More recent evidence suggests that the effect of advertising on price-sensitivity depends on competitors' reactions to a change in advertising: If competitors react by increasing their own advertising, brand comparisons are encouraged so price-sensitivity should increase, but price-sensitivity is reduced if competitors do not react because the brand experiencing higher advertising will be more widely remembered.[7] Additionally, the type of advertising that characterizes a market also appears to be a factor. Specifically, if the advertising focuses on building *awareness,* then the number of brands a consumer will consider tends to increase, so price-elasticity will increase. However, if the emphasis is on *positioning-oriented* advertising, the effect will normally be to differentiate the various brands, resulting in more inelastic demand.[8]

COST FACTORS

In Chapter 6 we discussed the pricing implications associated with economies of scale. Specifically, we discussed how lower prices also result in lower average costs if they lead to significant increases in volume: As volume increases, fixed costs are spread over more units. Therefore, the gains from economies of scale are greatest when fixed costs represent a high proportion of total cost. (Of course, if a firm is already producing close to its capacity, the economies of scale are already fully realized; such firms have little to gain from reducing prices.)

In many firms, current or anticipated average costs serve as the primary basis for pricing. Specifically, many firms use the *cost-plus* approach, in which the price is determined by taking the cost per unit and then adding a dollar or percentage-target-contribution margin.

To illustrate one version of the cost-plus approach, consider the data in Table 9-7, which presents the cost structure for a case of a liquid dishwashing detergent brand. In arriving at the manufacturer's price (the price per case paid by the retailer), a firm using cost-plus would usually take the variable costs of producing the detergent and then add on an estimate of each case's share of fixed overhead costs and of estimated advertising and selling costs.

---

[6] See Hubert Gatignon, "Competition as a Moderator of the Effect of Advertising on Sales," *Journal of Marketing Research,* November 1984, pp. 387–398, for a succinct overview of these issues.
[7] Ibid.
[8] John Hauser and Birger Wernerfelt, "The Competitive Implications of Relevant-Set/Response Analysis," *Journal of Marketing Research,* November 1989, pp. 391–405.

Note that in order to estimate the fixed cost per case, the company must have some estimate of the number of cases that will be sold because

$$\text{Fixed cost per case} = \frac{\text{total fixed cost}}{\text{number of cases sold}}$$

Subsequently, a target profit (usually expressed as a percentage of total costs) is added on—hence the name "cost-plus."

A key issue in using the cost-plus method is the determination of the true unit cost. In many cases, some costs are allocated arbitrarily. For example, fixed costs (such as those shown in Table 9-7) will often include direct fixed costs plus some contribution to company overhead. Additionally, since the amount of fixed costs must be based on some estimate of the number of units sold, the company is implicitly assuming demand will not vary dramatically with any change in the factory price. For example, assume total annual advertising and selling expenses are expected to be $26 million. In order to determine the share of these costs to assign to each case sold, a manager must have some estimate of the expected sales volume, even though the total cost (and thus the final price) has yet to be determined. In our Table 9-7 example, the $6.50 allocation per unit must mean sales are expected to be 4 million cases. That is,

$$\$6.50 = \frac{\$26 \text{ million}}{4 \text{ million cases}}$$

Marketers should recognize, however, that there are two alternative approaches to cost-plus pricing. The previous example illustrated the use of a full-cost approach, in which all costs are considered in setting the minimum price. Alternatively, our detergent manufacturer could also consider a variable-cost pricing approach. As we discussed in Chapter 6, a firm operating in a price-elastic market at less than full capacity may be able to improve total profitability through pricing below the average unit cost. That is, as long as the company is pricing the product above variable costs, each unit sold makes some contribution to fixed costs. Accordingly, if sales stagnate below the expected volume (that is, the volume used to compute average fixed costs), the

| TABLE 9-7 | AN ILLUSTRATION OF COST-PLUS PRICING FOR A LIQUID DISHWASHING DETERGENT |

Variable costs per case (materials, packaging)	$ 6.80
Plus allocated share of manufacturing overhead	1.70
Plus allocated share of advertising	6.50
Total unit cost	$15.00
Plus target profit per case	2.00
Manufacturer's selling price to retailer	$17.00

detergent maker will be better off to lower the manufacturer's price (assuming demand is elastic) below $17 as long as the price exceeds $6.80 per case (the variable costs). However, if managers assume demand is inelastic, they are not likely to pursue this course of action.

TYPES OF PRICING PROGRAMS

Managers can select a pricing program once they have established the pricing objective and the elasticity of demand and once they have assessed their competitive and cost situation. Essentially, there are three basic types of programs for pricing individual products: penetration, parity, and premium. (Later in this chapter we will give example programs for product-line pricing.)

Penetration Pricing

A pricing program designed to use low price as the major basis for stimulating demand is a penetration pricing program. When using these programs, firms are attempting to increase their product's degree of penetration in the market either by stimulating primary demand or by increasing market share (acquiring new customers) on price.

The success of a penetration pricing program requires that either market (primary) demand or company (selective) demand be elastic. If market demand is elastic, market demand and total industry revenue will grow with a reduction in industry prices. Thus, even if competitors match our price cut, the increase in market demand will make all competitors better off. If economies of scale exist or the product has many complements, the benefits of increased volume are even greater.

If market demand is inelastic, then penetration pricing can make sense only if company demand is elastic (so buyers will change suppliers on the basis of price) and if competitors cannot or will not match the lower price. The failure of competitors to match the lower price could reflect a lack of competitiveness on costs or a willingness to concede market share (at least for a while) in exchange for higher profits, or because the low price appeals to a minor segment of the market. Consider, for instance, the case of Dover Publications.

> While mass market paperbacks often sell for $5.95 or more, the privately held publisher Dover Publications sells paperbacks for as little as $1. Similarly, Dover's hardbacks normally run 30% below competitors' prices. In part, Dover's ability to keep prices down is due to lower overhead and lower distribution costs. Additionally, Dover focuses heavily on a list of specialized titles in art, science, crafts, music, and architecture. Large publishers (who generally operate with higher overhead costs) generally avoid these categories because volume is not great. In effect the large publishers are willing to concede these market segments to Dover because price competition and low volume make them less attractive.[9]

[9] Fleming Meeks, "Mom-and-Pop Publishing," *Forbes*, Sept. 17, 1990, pp. 170–171.

| TABLE 9-8 | CONDITIONS FAVORING A PENETRATION PRICING PROGRAM |

1. Market demand is elastic.
2. Company demand is elastic, and competitors cannot match our price because of cost disadvantages.
3. The firm also sells higher-margin complementary products.
4. A large number of strong potential competitors exist.
5. Extensive economies of scale exist so that the variable-cost approach can be used to set the minimum price.
6. The pricing objective is to accomplish either of the following:
   - Build primary demand
   - Acquire new customers by undercutting competition

Table 9-8 summarizes the conditions most favorable to penetration pricing programs.

Parity Pricing

Parity pricing means setting a price at or near competitive levels. In effect, parity pricing programs attempt to downplay the role of price so that other marketing programs are primarily responsible for implementing the marketing strategy.

Frequently, this approach will be selected when company demand is elastic, industry demand is inelastic, and most competitors are willing and able to match any price cut. In such situations, managers should avoid penetration pricing because any price cuts will be offset by competitive retaliation (precluding any market-share gains). The resulting lower industry prices will not yield a significant gain in industry sales, and so total revenues and profit margins will decline. Table 9-9 summarizes the conditions that generally favor a parity pricing program.

Parity pricing is highly compatible with cost-plus pricing, especially when average costs are based on the full-cost approach. In many industries, cost structures will be very similar for the various competitors, especially when similar labor contracts, raw materials, production technologies, and distribution channels are used. In such situations, firms who perceive that market

| TABLE 9-9 | CONDITIONS FAVORING A PARITY PRICING PROGRAM |

1. Market demand is inelastic, and company demand is elastic.
2. The firm has no cost advantages over competitors.
3. There are no expected gains from economies of scale, so that the price floor is based on fully allocated costs.
4. The pricing objective is to meet the competition.

demand is inelastic and that competitors' costs are comparable are hardly likely to anticipate major volume gains from penetration pricing, because they expect competitors to retaliate. Thus, the potential gains of any economies of scale would go unrealized, meaning a variable-cost price floor is impractical.

Unfortunately for some manufacturers, there are industries in which the conditions for parity pricing seem to exist, but penetration pricing is the reality. For example, in the markets for television sets, passenger air travel, and salty snacks there are a few large competitors with significant economies of scale and elastic company demand. But the resources committed in these industries by the leading firms are so great that even firms who have higher costs feel the need to meet low competitive prices in order to stay in business. If market demand is inelastic (either because industry sales are approaching market potential or because of recession), penetration pricing results in destructive industry price wars.[10]

Premium Pricing

Premium pricing involves setting a price above competitive levels. (In the case of a new product form or class where there are no direct competitors, premium pricing involves setting a price at a level that is high relative to competing product forms.) This approach will be successful if a firm is able to differentiate its product in terms of higher quality, superior features, or special services, thereby establishing an inelastic company-demand curve—at least within one or more target segments. Firms that are successful in implementing this approach will generate higher contribution margins and, at the same time, insulate themselves from price competition. However, even if this effort is initially successful, managers should continue to monitor the marketplace to determine whether a differential advantage is being maintained and whether the importance of price (relative to quality or special services) remains unchanged in the target segments. Table 9-10 summarizes the conditions that usually favor a premium pricing program.

Importantly, premium pricing can be implemented even in markets that would appear to be very price driven if special services can be added that provide demonstrated added value.

[10] Bill Saporito, "Why the Price Wars Never End," *Fortune*, Mar. 23, 1992, pp. 68–71.

TABLE 9-10	CONDITIONS FAVORING A PREMIUM PRICING PROGRAM

1. Company demand is inelastic.
2. The firm has no excess capacity.
3. There are very strong barriers to entry.
4. Gains from economies of scale are relatively minor, so that the full-cost method is used to determine the minimum price.
5. The pricing objective is to attract new customers on quality.

Consolidated Freightways Inc., one of the nation's largest trucking companies, has successfully charged premium rates for its trucking services even in a deregulated environment that has driven industry prices downward. Consolidated specializes in less-than-truckload shipments and has been a technological leader with its sophisticated computer systems. Such technology allows Consolidated's terminal managers to know three days in advance how much freight is coming in, and allows customers to monitor each shipment closely from pickup to delivery.[11]

PRICING PROGRAMS FOR A LINE OF SUBSTITUTES

When a firm markets a line of products that essentially serve the same needs, an increase (decrease) in price for one member of the line will result in an increase (decrease) in demand for the other products in the line. In such cases the *cross-elasticity of demand* is said to be positive. Basically, there are two kinds of situations in which positive cross-elasticities can exist.

In some situations, the various products serve different segments that are clearly demarcated in terms of major differences in the product's function or benefits. In such cases, the primary pricing objective is to distinguish the product from the rest of the line and focus on competing within that segment. Generally, this will result in major price differentials within the product line and differences in brand name or distribution to match. Thus, Marriott prices its full-service hotels as much as $75 per night above its Fairfield Inns, which have smaller rooms and fewer amenities. Similarly, Compaq designed a new line of Prolinea personal computers to serve the mass market while continuing to offer its DeskPro line (at prices $1000 to $1500 higher than Prolinea models) for customers desiring more upgrades, high performance add-ons, and greater memory.[12]

Alternatively, in some product lines, the various members may be much more similar, differing from one another on a single dimension. A typical L. L. Bean catalog, for example, offers three grades of men's chino pants; a line of rider mowers may vary primarily in terms of horsepower. In such cases, a primary objective of pricing is usually to encourage demand for the higher priced product.

Because of this difference in pricing objectives, managers need to have some understanding of the impact variations in price differentials will have on demand. In developing this understanding two key psychological concepts must be considered: anchoring and subjective price scales.

Anchoring is the effect a price stimulus has on the reference points buyers use to assess prices. Specifically, buyers evaluate a price in the context of the entire range of prices with which they are confronted. Thus, adding a product at a new price at either the high or low ends of a market will change the

---

[11] Marc Beauchamp, "Skillful Driving," *Forbes*, Aug. 22, 1988, p. 98.
[12] Catherine Arnst and Stephanie Andersen Forest, "Compaq: How It Made Its Impressive Move Out of the Doldrums," *Business Week*, Nov. 2, 1992, pp. 146–151.

standards by which customers evaluate each item in a line. For example, if a catalog retailer offers a line of men's chino pants at prices of $20, $28, and $36, the addition of a new pant priced at $45 will raise the price standard by which other pants are judged: The perceived quality of the lowest priced pants will be somewhat diminished, and some customers will trade up to the $36 pant as well as to the new pant. Similarly, the introduction of a new item at the low end will enhance the quality image of the products that formerly were at the low end of the line.[13]

Subjective price scales are the psychological scales on which buyers code price information. Because this scale resembles a logarithmic scale rather than a natural arithmetic scale, equal price differentials are not perceived as being equal. Rather, price differentials should reflect *relative* rather than absolute differences among prices. For example, in our earlier example, the $28 pant is priced 40 percent above the $20 pant, but the $36 pant is priced only 28 percent above the $28 pant. Research on price perceptions suggests that, assuming the perceived difference in quality between the top- and middle-priced pants is *equal* to the perceived difference in quality between the low- and middle-priced pants, the higher priced pant should also be priced at a 40 percent differential, yielding a price of $39.20.[14]

PRICING PROGRAMS FOR A SET OF COMPLEMENTS

As we indicated in Chapter 6, complementary products and services are those that experience a sales increase when related products (services) experience a price decrease. Thus, as prices are reduced on compact disk players, not only do compact disk player sales grow, but sales of disks (a complement to disk players) grow as well. In such cases, there is a negative cross-elasticity between the products.

Analyzing the effect a price change on one product has on the sales of complementary products can often be difficult. However, managers can attempt to take advantage of complementary relationships through either of two special product-line pricing programs: leader pricing or price bundling.

LEADER PRICING

If the demand for a product is elastic, and if that product has a number of complements either that enhance its value or that can be purchased more conveniently by buying from the same source, that product may then be used as a leader. Leader pricing simply involves setting and then promoting a penetration price on the leader. The expectation is that sales of complements to new customers will increase more than enough to offset the reduced profit on the leader.

[13] Nagle, op. cit., p. 187.
[14] Kent B. Monroe and Albert Della Bitta, "Models for Pricing Decisions," *Journal of Marketing Research*, August 1978, pp. 413–428.

TABLE 9-11	CHARACTERISTICS OF A GOOD PRICE LEADER

1. The product is widely used by individual buyers in the target market.
2. The product's prevailing market price is well known.
3. The product has a high degree of price-elasticity.
4. The product has many complements, which enhance the value of the leader or are convenient to purchase when buying the leader.
5. The product has few or no substitutes.
6. The product is not usually bought in large quantities and stored.

Adapted from J. Barry Mason and Hazel F. Ezell, *Marketing: Principles and Strategy*, Business Publications, Plano, Tex., 1987, p. 392.

Table 9-11 lists the major characteristics that make for a good leader product. Note that in selecting a leader, managers are generally advised to avoid products that customers are likely to stock up on during the special prices or where strong substitution effects will lead to simple shifts in sales from high-margin to low-margin products.

PRICE BUNDLING

Price bundling is marketing two or more products or services together for a special price.[15] Technically, most firms employ mixed price bundling: Buyers are given the choice of buying two products in a package or buying the products individually. Buyers who place a low value on one of the two products will avoid the bundle. However, the economic incentive of a lower price on one item will lead to additional sales of both products to some buyers who otherwise would buy only one. When complementary relationships are very strong, the effects of the special price are even greater.

Mixed price bundling can be accomplished through either of two approaches. In the *mixed leader* form, the price of a lead product is discounted on the condition that a second product be purchased. In *mixed joint* bundling, two or more products or services are offered for a single package price. For example, assume a bank offers a VISA credit card at an annual fee of $15 and a safe deposit box for $25 per year. A mixed leader bundling option would be to discount the VISA to $5 per year on the condition that a customer also rent a safe deposit box at the regular price. The comparable mixed joint bundling option would be "a VISA card and safe deposit box for $30 per year."

Both forms of bundling could be used to achieve the objective of expanding the range of products bought by existing customers. For our bank, the mixed leader option would then make sense if we had a large VISA base and a small safe deposit box base: The discounted VISA would serve as an incentive for renting the safe deposit box. The mixed joint option would be more useful if our customers tended to buy either one or the other product. Safe deposit box holders would then have an incentive to buy a VISA, and vice versa.

[15] This section draws heavily on Joseph Guiltinan, "The Price Bundling of Services: A Normative Framework," *Journal of Marketing*, April 1987, pp. 74–85.

TABLE 9-12	CHARACTERISTICS OF SUCCESSFUL MIXED PRICE BUNDLING PROGRAMS

MIXED LEADER PROGRAMS

1. Demand for the lead product should be price-elastic.
2. Complementarity is based on the leader being enhanced by the other product(s) or on convenience.
3. If the objective is to cross-sell complements to regular customers,
   - The leader is the lower margin product (so that the lost profit from the price reduction is minimized).
   - Sales volume for the leader exceeds that of other products.

MIXED JOINT PROGRAMS

1. Demand for the total package is price-elastic.
2. Complementarity is bidirectional (each product in the bundle enhances the value of the others) or is based on convenience.
3. If the objective is to cross-sell complements to regular customers, the various products in the bundle are approximately equal in volume and in profit margins so that sales gains from regular purchasers of any product are about equal.

If bundling is to be used to attract new customers, both approaches are feasible. In making a choice between mixed leader and mixed joint bundling, managers should consider the demand-elasticity and complementarity characteristics listed in Table 9-12. In general, the characteristics leading to successful mixed leader bundling are similar to the characteristics leading to successful leader pricing policies. However, mixed joint bundling may be used when there is no natural sales-volume leader and when two or more products or services have a mutually reinforcing complementarity. Illustrative of such situations are home entertainment centers (packaging electronic audio and video products into a total system) or vacation packages (incorporating airline, car rental, and hotel arrangements).

ADDITIONAL PRICING CONSIDERATIONS

Political-Legal Environment

The political and legal environment can pose significant constraints on pricing decisions. Many of these constraints involve direct price regulation: Public utilities, airlines, trucking, and cable television are examples of industries that are or have been directly regulated with respect to prices.

Additionally, state and federal tax policies can have an impact on the effect of various pricing policies. For example, in 1990 the federal government levied special excise taxes on luxury automobiles and boats. Distilled spirits and cigarettes are taxed substantially, although the amount varies by state.

(For cigarettes, research suggests that a 10 percent hike in the net cost of cigarettes reduces long-term consumption by 7.5 percent.)[16]

Finally, in fields like health care where government pays a substantial portion of the total bill, pressure is often levied on hospitals and other medical facilities to reduce costs. This can lead these organizations to emphasize price in their buying decisions. For instance, General Electric is discounting its magnetic resonance imaging machines and CT scanners in order to allow hospitals to reduce the diagnostic fees they charge patients. Indeed, the price of CT scanners dropped from approximately $1 million in the early 1980s to $700,000 by the early 1990s.[17]

Finally, managers should be aware of government regulations that are designed to preserve competition and apply to virtually all industries. Based on the Sherman Antitrust Act, the Federal Trade Commission Act (Section 5), and the Robinson-Patman Act, federal regulations limit pricing behavior in two ways. Collusive behavior (agreements among competitors) is the most fundamental unlawful action in pricing. All the collusive practices listed in Table 9-13 are automatically illegal. Also, companies that distribute through retailers and wholesalers should be aware of the issue of price discrimination if different prices are charged to different resellers. Price discrimination is not automatically illegal. However, it will be illegal if these price differences fail to pass at least one of the criteria given in Table 9-14.

International Considerations

The firm's competitive situation and cost structure must also be evaluated in the context of several special international considerations. Even if the firm has no overseas business, foreign firms are likely to be competing in the domestic market, and the ability to compete with foreign-based firms on price is often influenced by nation-specific cultural, political, and economic factors.

Certainly prices are influenced by the cost of doing business in various nations. Firms that can attract capital, labor, or raw materials at lower cost will have an advantage in pricing. For example, the *cost of borrowing* was significantly lower in Japan than in the United States during the 1980s, allowing

---

[16] "Economic Trends," *Business Week*, June 18, 1990, p. 20.
[17] Amal Naj, "Diagnostic Equipment Field in Squeeze," *The Wall Street Journal*, Sept. 6, 1990, p. B1.

| TABLE 9-13 | EXAMPLES OF COLLUSIVE PRICING PRACTICES |

1. Agreement to reduce prices in order to injure competitors
2. Agreement on selling prices, bids, discounts, or credit policies
3. Agreement upon and enforcement of resale prices
4. Agreement to fix price differentials, discounts, or important terms of sale to designated groups of customers
5. Agreement to rotate bids among competitors

| TABLE 9-14 | SITUATIONS IN WHICH DIFFERENT PRICES MAY LEGALLY BE OFFERED TO DIFFERENT RESELLERS |

1. The products sold are not of "like grade and quality" in technical content and features.
2. Price differences do not result in injury to competition.
3. Price differences can be justified by differences in the cost of serving the different customers.
4. Price differences are made in good faith to meet equally low prices of competitors in retaining customers and where the competitor's price is not discriminatory.
5. Discounts and allowances are offered on proportionately equal terms to all competing resellers.

Japanese firms to price products slightly lower to get the same profit return as their U.S. counterparts.

Additionally, when exporting products to other nations, *tariffs* or *import fees* must be considered. It is still not unusual to find tariffs of 20 or 30 percent applied to selected imported goods when a nation is trying to protect a domestic industry from price competition.

The most problematic global force for business is the *currency exchange rate*. The rates at which currencies of different nations are exchanged fluctuate over time, and a sharp unexpected change (or even a significant long-term change) can create problems for a firm. For example, a Waterford crystal wine decanter made in Ireland and sold in the United States for $150 in 1985 would have brought the seller 148 Irish pounds at the then-prevailing exchange rate. By late 1992, the U.S. dollar's value relative to the Irish pound had declined to the rate of 1.66 U.S. dollars per pound. Thus, a $150 sale in the United States yielded only 90 Irish pounds (150 ÷ 1.66 = 90).

Price Elements of Other Marketing Programs

As we have frequently suggested in this book, the various marketing programs are usually interrelated. This chapter has focused on the basic list-price strategy. In subsequent chapters, other programs relating directly or indirectly to price will be addressed. These programs are summarized in Table 9-15.

| TABLE 9-15 | PRICE ELEMENTS OF OTHER MARKETING PROGRAMS |

SALES-PROMOTION PROGRAMS	SALES AND DISTRIBUTION PROGRAMS
Coupons	Quantity discounts
Cents-off deals	Cash discounts
Promotion allowances	Credit or financing assistance
Rebates	Long-term contracts
	Negotiated pricing

Although these programs involve modifications of the list price, managers usually employ them to achieve different kinds of program objectives. Decisions regarding the use of these elements are usually made by different managers. Accordingly, they will be treated in subsequent chapters.

CONCLUSION

Management's recognition of the importance of price decisions has increased in recent years. Deregulation, greater international competition, changes in technology, and occasionally inflation have all created changes in the patterns of price competition in one industry or another.

However, the process of developing a basic pricing program and arriving at a specific price remains a difficult one. As we have indicated in this chapter, there are no simple rules of thumb managers can use to guarantee a correct price. However, by employing the process this chapter has suggested, managers should be able to devise a pricing program that is consistent with their marketing strategy. While the pricing program may be modified by sales-promotion programs and by sales and distribution programs, the basic role pricing will play in implementing a marketing strategy should be determined by (1) establishing clear pricing objectives, (2) analyzing price-elasticity, com-

FIGURE 9-3

Relationship of pricing programs to the situation analysis, marketing strategy, and other marketing programs.

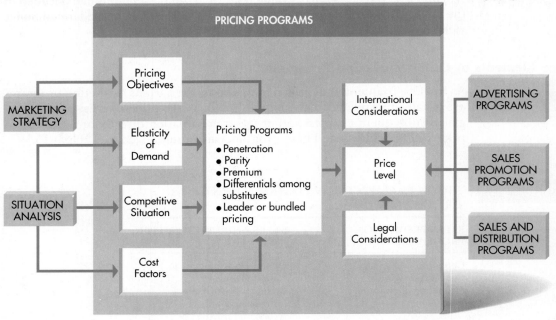

SOUTHWEST AIRLINES: A SUCCESSFUL PENETRATION PRICING PROGRAM*

Southwest Airlines began its corporate existence as a cut-rate airline based at Love Field in Dallas and flying to Houston and San Antonio. Love Field is located near downtown Dallas, unlike the city's major airport (Dallas-Fort Worth Airport), which is located 20 minutes to the west.

When the federal government began to deregulate the airline industry in 1978, Southwest launched an expansion, and today the airline serves thirty-two cities from Detroit to Houston to San Francisco. But one of the critical elements in Southwest's growth has been the continued use of second tier terminals such as Midway in Chicago, Hobby in Houston, City in Detroit, and Ontario or Burbank in Los Angeles. These lower-traffic airports allow Southwest to have faster turnaround for its airplanes so they spend a greater percentage of their time in the air. (Seventy percent of Southwest's flights have a turnaround time of 15 minutes.)

Too, Southwest's planes emphasize high-frequency, short-haul flights; all flights are under 2 hours. This allows Southwest to avoid the expense of serving meals and gives it the ability to be a leader in convenience. (Southwest has eighty-three flights per day between Dallas and Houston.) The short-distance, low-fare strategy also means Southwest is competing not just with other airlines but with the automobile as well. Air traffic often doubles or triples when Southwest enters a market with its often astoundingly low prices.

The low prices are made possible by the fast turnaround time plus other cost-saving prac-

tices. Southwest doesn't transfer baggage to other airlines; the airline does not subscribe to any central reservation system (CRS), because the booking fees are too high relative to prices (while 80 percent of all airline tickets are sold by travel agents who receive commissions, the figure for Southwest is 55 percent because of the absence of CRS links); Southwest uses only one type of jet—the Boeing 737—which reduces maintenance costs and spare parts inventories. As a consequence of all these policies, Southwest's cost per passenger mile is $0.068 compared to $0.088 at American Airlines and $0.096 at United Airlines.

1. What marketing strategy and pricing objective best characterize Southwest Airlines?
2. Which of the conditions favoring a penetration pricing program appear to apply in this case?
3. Which approach to measuring elasticity would be most useful?
4. If you were competing in the same air routes as Southwest, what type of pricing program would you use? Why?

---

* Developed from Elaine Underwood, "Just Plane Hot," *Brandweek*, Aug. 24, 1992, pp. 17–18; Subrata Chakravarty, "Hit 'em Hardest with the Mostest," *Forbes*, Sept. 16, 1991, pp. 48–51; Catherine Reagor, "Southwest Airlines Expands While Others Contract," *The Business Journal-Phoenix*, Sept. 4, 1992, p. 5; James Flanigan, "Southwest Airlines Sends Goliaths Back to Flying School," *Los Angeles Times*, Mar. 24, 1992, p. D1; Mercedes Cardona, "Long and Short of It," *Travel Agent*, July 13, 1992, p. 16; "Southwest Flies High with Cut-Rate Niche," *USA Today*, May 7, 1992, pp. B1–B2.

petition, and costs, and (3) considering political-legal and international constraints. Figure 9-3 summarizes these steps and provides an overview of the relationships among them.

While the pricing program may not be a major component in the marketing strategy of every firm, it is certainly a critical component in Southwest Airline's strategy.

QUESTIONS AND SITUATIONS FOR DISCUSSION

1. A marketing manager for a consumer electronics company is considering a reduction in the price of one of its VCRs from $220 to $199.99. Currently, sales of this model are averaging 15,000 units per month.

  a. If sales increased to 17,000 units per month, would this imply demand is inelastic or elastic?

  b. What other factors must the manager consider in determining whether the change in demand truly reflects the degree of price-elasticity?

2. Would the *market* demand for each of the following products be elastic or inelastic with respect to price? Why?

  a. Open heart surgery

  b. Airline tickets for a vacation

  c. A yacht

  d. Gasoline

3. For each of the following procedures, do you think *company* demand would typically be elastic or inelastic with respect to price? Can there be exceptions to your answer for any of these producers?

  a. A paint manufacturer

  b. A hairstylist

  c. A manufacturer of electric razors

  d. A textbook publisher

4. In which of the following situations would historical ratios be most useful in estimating price-elasticity of demand? Why?

  a. Setting prices on a new line of microwavable frozen dinners

  b. Pricing blank videocassette tapes

  c. Ticket prices for the Boston Celtics basketball team

5. A number of firms around the world are developing sophisticated new high definition television systems (HDTV) that will offer incredibly improved picture quality. Such systems are now available in Japan at prices in the order of $8000. While much patented technology is involved in the development of HDTV, the federal government will insist that any technology approved for use in transmitting and receiving HDTV signals be available to all potential television set manufacturers.

Based on this information, what type of pricing program would you recommend to firms who decide to enter this market?

6. In each of the following situations, what type of pricing program would typically be appropriate?

  a. Market demand is inelastic, and company demand is elastic.

  b. A firm has a distinct quality advantage.

  c. A firm is not producing at full capacity, and company demand is elastic.

7. For each of the following situations, discuss the kinds of product-line issues that should be considered in making pricing decisions.

  a. A publisher offers a book in both hardcover and softcover versions and must set a price on each one.

b. A sporting goods store carrying a wide assortment of goods wants to attract customers who will buy a variety of Christmas presents at the store.

c. A camera manufacturer who also produces and sells the film for its cameras is considering a reduction in the price of its lowest-priced model.

8. TWA offers a "get-away" vacation package that includes airfare, lodging, and side trips to historical sites in Europe. IBM sells personal computers, software, and maintenance contracts in one package. What demand-oriented pricing practices are TWA and IBM practicing? What are the benefits to consumers? To the companies?

9. In recent years, the interstate trucking, banking, and long-distance telephone industries have been deregulated, resulting in the rise of new competitors, increased price competition, and the demise of some old competitors.

a. Which of the conditions favoring penetration pricing do you think are most responsible for these results?

b. Are there potential negative consequences of deregulation? Explain.

10. In 1989, a group of British companies launched "telepoint" mobile telephone services. Using a pocket-calculator-sized handset, subscribers to the service could make calls within 200 meters of base stations located at clearly marked sites. In effect, the concept was designed to create a cheap "public telephone in your pocket" service with sound quality superior to that of cellular phones but at lower rates. The only drawback relative to cellular was that subscribers could make calls but not *receive* calls. (This restriction was imposed by Britain's Department of Trade and Industry—the nation's telecommunications licensing authority.) The product was introduced in 1991 with the price of a handset at about £190 (more than some of the cheaper cellular phones). Users also paid a one-time £20 connection fee and a monthly charge of £10. Charges for long-distance calls were slightly higher than those that either cellular or public telephone systems charged. Evaluate the telepoint pricing program.

SUGGESTED ADDITIONAL READINGS

Cavusgil, S. Tamer, "Unraveling the Mystery of Export Pricing," *Business Horizons*, May–June 1988, pp. 54–63.

Curry, David J., and Peter Riesz, "Prices and Price/Quality Relationships: A Longitudinal Analysis," *Journal of Marketing*, January 1988, pp. 36–51.

Dolan, Robert, and Abel Jeuland, "Experience Curves and Dynamic Demand Models: Implications for Optimal Pricing Strategies," *Journal of Marketing*, Winter 1981, pp. 52–73.

Farley, John U., James M. Hulbert, and David Weinstein, "Price Setting and Volume Planning by Two European Industrial Companies: A Study and

Comparison of Decision Processes," *Journal of Marketing*, Winter 1980, pp. 46–54.

Guiltinan, Joseph, "The Price Bundling of Services: A Normative Framework," *Journal of Marketing*, April 1987, pp. 74–85.

Monroe, Kent B., and Andris Zoltners, "Pricing the Product Line during Periods of Scarcity," *Journal of Marketing*, Summer 1979, pp. 49–59.

Nagle, Thomas, "Pricing as Creative Marketing," *Business Horizons*, July–August 1983, pp. 14–19.

Tellis, Gerard J., "Beyond the Many Faces of Price: An Integration of Pricing Strategies," *Journal of Marketing*, October 1986, pp. 145–160.

Wilcox, James B., Roy D. Howell, Paul Kuzdrall, and Robert Britney, "Price Quantity Discounts: Some Implications for Buyers and Sellers," *Journal of Marketing*, July 1987, pp. 60–70.

Wind, Jerry, "Getting a Read on Market-Defined Value," *Journal of Pricing Management*, Winter 1990, pp. 5–14.

CHAPTER 10

ADVERTISING PROGRAMS

OVERVIEW

As seen in previous chapters, marketing management entails developing the appropriate products and services for the target markets at the right price and making them readily available. However, in order to persuade consumers to buy the product or service, it is necessary to communicate a considerable amount of information about the company, its products, and the price structure and distribution to a variety of audiences. Included among these audiences are consumers, distributors, and the media. Effective communication is often a prerequisite for successful marketing and can offer a significant advantage that may distinguish the product or service from that of the competition.

The term *promotion* is often used to summarize the various activities that are associated with marketing communications. Promotion strategy has been described as a "controlled, integrated program of communication methods and materials designed to present an organization and its products to prospective customers; to communicate need-satisfying attributes of products to facilitate sales and thus contribute to long-run profit performance." For management to develop an effective promotional strategy, it is necessary that they have an understanding of the buying process, competition, market segments, and product positioning.

Of the various promotion activities, advertising is clearly the most visible. Indeed, many consumers tend to equate advertising with the term *marketing*. This is partially explained by the large amount of dollars spent on advertising by both profit and not-for-profit organizations.[1] For instance, in 1993 advertising expenditures in the United States were expected to exceed \$132 billion.[2] Outside the United States, advertising expenditures increased from \$55 billion in 1980 to \$265 billion by 1990.[3]

Unfortunately, this preoccupation with advertising sometimes leads people to ascribe a level of effectiveness to advertising that may far exceed the level

[1] James F. Engel, Martin R. Warshaw, and Thomas L. Kennew, *Promotional Strategy*, Irwin, Homewood, Ill., 1987, p. 6.

[2] Martha Moore, "Forecast Brightens for '93 Ad Spending," *USA Today—International Edition*, Dec. 9, 1992, p. 10B.

[3] "Survey of World Advertising Expenditures: Twenty-Fourth Edition," Starch INRA Hooper & the Roper Organization, New York, 1991.

actually achieved. Probably the most important facets of advertising planning are the development of a clear understanding of what the impact of advertising might be on a specific product or service, and a clear statement of what the advertising objective should be. Put another way, advertising programs should be developed not only in the context of a clear marketing strategy but also in the context of the plans and expectations for the other communications-oriented programs such as sales promotion, personal selling, publicity, and public relations.

Generally, communications programs can achieve one or more of the types of effects listed in Table 10-1. Advertising and communications theorists have developed a number of frameworks for discussing the relationships among these effects.[4] However, a generally agreed-on grouping (as Table 10-1 suggests) classifies these effects into three levels:

1. Cognitive responses—those which indicate that the message has been received
2. Affective responses—those that indicate the development of attitudes (liking or disliking) regarding the product or company
3. Behavioral responses—actual actions taken by the members of the target audience

As we shall see, each type of communications program has unique characteristics, and managers must consider these characteristics as well as the types

---

[4] For a discussion of these effects and the theoretical relationships among them, see Robert J. Lavidge and Gary A. Steiner, "A Model for Predictive Measurements of Advertising Effectiveness," *Journal of Marketing*, October 1961, pp. 59–62; and Thomas E. Barry, "The Development of the Hierarchy of Effects: A Historical Perspective," *Current Issues and Research in Advertising* 10, No. 2, 1987, pp. 251–296.

TABLE 10-1

EFFECTS OF COMMUNICATIONS AT VARIOUS STAGES OF RESPONSE

STAGES	SPECIFIC EFFECTS
1. Cognitive stage	Exposure to message Message recall Awareness of product Knowledge of product attributes and uses
2. Affective stage	Willingness to seek more information Interest in product Favorable evaluation of product or brand attributes Intention to try or buy
3. Behavioral stage	Product trial Product purchase

of effects they hope to achieve when designing each program. In this chapter, we will examine the first of these communications programs. Subsequent chapters will discuss sales promotion and personal selling.

Advertising consists of paid messages designed to inform or persuade buyers or users about a product, service, belief, or action. (An exception to this may be in the case of public service announcements where advertising space or time is donated by the media.) The purpose of this chapter is to present some concepts and procedures that managers can use in developing advertising programs (also called advertising campaigns) in order to implement the marketing strategy. In particular, we will examine (1) the process of setting advertising objectives, (2) procedures for developing advertising budgets, (3) the important considerations involved in devising a message and a media plan, and (4) various approaches for evaluating the effectiveness of a program.

It is important to note that the process of managing the advertising program can be exceedingly complex because of the number of people who may be involved. Much of the work of advertising is performed by outside organizations (such as advertising agencies). In addition, different kinds of managers are responsible for advertising programs in different firms. Accordingly, we will begin our discussion by examining the kinds of decisions involved in advertising programs and the ways of organizing advertising decision making.

ADVERTISING PROGRAMS: DECISIONS AND ORGANIZATION

Decisions regarding the advertising message (what to say and how to say it) and the media (where the message is to be presented and how many times) are fundamental to advertising programs. These decisions generally require highly specialized creative and technical skills and yet are made relatively infrequently. As a result, most organizations find that it is uneconomical to perform this work internally. Instead, these organizations often purchase the skills of advertising agencies independent specialists who perform tasks such as

- Developing creative copy ideas
- Creative artwork and photos
- Testing copy for consumer reactions
- Buying media time
- Researching audience readership or viewing habits

Although outside specialists or agencies can provide the needed skills economically, certain problems can result from using them. First, these specialists may not have a great deal of knowledge about the product's market potential, about the buying process, or about the various segments that exist. Further, they may not have knowledge of the profitability of the product to be advertised or of the product objectives and marketing strategy. Even when an in-house advertising agency exists, the number of products being advertised is usually so large that technical specialists will have little knowledge of the situation analysis and marketing strategy for each product. Additionally, advertising programs must be coordinated closely with other marketing programs and with pricing, sales, and sales promotion, as well as manufacturing capabilities. Failure to coordinate advertising programs with other activities can drastically reduce profits. For example, Klondike chocolate-covered vanilla ice cream bars initiated an expensive summer advertising campaign on national TV, which resulted in overselling the product. Even though Klondike's three manufacturing facilities produced 56,000 bars an hour, 21 hours a day, 7 days a week, the company ran out of the product just as the combination of heavy advertising and hot weather were stimulating consumer demand.[5]

Accordingly, message and media decisions can be made most effectively when advertising agencies, specialists, and in-house departments have some guidance on

■ How the advertising program is expected to contribute to the marketing strategy and relate to other programs
■ What level of advertising expenditures will be consistent with the firm's product mix allocation plan and with product profitability

This means that clearly specified advertising objectives are necessary to provide guidance on message and media decisions. These objectives should be developed by the managers who are responsible for developing and implementing the overall marketing strategy.

Responsibility for Advertising Programs

Organizations differ on the question of who should serve as the coordinator or liaison with the agency or with other advertising specialists. Because the primary purpose of this chapter is to provide insights and procedures for managing advertising programs (rather than for developing the creative and technical elements of advertisements), it is important to briefly identify the marketing positions and organizational approaches involved in advertising management.

The position of *advertising manager* or *advertising director* often exists in firms that are organized on a functional basis. In industrial firms, this individual may report to the sales manager, because advertising is often a small portion of the marketing effort and because its primary role is to support the sales function. Otherwise the advertising manager will typically report to a senior marketing manager.

[5] Kerry Hannon, "Meltdown," *Forbes*, Aug. 7, 1989, pp. 130–131.

The *product* or *brand manager* will be involved in advertising in firms that are organized on a product basis. When there are a large number of products in a firm, these managers tend to take on more of the responsibility for market analysis, short-run planning, and coordination with the other functions (such as sales and marketing research). In some companies, such as Procter and Gamble, there is an additional layer of management—referred to as the category manager—above the brand managers. This structure is designed to improve and coordinate efforts among groups of product categories.

Although advertising managers and product managers work most closely with outside agencies and specialists, their role in advertising management is often shared with the chief marketing executive or the divisional manager. There are two reasons why top management may become involved in these programs rather than delegate all responsibility to middle managers. First, advertising managers are staff personnel. Although they have expertise in selecting the advertising message and media, they are not directly responsible for sales or profits. Second, product or brand managers usually have sales or profit responsibility but are often seeking increases in advertising budgets—especially if they are responsible for sales volume but not profitability. However, this will vary company by company. For instance, Procter and Gamble has ninety brands and relationships with sixteen advertising agencies. In 1987 P&G eliminated the position of ad manager for most of its brands in an attempt to more effectively coordinate activities of brands that were in the same category. In 1989, they restored the ad manager position because they discovered that those brands that kept their ad managers outperformed those that didn't. At P&G, brand managers usually maintain close contact with the ad agencies whereas ad managers help set overall product-line strategy and approve all advertising and promotions.[6]

Consequently, in order to control the allocation of resources in accordance with product objectives, top management may make the major decisions regarding advertising expenditures, creative policy, or media plans (with the technical support of staff advertising specialists).

Elements of the Advertising Program

As we suggested in the preceding section, message development and media scheduling are not the only elements involved in advertising programs. In fact, as Figure 10-1 indicates, there are a number of decisions to be made in managing the advertising program. Although advertising agencies and other specialists are primarily involved in message design and media decisions, marketing managers in the firm doing the advertising must be somewhat involved in every step of the process.

Given the situation analysis and marketing strategy, these company managers are responsible for defining the objectives of the advertising program and

[6] Laurie Freeman, "P&G Keen Again on Ad Managers," *Advertising Age*, Sept. 25, 1989, p. 6; and Barry Brown, "P&G Hires 10 Shops," *Advertising Age*, Oct. 21, 1991, p. 38.

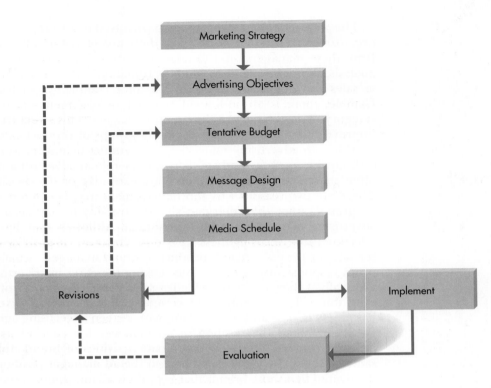

FIGURE 10-1
Basic elements of
an advertising
program.

for determining the budget. Subsequently, the advertising agency or outside specialists can develop message and media decisions that are consistent with the objectives and the budget. Additionally, managers should be responsible for examining the proposed message and media plan for consistency with the marketing strategy and the product objectives. Finally, managers should evaluate the program to see if objectives are being attained and to determine whether any elements of the program should be revised.

ADVERTISING OBJECTIVES

There are two basic reasons for establishing objectives for advertising programs. First, as suggested already, the advertising objectives can provide guidance for the development of message and media decisions. Second, advertising objectives serve as standards for evaluating the performance of the advertising program. Unless managers have defined what the advertising effort is designed to achieve, there will be no fair way of evaluating the results.

Of course, over the long run, firms would not spend money on advertising unless they expected that their expenditures would help to achieve sales, market-share, and profitability objectives. But sales and profits are generally inappropriate objectives for advertising programs for several reasons. First, sales generally respond rather slowly to advertising. This is especially true for products that are infrequently purchased. But it is also true for frequently purchased products, because most advertisements must be seen more than once before the message is received and acted on. Second, changes in sales and market share are often influenced by environmental factors and competitive actions. An advertising message may be very effective in communicating a particular product benefit about an automobile, but if interest rates rise or if unemployment rises, industry sales and company sales may decline in spite of the advertising effort.

For example, Nissan introduced its luxury Infiniti car with a $60 million campaign. The objectives of the campaign were to create high levels of awareness and interest among prospects for a luxury sports sedan. All of Nissan's measures of awareness, brand identification, and showroom visits indicated these objectives had been met. However, instead of the 2500-unit monthly sales called for in the marketing plan, only 1700 cars were sold during the first two months. Analysts indicated that this occurred because Toyota had introduced its luxury sports sedan Lexus two months prior to the Infiniti, and Nissan had underestimated the competition it would face from other luxury car companies such as BMW, Mercedes, and Volvo.[7]

Additionally, sales and market-share objectives provide very little direction for developing messages and selecting media. Indeed, as we suggested at the outset of this chapter, motivating an action (such as purchase) is only one of the possible types of effects of communications programs.

What advertising can do, however, is to help implement the marketing strategy for a product or service. That is, managers can establish other types of advertising objectives that can guide the selection of messages and media, permit program performance to be evaluated, and make a specific contribution to achieving the marketing strategy.

Types of Advertising Objectives

Although no single typology of advertising objectives is considered to be standard, we can identify eight basic types of advertising objectives.[8]

However, it is possible to achieve more than one objective during a given campaign, although this can be very difficult and costly. Moreover, each objective is generally most useful for implementing a particular type of marketing strategy. For instance, for the same product, there may be different advertising objectives for different customer groups. Obtaining trial of a

---

[7] Kenneth R. Sheets, "Infinities Art of Pacific Persuasion," *U.S. News & World Report*, Nov. 13, 1989, p. 67; and Bradley A. Stertz, "Nissan's Infiniti Gets Off to a Slow Start," *The Wall Street Journal*, Jan. 8, 1990, p B6.

[8] For additional background on these objectives, see Harper Boyd, Michael Ray, and Edward C. Strong, "An Attitudinal Framework for Advertising Strategy," *Journal of Marketing*, April 1972, pp. 27–33; and Kenneth A. Longman, *Advertising*, Harcourt, New York, 1974.

particular product or brand may be the objective for nonusers and/or new entrants into the market. However, for present users, the objective may be to obtain preference or loyalty for the product or brand. In addition, the promotion objective might be to stimulate demand for the entire product class, for example, electric shavers, and for a particular brand, for example, Braun electric shavers. Consequently, if more than one objective is employed, it is important to make sure that the various objectives are compatible with the marketing strategy.

The basic types of objectives include

1. Awareness
2. Reminder to use
3. Changing attitudes about the use of the product form
4. Changing perceptions about the importance of brand attributes
5. Changing beliefs about brands
6. Attitude reinforcement
7. Corporate and product-line image building
8. Obtaining a direct response

AWARENESS

Frequently the primary advertising objective is simply to generate or increase recognition of a brand name, a product concept, or information regarding where or how to buy a product. This can be an important objective in several different situations.

First, when a brand enters the market it will often be difficult for buyers to develop an attitude if the brand and its basic product concept are not known. That is, awareness of the product and comprehension of its basic concept must exist before favorable attitudes toward the brand can be developed.

Second, managers should also employ awareness objectives when customers need information about how to buy or how to get more information about a product. Managers of consumer products with highly selective distribution systems may need to emphasize this objective, especially if competing brands have more intensive distribution. Advertisements for Curtis-Mathes televisions, John Deere lawn mowers, and many other brands usually identify local dealers at the end of the commercials. Similarly, industrial marketers—especially those with small sales forces—may include inquiry slips or toll-free phone numbers in their advertisements to enable interested potential customers to obtain more detailed information, thus providing potential prospects for the sales force.

Finally, awareness and brand-name recognition are usually essential objectives in marketing low perceived-risk products when little deliberation or search is involved. In these situations, buyers will make brand selections largely on the basis of brand familiarity. That is, the brands that are most widely recognized will tend to have the largest market shares.

REMINDER TO USE

For discretionary items with irregular usage patterns, an appropriate marketing strategy may be to stimulate primary demand by increasing the rate of usage. The primary role of advertising in implementing this strategy is to remind buyers to use the product or to restock the product. That is, purchases may decline because the product is highly discretionary and consumers have no remaining stock to remind them to use it. For example, H. J. Heinz's Ore-Ida division designed an advertising program to build frequency of usage for french fries by showing that the product fits in with a fast-moving, contemporary everyday family lifestyle. Research had indicated that even though the quality of Ore-Ida was good, consumers didn't see french fries as a regular part of their contemporary lifestyle.[9]

CHANGING ATTITUDES ABOUT THE USE OF THE PRODUCT FORM

This objective is designed to support primary-demand strategies for attracting new users or for increasing the number of uses. Advertising programs to implement these strategies usually take one of two basic forms. First, advertising campaigns may demonstrate new ways to use the product or new usage occasions. Thus, Arm & Hammer has used advertisements showing the use of baking soda to eliminate odors in carpets, ashtrays, and refrigerators, and A-1 Steak Sauce has been promoted as an alternative to ketchup for use on hamburgers. Second, some advertising campaigns have been designed to overcome negative perceptions about product categories.

Oldsmobile, realizing that its customer base was getting smaller and older, decided to attack Oldsmobile's fuddy-duddy image directly with its "New Generation" advertising campaign. The "New Generation" ads featured celebrities of the 1950s and 1960s and their children in a series of playful vignettes with Oldsmobile cars. Surveys indicated positive responses to the campaign among consumers aged 35 to 44, which was the target audience Olds desired. Although there was not a measurable sales increase after the first year, Oldsmobile marketing executives contend that this is because it takes about 3 years for an advertising theme to work its way down to sales. Nevertheless, Cutlass Supreme buyers who were on average 50 years old when the car was introduced in 1987 now average 45 years old. In addition, dealers report more younger people coming into the showrooms.[10]

CHANGING PERCEPTIONS ABOUT THE IMPORTANCE OF BRAND ATTRIBUTES

An effective way of acquiring new customers through differentiated positioning is to advertise a "unique selling proposition." As suggested earlier, for an

---

[9] Warren Berger, "The Big Freeze at Heinz," *Adweek's Marketing Week*, Aug. 21, 1989, pp. 20–25.
[10] Joanne Lipman, "New Olds Ad Campaign Updates the Old," *The Wall Street Journal*, Aug. 23, 1989, p. 5; Raymond Serafin, "Olds Keeps the Faith," *Advertising Age*, Aug. 25, 1989, p. 50; and Joseph B. White, "New Ads Give a Boost to the Olds Image but Don't Help the Old Sales Woes Much," *The Wall Street Journal*, June 19, 1989, p. B1.

attribute to be determinant in the buyer's choice process, the attribute must be important and buyers must perceive that alternatives differ in the degree to which they possess the attribute. Therefore, if a brand or supplier has a unique attribute, advertising may be used to stress the importance of the attribute in order to make it determinant. For example, Listerine ads show how the brand helps prevent gingivitis. The objective is to persuade consumers to consider this attribute in forming their attitude toward mouthwashes and make evaluations of Listerine more favorable.

CHANGING BELIEFS ABOUT BRANDS

If an attribute (or benefit) is already considered important, buyers will examine the degree to which each alternative product or brand possesses that attribute or provides that benefit. Accordingly, the advertising objective may be to improve buyers' ratings of a brand on important attributes or to change the relative ratings of competing brands on the attribute. Because the attribute is not unique to a brand, advertising designed to demonstrate this relative superiority would be supporting a marketing strategy of head-to-head competition. For example, Con Agra introduced its *Healthy Choice* dinners and entrées illustrating the superiority of its products by attacking the nutritional merits of competitors' frozen dinners. In a $15 million advertising campaign, the company showed that *Healthy Choice* was healthier in terms of sodium, fat, and cholesterol. Sales of *Healthy Choice* were $150 million in the first year with more than 55 percent of initial purchasers buying the product again. In addition, on average consumers purchase three boxes of *Healthy Choice* compared to 1.5 boxes of most frozen meals.[11]

ATTITUDE REINFORCEMENT

Brands or suppliers with a strong market position and with no major competitive weaknesses are more likely to be concerned with customer-retention strategies. By reassuring customers that the brand or supplier continues to offer the greatest level of satisfaction on the most important benefits, advertising can reinforce attitudes and thus maintain brand preferences and loyalty. Accordingly, to achieve this kind of objective, Heinz displays the continued high level of thickness and quality of its ketchup by advertising the product's slow-pouring quality, and the Energizer bunny ads remind consumers of the batteries' long life.

CORPORATE AND PRODUCT-LINE IMAGE BUILDING

Frequently advertising is used to establish or change perceptions of organizations or broad product lines but without focusing on specific product attributes or benefits. General corporate advertising usually is designed to enhance a corporation's public image, ostensibly to make it more attractive to prospective stockholders. For example, Dow Chemical ran an extensive advertising campaign telling why Dow is a great place for young people to work and

[11] Steve Weiner, "How Josie's Chili Won the Day," *Forbes*, Feb. 5, 1990, pp. 57, 60, 62, 63.

emphasizing the corporation's efforts to improve the quality of life. It is possible that such advertising may increase awareness about certain corporate attributes, but many experts question its actual effectiveness and value.[12] However, Metropolitan Life Insurance's research suggested that insurance companies were measured by their trademark images. Accordingly, they licensed *Peanuts* cartoon characters from their creator. Met Life's campaign is intended to position them as a nonthreatening insurance company with a human side, while at the same time improving the awareness factor that gets agents in the door of prospective customers.[13]

On the other hand, product-line image building is frequently very effective. This type of objective usually becomes important when a firm offers a line of related products that have a complex set of benefits. In automobiles, computers, most consumer electronics products, and many other categories, many products (each with distinct features and positioning strategies) share a common brand name and a common distribution system. Product-line image advertising is used to provide an umbrella image for the specific attributes and benefits of each item in the line. Thus, in the automobile business, General Motors' Pontiac automobiles have been marketed under the "We Build Excitement" image, while Chevrolets were linked together by "The Heartbeat of America" theme. The Chevrolet program was designed to target the product line toward the middle of the market: Reasonably priced cars and trucks satisfying the "secret desires harbored in the Middle American heart."[14] Advertising designed to build product-line perceptions will then be augmented by advertising designed to build brand beliefs or attribute importance for individual products and models within the line.

OBTAINING A DIRECT RESPONSE

One of the fastest-growing sectors is that of direct marketing. In direct marketing the organization communicates directly with target customers with the objective of generating a response or a purchase. Although direct marketing is not solely a part of the promotional mix, it has become an integral part of the communications program. Direct response advertising is a method of direct marketing where the product or service is promoted through the advertisement, and the customer has the opportunity to buy or respond directly to the manufacturer.

In direct response advertising, merchandise is advertised in material mailed to customers, in newspapers and magazines, or on television. In 1991, over $200 billion in sales were made by direct response advertising. Firms using this approach range from major retailers, computer manufacturers such as Compaq, Dell, and Gateway, to financial services such as American Express and VISA. Trillium Health Products, for instance, markets a $289 electric appliance called Juiceman as well as a smaller $150 version. Annual revenues of

---

[12] Anne B. Fisher, "Spiffing Up the Corporate Image," *Fortune*, July 21, 1986, pp. 68–70.
[13] Dan Koeppel, "What Have Snoopy and Gang Done for Met Life Lately?" *Adweek's Marketing Week*, Nov. 13, 1989, pp. 2–3.
[14] "Those Heartbeat Ads Are a Hit in the Heartland," *Business Week*, Feb. 23, 1987, p. 107.

Trillium increased from $950,000 in 1989 to more than $75 million by 1992 largely through the use of "infomercials."[15] Most infomercials are designed to be viewed as regular TV shows, (consumers dial an 800 or 900 number to place an order). Infomercials range from as short as 3 minutes to as long as 60 minutes, with most being 30 minutes long. Research studies have found that 25- to 49-year-olds watch the most infomercials, and those having incomes between $30,000 and $40,000 viewing at an above-average rate.[16]

Stating the Objective

Once management has determined the most appropriate type of advertising objective, they should make a specific and measurable statement of objectives. Additionally, the target audience should be clearly defined in this statement.

For example, an awareness objective might be stated as follows: "Increase the percentage of males aged 25 to 44 who are aware of our brand from 30 to 50 percent." By stating the objective in this manner, management is accomplishing two things. First, the target audience is identified, enabling managers to select appropriate media. Second, the objective is stated in specific terms (50 percent). This will enable management to evaluate the degree to which the communications objective is being achieved if measures of awareness are conducted during and after the advertising campaign.

THE BUDGETING PROCESS

Establishing the advertising budget is one of the more difficult tasks facing marketing managers. As we suggested in our discussion of productivity analysis (in Chapter 6), it is extremely difficult to predict the impact of a given level of advertising expenditures on sales for several reasons: The relationship between advertising and sales is not likely to be a direct, linear relationship; competitive actions or environmental factors may offset the effectiveness of advertising efforts; and advertising effects are sometimes offset by changes in price, selling effort, or other marketing programs. An additional problem is that advertising effects tend to be cumulative. That is, expenditures in one year will have some immediate impact on sales, but they also have a longer term impact on sales in subsequent periods as seen in the case of Oldsmobile's campaign. Buyers who have been influenced to buy the product (or at least to become aware of it or develop favorable attitudes toward it) because of the first-year's advertising effort will often make purchases in subsequent years. A final difficulty revolves around the issue of efficiency. Increased advertising expenditures can never guarantee increased sales; that is, the additional money may be ineffectively spent because of a poor message design or inefficient media scheduling.

[15] Anne B. Fisher, "The New Debate Over the Very Rich," *Fortune*, June 29, 1992, p. 50.
[16] *Marketing News*, Jan. 20, 1992, p. 6.

In spite of these difficulties, it is important to establish a tentative budget in order to provide some guidance for message designers and media planners. These tasks cost money, and it is essential to have some feeling for the resources that will be available before reasonable message and media alternatives can be identified. (Figure 10-2 explores the development of a tentative advertising budget.)

Although the specifics of the advertising budgeting process will vary among companies, managers can use a general approach that includes the following steps:

1. Establish a baseline budget.
2. Based on the advertising objectives, estimate the message design and media cost required.
3. If time and resources permit, run experiments to obtain a rough estimate of the impact of the proposed program.
4. Revise the budget (or objectives) as necessary on the basis of the costs of the tasks, the results of any experiments, and the costs and expected impact of other marketing programs.

FIGURE 10-2
Developing a tentative advertising budget.

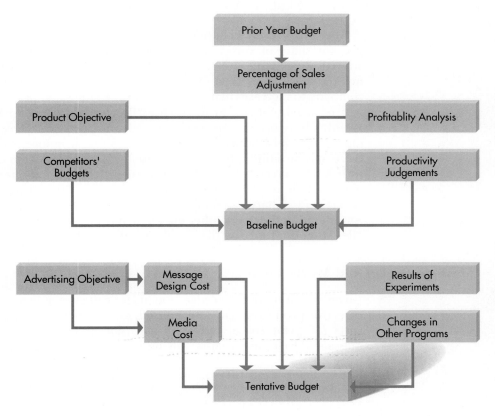

Establishing Baseline Budgets

In most organizations, the total advertising budget does not vary greatly from year to year, and so a possible baseline is to use the previous year's budget, or industry advertising-to-sales ratios as a guideline (see Table 10-2).[17] More realistically, managers will adjust budgets each year because of a number of factors.

1. *Product objectives* (based on the product portfolio analysis) determine which products should receive increased, sustaining, or reduced support. Accordingly, managers may modify budgets to reflect any changes in product objectives, with problem children receiving increased amounts, for example, and dogs receiving declining amounts.
2. *Product profitability* should be a major consideration in budgeting. The greater the contribution margin, the smaller the increase in sales that will be needed to cover the costs of increased advertising budgets.
3. *Productivity judgments* (especially when combined with profitability analyses) can be useful in determining the effects of changes in budgets. As discussed in Chapter 6, managers may decide that the level of advertising needs to be increased just to maintain the market share at the current level.

Many advertisers believe that it is necessary to keep their advertising budgets (or share of voice) at a consistent ratio of expenditures with the total advertising expenditure of the product category if they are to maintain their market share. This type of competitive parity approach would require the company to increase their "share of voice" to the same percentage level as the desired market share. Firms such as Procter and Gamble, McDonald's, and Wendy's have been reported to use such an approach.[18] This form of budgeting may be misleading for two reasons. First, it ignores the possibility that there may be limits to the market share that is attainable. For example, a brand with a 10 percent share could not reasonably be expected to increase its market share to 50 percent simply by spending 50 percent of the category's advertising dollars. Second, this approach to budgeting doesn't take into consideration the many other buying behavior factors influencing the brand's sales response function that we discussed in Chapter 6.

Message-Design and Media Costs

Given an advertising objective, a manager can estimate message-development costs (for production costs, technical fees, royalties to participants) and media costs (of print space, radio, or television time) fairly quickly. Generally, message-development costs will be a minor proportion of total cost, with

---

[17] Ratios from *Business Marketing*, November 1991, pp. 111–113.
[18] M. L. King, "Wendy's New Management Cooks Up Plans for Growth and Diversification," *The Wall Street Journal*, Mar. 27, 1981, p. 34.

TABLE 10-2

ADVERTISING-TO-SALES RATIOS (by industry), 1991

INDUSTRY	AD DOLLARS AS PERCENT OF SALES	AD DOLLARS AS PERCENT OF MARGIN	INDUSTRY	AD DOLLARS AS PERCENT OF SALES	AD DOLLARS AS PERCENT OF MARGIN
Abrasive, asbestos, misc minerals	1.1	3.9	Computer communication equipment	1.9	4.0
Adhesives & sealants	2.7	5.9	Computer peripheral equip, NEC	1.9	4.1
Agriculture chemicals	0.7	3.1	Computer storage devices	1.4	4.8
Agriculture production-crops	2.2	7.1	Computers & software-wholesale	0.6	5.2
Air cond, heating, refrig equip	1.7	6.5	Construction, mining, matl handle equip	4.4	12.9
Air courier services	1.2	9.9	Convert paper, paprbd, ex boxes	2.3	5.2
Air transport, scheduled	1.9	65.5	Dairy products	4.1	11.2
Aircraft & parts	0.6	3.1	Drug & proprietary stores	1.6	5.6
Aircraft parts, aux equip, NEC	0.8	3.1	Durable goods-wholesale, NEC	3.6	7.6
Auto & home supply stores	2.2	8.9	Educational services	6.9	15.7
Auto rent & lease, no drivers	2.4	3.6	Electrical indl apparatus	2.0	6.2
Automatic regulating controls	3.3	11.5	Electrical measure & test instruments	2.6	5.4
Bakery products	8.0	47.6	Electr, other elec equip, ex computrs	2.2	5.6
Beverages	8.6	14.6	Electric lighting, wiring equip	2.5	8.5
Books: publng & printing	2.9	6.0	Electromedical apparatus	1.3	2.2
Broadwoven fabric mill, cotton	4.3	21.7	Electronic comp, accessories	0.7	2.3
Business services, NEC	2.7	6.5	Electronic components, NEC	1.0	3.4
Cable & other pay TV services	2.9	6.0	Electronic computers	3.6	7.2
Calculate, acct mach, ex comp	1.7	4.4	Electronic connectors	1.0	4.2
Catalog, mail-order houses	6.9	17.7	Electronic parts, equip-whsl, NEC	2.0	7.5
Chemicals & allied prods-whsl	4.2	18.0	Engineering services	0.4	1.9
Chemicals & allied products	2.3	6.1	Engines & turbines	1.3	6.6
Cmp programming, data process	0.2	0.6	Engr, acc, resrch, mgmt, rel svcs	1.4	6.7
Computer & comp software stores	0.6	3.1	Equip rental & leasing, NEC	0.7	2.4
Computer integrated system design	1.5	4.1	Fabricated plate work	1.0	3.7
Computer processing, data prep svc	1.5	2.9	Fabricated rubber products, NEC	0.7	3.9
Computer programming service	1.7	8.9	Facilities support mgmt svcs		11.6
Commercial printing	2.7	10.4	Farm machinery & equipment	1.9 1.1	4.5
Communications equipment, NEC	2.1	4.9	Finance-services	0.8	6.9
Communications services, NEC	1.3	3.2	Food & kindred products	6.3	14.9
Computer & office equipment	1.6	3.3			

From *Business Marketing Magazine*, November 1991, pp. 111–113.

media costs constituting the major component. As discussed in detail later in this chapter, media costs are influenced by the size of the target market, the size or length of the advertisement, the number of times the advertisement is presented, and the specific costs of each media vehicle.

Experimentation and Revisions

When feasible, the proposed advertising program should be tested in a limited market area to determine whether the advertising objectives are being achieved and to estimate the sales response. These tests can provide insights into whether historical advertising effects on sales are optimistic or pessimistic relative to the present program. But experiments usually indicate only the short-run effects of a program because the length of an experiment is usually limited. However, experiments can be particularly useful in determining the effect of alternative copy and media schedules. If different media or different numbers of advertisements are used in different markets, the value of each medium and of different levels of audience exposure to a message can be measured. These measures may enable managers to adjust budgets to obtain the most efficient media schedules.

Revisions may also be necessary because of the impact of other programs. To some degree advertising competes with sales, sales promotion, and product development for funds. Further, price changes will lead to changing contribution margins. Accordingly, changes in the budgets for other programs may force managers to modify the advertising budget to stay within the resources available for a product. For instance, Sprint reduced its ad spending from $81 million to $68 million in 1991 while its competitor MCI was increasing its ad budget from $56 million to $94 million. MCI's market share increased from 14.2 percent to 16 percent while Sprint's decreased from 9.7 percent to 9.5 percent.[19]

DESIGN

An increasing number of advertising researchers seem to believe that the creative component (the message design) of advertising is far more important than the rate or pattern of advertising expenditures.[20]

The advertising message includes two basic elements: the appeals (or copy claims) that represent the central idea of the message and the method of presentation (or execution style) that is used to present the copy claims.

[19] Terry Lefton, "The Man from Mar's Game Plan for Sprint," *Adweek's Marketing Week*, May 25, 1992, p. 12.
[20] Joseph Eastlack and Ambar Rao, "Modeling Response to Advertising and Pricing Changes for V-8 Cocktail Vegetable Juice," *Marketing Science*, Summer 1986, pp. 245–259.

Although message design is primarily the responsibility of the advertising agency or of other creative specialists, the advertising director or product managers can provide significant input to see that the message design is appropriate for the marketing strategy and advertising objectives. In particular, information regarding the demographic and lifestyle characteristics of the target audience is useful in deciding what kinds of individuals might be portrayed in the advertisement.

For instance, the Department of Defense needs to recruit over 200,000 young men and women each year. The target audience is intelligent, well educated, motivated, and committed to the defense of the nation. Pentagon messages such as "Be all that you can be" or "Full speed ahead," emphasizing attractive elements of military service such as money for college and skill training, are the focus of the 1993 advertising budget of $117 million.[21]

Product usage situations and usage problems can be used to establish a setting or context in which the advertisement takes place. Factors limiting the willingness to buy can be considered by message designers, and the advertisement can be structured so that the existence or significance of these factors can be reduced. In addition, a knowledge of buyer perceptions of competing alternatives and of objective differences among alternatives will be useful.

Contents of an Effective Message

Information on the buying process can help the agency or specialists to deal with the three major requirements of an effective message: desirability, exclusiveness, and believability.[22] The use of desirability and exclusiveness criteria is simply a way of saying that a firm should try to emphasize those determinant attributes on which it has an advantage. If desirability is a problem, the usefulness of the product in solving a usage problem might be portrayed. Exclusiveness may be demonstrated through comparisons (direct or indirect) once the real and perceived product differences are known. Believability will become important in those situations where the product benefit or attribute is difficult to demonstrate or is highly subjective, or where it requires a major change in usage patterns. For example, Del Monte Foods scrapped a new shelf-stable yogurt, Little Lunch, after consumer research revealed that yogurt buyers refused to accept the idea that yogurt could be kept unrefrigerated. Early research indicated that the concept was viewed as desirable and unique, but the cost of achieving believability was finally judged too high after lengthy test marketing with various types of messages.[23]

[21] Cyndee Miller, "Military Ad Budget Takes A Shelling," *Marketing News*, Oct. 12, 1992, p. 19.

[22] Dik Warren Twedt, "How to Plan New Products, Improve Old Ones and Create Better Advertising," *Journal of Marketing*, January 1969, pp. 53–57.

[23] Sally Scanlon, "Calling the Shots More Closely," *1978 Sales and Marketing Plans*, Sales and Marketing Management, 1979, p. 90.

Copy-Claim Alternatives

The copy claims (or basic appeals of the message) are the motivational arguments or descriptive statements contained in the message. These claims can be of three types:

- Claims that describe the *physical* attributes of the product
- Claims that describe the *functional* benefits that can be obtained from the product
- Claims that *characterize* the product in terms of the types of people who use it, the results of obtaining the functional benefits or moods

In choosing the type of copy claim to use for a given advertising program, creative specialists should first of all be guided by the statement of the firm's advertising objective. That is, the advertising objective should clearly state the specific features that buyers are to be made aware of or the specific attributes or benefits on which perceptions are to be changed or reinforced. In addition, some advertising objectives may focus on exclusiveness, while others may emphasize the desirability (importance) of an attribute. Given the advertising objective, creative specialists can then select a copy approach that will support the desirability, exclusiveness, or believability (or any combination of these) of the attribute or benefit being featured. For instance, Compaq has set its worldwide objective as consistently ranking number two for business personal computers. Advertising's role in attaining the objective is to make Compaq's leadership believable. To accomplish this, Compaq has planned its ads around its fast growth.[24]

In developing the copy, creative specialists must also consider the type of brand concept involved. Products can be classified as relating to one of the following types of needs.[25]

1. *Functional needs*—products which resolve consumption-related problems that are brought on by the individual's environment (lawn mowers, for example)
2. *Symbolic needs*—products that fulfill internally generated needs, such as self-enhancement or ego identification (automobiles, for example)
3. *Experiential needs*—products that provide sensory pleasure, variety, or other kinds of stimulation (such as food or entertainment)

Clearly, characterization becomes a more important element of the copy when symbolic or experiential needs are involved. In addition, the type of need is often a significant influence in selecting an execution style.

[24] Richard I. Kirkland, Jr., "Europe Goes Wild for Yankee PCs," *Fortune*, June 5, 1989, pp. 257–260; and Jennifer Lawrence, "Compaq Prepares for European Push," *Advertising Age*, June 12, 1989, p. 38.
[25] C. Whan Park, Bernard Jaworski, and Deborah MacInnis, "Strategic Brand Concept-Image Management," *Journal of Marketing*, October 1986, pp. 135–145.

Execution Style

The execution style is the specific method of presenting the copy claim that is used to provide an environment for enhancing the copy. Although the details of the selection of execution style are beyond the scope of this book, an array of options and their uses can be examined.[26]

Humor may be used to draw attention to the message. However, to be effective, the basis for the humor should be related to the product's benefits. Humor also appears to have negative effects when applied to "serious" products or problems, and it may obscure the basic message. Further, humorous ads tend to lose their effect more quickly than other types. Similarly, exaggeration attracts attention and increases the memorability of advertising content.

Symbolic associations may provide a means of dramatizing intangible attributes or benefits by associating the product or service with a certain type of individual (usually the case in automobile advertisements) or a tangible object. (Note the symbols of assurance used by insurance companies: sentries, shields, the Rock of Gibraltar, and so forth.)

Functional benefits can be communicated in a variety of ways. *Testimonials* are employed to support the believability of benefits by using celebrities with some tie to the product category (in vocation or reputation) or with some special credibility with the target segment. *Product demonstrations* or recipes are used to show how a particular buyer problem can be solved to enhance desirability. *"Slice of life"* sequences portraying buyers in problem-solving situations are similar to demonstrations that provide a vehicle for showing product benefits. *Case histories* documenting the benefits of a product (such as flashlight batteries that burn all night) provide both credibility and a demonstration of product benefits.

If the copy claims focus on product attributes, *documentation* of the product's attributes (by presumably unbiased organizations) may be employed. More recently, *comparison advertising* formats (in which two or more brands are compared on one or more attributes) have enjoyed wider utilization as a means of demonstrating the uniqueness or believability of a product-attribute claim.

One of the most successful U.S. comparative ad campaigns has been the "Pepsi Challenge"—comparing the taste of Coke and Pepsi. However, in Japan, where commercials showing Japanese consumers taking the "Pepsi Challenge" were shown, the networks made Pepsi cover up Coke's name, diminishing the impact of the advertisement. Japanese consumers consider it arrogant to compare one product against another, and most Japanese business people believe that openly challenging competition is unethical. Later, Japan's Fair Trade Commission lessened restrictions against comparative advertising, and Pepsi then aired a comparative spot using rap singer M.C. Hammer. In the two months during which the spot aired on the five major

---

[26] An extended discussion is available in George E. Belch and Michael A. Belch, *Introduction to Advertising and Promotion*, Richard D. Irwin, Homewood, Ill.,1993, pp. 351–382.

commercial stations, Pepsi sales increased 50 percent. This was attributed to the popularity of M.C. Hammer and the heavy soft drink consuming youth population. However, additional spots were rejected by TV stations, and the future of comparative advertising in Japan is uncertain.[27]

As the preceding discussion has indicated, a great many options are available to creative specialists. However, they are more likely to select effective copy and execution styles if they understand the advertising objective and if they understand the buying process. Accordingly, it is more important for managers to state these objectives and to provide these specialists with the insights gained in buyer analysis.

MEDIA SCHEDULING

Media scheduling decisions are extremely important for two reasons. First, purchases of radio and television time and of newspaper and magazine space represent the largest element of cost in the advertising budget. For instance, the cost of a single 30-second spot on network TV during the evening averaged $122,000 in 1991. The National Football League's 1993 championship Super Bowl game advertising rate was between $850,000 and $900,000 for a 30-second commercial. In addition, the costs of producing a 30-second commercial for a national brand average nearly $200,000.[28]

Second, the success of an advertisement in achieving the advertising objectives depends largely upon how well each show or magazine reaches buyers in the target market segment. Because the cost and the audience size and characteristics of each media alternative are generally known, managers can employ some quantitative tools in media scheduling. However, as we will demonstrate, managers must also employ judgment in media scheduling decisions, because some of the attributes of media are not easily measured.

In this section, we will present the major steps involved in developing the media schedule. In particular, we examine each of the following kinds of decisions:

- Selecting the type of medium to use
- Selecting specific vehicles for consideration
- Determining the size, length, and position of an advertisement
- Determining the desired reach and frequency distribution of messages

---

[27] "Pepsi, Coke Spar in Japan Over Comparative TV Ad," *The Wall Street Journal*, Mar. 8, 1991, p. B6; Yukimo Ono, "Pepsi Challenges Japanese Taboo as It Ribs Coke," *The Wall Street Journal*, Mar. 6, 1991, pp. B1, B3; and David Kilburn, "Pepsi's Challenge: Double Japan Share," *Advertising Age*, Dec. 10, 1990, p. 36.

[28] "Trends in Media," Research Report by Television Bureau of Advertising, New York, July 1991; "Super Bowl Pumps Up Ads' Prices," *Orlando Sentinel*, Jan. 21, 1993, pp. C1, 4; and Janet Meyers and Laurie Freeman, "Marketers Police TV Commercial Costs," *Advertising Age*, Apr. 3, 1989, p. 51.

After these decisions have been made, one or more media schedules can be developed. Managers should then examine the media schedule to determine if it will be adequate for achieving the objective and if revisions in the tentative budget will be needed.

As in the case of message design, advertising managers and product managers may not make each of the detailed decisions involved in this process. However, these managers should review and analyze those decisions to be sure that they are consistent with the type of advertising objective and that they will be appropriate for the target market and the message design. We provide some guidelines for making these reviews and evaluations in this section of the chapter.[29]

Selecting the Type of Medium

Each medium (TV, radio, newspaper, magazine) has unique characteristics that may or may not be appropriate for the kind of message to be presented and for the kind of target segment to be reached. For instance, when using direct mail advertising, a firm usually relies on a mailing list containing the names of individuals with some common characteristic such as age (for example, senior citizens), occupation (student or doctor, for example), geographic area (such as suburban locations), or product ownership (such as homeowners).

Where to promote often is related to geographic considerations. Advertising expenditures may be allocated according to the market potential of an area if sales vary from one area to another. Advertising expenditures may be allocated to those areas where the product is already a leader to help maintain market share or to those areas where there is more potential for growth. Media planners often use indexes to help in this decision. In addition to indexes such as the Survey of Buying Power, Brand Development Index (BDI), and Category Development Index (CDI) discussed in Chapter 5, firms may rely on secondary information such as that provided by Simmons Market Research Bureau (SMRB) or Mediamark Research, Inc. (MRI). These sources provide syndicated data and audience size and composition for approximately 100 publications as well as data on broadcast exposure and usage of over 800 consumer products and services. In addition, they provide lifestyle information as well as media usage characteristics of the population. For instance, Chrysler Corp. mailed a videocassette promoting changes in its 1991 minivan to 400,000 current minivan owners, and Cadillac sent a mail offering of a videocassette to 170,000 young and affluent consumers.

Because the audience is narrowed down, this tends to be an economical way of reaching specific target segments with complex messages. Alternatively,

[29] Dennis Gensch, "Media Factors: A Review Article," *Journal of Marketing Research*, May 1970, pp. 216–225; and Leo Bogart, "Mass Advertising: The Message, Not the Measure," *Harvard Business Review*, September–October 1976, pp. 107-116.

managers may use media such as billboards, posters, and advertising on mass-transit vehicles when short, clear messages are presented to a (typically) nonselect audience.

Selecting Possible Vehicles

A *vehicle* is a specific magazine, newspaper, or radio or television program. In selecting a specific set of vehicles, managers should understand each vehicle's ability to reach the target market segments. Rating services and special research provided by the vehicles or by advertising agencies provide information on the audience size and demographics for each vehicle. Additionally, some magazines provide separate editions for reaching specific demographic groups. For example, *Time* magazine provides separate editions containing special advertising for doctors, educators, business executives, and students.

Additionally, vehicles should be evaluated on their likely effectiveness for the specific product and message. For instance, the editorial climate of a respected vehicle (such as *Time* or *Newsweek*) may enhance the credibility of an appeal because the vehicle is perceived as trustworthy. Similarly, a vehicle that is recognized for its prestige or expertise on a given subject may be an excellent choice for certain products (for example, *Sports Illustrated* for athletic equipment). Or the technical ability to adequately deliver the message (because of its use of color, available page size, or amount of commercial clutter in the program) may influence the selection of a specific vehicle.

Media availability and conflicting national regulations vary dramatically around the world. For instance, in certain countries commercial television and radio are not available, or are limited in use. Print media account for 100 percent of advertising expenditures in Oman and 97 percent in Norway.[30] In addition, there are conflicting national regulations that may include limits on the amount of time available for advertisements on television ranging from complete prohibition (Sweden) to 15 to 20 minutes a day in blocks of 3 to 5 minutes (West Germany). In some cases it may be necessary for companies to wait up to 18 months for allocation of airtime in those countries where the percentage of revenues that state monopoly systems can derive from advertising is limited (France and Italy). In addition, different nations have varying restrictions on comparative claims and gender stereotypes and many of these regulations may be standardized by the European Community in the near future.

By examining audience characteristics and effectiveness, managers can reduce the number of potential vehicles to a more manageable number for subsequent analyses. In addition, the cost per insertion in various media can be obtained from direct contact with media personnel, from media buying specialists (who are often able to obtain discounts on these rates), and from Standard Rate and Data Service publications.

---

[30] Lena Vanier, "U.S. Ad Spending Double All Other Nations Combined," *Advertising Age*, May 16, 1988, p. 36.

Cost will be an important consideration in the final media scheduling decision. However, except in the case of vehicles that are unusually costly relative to the size of the advertising budget, managers will not generally eliminate specific vehicles from further consideration at this point. Additionally, the actual cost per insertion will depend on the size, length, and position of the advertisement.

Determining Size, Length, and Position

In general, the probability that an advertisement will be seen varies with the size and length of a commercial or with different positions in a magazine (such as the back cover or inside the front cover). Additionally, these differences can influence recall. For instance, a 30-second commercial has about 60 to 75 percent of the recall value of a 60-second commercial.[31] However, these effects vary among types of products. That is, size, length, and position effects will be more important for low perceived-risk products because buyers are less active in searching for information and less quick to notice advertisements for those kinds of products.

The cost of an insertion is also influenced by the size, length, and position of the advertisement. After a particular size, length, and position decision has been made, managers will calculate the cost of each vehicle relative to the size of the audience reached. The typical measure used is cost per thousand (called CPM).

Agencies tend to use some variation of a weighted or demographic cost per thousand, which calculates the CPM using only that portion of a medium's audience that falls in a particular prime-prospect category. For instance:

$$CPM = \frac{ad\ cost \times 1000}{circulation}$$

Cosmopolitan has a circulation of 5,000,000 and a four-color page rate of $65,800. Thus,

$$CPM = \frac{(\$65,800 \times 1000)}{5,000,000} = \$13.16$$

If the advertiser is only interested in reaching women with 4 years of college education, we may find 2,200,000 readers in this category. Then

$$Demographic\ CPM = \frac{(\$65,800 \times 1000)}{2,200,000} = \$29.90$$

The basic measure of television is the rating point. This is the percentage of TV households in the market a TV station reaches with a particular program.

---

[31] Jack Z. Sissors and E. R. Petray, *Advertising Media Planning*, Crain Books, Chicago, 1976, p. 185.

This rating is calculated as:

$$\text{Rating} = \frac{\text{program audience}}{\text{total TV households}}$$

A household rating of 17 for a program would mean that 17 percent of all households in a particular market tuned their sets to that program.

Determining the Desired Distribution of Messages

For a given planning period, advertising expenditures can be distributed in different ways: according to the timing of the expenditures or according to reach and frequency.

TIMING OF EXPENDITURES

Timing reflects the manner in which expenditures are distributed over the course of the planning period. Many products and services have highly seasonal sales patterns. Toy sales peak in November and December, cold tablet sales in winter, greeting card sales before major holidays. To the extent that seasonal patterns are known, managers can schedule advertising so that the bulk of the dollar expenditures coincides with (or slightly leads) the peak sales period.

An additional timing consideration (especially for smaller advertisers) is the idea of *flighting*. When the total number of dollars available for advertising is very limited, some firms believe that these funds should be spent in lump sums that are adequate to generate sufficient impact. That is, if a small budget is spread evenly over the planning period, the weekly or monthly level of advertising might be too low to be noticed. By placing larger chunks of advertising intermittently, many managers believe that the visibility of the advertising will be greater than if the same dollars are spent in smaller but more frequent amounts. For instance, Porsche Cars North America scheduled virtually its entire $5 million fall ad budget behind two 2-minute commercials and a twenty-page insert in selected magazines. Because Porsche couldn't match competitors' total spending levels, they attempted to create impact and memorability through this concentrated burst of effort.[32]

MEASURING REACH AND FREQUENCY

Managers must also determine how to distribute expenditures among members of the target audience according to reach and frequency. *Reach* represents either the number or the percentage of target audience members who will be exposed to a message. *Frequency* represents the average number of times a member of the target audience is exposed to the message.

[32] Raymond Serafin, "Porsche Ads Go for High Impact," *Advertising Age*, Sept. 11, 1989, p. 25.

Reach and frequency measures are based on estimates of the size of an audience as calculated by independent rating services. When possible, these measures should be calculated in terms of the target audience rather than in terms of the total audience.

For example, assume that a magazine has a circulation of 1 million, of which 800,000 subscribers are in a target audience defined as females aged 15 to 24. Defined in terms of the target audience, the reach of one insertion in that magazine would be 800,000. If an advertiser made one insertion in that magazine in each of 4 weeks, the total reach would be 4 × 800,000, or 3.2 million. Advertisers use the term *gross impressions* to indicate the number of target audience members reached by a given advertising plan. Therefore, 3.2 million can be referred to as the number of gross impressions resulting from four insertions in this magazine.

However, reach can also be calculated in terms of the percentage of the target audience. If the total target audience consists of 20 million females, each issue of this magazine reaches 800,000 out of the 20 million, or 4 percent of the target audience. Advertisers use the term *gross rating points* (or GRPs) to indicate the reach in percentage terms. Therefore, if a firm advertised in four issues of this magazine, the number of GRPs would be calculated as 4 percent per issue multiplied by four issues, or 16 gross rating points.[33]

Both of these measures can be used to describe the total reach of a combination of media as well as of a single vehicle. Figure 10-3 illustrates the relationship of reach, frequency, and GRPs using different media. For instance, a schedule of 200 GRPs using magazines would reach 66 percent of the households. However, there will be some overlap in media usage among target audience members. That is, some readers of *Time* magazine also read *Newsweek*. Therefore, in determining the total number of individuals reached one or more times by these magazines, some measure of the duplication in audience coverage is needed. The terms *net coverage* and *combined coverage* indicate the total reach of a combination of vehicles after adjustments for overlapping coverage.[34]

Once the net coverage (the total number of audience members reached at least once) is known, the frequency can be calculated as follows:

$$\text{Frequency} = \frac{\text{gross impressions}}{\text{net coverage}}$$

USING REACH AND FREQUENCY

Managers often use measures such as gross impressions and gross rating points in order to rank alternative vehicles or combinations of vehicles by their

[33] This section is based on Sissors and Petray, op. cit., pp. 97–118; and Grossman, *The Marketers Guide to Media Vehicles, Methods and Options*, Quorum Books, Westport, Conn., 1987, chap. 1.
[34] Some procedures for measuring duplication are discussed in David B. Montgomery and Glen L. Urban, *Management Science in Marketing*, Prentice-Hall, Englewood Cliffs, N.J., 1969, pp. 98–100.

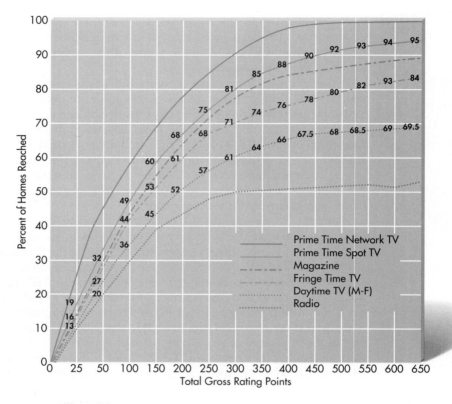

FIGURE 10-3
Relationship of reach, frequency, and GRPs. (Source: Michael L. Rothschild, *Advertising, from Fundamentals to Strategies,* D.C. Heath and Company, Lexington, Mass., 1987, p. 381.)

coverage of the audience. However, many advertisers and agencies believe that some vehicles are more effective than others in gaining actual audience perception—for the reasons cited earlier. Thus, these vehicles may receive more positive consideration even if they generate a slightly lower number of gross impressions than other vehicles.

Reach is, of course, desirable because the advertiser would prefer to reach as many individuals in the target audience as possible. In general, broader net coverage can be achieved by using a number of different vehicles, since different vehicles are likely to reach different members of the target audience.

On the other hand, it is generally recognized that some level of repeated exposure to a message is necessary before the message has any impact. And in general, repetition of the same advertisement in the same vehicle will tend to reach the same audience members. Therefore, by using only a limited number of vehicles, an advertiser may reduce net coverage but increase frequency.

Further, average frequency figures may be misleading. In reality some audience members are heavier readers or viewers than others, and so the distribution of frequency of potential exposure is usually unbalanced. Consider for example Figure 10-4. In this example, the average frequency of exposure is 1.67 times. But nearly a third of those reached were exposed (potentially) only once.

The critical question regarding frequency is, "How much is enough?" It can usually be established that, up to a point, repeated exposures increase brand awareness and foster favorable attitudes (assuming appropriate copy exists).[35] On the other hand, excessive repetition can lead to the phenomenon of wear-out. The average U.S. adult is subjected to 3000 marketing messages a day, and Video Storyboard Tests say that viewer retention of television commercials has decreased dramatically. Whereas 64 percent of those surveyed in 1986 could name a TV commercial they had seen in the previous 4 weeks, this had dropped to just 48 percent by 1990.[36] That is, continued repetition of an advertisement may not only be a waste of money but may actually lead to a decline in awareness or positive attitudes toward the product.[37]

Setting the Media Schedule

As indicated in Figure 10-5, the preceding steps provide the basic management inputs to the media scheduling decision. Computer routines, based on budget limitations, the target audience for the commercial, the desired frequency and reach, the cost per insertion for a given length and position, and the audience size and demographics for each acceptable vehicle, are typically

[35] See David Aaker, "ADMOD: An Advertising Decision Model," *Journal of Marketing Research*, February 1975, pp. 37–45; and Michael Ray and Alan Sawyer, "Repetition in Media Models: A Laboratory Technique," *Journal of Marketing Research*, February 1971, pp. 14–20.
[36] "What Happened to Advertising," *Business Week*, Sept. 23, 1991, pp. 66–72.
[37] See, for example, C. Samuel Craig, Brian Sternthal, and Clark Leavitt, "Advertising Wearout: An Experimental Analysis," *Journal of Marketing Research*, November 1976, pp. 365–372.

FIGURE 10-4
Example of a distribution of frequency of exposure.

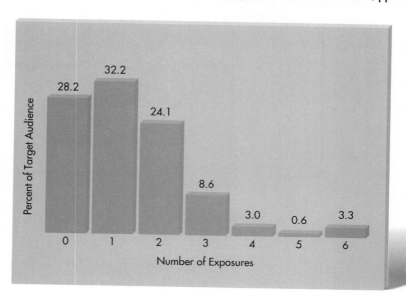

used to allocate the budget among the acceptable vehicles. Generally, these routines will yield a set of media schedules that provide the largest number of gross impressions for the given budget, with slight variations in reach and with frequency trade-offs among the alternative media schedules.

Table 10-3 provides an example of a media schedule for a product that is a frequent gift item for men. In examining the table, we can see that advertising tends to be heaviest during the Easter, graduation, and Christmas periods. Reach (as measured by gross rating points) and frequency levels are provided for each month. (The specific magazines and television programs selected were examined for consistency with the product.) The resulting schedule was then determined by examining the budget constraint and the cost per insertion using a computerized scheduling model.

Although a number of media scheduling models have been developed by using a variety of mathematical procedures,[38] it is important to recognize that

---

[38] An excellent overview of alternative approaches is contained in Dennis Gensch, *Advertising Planning: Mathematical Models in Advertising Media Planning*, Elsevier Scientific, Amsterdam, 1973.

FIGURE 10-5
Developing the media schedule.

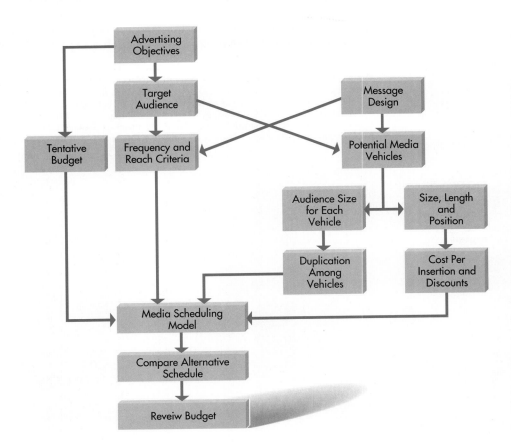

| TABLE 10-3 | MEDIA PLAN FOR A MEN'S GIFT PRODUCT |

MEDIA PLAN FOR A MEN'S GIFT PRODUCT

		MEN 25–49	
MONTH	MEDIUM	REACH	FREQUENCY
March	Television	78	3.1
	Magazines	69	2.1
	Combined	93	2.4
April	Television	78	3.1
	Magazines	33	1.3
	Combined	84	3.4
May	Magazines	34	1.3
June	Magazines	34	1.3
	Radio	38	5.3
	Combined	59	4.1
July	Radio	38	5.3
September	Magazines	35	1.3
October	Magazines	59	1.7
November and December	Television	81	3.5
	Magazines	32	1.2
	Radio	38	5.3
	Combined	92	5.7

From Michael L. Rothschild, *Advertising Firm Fundamentals to Strategies,* DC Heath and Company.

the use of such models does not serve as a substitute for managerial judgment. Rather, these models merely serve to display the best schedules based on the budget and on prior management decisions regarding message and objectives and size, length, and position. In fact, even the most sophisticated models available to advertisers require very extensive inputs by advertising or product managers.[39]

EVALUATING EFFECTIVENESS

Advertising frequently consumes a large proportion of the marketing budget and is often a critical ingredient in the success of a product. Accordingly, managers should attempt to evaluate the effectiveness of advertising to determine whether advertising expenditures are being well utilized. In particular, they should evaluate the effectiveness of individual messages (before or during the implementation of the program) and the effectiveness of the overall advertising program in achieving advertising objectives.

The role of advertising managers and product managers in the evaluation process is critical—especially in regard to monitoring the achievement of

[39] John D. C. Little and Leonard M. Lodish, "A Media Planning Calculus," *Operations Research,* January–February 1969, pp. 1–35.

objectives. Advertising agencies and creative specialists are likely to be more skilled and very objective in evaluating individual messages to determine the most effective copy. But advertising managers, product managers, and top-level marketing managers should attempt to determine whether the message will create the desired effect on awareness or attitudes. Advertisements well liked by the ad industry and recalled by viewers do not necessarily move product. For instance, Pepsi's 1991 "chill out" campaign achieved very strong results in terms of memorability and consumers' strong liking of the ads. However, Pepsi's sales during this period grew at a significantly lower rate than did those of Coke.[40]

Further, advertising and product managers should be primarily responsible for evaluating the effectiveness of the total program, for two reasons. First it will be nearly impossible for agencies to be perfectly objective. Second, even when clearly specified communications-oriented objectives have been established, awareness and attitude results may still be influenced partly by other factors (such as changes in distribution availability, prices, and competitors' actions). Only the marketing managers in the firm doing the advertising can properly assess the impact of those factors.

One other point regarding evaluation is important. When possible, evaluation should be diagnostic. That is, it should not merely indicate which of two alternative messages is superior or how well the advertising objective is being achieved, but it should also provide insights into the specific remedial actions needed.

Procedures

As indicated in Table 10-4, a number of alternative procedures for evaluating advertising effectiveness are available.[41] Some of these procedures must be implemented by the advertiser or its agency, while others are available from syndicated research services such as those indicated in the table. Advertising effectiveness techniques used in international markets do not differ from those used domestically. However, costs of advertising research are usually higher because syndicated services may not be available, and audience measurement technologies and analyses may vary from country to country.[42]

It is important to recognize that different procedures are used for different kinds of evaluations. In particular, three kinds of effectiveness evaluations can be made:

[40] "Pepsi: Memorable Ads, Forgettable Sales," *Business Week*, Oct. 21, 1991, p. 36.

[41] Joanne Lipman, "Single-Source Ad Research Heralds Detailed Look at Household Habits," *The Wall Street Journal*, Feb. 16, 1988, p. 35; D. Dalbey et al., *Advertising Measurement and Decision-Making*, Allyn and Bacon, Boston, 1968; also see: Bernard Ryan, Jr., *It Works! How Investment Spending in Advertising Pays Off*, American Association of Advertising Agencies, New York, N.Y. 1991, pp. 1–63.

[42] Joseph T. Plummer, "The Role of Copy Research in Multinational Advertising," *Journal of Advertising Research*, October–November 1986, pp. 11–15; and Nancy Giges, "Europeans Buy Outside Goods, but Like Local Ads," *Advertising Age International*, Apr. 27, 1992, pp. I1, 26.

| TABLE 10-4 | PROCEDURES FOR EVALUATING ADVERTISING PROGRAMS |

PROCEDURES FOR EVALUATING SPECIFIC ADVERTISEMENTS

1. Recognition tests:
   Estimate the percentage of people claiming to have read a magazine who recognize the ad when it is shown to them (for example, Starch Message Report Service).
2. Recall tests:
   Estimate the percentage of people claiming to have read a magazine who can (unaided) recall the ad and its contents (for example, Gallup and Robinson Impact Service; various services for TV ads as well).
3. Opinion tests:
   Potential audience members are asked to rank alternative advertisements as most interesting, most believable, best liked.
4. Theater tests:
   Theater audience is asked for brand preferences before and after an ad is shown in context of a TV show (for example, Schwerin TV Testing Service).

PROCEDURES FOR EVALUATING SPECIFIC ADVERTISING OBJECTIVES

1. Awareness:
   Potential buyers are asked to indicate brands that come to mind in a product category. A message used in ad campaign is given, and buyers are asked to identify brand that was advertised using that message.
2. Attitude:
   Potential buyers are asked to rate competing or individual brands on determinant attributes, benefits, characterizations using rating scales.

PROCEDURES FOR EVALUATING MOTIVATIONAL IMPACT

1. Intentions to buy:
   Potential buyers are asked to indicate likelihood they will buy a brand (on a scale from "definitely will not" to "definitely will").
2. Market test:
   Sales changes in different markets are monitored to compare effects of different messages, budget levels.

- Evaluating individual advertising messages (copy and format) in order to choose the best of two or more alternatives or to measure the degree to which the message is being received by the audience
- Evaluating the achievement of awareness and attitude objectives
- Evaluating the motivational impact of the advertising program as reflected in sales or intentions to buy

Note that when measuring awareness, attitudes, intentions to buy, and sales, managers should make these measurements before a campaign begins and again at intervals of time during the campaign.

AT&T ran a series of advertisements that portrayed angry or frightened business people coping with telephone and computer problems. These ads portrayed business people who were not always nice and polite when purchasing a phone system. The ads were developed and monitored using a variety of research methods. Focus groups were conducted and led to the original concept. Later, in-house tests were conducted to measure persuasion and recall of the advertisements that had been developed. Prior to breaking the ad campaign, additional focus groups were conducted to see if they supported the results of the in-house testing of the advertisements. Throughout the campaign, results were monitored and research was conducted with salespersons.[43]

A procedure such as AT&T's enabled management to catch problems and think of possible modifications in message design or media scheduling at as early a time as possible. Further, managers should note that those tests which provide diagnostic information are generally most useful in determining what specific modifications are necessary. For example, recall tests help to diagnose weaknesses in a message by indicating which copy claims are not recalled. Additionally, differences in recall between vehicles can reveal differences in the effectiveness of vehicles (or in the effects of size, length, and position factors, if these differ). Similarly, attitude tests can serve to tell whether the copy is effective in changing perceptions and whether unintended changes in perception have resulted from the copy.

LOCATION

The global approach has received considerable attention; it views the world as one market rather than as a collection of many national or regional markets.[44] This orientation employs a uniform marketing approach and standardized products. The advantages of this highly standardized approach include lower production costs, higher quality products, a consistent worldwide image, and more efficient marketing. As previously discussed in Chapter 7, it has been argued that advances in communication, transportation, and entertainment technology have brought about more homogeneous world tastes and wants. The biggest hindrance to global marketing may still be cultural differences. There is little evidence to support the contention that world consumers are becoming more alike. In fact, as people become more affluent and better

---

[43] Thornton C. Lockwood, "Behind the Emotion in Slice of Death Advertising," *Business Marketing*, September 1988, pp. 87–93.

[44] Robert D. Buzzell, "Can You Standardize Multinational Marketing?" *Harvard Business Review*, November–December 1968, p. 102. Professor Buzzell was one of the first persons to raise the question of how much multinational marketing could be standardized. Theodore Levitt, "The Globalization of Markets, *Harvard Business Review*, May–June 1983, pp. 92–96, declared the approach appropriate for all firms. See also "Differences, Confusion Slow Global Marketing Bandwagon," *Marketing News*, Jan. 16, 1987, p. 1. In a study of 100 advertisers selling products overseas, only 9 percent used a global marketing approach.

educated, their tastes diverge, and it may become necessary to make greater adjustments for local culture and conditions. The Grey Advertising Agency has identified three questions that companies should ask when selling products in foreign markets. A negative answer to any one of these would suggest that a global marketing strategy is not appropriate.[45]

- Are consumer targets similar in different nations? For instance, Kentucky Fried Chicken may be viewed as an ordinary meal in the United States while considered a treat in Japan.
- Do consumers share the same wants and needs around the world? General Foods successfully positioned Tang as a substitute for orange juice at breakfast but found that in France people drank little orange juice and almost none at breakfast.
- Has the market developed in the same way from country to country? For instance, Kellogg's Pop-Tarts failed in the United Kingdom because toasters were not widely used, whereas a toaster is a common household appliance in the United States.

The most visible of the firm's marketing activities in international markets may be its advertising effort. The same advertising may be used in different countries or country-to-country variations may be made. For example, Gillette used one ad campaign to support the new Sensor shaving system.[46] Gillette felt the product category enabled it to market across multinational boundaries as if they were one country. Previously, Gillette had introduced Contour Plus (called Atra Plus in North America) in fifteen European nations with identical commercials in each country. The European commercial differs from the North American execution only in that it used the Contour Plus name and featured sports footage that better reflected European culture.

However, in the majority of cases, differences among countries require that the promotional effort be tailored to reflect local considerations. In Gillette's case this meant using a different brand name. Similarly, Sara Lee's best-selling herbal bath soap in Great Britain is Radox. However, many Europeans confuse this name with Raid, the bug killer, and Radox comes across as being unsuitable as a product to put on your skin. In place of Radox, Sara Lee promotes Sanex, a Spanish soap that is seen by Europeans as a brand that lathers nicely and kills germs. However, in the big British market it sounds like "sanitary" and has the wrong connotations. Other names such as L'eggs do not translate for many European markets. For instance the word for L'eggs in France would have to be Les Oeufs (the eggs).[47]

---

[45] Ronald Alsop, "Efficacy of Global Ad Projects Is Questioned in Firm's Survey," *The Wall Street Journal*, Sept. 13, 1984, p. 1.
[46] Allison Fahey, "International Ad Effort to Back Gillette Sensor," *Advertising Age*, Oct. 16, 1989, p. 34.
[47] Steve Weiner, "How Do You Say L'eggs in French?" *Forbes*, Nov. 27, 1989, pp. 73–77.

CONCLUSION

Although the process of developing and implementing advertisements is often the primary responsibility of an advertising agency, it is critical that advertising managers, product managers, and top-level marketing management personnel take an active part in this process. In particular, it is essential that managers set advertising objectives that are (1) consistent with the marketing strategy, (2) specific enough to provide guidance to the copy and media people, and (3) measurable so managers can effectively evaluate the program's effectiveness.

The importance of taking an active role in the development of an advertising program seems obvious. But far too many firms, especially smaller ones, allow their agencies too much freedom in developing the program. In effect, creative concerns often receive more attention than managerial concerns. Of course, agencies or other specialists are essential to the advertising process. But by taking an active role in specifying the marketing strategy, the target market, the advertising objectives, and the basis for evaluating effectiveness, managers can assure that advertising programs are viewed as part of the marketing effort (rather than vice versa) by the agency.

In this chapter, we have presented several guidelines and procedures for developing effective advertising programs. Additionally, we have presented a process within which these guidelines and procedures can be most effectively

FIGURE 10-6
Relationship of advertising programs to situation analysis, marketing strategy, and other marketing programs.

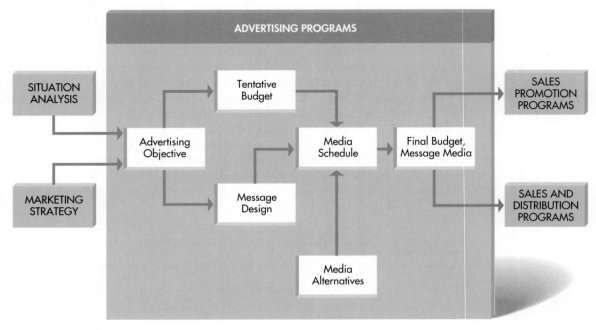

RENAMING NEW COKE*

For 20 years the Coca-Cola Company and Pepsi-Cola have competed for leadership in the soft-drink market. These two companies account for 70 percent of industry sales and spend hundreds of millions of dollars on advertising each year. Each percentage point of market share is equal to $460 million in retail sales in the $44.4 billion soft drink industry.

In April 1985, Coca-Cola changed the formula of its product and introduced *New Coke*. This resulted in a strong protest from loyal customers of the old brand and led to the reintroduction of the original Coke as *Coca-Cola Classic* a short time later. In addition, *New Coke* never attained the market-share goals that had been established and was relegated to obscurity, although continuing to be distributed in markets where Pepsi was strong, such as Spokane, Washington, and southern California. Coke marketers, exploring ways to obtain younger drinkers who prefer a sweeter flavor, decided to revive *New Coke* and reintroduce it as *Coke II*.

The city of Spokane, Washington, was chosen as a test market to research reintroduction of this brand. Spokane was selected because of its relatively isolated media market with sophisticated market-research facilities and high Pepsi market share. In the test, Coke countered Pepsi's rap ads with its own as well as with special 16 oz. cans at 12 oz. prices. Coke II advertising emphasized its "real cola taste—plus the sweetness of Pepsi."

Pepsi responded to Coke advertisements with ads aimed at consumer confusion about what seemed like three types of Coke. Before and during the ads Coca-Cola conducted focus groups, weekly phone surveys, man-in-the-mall surveys, and studies of comparative local ads for Coke II and Pepsi. This research was designed to learn what it would take to convert a loyal Pepsi fan to the new Coke formula.

When the test began in March 1990, *New Coke* had a 1.3 percent share in Spokane. A month after the test began, *Coke II* had a 4.7 percent share, and by May was 2.4 percent. During this same time, *New Coke's* national share was 0.6 percent. In addition, both Coke

and Pepsi's overall sales increased due in large part to price cuts.

After the tests, Coke decided to reposition New Coke as Coke II nationally. TV ads, showing a can of Coke II with a voice-over informing viewers that *New Coke* is now called *Coke II* and has a real cola taste with the sweetness of Pepsi, were run. These ads suggested that those drinking Pepsi should give *Coke II* a try and reminded the viewer that *Coca-Cola Classic* hadn't changed.

Research Systems Corp. (RSC) found that 24 percent of the viewers of these ads were able to play back the new name message. The research was conducted in four geographically dispersed markets and involved 832 soft-drink purchasers. RSC investigated how persuasive these ads were. This was done by measuring the change in brand preference that resulted from being exposed to the ad. RSC's experience with similar studies led it to conclude that the ads alone would not generate the share increase desired. Interviews were conducted with those soft-drink purchasers participating in the persuasion tests three days later. By that time, only 57 percent of the respondents were able to recall the key message of the ad. This led RSC to conclude that Coke would need to use a number of different ads so they could replace each spot as its recall declined. This would maximize the persuasion level for the GRPs under Coke II's media budget.

1. What seem to be Coca-Cola's objective(s) for the Coke II advertising spots?
2. What would be the advantages/disadvantages of testing the Coke II campaign in Spokane?
3. How would reach and frequency be important in scheduling the Coke II campaign?

* This case was developed from Laura Bird, "Coke II: The Sequel," *Adweek's Marketing Week*, July 30, 1990, pp. 6–7; "Coke II Spot Goes Flat on Persuasion," *Advertising Age*, Sept. 7, 1992, p. 9; Patricia Winters, "Jury Still Out on Future of Coke II," *Advertising Age*, July 16, 1990, p. 44; Patricia Winters, "Pepsi Yawning Over Relaunch Plans for Coke II," *Advertising Age*, March 1990, pp. 3–77; John Lippman, "Coca-Cola Pours More Energy into Ads," *Los Angeles Times*, Sept. 5, 1991, pp. D1, 7.

used. Figure 10-6 summarizes this process and indicates the relationship between advertising programs and the other elements of the planning process. As this figure indicates, advertising programs are closely related to the other kinds of marketing programs. Sales-promotion programs must often be communicated through advertising. Further, sales promotions and advertising should be closely coordinated, for reasons discussed in Chapter 11. Additionally, advertising and personal selling efforts should be coordinated as well, because advertising is often a means of paving the way for the sales force. This relationship will be discussed in greater detail in Chapter 12.

QUESTIONS AND SITUATIONS FOR DISCUSSION

1. Would you expect a direct marketer of personal computers, such as Dell or Gateway, to develop an advertising campaign that emphasizes the cognitive, affective, or behavioral response stage? Explain.

2. In which of the following cases would it be most reasonable to use sales volume as a primary advertising objective?

a. A small software firm is planning an advertising program in leading business magazines.

b. Kellogg's is introducing a new anticholesterol cereal product to the market.

c. Marshall Fields is advertising its private-label line of men's sports coats.

3. Upjohn Company has taken a low-key approach to advertise its hair-loss remedy, Rogaine. The advertisements do not mention either Rogaine or Minoxidil, its active ingredient. The U.S. Food and Drug Administration prohibits the mention of drugs in advertisements unless there is full disclosure of any warnings and side effects. The ads appear in male-oriented magazines such as *Golf Digest*, *Sports Illustrated*, and *Gentlemen's Quarterly*. In addition to not using the name, the treatment in the ad isn't even referred to as a drug. The result is that the audience does not know if the treatment is a hair weave, a transplant, or a drug. The message is "if you're concerned about hair loss you should see your doctor." What are the advertising objectives Upjohn seems to have for their campaign for Rogaine? What are the advantages of advertising in magazines as opposed to broadcast media for a high-involvement product such as Rogaine?

4. What effect does the product life cycle have on the advertising a company employs?

5. Coca-Cola beat out PepsiCo. to become the exclusive soft-drink sponsor for the 1992 Universal Exhibition in Seville, Spain. Coca-Cola paid $8.4 million to be the official sponsor and another $5.3 million to be a "collaborating company," financing certain facilities and services. In addition, Coca-Cola paid $650,000 to be able to sell soft drinks on the fairgrounds. In exchange,

Coca-Cola can use the exposition's official logo and Curro mascot (a bird with a crest of rainbow colors) on promotions of products approved by the exposition. Coca-Cola's communications director said the "only reason we are taking part in Expo is to impede competitors from getting the upper hand." Does this appear to be a reasonable objective for Coca-Cola?

6. Since 15-second commercials were first introduced in 1986, they have increased to where they now account for 41 percent of all daytime television spots. How would you expect the shift from 30- to 15-second spots to influence the design of messages? Studies have shown that 15-second ads are generally 70 percent as effective as longer ads. Would this have any implications on establishing the baseline advertising budget?

7. Suppose an advertiser is considering two markets for the TV schedule. These markets are Los Angeles and Chicago:

MARKET	TV HOMES (000's)	AVG. COST PER SPOT	AVG. PRIME TIME RATING
Los Angeles	4200	$3000	20
Chicago	2000	$2000	20

The advertiser is contemplating buying three prime-time spots in each of these markets.

  a. How many household impressions in each market would such a schedule deliver?

  b. What is the cost per rating point (CRP) for Los Angeles and Chicago?

  c. What other factors would you consider in comparing GRPs from markets for different sizes?

8. Abacus, Inc., had been formed by three recent MIT graduates who had developed a quiet and powerful disk-drive system. This disk system was 100 percent compatible with the Apple II and Apple IIe personal computers. The Abacus system had a 5-year electromechanical design life with a full, 1-year parts-and-labor warranty. In addition, standard equipment included three software programs and a handsome portable carrying case.

In developing their marketing program for this system, the founders had chosen to utilize some print media. Faced with a limited budget, they were trying to choose between two magazines. Magazine *Alpha* had 1 million readers and charged $200 for a full-page ad, while magazine *Beta* had 1.5 million readers and charged $2500 for the full-page ad. In addition, they knew that *Alpha* readership consisted of 10,000 personal computer owners and that *Beta* readership included 15,000 personal computer owners.

  a. If you had to choose between *Alpha* and *Beta*, which would you use, given the above information?

  b. What additional information would you feel necessary prior to making such a decision?

SUGGESTED ADDITIONAL READINGS

Dickson, Peter R., "GRP: A Case of a Mistaken Identity," *Journal of Advertising Research*, February–March 1991, pp. 55–59.

Gronhaug, Kjell, Olan Kvitastein, and Sigmund Gronmo, "Factors Moderating Advertising Effectiveness as Reflected in 333 Tested Advertisements," *Journal of Advertising Research*, October–November 1991, pp. 42–58.

Hite, Robert E., and Cynthia Fraser, "International Advertising Strategies of Multinational Corporations," *Journal of Advertising Research*, August–September 1988, pp. 9–17.

Jones, John P., "Ad Spending: Maintaining Market Share," *Harvard Business Review*, January–February 1990, pp. 38–42.

Kashani, Kamran, "Beware the Pitfalls of Global Marketing," *Harvard Business Review*, September–October 1989, pp. 91–98.

McMeekin, Gordon C., "How to Set Up an Advertising Budget," *Journal of Business Forecasting*, Winter 1988–1989, pp. 22–26.

Peltier, James W., Barbara Mueller, and Richard G. Rosen, "Direct Response versus Image Advertising: Enhancing Communication Effectiveness through an Integrated Approach," *Journal of Direct Marketing*, Winter 1992, pp. 40–48.

Plummer, Joseph T., "The Role of Copy Research in Multinational Advertising," *Journal of Advertising Research*, October–November 1986, pp. 11–15.

Rice, Marshall D., "Estimating the Reach and Frequency of Mixed Media Advertising Schedules," *Journal of the Market Research Society*, October 1988, pp. 439–451.

Schroer, James C., "Ad Spending: Growing Market Shares," *Harvard Business Review*, January–February 1990, pp. 44–48.

Zaltman, Gerald, and Christine Moorman, "The Management and Use of Advertising Research," *Journal of Advertising Research*, December 1988–January 1989, pp. 11–18.

CHAPTER 11

SALES-PROMOTION PROGRAMS

OVERVIEW

A sales promotion is any *short-term* offer or incentive directed toward buyers, retailers, or wholesalers that is designed to achieve a *specific, immediate response*. The two basic classifications of sales promotion are *consumer promotions*, including coupons, free samples, premiums, and special exhibits, and *trade promotions*, in which cash, merchandise, equipment, or other resources are awarded to retail or wholesale firms or to their personnel.

Consumer sales promotions are often communicated through or coordinated with advertising programs. Consequently, they may assist advertising in increasing awareness or changing or reinforcing attitudes. But the main value of both consumer and trade promotions lies in their effectiveness in stimulating *behavioral responses*.

Specifically, sales promotions have a number of benefits as marketing tools:

- They are useful in securing trial and in defending shelf space against new or existing competitors.
- They reduce the retailer's and wholesaler's risk in stocking new items.
- They can add excitement to the in-store merchandising of mature or mundane products.
- They allow small, regional firms to recover their limited marketing expenditures more quickly than advertising would.
- They allow manufacturers to make short-term reductions in idle capacity or excess inventory while maintaining list prices.
- They allow manufacturers to reach segments with differing degrees of price sensitivity.[1]

The importance that U.S. firms attach to sales promotion is at least partially reflected by Figure 11-1. In 1991, packaged-goods manufacturers spent about $72 billion on advertising and sales promotion combined. Of this amount, half went to trade promotion and one-fourth to consumer promotion; only one-

---

[1] Robert Buzzell, John Quelch, and Walter Salmon, "The Costly Bargain of Sales Promotion," *Harvard Business Review*, March–April 1990, pp. 141–149.

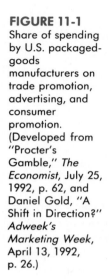

FIGURE 11-1
Share of spending by U.S. packaged-goods manufacturers on trade promotion, advertising, and consumer promotion. (Developed from "Procter's Gamble," *The Economist,* July 25, 1992, p. 62, and Daniel Gold, "A Shift in Direction?" *Adweek's Marketing Week,* April 13, 1992, p. 26.)

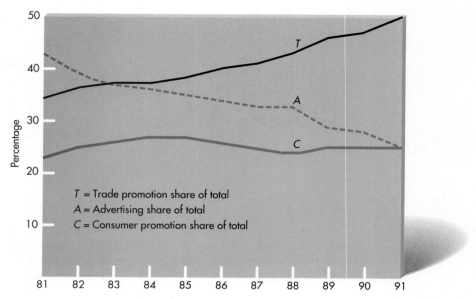

T = Trade promotion share of total
A = Advertising share of total
C = Consumer promotion share of total

fourth went to advertising. By comparison, advertising represented 43 percent of this total 10 years earlier.[2]

While a number of explanations have been offered for this shift, it seems as though five basic forces were most responsible:

1. Slow population growth has intensified the competition for market share in packaged-goods industries where promotions are most widely used.
2. Increased audience segmentation and media costs have made advertising less cost effective, while the development of targeted data bases (as discussed in Chapter 5) has made consumer promotion more cost effective.
3. More products have reached the maturity stage of the life cycle, so opportunities for differentiation decrease and price becomes more important.
4. Large retailers and wholesalers placed increasing demands on manufacturers for promotions because special cash and merchandising allowances were a significant contribution to their profits.
5. Price promotions have usually been more reliable than advertising for boosting short-term earnings, which is appealing to firms whose stock prices are under pressure to show such bottom-line results.[3]

Today numerous signs suggest trade promotion budgets may have passed their peak. For example, in 1992 Procter & Gamble decided to phase out most

[2] "Procter's Gamble," *The Economist,* July 25, 1992, pp. 61–62.
[3] Paul Farris and John Quelch, "In Defense of Price Promotion," *Sloan Management Review,* Fall 1987, p. 63.

trade promotions in favor of stable but lower list prices.[4] Nevertheless, many firms are likely to continue to spend relatively large amounts of their marketing budgets on promotion. Table 11-1 summarizes the reasons why some brands spend more heavily on promotion while others spend more heavily on advertising.

In this chapter, we will examine the ways in which managers can use sales-promotion programs to implement a marketing strategy. In particular, we will examine (1) the objectives various kinds of sales-promotion programs can achieve, (2) the factors that should be considered in selecting a specific sales-promotion alternative, and (3) procedures for developing the sales-promotion budget.

SALES-PROMOTION OBJECTIVES

The array of specific sales-promotion ideas, tactics, and activities that have been used is enormous, and it seems to grow weekly as creative marketing minds generate still more new promotions. As was the case with advertising programs, however, a sales-promotion program should not be designed until

[4] Valerie Reitman "Eliminated Discounts on P&G Goods Annoy Many Who Sell Them," *The Wall Street Journal*, Aug. 11, 1992, pp. A1, A6.

TABLE 11-1 **REASONS FOR DIFFERENCES IN RELATIVE ADVERTISING AND SALES-PROMOTION EXPENDITURES**

Lower levels of promotion relative to advertising are associated with brands that:
1. Have a profit-contribution rate above the company average
2. Have a high level of brand loyalty
3. Have a strong competitive differentiation
4. Have a high degree of perceived risk associated with purchase
5. Are in the growth and maturity stages of their life cycle
6. Have a large market share

Higher levels of promotion relative to advertising are associated with brands that:
1. Have a profit-contribution rate below the company average
2. Have little brand loyalty
3. Have little competitive differentiation
4. Are directed to children
5. Are purchased with little planning
6. Are at the introductory or decline stage of their life cycle
7. Have a marked seasonal sales pattern
8. Have a small market share
9. Face promotion-oriented competitors
10. Are in a market where private labels are important

Source: Roger Strang, *The Relationship between Advertising and Promotion in Brand Strategy*, Marketing Science Institute, Report No. 75–119, p. 13, Cambridge, MA. Reprinted by permission.

the objective is clearly understood. Moreover, the sales-promotion objective should be consistent with the marketing strategy.

Although the number of possible specific sales-promotion objectives is very large, there are a limited number of basic types of objectives that may be established.[5] Tables 11-2 and 11-3 list these types of objectives and indicate some typical programs that can be used to achieve each objective.

Objectives Directed at Final Buyers

There are five basic types of buyer actions that can be stimulated by sales promotions: inquiries, product trial, repurchase, traffic building, and increasing the rate of purchase.

STIMULATING INQUIRIES *CL*

Inquiries can include returning a form requesting additional information about a product or service or visiting an exhibit at a trade association meeting.

[5] See, for example, Ovid Rose (ed.), *The Dartnell Sales Promotion Handbook*, 6th ed., Dartnell Corp., Chicago, p. 128; and William H. Lembeck "Selecting the Right Strategy for a Successful Promotion," *Marketing and Sales Promotion: A Special Report*, Bill Publications, New York, 1978, pp. 2–4.

TABLE 11-2 **SALES-PROMOTION OBJECTIVES AND ALTERNATE PROGRAMS DIRECTED AT FINAL BUYERS**

OBJECTIVE	ALTERNATE PROGRAMS
Inquiries	Free gifts Mail-in coupons for information Catalog offers Exhibits
Product trial ■ New products ■ Related products ■ Brand switchers	Coupons Cents-off specials Free samples Contests Premiums Demonstrations
Repurchase	On-pack coupons Mail-in coupons for rebate Continuity premiums
Traffic building	Special sales Weekly specials Entertainment events Retailer coupons Premiums
Increased rate of purchase ■ Inventory building ■ Increased usage rate	Multipacks Special price on twos Information on new usage situations

TABLE 11-3	SALES-PROMOTION OBJECTIVES AND ALTERNATE PROGRAMS DIRECTED AT THE TRADE

OBJECTIVE	ALTERNATE PROGRAMS
Inventory-building	
■ New-product acceptance	Returns allowances
■ Increased space allotment	Merchandise allowances
	Slotting allowances
Promotional support	
■ Local ad feature	Promotional allowances
■ Displays	Cooperative promotions
■ Price special	Reusable display cases
	Sales contests
	Merchandise allowances

Managers can generate inquiries by offering such things as a free catalog or some premium or prize. (Often, the incentive is offered in the context of some advertising message designed to introduce the product benefits. Accordingly, such promotions must be closely coordinated with advertising programs.) A manager will often select this objective when attempting to identify and attract new prospects for a product or service. This objective is especially important when clients or customers must be periodically replenished (a problem facing colleges and the military). In addition, it is often important to attract only high-interest prospects, especially when the potential buyers are few and hard to identify. In these cases, firms that are effective in stimulating inquiries will be able to focus their follow-up sales and other marketing activities on high-interest prospects. Further, when new models or versions of a product or service are being offered, sales promotions may be designed to stimulate inquiries from past customers in order to maintain contact with prospects.

GENERATING PRODUCT TRIAL

A product trial objective is certainly appropriate in marketing new products. Free samples and coupons are usually useful in stimulating trial for low perceived-risk products because they generate a low-cost usage experience that may lead to favorable attitudes faster than advertising. For more complex, higher priced products (such as durable goods or many services) in-store demonstrations appear to be most useful. For houseware items, demonstrations have been known to increase sales by 80 to 300 percent during the week of the demonstration.[6]

Additionally, firms that market a number of different products (such as franchise extensions or complements) may use techniques such as cross-couponing to build trial for these other products. Thus, a package of Gillette

---

[6] Elaine Appleton, "Houseware Companies Are Convinced That Seeing Is Believing," *Adweek's Marketing Week*, Oct. 9, 1989, pp. 20–21.

razor blades might contain a coupon for a new Gillette Foamy shaving cream line extension.

ENCOURAGING REPURCHASE

To the extent that habit building will lead to brand loyalty (especially for low perceived-risk products), promotional incentives that "tie" a buyer to a seller may be desired. For example, coupons contained in the package that can be redeemed on the next purchase can have this type of impact and will be especially valuable in implementing retention strategies. Similarly, retailers may encourage store loyalty (or at least continued visits to the store) through special sales offered to charge-account customers or through continuity promotions. *Continuity promotions* include trading stamps, games, and contests that run over a period of weeks, or gifts distributed in increments over time (such as encyclopedias or sets of dishes). These promotions stimulate repurchase from a retail store because customers must continue to return to the store to obtain the full value of the program. Additionally, "frequent patron" programs (such as frequent shopper or frequent flyer programs) are a form of continuity promotion.

TRAFFIC BUILDING

Retailers employ sales promotions as vehicles for stimulating more store traffic from new buyers as well as for the repurchase objectives already cited. Special entertainment events (such as having authors autograph copies of their books) and special attractions placed in shopping malls may attract customers, who will then make some purchases. Additionally, by establishing price specials on so-called *leader* products (as we discussed in Chapter 9), retailers may draw customers who purchase the leader plus complementary products (at nonsale prices).

INCREASING RATES OF PURCHASE

Often the major desired effect of a promotion is to get more purchases from existing buyers. But there are two alternative strategic purposes underlying this objective: consumer loading and increased consumption rate. *Consumer loading* reflects a retention-oriented marketing strategy in which the main goal is to get buyers to stock up on the product. A buyer who is carrying above-normal stocks of a product is not likely to buy competing products. Thus, multipacks and similar promotions may be used just before new competing products are introduced or in anticipation of increased competitor promotional activity. Alternatively, the promotion may stimulate primary demand if the lower prices encourage a higher rate of consumption (often the case with products such as soft drinks or some meat products). Additionally, if the promotion includes information pertaining to new ways of using the product or new usage situations, this can complement and reinforce the price incentive to use more of the product.

Additionally, a well-known method of increasing purchase rates is the use of in-store displays. Even when displays are not combined with special prices, sales usually go up dramatically. By examining scanner data for periods covering both the use and nonuse of displays, Information Resources Inc. reports that displays are especially effective for snack foods, soft drinks, and apple juice. However, the company also reports weekly sales gains of 100 to 200 percent for other products, including soups and laundry detergents.[7]

Trade-Promotion Objectives

The fundamental purposes of trade promotions are to *push* the product through the marketing channel by getting resellers (retailers and wholesalers) to market the product aggressively and to help ensure the success of consumer promotions designed to *pull* the product through the channel. These two purposes are reflected in two types of sales-promotion objectives.

ENCOURAGING TRADE INVENTORY BUILDING

Marketers who are developing extensive consumer-oriented promotions will nearly always want to pursue this objective simultaneously. If the consumer promotion is expected to build short-run demand, retail stockouts must be avoided. Thus, manufacturers may offer special margins or extra merchandise at no extra cost to induce an increase in retailer or wholesaler inventories. In addition, special returns allowances—higher-than-usual prices paid to retailers who want to return unsold goods—may also be used to encourage retailers to risk higher inventories.

With respect to building acceptance for new products, manufacturers have increasingly encountered retailer demands for so-called slotting allowances. These allowances are either straight cash payments or free cases of the product, which are given to retailers in exchange for stocking a new product for a specified period of time. According to one source, it can easily cost $70,000 to get a truckload's worth of a new product line accepted into a chain with fifty stores. The cause of the rise in slotting allowances is the proliferation of new grocery products. In a typical supermarket the number of items carried grew from 13,000 to 26,000 during the 1980s. Retailers seeking these slotting allowances argue that most new products fail while others merely draw sales from established products within the store. In both cases, the retailer has little to gain.[8]

---

[7] Kathleen Deveny, "Displays Pay Off for Grocery Marketers," *The Wall Street Journal*, Oct. 15, 1992, p. B1.
[8] Lois Therrien, "Want Shelf Space at the Supermarket? Ante Up," *Business Week*, Aug. 7, 1989, pp. 60–61.

OBTAINING DISTRIBUTOR PROMOTIONAL ASSISTANCE

The objective of obtaining distributor promotional assistance must usually be achieved by coordinating sales promotion with personal selling. However, it is often the purpose of sales promotions offered to distributors. Sales contests and special cash or merchandise allowances may be offered in return for distributor agreements to provide special display space or to provide additional selling or advertising effort. If successful, these programs may help to ensure the success of a consumer promotion. For example, retailers may have a limited amount of space to devote to special displays. Consequently, trade-promotion incentives (usually in the form of free cases of the product being displayed) are essential to gain retailer support.

Relationship of Sales-Promotion Objectives to Marketing Strategy

As we have indicated, different types of sales promotions serve different sales-promotion objectives. In turn, each of the sales-promotion objectives is more appropriate for some marketing strategies than for others.

With respect to promotions directed toward final buyers, inquiries and product trial are generally more appropriate when the marketing strategy is either to increase the number of product-form users or to acquire new customers. Repurchase-oriented promotions support a retention strategy. Promotions for increasing the rate of purchase may support a primary-demand strategy (through increasing the rate of usage) or a retention strategy, as we discussed above. Traffic building is a broad objective and may serve any of the basic strategies, depending on the specific nature of the promotion: Weekly specials tend to stimulate retention while unique exhibits may attract new customers. Finally, trade promotions must be viewed as a means rather than an end. The basic purpose of trade promotion is to support advertising or consumer sales promotions. Thus, the different trade-promotion objectives may ultimately serve any of the marketing strategies.[9]

SELECTING A SPECIFIC SALES PROMOTION

As we suggested in the previous section, managers should establish the sales-promotion objective before selecting a specific type of sales-promotion incentive. Further, the sales-promotion objective should support the marketing strategy for the product.

A number of alternative types of incentives may be used to try to achieve the sales-promotion objective. In selecting a specific sales-promotion program, it is essential that managers examine the buying process in order to

---

[9] Kenneth Hardy, "Key Success Factors for Manufacturers' Sales Promotion in Package Goods," *Journal of Marketing*, July 1986, pp. 13–23.

understand the likelihood of response to a type of incentive. In this section, we will examine some of the most important buying process factors managers should consider in developing consumer promotions, promotions to distributors, and promotions directed at organizational buyers.

Consumer Promotions

Although relatively little research has been reported on consumer responses to specific types of promotions, managers should closely examine three facets of the consumer decision process (deal proneness, level of involvement, and purchase patterns) and two basic aspects of the promotion (method of distribution and extent of consumer franchise building), as presented in Figure 11-2.

DEAL PRONENESS

Markets can frequently be segmented in terms of *deal proneness*—the degree to which consumers are likely to search out and respond to sales-promotion incentives or "deals." Few generalities can be stated about consumer responses to sales promotions. In particular, early research is unclear about who deal-prone consumers really are. However, most recent studies suggest affluence is correlated with deal-proneness. For example, 38 percent of households with incomes over $40,000 are heavy coupon users, compared to 19 and 24 percent of households in the "under $10,000" and "$10,000 to $15,000" income categories, respectively.[10] Accordingly, a number of consumer-goods firms have used manufacturers' coupons designed and promoted by Donnelley

[10] "How Consumers Use Coupons," *Adweek's Marketing Week*, Sept. 25, 1989, special "Promote" supplement, p. P20. See also Robert Blattberg et al., "Identifying the Deal-Prone Segment," *Journal of Marketing Research*, August 1978, pp. 369–377.

FIGURE 11-2
Factors influencing consumer response to sales promotion.

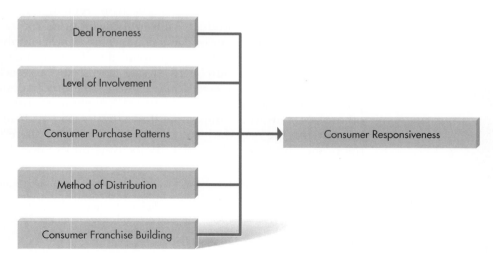

Marketing, Inc. Donnelley uses a mailing list of persons selected for "upscale demographic qualities" who tend to be heavy users of mass-distribution goods.

Additionally, coupon-prone consumers have been shown to be younger and less store loyal and brand loyal, and they are more likely to live in urban areas.[11]

LEVEL OF INVOLVEMENT

The consumer's level of involvement in the search process will have some impact on the kind of response management can anticipate. Recent research evidence suggests that the degree to which product trial leads to changing preferences depends on the type of promotion. For example, one recent study suggests that sustained loyalty to a brand that is first purchased during a sales promotion will be greater where the effort involved in trying the brand is *high* relative to the economic value obtained. This suggests coupons requiring some consumer effort to cut out, save, and redeem may be more effective in the long run than simple on-package or on-shelf price deals because they may increase the likelihood of conversion to the new brand.[12]

Additionally, when consumer involvement is low, behavioral learning theory suggests that, in general, reinforcers (such as coupons and premiums) work best when they are immediate rather than delayed. This implies that mail incentives will be weaker than in-package, on-package, or cents-off incentives when involvement is low.[13]

CONSUMER PURCHASE PATTERNS

Frequently, the effectiveness and efficiency of a program can be increased by knowing buyer purchase rates. That is, incentives should be available long enough to allow all heavy buyers an opportunity to respond during their normal purchase cycles. However, if the program lasts too long, all potential new buyers will have had an opportunity to buy. As a result, most sales in the later stages of the program will come from regular buyers who are simply stocking up on the product while the lower price (or other incentive) is available. (One advantage of using coupons instead of simply offering a lower sales price is that the number of coupons distributed is the upper limit on the quantity that can be purchased at sale prices, and so stocking up is more difficult.) Similarly, size loyalty may exist in some product categories, so that a promotion on one size may not attract competitors' customers who prefer other sizes. This would imply that if size loyalty exists, a firm should offer the incentive on the size in which it has the *lowest* market share if the purpose of the promotion is to induce trial. By focusing on its lowest market-share size,

[11] Kapil Bawa and Robert Shoemaker, "The Coupon-Prone Consumer: Some Findings Based on Purchase Behavior across Product Classes," *Journal of Marketing*, October 1987, pp. 99–110.
[12] Joe Dodson, Alice Tybout, and Brian Sternthal, "Impact of Deals and Deal Retraction on Brand Switching," *Journal of Marketing Research*, February 1978, pp. 72–81.
[13] Michael Rothschild and William Gaidis, "Behavioral Learning Theory: Its Relevance to Marketing and Promotions," *Journal of Marketing*, Spring 1981, pp. 70–78.

the firm will reduce the proportion of coupons used by its regular customers and will be more likely to attract competitors' customers.[14]

METHOD OF DISTRIBUTION

Consumer response to sales promotions will, in large part, depend on the amount and type of search effort required of the consumer. For example, in-pack or on-pack coupons generally have the highest redemption rate because regular users do not have to exert much effort to acquire these coupons and because these customers are already favorably disposed to the product. In general, however, redemption rates have fallen over the past decade from 6 percent to 2 percent for the direct mail and free-standing insert coupons that are most popular with manufacturers. Consequently, increased emphasis has been placed on focusing promotions more precisely using two key techniques:

- *Consumer data bases* (such as those of Land's End and Nestlé, described in Chapter 7). Such data bases allow firms to target regular customers or heavy users of the product category, thus ensuring greater response to the promotional offer.
- *In-store promotion systems* (such as Catalina Marketing's Checkout Coupon System or Vision Value Club). These systems provide coupons or other incentives in the store based on actual purchases. For example, in the Catalina system, as checkout scanners read bar codes, a Catalina computer spits out coupons for competitive or complementary products, or even for the same product, depending on the objective of the manufacturer using the system. Catalina reports attaining an average redemption rate of 7.5 percent.[15]

CONSUMER FRANCHISE BUILDING

A major distinction among sales promotions directed at buyers is the degree to which the promotion is supportive of brand attributes, benefits, or characterization—*consumer-franchise-building* (CFB) promotion—as opposed to being a straight economic incentive (non-CFB promotion). CFB promotions are free samples, premiums, demonstrations, or coupons that are presented through an effective sales message that reinforces the brand image. For example, General Foods offered a free stoneware mug as a mail-in premium in a promotion in which its Maxim brand (a freeze-dried instant coffee) was described as "the spoonful rich enough for a mug full." A more complex example involving the same company is a data-based promotion directed at households with children aged 3 to 12.

---

[14] P. J. Robinson et al., *Promotional Decisions Using Mathematical Models*, Allyn and Bacon, Boston, 1967, pp. 79–81.
[15] Michael McCarthy, "P&G Takes Back the Supermarket," *Adweek's Marketing Week*, Apr. 13, 1992, p. 4, and "Buy Theirs, Get Ours Free," *The Economist*, Sept. 5, 1992, p. 68.

General Foods created a data base of four million households composed mainly of users of its Kool-Aid product and of heavy pre-sweetened cereal users. The company then produced a magazine for kids called *What's Hot* containing educational articles, free posters, and a page for parents. The data base was used for several promotions. One for Post pre-sweetened cereals involved sending books and games designed to build brand image along with coupons. Results indicated Post received three times the sales results that were typical for direct mail coupons. At the same time, 90 percent of mothers in the target households said they would welcome additional promotions of this type.[16]

The use of CFB-type promotions is often viewed as a way to maintain a brand's image and to reduce the chances of building a high degree of *price-sensitivity* among consumers. This is an especially important consideration for products in the growth and maturity stages, because as consumers become more familiar with alternative brands and as products become more technologically mature, price may come to be a primary factor in the choice process. Even those brands with strong quality images may suffer losses in sales if extensive non-CFB promotions are used, unless they have been clearly differentiated on a product attribute or unless they have vastly superior distribution.

Promotions to Resellers

As discussed earlier, trade promotions (those directed at retailers or wholesalers) are designed to achieve either inventory building or promotional support. Indeed, it may be necessary to achieve both of these sales-promotion objectives to ensure the success of consumer promotions.

Unfortunately, many trade promotions are not achieving these objectives. Specifically, there is evidence of three major problems with trade sales promotions.

1. Many trade buyers respond to promotions by purchasing for normal inventory. In some cases, buyers buy in large volume during deals to avoid buying at normal prices.
2. Trade buyers often accept the incentive but fail to perform the promotional requirements expected.
3. Some retailers make purchases beyond their own requirements during price "deals" and then resell the discounted merchandise to other retailers at a profit.[17]

Although these problems are not easily resolved, managers can take several steps to reduce the severity of them.

[16] Jock Bickert, *Adventures in Relevance Marketing*, 2nd ed., Briefcase Books, Denver, 1991, p. 37.
[17] John Quelch, "It's Time to Make Trade Promotion More Productive," *Harvard Business Review*, May–June 1983, pp. 130–136.

First, managers must understand the distributor's needs with respect to the product category. Some understanding can be gained by knowing the kinds of pricing programs the distributor uses. For example, price-oriented promotions (such as merchandise allowances) may be more effective in gaining support from retailers who are volume-oriented. Similarly, promotions that help to build a retailer's image on quality may be more important for margin-oriented retailers.

In the latter case, cooperative advertising programs may be more effective because these promotions are similar to consumer franchise building. Indeed one recent study suggests retailers are more likely to use trade allowances for advertising than for deep price cuts or for display.[18]

Managers should also recognize the profit impact of a sales promotion on a dealer's space and inventory constraints and on the retailer's assortment of products. For example, many manufacturers may attempt to run promotions simultaneously. When a large number of products in a similar category are promoted at the same time, distributor attention, space, and inventory investment will all be divided. Accordingly, off-season promotions are more likely to generate distributor support. Because resellers are likely to vary along these and other dimensions, most experts now believe greater flexibility should be provided in defining the promotional performance requirements expected of retailers. Thus, firms such as Procter & Gamble often allow retailers to decide whether to support a product through cooperative advertising or special displays or by means of some other mechanism, depending on which will best fit that retailer's needs.

The advent of electronic scanning has certainly improved the ability of firms to assess the impact of consumer promotions on retailer performance as well as on the performance of the brand. Thus, managers are increasingly aware of which kinds of trade efforts will pay off. If manufacturers can show how a given promotion affects *total* sales for a given retailer it will be easier to gain trade acceptance. For example, Procter & Gamble salespeople were able to gain extensive support for featuring Liquid Tide when they presented scanner results showing that the product attracted shoppers who spent more on that shopping trip.[19]

International Considerations

In many cases, managers will find that sales-promotion programs will be more difficult to globalize than other programs. Specifically, there are three fundamental reasons why promotions tend to be localized: cultural differences in product usage and perceptions; large variations in retailing and distribution

---

[18] A useful discussion of these steps is in Rockney Walters, "An Empirical Investigation into Retailer Responses to Manufacturer Trade Promotions," *Journal of Retailing*, Summer 1989, pp. 253–272.

[19] Laurie Petersen, "Getting Smart," *Adweek's Marketing Week*, Jan. 8, 1990, special "Promote" supplement, p. P8.

structures and practices; and inconsistent legal treatment of promotions. To illustrate the impact of these factors, consider the following examples and facts confronting consumer packaged-goods marketers in the European community.

Cultural differences. Countries differ in terms of the degree to which price promotions would hurt a brand's quality image. For example, in Spain beer is simply a refreshing beverage, but in northern Europe beer is a part of the national heritage.

Distribution structure and practices. In France, retailing is heavily concentrated in large "hypermarket" stores that carry everything from auto parts to clothing to groceries, but in Spain most of the population shops in small rural stores where sales-promotion activity is modest.

Legal restrictions. While there are virtually no restrictions on sales-promotion practices in Great Britain, Germany has extensive legal barriers. Additionally, differences exist in the application of "value-added" (sales) taxes. A recent Italian law was designed to place a 45 percent tax levy on premiums, for instance. Presently, there is little uniformity governing the application of these taxes, which vary across nations on regular sales as well.

SALES-PROMOTION BUDGETS

The answer to the question, "How much should be spent on sales promotion?" is an elusive one. Just as in the case of advertising, the sales results of a given level of expenditure are difficult to predict. In fact, managers often find it difficult to estimate the costs that will be incurred by a sales-promotion program. However, it is both necessary and possible to analyze the profitability impact of a sales promotion in order to establish a sales-promotion budget.

In this section, we will review the basic elements that should be considered in the budgeting process. These elements are depicted in Figure 11-3. Additionally, we illustrate the approaches that can be used in developing the budget. Because consumer promotions are the most widely used, and because they are generally the most complex from a budgeting perspective, our discussion will focus on the budgeting process for those types of promotions.

Determining Costs

Most promotions will incur direct fixed costs and variable costs. Among the direct fixed costs are the costs of physically distributing samples, mailing coupons, and placing advertisements carrying coupons, inquiry slips, and premium offers. Additionally, contribution margins may be reduced, because the value of the coupon or cents-off special is effectively a price reduction. Further, when coupons are used, retailers must be remunerated for each coupon redeemed (usually at the rate of 7 cents each), and this represents an increase in the variable cost per unit.

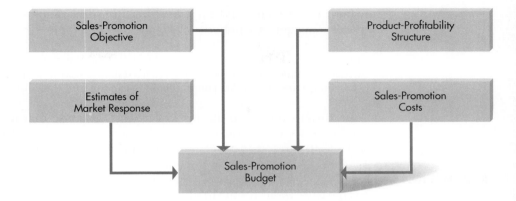

FIGURE 11-3
Factors to be considered in developing the sales-promotion budget.

One key problem in estimating costs is that contribution margins are reduced only on those items actually purchased at promotional prices. Therefore, some estimate of sales response will be necessary to determine the actual reduction in contribution margins.

Additionally, when coupons are used, some retailers will redeem coupons even when the product is not actually purchased and then redeem the face value of the coupon, as well as receiving the 7-cent handling charge. While this procedure (called *misredemption*) is a fraud, it is believed to be very extensive and is highly costly to manufacturers. Thus, some provision for estimating the level of misredemptions should be considered in projecting costs.

Estimating Market Response

In Chapter 10, we suggested that managers must have some estimate of sales response in order to set the tentative advertising budget. These estimates are even more critical in sales-promotion budgeting, for two reasons. First, as noted already, some costs cannot be estimated without estimates of sales response. Second, unlike advertising objectives, sales objectives generally have a very direct link to sales volume. Product-trial, repurchase, increasing the rate of purchase, and traffic-building objectives are specifically sales-oriented. Promotional support and inquiries can be expected to result in increased sales with a small time lag. Consequently, the ability to predict response will enable the manager to assess not only the profitability consequences but also the degree to which the program objective will be achieved.

In developing estimates of market response, managers generally rely on judgment. These judgments should reflect a manager's understanding of the buying process (as discussed earlier in this chapter) and the firm's experience in promoting the product (or in promoting similar products). Additionally, managers may use experiments to estimate market response. This approach is especially useful for organizations that have limited experience in sales promotion and for comparing two or more alternative incentives. In particular, electronic scanner data results (as discussed in Chapter 6) are extremely useful for both experiments and for extracting historical ratios. As the promotion services manager of Kimberly-Clark put it:

> Before it was more of a guess, a gut feeling. Traditional wisdom entered into the decision-making process. Now we have hard data supporting our planning process. We can accurately predict coupon liability even before the coupon drops.[20]

Specifically, there are six types of market response that managers should examine: (1) redemption rates, (2) displacement rates, (3) acquisition rates, (4) stock-up rates, (5) conversion rates, and (6) product-line effects.

REDEMPTION RATES

This measure indicates the total number (or percentage) of buyers responding to the incentive. As suggested earlier in the chapter, the percentage of coupons that will be redeemed is largely a function of how they are distributed. However, there are a number of other factors that will determine the percentage of coupons redeemed or the number of buyers responding to other kinds of incentives (such as games, premiums, or cents-off deals). Specifically, redemption rates will be higher when[21]

- The product or brand is well established so that the value of the incentive is well understood.
- The product is widely distributed or easy to obtain so that coupon redemption is easy or there is a low effort required to acquire the incentive.
- The product form is used by a large percentage of households or organizations.
- The frequency of purchase of the product form is high.
- The value of the incentive is high (although coupon users will buy their regular brand using 25-cent coupons, the average face value necessary to obtain trial for a new brand is 58 cents, according to one recent study).[22]

Additionally, it appears as though the impact of the value of the incentive depends upon the brand and the product category. That is, recent research on price promotions suggests that

- High market-share brands are more inelastic with respect to a brand price promotion than low-share brands.
- A brand's sales are more inelastic with respect to a price promotion if the brand or category is one that receives frequent store display.

---

[20] Amy Gross, "Kimberly-Clark Masters the Science of Couponing," *Adweek's Marketing Week*, Jan. 8, 1990, special "Promote" supplement, p. P9.
[21] For additional discussion see Don E. Schultz and William A. Robinson, *Sales Promotion Essentials*, Crain Books, Chicago, 1982, pp. 29–31.
[22] "How Consumers Use Coupons," *Adweek's Marketing Week*, Sept. 25, 1989, special "Promote" supplement, pp. P20–P21.

■ A brand's sales are more elastic with respect to a price promotion if the brand or category is frequently featured in local newspaper ads.[23]

DISPLACEMENT RATES

Some of the sales made during a promotion will simply displace sales that would otherwise have been made to regular buyers at the normal price. In fact, studies show that 75 percent of coupons are redeemed by consumers who already use the couponed brand.[24] Accordingly, managers must determine the amount of the lost contribution margin that results from selling to regular buyers at discounted prices. In general, regular buyers of a brand will be more likely to take advantage of coupons or cents-off specials than will nonregular buyers. Consequently, the redemption rate will typically be a percentage that is somewhat greater than the product's market share. Additionally, the displacement rate will depend on the method of coupon distribution or the method by which potential buyers are made aware of a promotion. For example, in-pack coupons "good on next purchase" and incentives handed out or mailed out to regular customers are likely to create very large displacement rates (perhaps intentionally if the objective is simply to build repurchase rates).

ACQUISITION RATES

Some of the buyers purchasing during a sales promotion will be nonregular buyers who purchase the specific brand or product because of the incentive. Note that this group can include buyers who usually purchase another brand and buyers who previously were nonusers of the product form. The percentage of redeemers who are not regular buyers will normally be greater when

■ Average purchase quantity is high.
■ Perceived risks and prices are generally low for the product form.
■ The incentive is directed toward demographic groups or geographic areas in which the product or firm's market share is relatively low.
■ Direct mail is used to distribute coupons or other information about a promotion (as mentioned earlier in this chapter).[25]

Managers should note that the displacement rate and the acquisition rate may not add up to 100 percent of the number of redemptions. That is, there is one more category of response that managers must consider when identifying redeemers—stock-up effects.

[23] Ruth Bolton, "The Relationship between Market Characteristics and Promotional Price Elasticities," *Marketing Science*, Spring 1989, pp. 153–169.
[24] Liz Murphy, "Redemption Isn't Always Salvation in Couponing," *Sales and Marketing Management*, Jan. 13, 1986, p. 46.
[25] Some findings that support these conclusions are available in Karl Irons, John D. C. Little, and Robert L. Klein, "Determinants of Coupon Effectiveness," in *Advances and Practices of Marketing Science* (1983 Proceedings of the ORSA/TIMS Marketing Science Conference), pp. 157–164.

STOCK-UP RATES

If an incentive is sufficiently large, some of the sales made during a promotion period will reflect "borrowed" sales from future sales periods, as buyers stock up on the product while special prices are in effect. Although this effect may be desirable when the sales-promotion objective is to build buyer inventories, managers should recognize that this will result in some reduction in sales in the postpromotion period. Additionally, the borrowed sales are made at a lower contribution margin than would be obtained if the stock-up did not occur. Consequently, as in the case of displaced sales, managers should determine the reduction in total contribution resulting from these sales. In attempting to estimate the magnitude of stock-up effects, managers should recognize that stock-up effects will be greater when

- Buyers are reasonably sure that they will use the extra amounts purchased in the future.
- Buyers will not have a large amount of space or money tied up in inventory.
- The risk of spoilage or obsolescence is low.
- Promotions are directed toward regular buyers or large market-share territories.
- No limits on volume (such as two to a customer) are established.

Importantly, coupons and in-store price promotions have been shown to change stock-up rates differently. A price promotion is only temporary and usually applies to multiple purchases, so stock-up effects are generally high. By contrast, coupons (usually) do not have short-term expiration dates and are only good for one purchase, so the incentive to stock up is less.[26]

CONVERSION RATES

When the marketing strategy is to build market share, the role of sales promotion is normally to build a larger customer base. Additionally, even large market-share firms may find they can improve their share among demographic groups or geographic areas in which their market share is lower than it is overall. In these cases, the primary objective of sales promotion is to build product trial in order to convert nonregular buyers into regular buyers. Indeed, the primary justification for sales promotion in this case is to gain converts for a product or brand. Accordingly, managers should attempt to estimate the level of postpromotion sales that will come from customers acquired during the promotion period. (As suggested earlier in this chapter, conversion rates appear to be higher for promotions requiring high degrees of customer effort relative to the value of the incentive. However, conversion rates are very difficult to estimate without some base of historical experience to draw upon.)

[26] See Robert Blattberg, Gary Eppen, and Joshua Lieberman, "A Theoretical and Empirical Evaluation of Price Deals for Consumer Nondurables," *Journal of Marketing*, Winter 1981, pp. 116–129.

Most of the results from research on the effects of couponing, however, suggest that brand-switching consumers generally revert to their own brands after making a coupon redemption or a promotion purchase.[27] Thus, managers should make conservative assumptions about conversion rates when attempting to project the outcome of a given price promotion.

PRODUCT-LINE EFFECTS

Managers should recognize that sales promotions are very similar to price cuts. Consequently, cross-elasticities of demand may exist between the promoted product and complementary or substitute products. Retailers and other firms that offer many complementary products should, therefore, attempt to identify increases in sales of these products (that is, drag-along sales) due to increased sales in the promoted leader product. Similarly, if the promotion creates sales shifts among different sizes or models of a product, such cannibalized sales should be considered in evaluating the total impact of the promotion.

Recent evidence suggests that complementary effects can be very strong. Especially if consumers stockpile promoted products, like cake mixes and spaghetti sauce, sales of complements (cake frosting and spaghetti) are likely to increase even though these products are not on sale.[28]

Figure 11-4 summarizes the relationships among the six types of responses to be estimated.

Assessing Profitability Implications

If managers can identify the direct costs associated with a sales promotion and can develop some rough estimates of market response, the profitability implications of a given promotion can be assessed by comparing the "normal" contribution over the period of the promotion with the expected promotional contribution. As Figure 11-5 indicates, there are three steps involved in assessing profitability implications: (1) Estimate the reduced contribution from displaced and stock-up sales; (2) estimate the increased contribution from incremental sales to new buyers; and (3) subtract the direct costs of the sales promotion. These steps are illustrated in the following example.

Linkster (introduced in Chapter 6) produces a line of golf apparel and accessories. In trying to expand sales of its specially designed golf sweaters (currently selling at a rate of 40,000 per year), the company is taking out a full-page advertisement in *Golf Digest* (circulation 1.4 million). The total cost (including artwork) of the ad is $96,000. Part of the advertisement contains a $20 coupon on any Linkster sweater.

[27] Kapil Bawa and Robert Shoemaker, "The Effects of a Direct Mail Coupon on Brand Choice Behavior," *Journal of Marketing Research*, November 1987, pp. 370–376.

[28] Rockney Walters, "Assessing the Impact of Retail Price Promotions on Product Substitution, Complementary Purchase, and Interstore Sales Displacement," *Journal of Marketing*, April 1991, pp. 17–28.

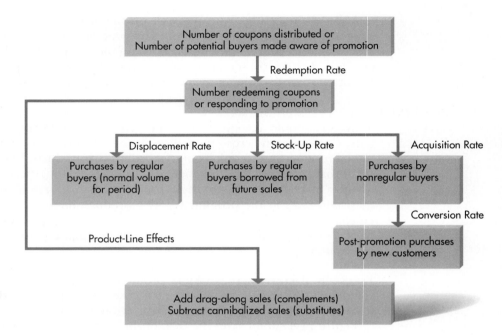

FIGURE 11-4
Relationship among types of market responses to sales promotions.

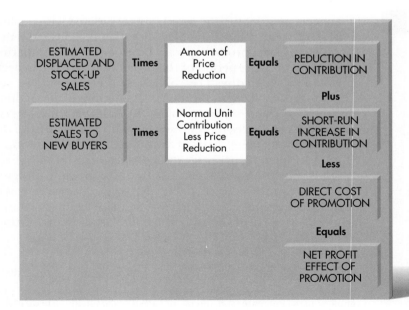

FIGURE 11-5
Assessing the profitability of a sales promotion.

As indicated in Chapter 6, the normal unit contribution on a sweater is $37. Linkster will reimburse its dealers for the $20 coupon plus 25 cents for the expense of handling the redemptions. Thus, Linkster's contribution margin on coupon sales will be:

$$\$37.00 - \$20.00 - \$0.25 = \$16.75$$

Based on information from *Golf Digest* and industry experience, Linkster's marketing manager anticipates that 0.5 to 1 percent of the coupons will be redeemed and that 15 to 20 percent of the redemptions will be displaced sales. Given these estimates, the estimated sales resulting from the coupon promotion will be between

$$1.4 \text{ million} \times .005 = 7000$$

and

$$1.4 \text{ million} \times .01 = 14,000$$

The profitability consequences of this promotion can be identified in Table 11-4. While each sale to a new buyer generates $16.75 in incremental contribution, each displaced sale reduces Linkster's contribution by $37.00 − $16.75, or $20.25. Subtracting the direct costs of $96,000 and the lost contribution on displaced sales from the incremental revenue from new buyers yields the expected net impact in total contribution. As we can see, the consequences are quite sensitive to our estimates of redemption rate and displacement rate. Under the best conditions, the promotion generates a $60,800 gain, but under the most pessimistic estimates (that is, lower redemp-

TABLE 11-4

ESTIMATING THE LIKELY PROFIT CONSEQUENCES OF LINKSTER'S PROMOTION

	0.5% REDEMPTION		1% REDEMPTION	
	15% DISPLACED	20% DISPLACED	15% DISPLACED	20% DISPLACED
Total redeemed	7,000	7,000	14,000	14,000
■ New buyers	5,950	5,600	11,900	11,200
■ Displaced sales	1,050	1,400	2,100	2,800
Increased contribution on sales to new buyers (at $16.75)	$99,663	$93,800	$199,325	$187,600
Minus lost contribution on displaced sales (at $20.25)	$21,263	$28,350	$42,525	$56,700
Minus increase in direct costs	$96,000	$96,000	$96,000	$96,000
Net impact on total contribution	($17,600)	($30,550)	$60,800	$34,900

tion and higher displacement), the promotion results in a $30,550 decrease in contribution.

Importantly, however, this (or any) promotion should not be judged solely on the profit consequences. Some reduced profitability may well be acceptable to management if the promotion has achieved its primary objective of acquiring new customers. In this particular case, nonregular buyers are expected to purchase between 5600 and 11,900 sweaters during the promotion, and many of these new customers are likely to purchase additional sweaters in the future. Of course, Linkster's marketing manager should also examine the company's experience and the buying process to determine whether the promotion will cannibalize sales of other products or create any drag-along sales from complementary products.

In sum, the Linkster example indicates several of the problems faced by sales-promotion managers. Although the profitability consequences of sales-promotion programs can be calculated, they will often be based on very rough estimates of market response. Firms that use a given sales-promotion device frequently, and that carefully monitor the results in terms of these types of market response, will be able to develop a fairly high degree of accuracy in projecting the effects of the sales promotion. Firms with limited experience can use management's knowledge of market share and of the buying-process factors in order to project displacement, conversion, and stocking-up effects. All firms can also use the experience of sales-promotion specialists in estimating coupon-redemption rates. But they must always regard these figures as rough estimates, and be prepared for a range of results.

Testing and Monitoring the Program

In addition to using experience and judgment, managers can use test-marketing experiments to predict the kind of market response that will occur—at least in terms of total sales and in terms of coupon redemptions.

In order to obtain precise information on displacement and conversion rates, however, managers should supplement test marketing by employing other research techniques. For example, panels of consumers may be employed. By monitoring specially selected households' purchasing patterns over time, brand-switching behavior and changes in purchase rates can be measured to estimate conversion and displacement effects. Additionally, when industry sales data are known, changes in competitors' retail sales and market shares can be measured by using syndicated services such as A. C. Nielsen. Increasingly, however, large packaged-goods firms are relying on electronic test markets (discussed in Chapter 6) for detailed tracking of sales promotions because such services provide the most comprehensive information.

Additionally, managers are finding that the effectiveness of sales promotions for a given product may vary substantially across geographic areas. As we saw in Chapter 5, product consumption rates can vary dramatically across ZIP code clusters. Thus, it is generally wise to test different versions of promotions (when feasible) in different markets and to measure performance in a way that allows management to observe any geographic differences in response.

CONCLUSION

The recent rate of growth in sales-promotion activity appears to reflect the effectiveness of this marketing tool in influencing demand. However, several cautionary notes are in order to users of sales promotions.

First, the long-term impact of sales promotions on brand equity is not certain. Some feel promotion can damage the brand image, especially if it is not combined with consumer-franchise-building activity. A judicious mix of advertising and sales promotion would generally be advisable. This means management should stimulate closer coordination between advertising and sales-promotion programs and should involve advertising agencies in the sales-promotion decision process.

Second, managers have much to learn about the ways in which buyers and distributors respond to promotions. For a given objective, a number of sales-promotion alternatives are usually available. In order to make intelligent choices among these options, more research is needed to determine the relative effectiveness of various programs.

Third, sales promotions must be coordinated with advertising programs (to communicate the special offer) and with sales programs (to follow up on customers' inquiries and trade support). This means clearly defined objectives

FIGURE 11-6
Relationship of sales promotion to marketing strategy, situation analysis, and other marketing programs.

SARDUCCI PASTA SAUCE: PROMOTING A LINE EXTENSION

Sarducci is a regional marketer of premium heat-and-serve pasta sauces. In 1992, the company introduced a new "Extra Hearty" version of its tomato-based pasta sauce to go with its regular tomato sauce and meat sauce offerings. Together the existing products held a 10 percent share of the regional pasta sauce market. Extra Hearty was priced to the consumer at $2.19 per jar, compared with $1.89 for the regular tomato-based sauce. Retailers paid Sarducci $20 for a case of twelve jars of Extra Hearty and $17.25 for a case of twelve jars of regular tomato sauce. Sarducci's variable cost per jar was 60 cents on Extra Hearty and 50 cents on regular.

To introduce the new product, Sarducci planned to distribute 8 million coupons worth 30 cents on the purchase of Extra Hearty sauce, using a cooperative direct mail service. The Sarducci coupon would be in a package with several other coupons, targeted to selected carrier routes in certain ZIP codes. The cost of printing and distributing coupons would be $50,000 plus 7 cents (to retailers) for each coupon redeemed.

Based on the firm's experience in prior coupon promotions, Sarducci's marketing manager expected redemptions to run between 2 and 4 percent. Additionally, Sarducci expected to spend $20,000 for in-store displays to introduce the new item, $25,000 in merchandise allowances for retailers who set up the displays, and $150,000 in spot television advertisements announcing the new product.

1. Set up a worksheet along the lines of the one in Table 11-4 for projecting the likely profitability consequences of this promotion.
2. a. For each set of assumptions in your worksheet, what level of repeat future purchases is necessary to cover the cost of the promotion?
   b. How would you go about assessing the likelihood that these levels of repeat will be realized?
3. Assume the average pasta sauce buyer purchases the product about once every 3 weeks. One month after the coupons are delivered, redemptions total 180,000, and sales of Sarducci's regular tomato sauce are 45,000 units lower than would be expected if the new product had not been brought out. Is this information sufficient for management to evaluate the short-run effects of the promotion? If yes, what has management learned? If no, what other information is needed?

and logically developed programs will be essential if these programs are to work in a synchronized way to implement the marketing strategy.

In this chapter we have presented several concepts and tools managers can use to develop effective sales promotions. In addition, we have described a process for combining various kinds of information in order to select programs that will be consistent with the marketing strategy and with a product's profitability requirements. This process is summarized in Figure 11-6.

To review some of these elements and their relationships to one another, consider the sales-promotion program of Sarducci Pasta Sauce.

QUESTIONS AND SITUATIONS FOR DISCUSSION

1. What sales-promotion objective and program would be most appropriate for each of the following? Why?
   a. A leading brand of spaghetti
   b. A new substance-abuse health care facility
   c. A lawn-care company
   d. A sports magazine

2. Two banks (in different markets) are offering a set of silverware as a premium. One bank is offering the premium at no charge to customers who deposit $500 in an account. The other bank is offering the premium for $5 plus a deposit of $500. Taking into account the buying process factors discussed in this chapter, discuss reasons why the $5 offer may be as effective as (or even more effective than) the no-charge premium offer in generating a response.

3. In the March of Dimes' January 1993 annual fund-raising drive, 850,000 volunteers agreed to hand out booklets of manufacturers' coupons to 14 million homes targeted for appeals. Manufacturers who participated paid $140,000 to the March of Dimes for each coupon inserted in the booklet. What are the advantages of this promotion to the March of Dimes? To manufacturers who participate?

4. For which of the following brands would the level of promotion be lowest relative to the level of advertising expenditure? Explain your answer.
   a. K-Mart paint
   b. Jell-O pudding
   c. Minute Maid frozen orange juice

5. Giorgio of Beverly Hills had the top selling perfume on the market, *Giorgio*, in 1989 when it decided to introduce a perfume for a slightly older and wealthier target. The new perfume was called *Red*, and the company relied heavily on a sampling campaign to introduce it. Giorgio's research had revealed that, if a woman wore a fragrance at least three times, she was more likely to buy it. The company obtained mailing lists of department stores' preferred charge customers and mailed them a three-day supply of *Red* in red tubes along with an announcement that the product would be available at their department store in two weeks. *Red* achieved a $90 million sales volume in its first year, and became the leading seller.
   Discuss the aspects of this promotion that contributed to its success.

6. In general, which of the following kinds of sales responses do you think would be most *difficult* to predict for a firm with extensive experience in sales promotion?
   a. Displacement rates
   b. Conversion rates
   c. Coupon redemption rates

7. General Foods has begun to consider more carefully regional differences in brand sales before embarking on sales promotions. For example, Country Time Drink Mix was experiencing a declining share of market nationally but was sufficiently strong in certain regions to warrant continued support. Accordingly, promotions were developed at a regional level in order to appeal to consumers and to retail buyers more effectively. For example, in Dallas, the company ran a picnic to accompany a Willie Nelson concert. The firm offered 40-cent coupons on Country Time products in a print ad describing Nelson's Fourth of July picnic. Additionally, a local country music station promoted a contest in which anyone at the picnic spotted with any Country Time label would win $25 in groceries at selected supermarkets. To participate, supermarkets had to meet certain product display requirements. The promotion boosted sales volume by 65 percent.

Discuss the facets of this program that helped make it successful in terms of short-run sales. Are there any features of the program that would also lead to enhanced long-term sales?

8. In the fall of 1990, Quaker Oats Company launched Quaker Direct, a system that delivers coupons for Quaker products to households that are individually targeted based on a promotional data base run by Computerized Marketing Technologies of New York. Thus, only households with dogs will receive coupons for Gaines Burgers. Moreover, coupon values will vary by household. Finally, because each coupon is coded, Quaker can track redemptions by households. The system also permits Quaker to design surveys to detect changing customer needs. To attract and retain these households, Quaker will also run sweepstakes and contests for participants.

The cost of Quaker Direct is about $27.50 per 1000 households reached. This is double the rate of independent targeted-household services and four times the cost of distributing free-standing inserts. Given this higher cost, what offsetting benefits might Quaker receive that relate to enhanced future sales-promotion opportunities?

9. McDonald's is one of the leading practitioners of sales promotion in the world. Not only are national promotions such as games, contests, and special meal combinations offered frequently, but individual stores and regions offer a wide array of local promotions, such as special celebrity appearances and tie-ins with local charities. When combined with extensive advertising, these programs create a high level of awareness of the company and its products. Nevertheless, eating at McDonald's is a discretionary activity, and the competition in the restaurant business is intense. Thus, most promotions are designed to do more than build awareness.

In January 1989, McDonald's implemented a "$.99 Big Mac" promotion to celebrate the twentieth anniversary of that sandwich. National television and radio ads ran for the first 2 weeks of the 3-week promotion period. The ad campaign was funded out of the cooperative advertising funds provided by franchisees. (The actual promotion lasted for 3 weeks.) Local stores were responsible for buying in-store displays and point-of-purchase materials to remind customers of the promotion. Additionally, each store was responsible for adding the extra labor required because of the increased business such promotions generate. In a typical store this might amount to $2000 for a 3-week promotion of this sort.

The results of the Big Mac promotion in one Florida outlet are given below. The sales data contrast the 3 weeks prior to the promotion with the promotion period's sales. Both of these periods are normally high-volume periods for the company.

    a. What were the probable sales-promotion objectives of this promotion?

    b. Why would McDonald's run a promotion of this magnitude during what is normally a high-volume period?

    c. How would the various issues discussed under "Selecting a Specific Sales Promotion" in this chapter have been useful in considering the design of the Big Mac promotion?

    d. Outline the various categories of sales and costs that would need to be considered in evaluating the profitability of the Big Mac promotion. (Identify the additional data needed for a complete evaluation.)

	3 WEEKS PRIOR	PROMOTION PERIOD
Sales	$27,285	$33,184
Transactions	8692	10,745
Average check	$ 3.15	$ 3.09
Big Mac	1191	4221
Quarter Pounder	1033	800
McDLT	310	219
Nuggets	554	578
Salads	449	434
Filet	790	705
Regular fry	2322	2876
Medium fry	406	597
Large fry	1479	2084
Regular drink	1118	1304
Medium drink	1549	1731
Large drink	1047	1161
32-oz. drink	258	256

SUGGESTED ADDITIONAL READINGS

Bawa, Kapil, and Robert Shoemaker, "Analyzing Incremental Sales from a Direct Mail Coupon Promotion," *Journal of Marketing*, July 1989, pp. 66–78.

Blattberg, Robert, Thomas Buesing, Peter Peacock, and Subrata Sen, "Identifying the Deal-Prone Segment," *Journal of Marketing Research*, August 1978, pp. 369–377.

Bolton, Ruth, "The Relationship between Market Characteristics and Promotional Price Elasticities," *Market Science*, Spring 1989, pp. 153–169.

Buzzell, Robert, John A. Quelch, and Walter Salmon, "The Costly Bargain of Trade Promotion," *Harvard Business Review*, March–April 1990, pp. 141–149.

Fader, Peter, and Leonard Lodish, "A Cross-Category Analysis of Category Structure and Promotional Activity for Grocery Products," *Journal of Marketing*, October 1990, pp. 52–64.

Farris, Paul, and John A. Quelch, "In Defense of Price Promotion," *Sloan Management Review*, Fall 1987, pp. 63–69.

Hardy, Kenneth, "Key Success Factors for Manufacturers' Sales Promotions in Package Goods," *Journal of Marketing*, July 1986, pp. 13–23.

Jones, John Philip, "The Double Jeopardy of Sales Promotions," *Harvard Business Review*, September–October 1990, pp. 145–152.

Varadarajan, P. Rajan, "Cooperative Sales Promotion: An Idea Whose Time Has Come," *Journal of Consumer Marketing*, Winter 1986, pp. 15–33.

Walters, Rockney, "An Empirical Investigation into Retailer Response to Manufacturer Trade Promotions," *Journal of Retailing*, Summer 1989, pp. 253–272.

CHAPTER 12

SALES AND DISTRIBUTION PROGRAMS: ESTABLISHING OBJECTIVES AND APPEALS

OVERVIEW

Sales and distribution programs include all activities that involve direct personal contact with final buyers or with wholesale or retail distributors. Principally, these activities focus on three functions:

- Communicating individually-tailored sales messages
- Providing customer service—information or assistance regarding product features, order status, or complaints for individual customers
- Coordinating the scheduling and methods of product delivery

These activities are of paramount importance in executing a marketing strategy when individual buyers or distributors have highly complex and varied needs and wants. In such circumstances, personal interaction is critical to properly understand and respond to each customer's buying situation or problem.

Although the range of activities involved in sales and distribution programs seems rather broad, in reality these activities are all a part of the sales function in a typical organization. Indeed, individual salespeople often spend more time on the many customer service activities than on *selling* per se. Additionally, as we discuss later in this chapter, salespeople may find that the various terms associated with the frequency and size of product shipments are often as important as product quality or list price in making a sale.

These same basic activities take place whether a firm is selling direct to final buyers or to distributors or both. In smaller industrial firms in particular, the same salespeople or sales managers may have responsibility for both direct sales to buyers and for working with distributors.

Because the topics of personal selling, customer service, distribution-channel relationships, and physical distribution policy are so highly integrated, they must be viewed as parts of comprehensive sales and distribution programs. In some companies, employees from other areas of the company such

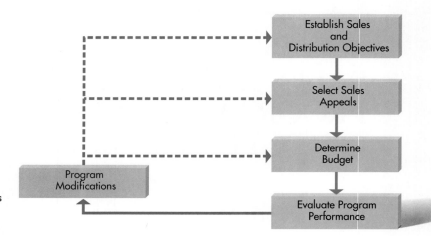

FIGURE 12-1
Elements of a sales and distribution program.

as marketing, finance, distribution, and operations have been assigned to coordinate with sales and work with key buyers to facilitate such coordination and integration. In this chapter and the next, we examine the process for developing and evaluating these programs. Four major steps are required in this process:

1. Defining sales and distribution *objectives* designed to implement the firm's marketing strategy
2. Identifying the most appropriate sales *appeals* to be used in accomplishing objectives
3. Determining and assigning the human and financial *resources* required for the program
4. Evaluating the program *performance* to adjust the program as necessary

The first two of these steps are examined in this chapter. In particular, we will present the kinds of objectives that can be used to guide the sales and distribution effort and the kinds of appeals the firms can employ. Subsequently, we will discuss the factors to be considered in selecting the best appeal and the best approaches that the sales force can use in presenting and gaining acceptance of the sales appeal. Finally, we will examine some of the unique considerations involved in selling through distributors.

Before examining sales and distribution objectives, however, it is important to understand the basic types of *sales and distribution systems* that can be employed by organizations. An understanding of these types of systems is important because the specific role of the sales force in implementing a marketing strategy will vary across these types of systems. (Figure 12-1 shows the main elements of a sales and distribution program.)

TYPES OF SALES AND DISTRIBUTION SYSTEMS

As summarized in Table 12-1, marketers can employ four basic types of sales and distribution systems, each of which differs in terms of the role played by personal selling.

DIRECT RESPONSE SYSTEMS

Direct response systems are essentially hybrid programs that may combine advertising, personal selling, and sales-promotion programs. However, because of their rapid growth and because they possess some special characteristics, they deserve to be viewed as sales and distribution systems. Specifically, direct response systems are characterized by the following:

- Unlike mass advertising, sales messages are directed to individually targeted customers, usually through telephone calls or direct mail.
- Customers are preselected from lists of individuals whose characteristics presumably indicate that they are good prospects. For example, the National Geographic Society has successfully sold globes, maps, videotapes,

TABLE 12-1	TYPES OF SALES AND DISTRIBUTION SYSTEMS	
	TYPES	**KEY CHARACTERISTICS**
	DIRECT SYSTEMS	
	1. Direct response systems	Products distributed directly to final buyer
		Sales message delivered to individual buyers by telephone or direct mail
		Primary function is to obtain orders
	2. Direct personal selling systems	Products distributed directly to final buyer
		Sales message delivered to individual buyers by face-to-face contact (Telephone selling may be used for order taking)
		Primary functions are to provide product information, technical advice, customer service; identify changing customer needs
	INDIRECT SYSTEMS	
	1. Trade selling systems	Products distributed through wholesalers or retailers who usually buy for resale to final buyers
		Sales message delivered by face-to-face contact (Telephone selling may be used for order taking)
		Primary functions are to obtain distributor support, provide product information, provide sales training and assistance to distributors
	2. Missionary selling systems	Products distributed through wholesalers or retailers who usually buy for resale to final buyers
		Sales message delivered by face-to-face contact
		Primary function is to provide product information and customer service directly to final buyer or to those who influence buyers

and travel magazines to subscribers who are interested in travel and geography.
■ Products are delivered directly to the final buyer.

Direct response marketing has grown dramatically in recent years. In large part, this growth is attributable to the fact that sales and distribution costs are substantially lower in such systems. Therefore, if only a small fraction of targeted customers responds with an order, direct response sales programs can be successful. For example,

> Paris-based Hermés, a retailer of exclusive women's fashions, has recently opened several stores in the United States and developed a mail-order catalog operation. Hermés sent out 300,000 catalogs to get around 4600 orders. But these orders generated $1.7 million in sales (about $375 per order), while the catalogs cost only $1.10 apiece.[1]

While historically direct response systems have been viewed by the general public to be very consumer-goods oriented, the use of direct response (especially telephone selling) has also grown rapidly in the industrial sector. Well over $100 billion worth of industrial products are sold by telephone each year with no clear limits on the kinds of products that can be effectively sold in this way, as General Electric's experience shows.

> General Electric's telemarketing operation grew to 45 telemarketing centers employing 2,000 employees under the management of Richard Huether. GE sells everything from medical accessories to hi-tech energy systems by telephone and, as Huether suggests, "We don't see this as some kind of selling function reserved for certain products."[2]

As is the case with consumer goods, economics has an important part to play in the growth of direct response in the industrial sector. Put simply, telemarketing is a more efficient way of contacting small-volume accounts than direct personal selling. Union Pacific Railroad, for instance, put its 20,000 smallest accounts on telephone hookups several years ago. Today these customers talk to Union Pacific telemarketers much more frequently than when called upon by reps. In addition, 84 percent of Union Pacific's customers rate its sales and marketing "very effective" as compared to only 67 percent prior to this change.[3]

Additionally, however, many firms (such as GE) have found that once telemarketing relationships are established, the amount of business generated from smaller customers often grows dramatically. Usually this occurs because customers begin to use the *inbound* telemarketing network to call for technical

---

[1] Phyllis Berman, "Mass Production? Yech!" *Forbes*, Sept. 22, 1986, pp. 182–183.
[2] Bill Kelley, "Is There Anything That Can't Be Sold by Phone?" *Sales and Marketing Management*, April 1989, pp. 60–64.
[3] Patricia Sellers, "How to Remake Your Sales Force," *Fortune*, May 4, 1992, p. 103.

advice or order information. To accommodate requests from consumers who wanted to order products anytime, Apple USA mailed a catalog featuring Apple software and some hardware products to over 1.1 million Apple computer users.[4]

DIRECT PERSONAL SELLING SYSTEMS

As with direct response systems, in direct personal selling systems products are shipped directly to the customer. However, unlike direct response systems most sales messages are delivered face to face. Note that this direct selling may be performed by a manufacturer's own sales force or by commissioned sales representatives. Technically, such representatives are wholesale distributors, but they perform only selling activities, so if they call only on final buyers they function as a direct sales force. Direct personal selling is used when the role of the sales force is more complex than the presentation of a simple sales message and asking for the order. Specifically, these salespeople focus their efforts on helping customers solve selected purchasing problems by demonstrating how a product (or service) can be used or adapted to fit customer needs. Additionally, they may also be responsible for identifying new products that might be developed to satisfy these needs. (Du Pont developed a flexible sales team recruited from all executive ranks to develop and sell new products. In 1990, this group identified the need for a new herbicide that corn growers could apply less often and created a product that had $57 million in sales its first year.[5]) Finally, they may also perform *customer service* activities such as following up on customer complaints; providing maintenance, repair, and operating (MRO) services; assuring reliable delivery; providing information on inventories and order processing; and assisting customers in managing spare parts inventories.

TRADE SELLING SYSTEMS

When organizations employ wholesalers and/or retailers to physically distribute products to final customers, a major role for the sales force is to assure that distributors are willing and able to support the marketing strategy. Accordingly, the sales force is usually called on to demonstrate to distributors how they can benefit from following specific policies that also enhance a manufacturer's sales. These policies can include promotion, service, space allocation, inventory, and production-assortment decisions. Additionally, this sales force may be responsible for providing distributors with the same kinds of customer service support that the direct sales force provides for the final buyer.

For example, RJR's Nabisco Biscuit runs a "direct store delivery" distribution system. Instead of shipping to central warehouses, company trucks deliver to 105,000 stores about three times a week. Nabisco's 400 merchandisers build store displays and organize shelves. The 2800 Nabisco sales reps use

---

[4] Carrie Goerne, "More Computer Marketers Taking the Direct Approach," *Marketing News*, Oct. 26, 1992, p. 6.
[5] "Smart Selling," *Business Week*, Aug. 3, 1992, p. 48.

hand-held computers to collect sales data for individual stores and help retail buyers configure their shelf space most productively. This system led to a change in Nabisco's new-product strategy, so that new products with high demand don't outstrip the bakery's ability to fill orders in a timely fashion.[6]

MISSIONARY SELLING SYSTEMS

Missionary selling also involves activities that enhance distributors' sales. However, these activities are primarily directed toward final buyers or toward individuals who influence the buying decision rather than toward distributors. For instance, a hospital-equipment manufacturer may use a wholesaler but will rely on its own missionary sales force to provide product information to key hospital personnel. Similarly, publishers use their own sales force to call on college professors, who influence students' purchases of textbooks, even though a local bookstore is used to distribute the product. These kinds of sales forces are employed when distributors' salespeople are inadequately trained or insufficient in number to provide the technical information required. Additionally, when distributors carry extremely wide and diverse product lines and when new products are developed at a high rate (as happens in the pharmaceutical industry), the missionary sales force will be especially useful.

The foregoing characterization suggests that there are significant differences in the role of the sales force across sales and distribution systems. However, there are also many differences in the role of the sales force *within* each type of system, as each selling organization has different products, customers, competitors, and strategies. Moreover, some organizations will employ more than one type of system. For example, in marketing personal computers IBM uses both direct response and direct personal selling systems, as well as in selling to the trade. Companies will use different distribution systems depending on their size as shown in Table 12-2. Finally, when selling through distributors, the type of system used will have a bearing on the design

---

[6] "This Cookie Is Tops in Food Sales," *Fortune*, May 4, 1992, p. 100.

TABLE 12-2 **COMPANIES USING DIFFERENT DISTRIBUTION ALTERNATIVES (by percent)**

SIZE OF COMPANY (SALES IN MILLIONS)	TELEMARKETING	MFG. REPS	DISTRIBUTORS/ WHOLESALER	MAJOR NATIONAL ACCOUNT REPS
less than $5	34.5	20.7	32.8	5.2
$5–25	21.6	52.6	48.5	5.2
$25–100	24.5	36.7	51.1	12.2
$100–250	44.0	20.0	48.0	16.0
$250 +	25.0	8.3	58.3	29.2

Adapted from "Twenty-Sixth Survey of Sales Force Compensation," The Dartnell Corp., Chicago, Ill., 1990.

of sales and distribution programs. We examine some distribution channel alternatives in the next section of this chapter.

DISTRIBUTION CHANNEL STRUCTURE

A *distribution channel* is a set of organizational units (such as manufacturers, wholesalers, and retailers) that performs all the functions required to get a product from a seller to the final buyer. The structure of the channel is determined by three elements: the *tasks* and activities to be performed by intermediaries, the *type* of distributor to be used, and the *number* of each type of distributor.[7]

TASKS

Firms use distributors to perform those marketing tasks that a supplier cannot perform as effectively or efficiently. The most widely performed distributor tasks include maintaining availability through local delivery or by having the product at locations convenient to the customer, providing customer financing and maintenance or repair services, and local selling and advertising of the product's benefits. These tasks are most likely to be performed by distributors rather than by suppliers when

- There are large numbers of buyers, each of whom purchases in small dollar amounts so that the cost of making personal sales calls on each one would be very high if performed by a manufacturer.
- A detailed knowledge of local market conditions and buyer needs is important because customers vary dramatically in their needs.
- Special emergency service is important.
- Competitors provide a high level of availability, and therefore convenience or speed of delivery is necessary to be competitive.
- Buyers purchase a wide assortment of related products in small volumes while the manufacturer provides only a narrow assortment and thus cannot meet the buyer's full range of needs.

In other words, the tasks that distributors must perform will depend on what is needed to competitively meet customer needs and on the relative economic efficiency of performing or delegating the task.

TYPE OF WHOLESALE-LEVEL DISTRIBUTOR

A manufacturer considering the use of wholesale-level distributors has a variety of options. The major differences among types of wholesalers are in the type and number of functions they perform. While all wholesale-level

---

[7] For a comprehensive examination of distribution channels, see Louis Stern, Adel El-Ansary, and James Brown, *Management in Marketing Channels*, Prentice-Hall, Englewood Cliffs, N.J., 1989.

distributors provide a selling function, only merchant wholesalers assume the risk associated with taking title to goods as they move toward the final buyer. Not surprisingly, these wholesalers also receive the largest margins on the sales they make—as high as 25 percent compared to 3 to 7 percent for most agents and brokers. This distinction in functions between merchant wholesalers and agents (or brokers) is the reason why merchant wholesalers are part of a trade selling system while agents are basically just substitutes for a manufacturer's sales force. Thus, when agents call on other distributors (as is the case with food brokers), they are part of a trade selling system. If they call on final buyers, they are part of a direct selling system.

TYPE OF RETAILER

Retailers differ in terms of two major factors: the extent of the product lines they carry and the type of consumer search effort they cater to. The type of retail intermediary employed will depend upon the firm's target markets. For example, in catering to a price-oriented market, stores that are classified as shopping goods-oriented are more likely to be chosen. In attempting to reach a market that is concerned with personal service and an image of quality, specialty stores are generally more appropriate.

At both the wholesale and the retail level, sales managers should target their efforts toward distributors who will perform the required tasks and who are of the type desired to reach the target market.

NUMBER OF DISTRIBUTORS

Channels may have an *intensive* pattern of distribution (in which a relatively large number of distributors exist for a given area) or a *selective* pattern of distribution (in which only a few distributors exist for a given area). At the extreme, a distributor may be designated the *exclusive* representative in an area. In general, the more functions a distributor is expected to perform, the more likely an exclusive or selective pattern of distribution will be necessary as a protective measure to provide the incentive for holding large inventories, for offering service, and for aggressive promotion. Selective distribution has other advantages for a supplier as well. When a firm has fewer distributors, the selling costs, delivery costs, and cost of monitoring distributor performance are usually lower. These advantages exist because fewer sales personnel are needed and because fewer points of delivery (normally with more economically sized loads) are required.

However, traditional exclusive distribution systems may be inappropriate if consumer shopping patterns and market conditions change. Goodyear Tire and Rubber in March 1992 announced plans to sell Goodyear brand tires through Sears and Roebuck as well as its exclusive network of 2500 independent dealers. Goodyear's decision was based upon its continual study of other distribution alternatives and the growth of large super retailers such as Sears, Kmart, Wal-Mart, and others. Since that announcement, hundreds of Goodyear dealers have adopted private brands, which offer them higher margins and lower their incentive to sell Goodyear Tires.[8]

On the other hand, to the extent that convenience in buying is very important to the buyer (especially for low-involvement consumer goods), more intensive distribution will be required. Accordingly, managers should be sure that the desired number of accounts in each market is considered before stating the specific number of new accounts to be developed.

Vertical Marketing Systems

The increased recognition of the importance of selling *through and not just to* the distributor had led many firms to develop highly coordinated channels. The term *vertical marketing system* is generally used to describe types of channels in which distributor actions are very highly coordinated with the manufacturer's marketing strategy because a strong, continuing, formal relationship has been established. These systems can be of three types: corporate, contractual, and administered systems.

Corporate systems are channels in which some degree of vertical integration has taken place. That is, if a retailer is owned by a supplier (or vice versa) then a corporate system exists. Today, many oil companies, tire companies, and clothing companies own at least some of their retail outlets. Although the cost of owning distribution outlets may be great, the sales representatives are generally assured that the distribution outlets will fully support the marketing strategy.

For instance, France is the only major market in the world where Coke owns the bottling business. Previously, Pernod-Ricard, a large spirits producer, controlled Coke's bottling in France for 40 years. France had the lowest per capita consumption of Coke in the European community, and Coke attributes this to Pernod-Ricard's promotion of its own brands at the expense of Coke and Coca-Cola's other products. After Coke's purchase of bottling operations, unit volume in France rose 23 percent the first year. This was the largest increase on the continent.[9]

Contractual systems include franchising programs and voluntary associations in which legally binding contracts are established that specify the tasks which each party will perform. Specifically, *franchise* programs are contractual arrangements between a manufacturer and a retail- or wholesale-level distributor that specify what assistance suppliers will provide as well as the obligations of distributors. In recent years, these programs have been dominant in such retail businesses as automobile sales, fast-food restaurants, automotive supplies and services, and in some wholesaling businesses (including soft-drink bottling). These lines of trade are similar in several respects: distributors rely

[8] Dana Milbank, "Independent Goodyear Dealers Rebel: Decision to Sell through Sears Proves Unpopular," *The Wall Street Journal*, July 8, 1992, p. B2.
[9] Patricia Sellers, "Coke Gets Off Its Can in Europe," *Fortune*, Aug. 13, 1990, p. 70.

primarily on one supplier, extensive capital investment is required of the distributor, and maintenance of quality service standards is important. Because of these features, suppliers and distributors are highly dependent on each other.

When this does not occur, such distribution arrangements deteriorate rapidly, as in the case of Burger King. A series of misdirected advertising campaigns and lack of new products led to franchisee revolts. Under new leadership now, store design, product development, and food research report to the CEO. This reorganization is designed to accelerate the introduction of new products and services that have been suggested by franchisees.[10]

Voluntary associations, on the other hand, are contractual systems organized by wholesalers to provide comprehensive merchandising and promotional programs to independent retailers. These programs are primarily designed to assist wholesalers' customers in maintaining a competitive posture with respect to franchised or vertically integrated chain retailers. IGA food stores and Western Auto stores are among the organizations falling into this category.

Administered systems are channels in which distributors have no contractual or ownership dependency on a supplier. Essentially, these manufacturers provide a wide range of incentives in exchange for extensive promotional support and for carrying large inventories and a full line of products. These systems are employed by firms such as O. M. Scott and Sons (lawn and garden products) and Kraft (food products) to provide distributors with comprehensive merchandising advice, protective provisions (such as exclusive distributorships), and direct financial assistance.

SALES AND DISTRIBUTION OBJECTIVES

Given a marketing strategy, managers can define one or more basic objectives for the sales and distribution program. Further, these objectives should be defined in specific terms in order to provide direction to the sales force and establish a basis for evaluating program success.

Of course, the most specific kind of objective that can be set and the easiest to measure is a dollar or unit-sales objective. And indeed, sales volume is an important program objective and a widely used basis for evaluating salesperson, sales-territory, and program performance. However, in most cases, sales volume will not be adequate as a program objective, for several reasons.

First, sales and distribution programs cost money. In many cases distribution costs, including selling costs, have been estimated to be as much as 30 to 40 percent of a product's cost.[11] Efforts designed to increase sales may not lead to increased profitability, for reasons discussed in Chapter 13. Accord-

---

[10] "Sid Fettenstein Is Having It His Way," *Business Week*, Nov. 23, 1992, p. 64.
[11] Rita Koselka, "Distribution Revolution," *Forbes*, May 25, 1992, p. 58.

ingly, a sales objective may not be consistent with a product objective of increased profitability. Second, sales results are often determined by competitors' actions, environmental forces, or other marketing programs outside the control of the sales force. Third, the primary role of a marketing program is to implement a marketing strategy. Because the marketing strategy defines target markets and the kind of impact on demand to be achieved, program objectives should reflect the marketing strategy, and simply establishing a sales or profit objective will not reflect the strategy very precisely. Fourth, and finally, a sales objective does not provide the sales force with any guidance on *how* to increase (or maintain) sales volume. Managers should be responsible for providing direction to the sales force by helping to identify the best opportunities for sales development.

In sum, although sales-volume objectives are useful—especially when a direct response system is employed—managers should also establish sales and distribution objectives that

- Reflect the marketing strategy
- Provide a focus for sales-force activities
- Can be used to evaluate sales-force efforts as well as results
- Identify the targets from which future sales volume will come

In general, four kinds of sales and distribution objectives can be employed (each of which should be stated in specific terms): account development, distributor support, account maintenance, and account penetration.

1. *Account-development* objectives are designed to emphasize the acquisition of new distributors or customers. Preferably, managers should identify specific targets for new accounts depending on the marketing strategy. For example, managers might identify: specific user groups or industries in a direct selling system; organizations of a specific size or consumers with special characteristics in a direct response system; specific types of retail outlets in a trade selling system.
2. *Distributor-support* objectives apply to trade selling and are designed to gain the cooperation of retail or wholesale distributors in implementing the marketing strategy. Specifically, manufacturers may seek a variety of types of support, such as distributor participation in cooperative advertising or special sales promotions, aggressive selling of the product, or providing extensive customer service. Distributor support is generally viewed as essential in indirect systems because the distributor is a key partner in the marketing effort. Indeed, when products are in the mature stage of the product life cycle, distributor support may well be the major marketing element in sales success because technically similar products may be broadly available.
3. *Account-maintenance* objectives typically take up the bulk of a salesperson's time in direct personal selling systems and in trade selling systems. These

objectives are emphasized when management is concerned with maintaining an effective selling position through regular sales calls designed to provide information about new products, acquire information on changing customer or distributor needs, and perform customer service activities. (For instance, Kraft's sales reps no longer limit their efforts to devising promotions in supermarkets. They now offer research and advice for improving a store's profits.)

4. *Account-penetration* objectives are designed to increase total sales volume or to increase the sales of more profitable products or complementary products to existing distributors or buyers. For example, direct response marketers often focus their selling efforts on offering different products to customers who have been good respondents in the past. (For example, Land's End mails a thirty-six-page specialty children's apparel catalog to the one-third of the people on their mailing list who have previously bought for kids. This costs the same as selling children's clothes on only twelve pages of the main catalog and has increased the response rate as well.)[12] Similarly, industrial firms often share the business of some customers with one or more competitors. (For instance, some automobile manufacturers will purchase tires from two or three suppliers.) An attempt by such firms to increase their share of a buyer's purchase volume reflects an account-penetration objective. Finally, firms that are attempting to get distributors to carry more inventory or allocate more selling space to a product are also pursuing account penetration.

Selecting an Objective

Managers should select a sales and distribution objective that is based on the marketing strategy for each product or product line, because the purpose of sales and distribution programs is to help implement these strategies. This means that managers should identify the needs of the target buyers or distributors and the marketing strategies to be implemented when selecting sales and distribution objectives.

Note that being able to "type" a product according to a portfolio model will not alone enable a manager to select a sales and distribution objective. Although account development is typically an important objective for new products and problem-child products, account penetration may also be employed in those cases. Similarly, reseller support may be an objective sought by managers of any of these types of products. Table 12-3 summarizes the marketing strategies that are typically associated with the various sales and distribution objectives.

Once the program objective has been established, management can then turn its attention to the question of how to achieve the objective. Specifically,

[12] "That's Show Biz," *Forbes*, July 6, 1992, p. 44.

TABLE 12-3	SALES AND DISTRIBUTION OBJECTIVES AND RELATED MARKETING STRATEGIES	
	SALES AND DISTRIBUTION OBJECTIVES	**HOW THEY IMPLEMENT MARKETING STRATEGIES**
	1. Account development	Increasing availability relative to competitors Gaining access to new segments Increasing ability to buy
	2. Distributor support	Increasing availability (inventory) Increasing consumption rate Reducing competitive opportunities Increasing promotional support relative to competition
	3. Account maintenance	Assuring user satisfaction Reducing competitive opportunities
	4. Account penetration	Simplification Increasing consumption rate and purchase volume Increasing ability to buy Head-to-head competition Complementary product sales

managers must identify the kinds of appeals that will be most effective in satisfying the benefit desired by the buyer or distributor.

SALES APPEALS

Sales appeals are the basic elements of the marketing offer that the sales force will communicate. That is, appeals reflect the benefits that a seller will offer in order to obtain the type of customer or distributor response stated in the program objective. Because the sales force communicates directly with final buyers and distributors, it is possible to particularize the appeal to a much greater degree than is possible with advertising. This attribute of selling is distinctly important because distributors may differ in the benefits they desire and because organizational buyers often differ in the criteria they use for selecting a supplier.

In general, six types of appeals may be employed in sales and distribution programs:

- Product appeals
- Logistical appeals
- Protective-provisions appeals
- Simplification appeals
- Price appeals
- Financial-assistance appeals

Product Appeals

Product appeals are the specific product-related benefits that buyers will gain from using a product or that distributors will gain from having the product in their assortments. The benefits of the product will almost always be important to the buyer or distributor. Accordingly, they will almost always be included in the sales message. However, in many cases a number of competing firms will be able to match product attributes or benefits. In those situations, other appeals are more likely to be determinant.

Product appeals are more likely to be determinant when noneconomic perceived risks are high. For example, if an industrial buyer purchases a component that is a major element in the quality of the final product, product quality and reliability will be the most critical attributes. For consumer goods, product appeals will be more important when social or psychological risks are paramount as the following example shows.

> BeautiControl Cosmetics has become the third largest direct selling women's cosmetics business, primarily by focusing on reaching career-oriented and professional women. The key appeal in the BeautiControl marketing plan is that the company offers free color analysis. This technique involves determining a woman's skin tone and then identifying what color cosmetics will look best.[13]

In the case of industrial products, product appeals generally include quality control, reliability, distinctive performance features, the ability to meet computer specifications, or compatibility with existing products and systems. In the case of selling to distributors, product appeals are those which demonstrate the impact that carrying the product has on total distributor sales. For example, some products may help to build store traffic, provide prestige to the distributor, or enable the distributor to offer a more complete product line. Of course, not all of these product benefits can be easily demonstrated. As we shall discuss at the end of the chapter, the ability of the sales force to effectively and credibly communicate these benefits will be a major factor in the success of product appeals.

Logistical Appeals

In recent years, the cost of holding inventory has risen sharply because of an increase in the number of models and lines offered and because of the higher cost of borrowing money. Accordingly, logistical appeals have become increasingly effective in dealing with distributors and industrial buyers. These appeals include providing fast processing of orders, providing frequent delivery, and offering expedited delivery.

[13] William Barrett, "See Dick and Jinger Sell," *Forbes*, Aug. 7, 1989, p. 48.

On-time delivery has become a key competitive advantage in most industries. In Europe, for instance, Nissan guarantees its dealers 10-day delivery, and Caterpillar delivers replacement parts within 72 hours 99.7 percent of the time. For direct response companies like Dell Computers, on-time delivery is a key element of their competitive strategy. Dell's promise of product shipment within 5 days of an order and 2-day delivery has been a key factor in their being rated first in their industry in customer satisfaction.[14]

Additionally, some manufacturers offer inventory-management appeals. For example, a buyer may guarantee a supplier that it will buy a minimum amount of a product over the course of a year. In exchange, the seller is responsible for providing very quick delivery (often within 24 hours) and also inherits the inventory-holding cost burden.

The primary effect of logistical appeals, therefore, is to help buyers or distributors reduce the amount of inventory they carry. In the case of K-Mart, the company was able to reduce the inventory carried in distribution centers by 20 percent while at the same time increasing sales by 15 percent through the addition of new information systems and distribution programs. This benefit is extremely important when any of the following conditions occur:

- Interest rates are high, so the cost of borrowing money to finance inventories causes a significant drain on profits.
- Demand for a product is difficult to predict, perhaps because demand is very sensitive to changes in economic conditions.
- The rate of product obsolescence is very high due to fashion changes, technological changes, or spoilage.
- Space constraints limit the amount of inventory that buyers or distributors are willing to carry.

For instance, Wal-Mart stores use only about 10 percent of their square footage for inventory, compared to the average store, which has 25 percent for nonselling uses.

A variety of techniques are available for helping customers with inventory problems. Some of these can be seen in the actions taken by A. M. Castle & Co.

A. M. Castle is an Illinois-based distributor of steel, aluminum, and other metal products to 30,000 industrial customers in a wide variety of industries and locations. During the 1990s, A. M. Castle will reduce from 18 to 12 the number of its regional warehouses. The surviving warehouses will be larger, however, and will stock more inventory to improve customer product selection. Additionally, improved locations for the warehouses will assure next-day delivery for the entire continental United States. At the same time, the company has linked its computer systems with those of

---

[14] Koselka, op. cit., p. 59; and Anil Kumar and Graham Sherman, "We Love Your Product, but Where Is It?" *Sloan Management Review*, Winter 1992, reprinted in *Business Edge*, October 1992, pp. 20ff.

customers to exchange information that enables Castle to help its customers track and manage inventory levels.[15]

Although logistical appeals may be very effective, the cost of these appeals can be very high. Accordingly, managers who wish to consider using these appeals should closely examine the profit impact that will result. Some procedures for evaluating this impact are discussed in Chapter 13.

Protective-Provision Appeals

Protective provisions represent specific policies designed to reduce buyer and distributor risk in accepting a product. For example, a supplier may offer *exclusive distributorships*. For instance, Haggar Corporation sells its "Brickerton by Haggar" line of men's slacks only to Dillard's Department Stores.

To protect resellers against the risk of poor sales, manufacturers may offer the product on *consignment*. In this procedure, the title and the inventory risk remain with the seller until the distributor actually sells the product. Or the seller may provide liberal *return allowances*. This provision allows a distributor to return all unsold merchandise to a seller at a high percentage of the original cost.

To protect buyers against price increases, sellers may offer *long-term contracts* that specify future price levels in exchange for a minimum order volume. To an increasing extent, buyers are becoming willing to accept such contracts even when specific *escalator clauses* are included. These clauses permit the seller to add certain kinds of cost increases (such as labor or material cost increases) to the contracted price.

Finally, *private branding* may be the appeal employed for protective provisions offered to distributors. A private brand is a product manufactured by one firm yet sold under a brand name controlled by a distributor (such as Wal-Mart's Sam's American Choice cola and chocolate chip cookies, which are made by Loblaw Co., the Canadian grocery chain). Frequently, manufacturers of cash cows will offer to produce private brands as a means of using excess capacity without incurring the cost of supporting a brand through heavy promotion. Distributors may be successful with a private brand in the maturity stage of the life cycle if a large segment of the market is price-sensitive. Additionally, by having a brand with no direct comparisons available, a distributor's risk of facing heavy price comparison is reduced.

In many product categories, an issue of major importance to retail and wholesale distributors is the existence of *gray marketers*, unauthorized outlets that sell branded products far below list price and often offer no service. Gray markets can come about when large buyers take advantage of discounts of 30 to 40 percent and then resell the products to unauthorized dealers at less than what small retail outlets might pay. IBM has protected its dealers from

---

[15] Flynn McRoberts, "Castle Fortified Metal Operations," *Chicago Tribune*, Aug. 7, 1989, p. B1.

such unauthorized competitors by insisting that dealers and large customers sign contracts agreeing not to resell to unauthorized dealers and by eliminating dealers or customers who violate these contracts.

Simplification Appeals

Simplification appeals are designed to enable the buyer or distributor to reduce the costs of handling, using, or promoting the product.

Manufacturers who sell to distributors often "preticket" merchandise (to save labor costs on the distributor's part) or provide specific promotional aids (sales training or displays). In some cases, big retailers demand that the manufacturer put price stickers on individual packages. Totes, Inc., for instance, was warned by one large retailer it would impose a $30,000 fine for errors in bar coding on products.[16]

Some manufacturers offer distributors a complete plan for merchandising the product, providing inventory and space-allocation guidelines and promotional programs specifically tailored to the distributor's market. Manufacturers of packaged-goods products offer a variety of simplification appeals to enhance sales of the product. Some, such as Kraft and Campbell Soup, help grocers rearrange shelves and displays to maximize profits. Others redesign products, packages, and delivery methods specifically for such wholesale clubs as Costco, Price, and Sam's. For example, Heinz bundles condiments like ketchup and relish into a single package and ships 64-ounce bottles on customized display pallets that are easy for stores to handle.[17]

In the case of industrial buyers, the provision of special maintenance, repair, and operating (MRO) services and inventory assistance constitutes a parallel to such merchandising plans. This approach simplifies a customer's problems in using the product. As a result, the seller may be able to develop greater buyer or distributor loyalty, because these programs may enable the buyer to use the product more satisfactorily or because they may lead to an increased dependence on the supplier.

Price Appeals

As suggested in Chapter 9, basic price-level decisions are developed by product managers or marketing managers on the basis of cost, demand, and competitive considerations and on the basis of the marketing strategy. The sales force often has an important impact on the final price paid by each buyer, however.

In the case of industrial goods, price *shading* is a commonly used appeal for closing a sale—especially when new accounts are being sought. That is, the

---

[16] "Clout: More and More, Retail Giants Rule the Marketplace," *Business Week*, Dec. 21, 1992, p. 68.
[17] Patricia Sellers, "Winning Over the New Consumer," *Fortune*, July 29, 1991, pp. 113ff.

sales force will often have some latitude on the actual price to be charged and may price "below list" if necessary. This practice is widespread among industrial goods firms. Additionally, under inflationary pressures, many firms develop price lists reflecting possible cost increases that might be incurred, and then systematically offer prices "off list" until cost increases catch up with the original list-price levels. In so doing, firms avoid the cost of frequent price-list revisions and also reduce buyer displeasure over rising prices.

Shading is not always an available option when manufacturers sell to distributors, because of the Robinson-Patman Act restraints on price discrimination that were discussed in Chapter 9. However, *quantity discounts* provide a mechanism for justifying lower prices to some distributors, and they also provide significant benefits to industrial buyers. The rationale for quantity discounts lies in the fact that buyers who order in large quantities do not require proportionately larger sales force, credit, or delivery costs to service the account. An additional possible benefit of quantity purchases to the seller is the reduction in inventory cost that results from shifting large volumes to the distributor or industrial buyer.

Financial-Assistance Appeals

In some cases, a buyer's working-capital, investment, or direct-expense requirements will be sharply increased as a result of a purchase. *Credit and cash discounts* are often provided when inventory requirements are large. Credit terms may range from 30 to 120 days (and often longer) and are designed to allow the distributor time to complete the resale of the product or to allow a buyer time for the production and sale of the final product in order to pay for the order. Cash discounts are designed to permit savings to firms that pay invoices quickly.

Additionally, sellers may offer special equipment free or at substantial savings to distributors in order to defray equipment and facilities investments. Signs, tools, service equipment, storage equipment, and many other inducements fall into this category.

More recently, new forms of financial assistance have been initiated that are designed to achieve special cooperation on stocking new products or building distributor sales support.

In 1989, IBM began the Flexible Funds Program for its 1900 dealers. In contrast to the old practice of giving special discounts, the new program offers financial aid for things such as new showrooms, special seminars on topics such as computer-aided design, and even paying the salaries of distributor employees designated to sell only IBM products.[18]

[18] Susan Gelford and Maria Shao, "The Power Surge at Computer Dealers," *Business Week*, July 17, 1989, pp. 134–135.

On the consumer packaged-goods side, the dominant new appeal in recent years is the *slotting allowance*, which is generally requested by supermarkets when the subject of stocking new products comes up.

Retailers initiated slotting allowances as a way of recouping part of the cost of setting up, handling, and stocking new products. In a typical supermarket, the number of items carried doubled between 1979 and 1990 and because many of these new items are line extensions or competing versions, the net gain in retailer revenue is usually modest. Accordingly, retailers have begun to require slotting allowances—upfront payments of $1,000 or more per store for each store in a chain to underwrite costs.[19]

The Relationship between Appeals and Objectives

As summarized in Table 12-4, a large number of appeals can be used as the focal point of the sales-force effort. Indeed, managers may elect to use several of these appeals simultaneously.

[19] Lois Therrien, "Want Shelf Space at the Supermarket? Ante Up," *Business Week*, Aug. 7, 1989, pp. 60–61.

TABLE 12-4	TYPES OF SALES APPEALS

TYPE OF APPEAL	EXAMPLES
Product	Technical features
	Performance features
	Impact on distributor sales
Logistical	Speed of delivery
	Inventory management
Protective provisions	Exclusive distributorships
	Consignment selling
	Return allowances
	Long-term contracts
	Private branding
Simplification	Preticketing
	Merchandising assistance
	MRO services
Price	Price shading
	Quantity discounts
Financial assistance	Trade credit
	Cash discounts
	Special equipment
	Slotting allowances

In general, nearly any type of appeal can be used to attempt to achieve a given sales and distribution objective. However, for a given type of objective, certain appeals do merit special consideration. For example,

■ Protective provisions, shading, and product appeals are very widely used for account development, especially if the buyers or distributors have limited knowledge of the seller's product.
■ Simplification and financial-assistance appeals are widely utilized to build distributor support, because these appeals are effective in stimulating cooperative attitudes on the part of distributors.
■ Logistical and simplification appeals are widely used in achieving account maintenance, especially if product features and prices do not vary a great deal among competing suppliers.
■ Quantity discounts and long-term contracts are often effective for achieving account-penetration objectives because they focus most directly on the issue of increased volume.

However, in selecting specific appeals for a customer or a market segment, it is important that sales managers and sales-force personnel understand what motivates a buyer or distributor. As we suggested earlier, one advantage of using a sales force is the ability to adapt the marketing offer to meet particular buyer or distributor requirements. Additionally, the success of a given appeal will depend on the type of power or influence relationship that exists between a seller and a buyer or distributor. Buyer-distributor requirements and power relationships are both discussed in the next section of this chapter.

SELECTING AND IMPLEMENTING APPEALS

As we suggested at the outset of this chapter, the distinctive feature of sales-force activities is the personal interaction between the sales force and the buyers and distributors. This personal interaction has two basic functions:

■ To develop an understanding of buyer or distributor requirements so that management can select appropriate appeals. (Figure 12-2 shows the process of selecting a sales appeal.)
■ To maintain a power or influence relationship with buyers or distributors in order to successfully *implement* the appeals.

Buyer or Distributor Requirements

Requirements here refers to the various benefits that organizational buyers or distributors desire from a seller to satisfy the needs of their businesses. In Chapter 3, several kinds of benefits were identified. However, these can be

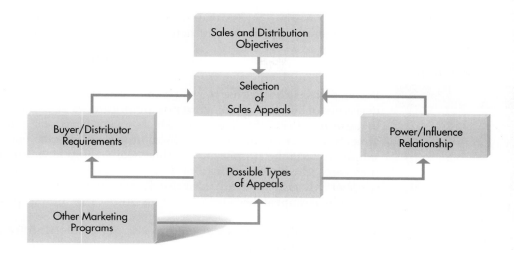

FIGURE 12-2

The process of selecting a sales appeal.

expected to vary on a segment-by-segment basis, and often on a customer-by-customer basis—especially when a number of individuals are involved in the buying center. Accordingly, sales and customer service personnel must assess how their products and services fit the needs of each account. In order to do this, the sales force must be able to answer questions such as the following:

- How significant is the performance or quality of the product to the operation or performance of the buyer's business or to the distributor's assortment or image?
- What special problems does a buyer have in using the product or a distributor have in selling or servicing the product?
- What is the price-elasticity in markets served by buyers or distributors?
- What related costs must buyers or distributors incur in order to maintain inventory or to promote the product?
- What costs (such as lost sales or production bottlenecks) are incurred by buyers or distributors as a consequence of late delivery or stockouts by the seller?
- How can the sales force help the company's distributors meet their financial objectives (regarding inventory turnover or gross-margin return on inventory investment) or their sales-growth objectives?

Additionally, the salespeople who call on buyers or distributors must understand not only the buyer/distributor *product* requirements but the customer's sales process as well. That is, each buyer is likely to have individual preferences or be in special situations that condition the amount and kind of information needed to make a purchase. Some may desire a short sales presentation while others may need extensive information and materials to use in gaining approval from their managers.[20]

Power Relationships

Power reflects the degree to which one firm can influence the actions and decisions of another firm. Power is significant in the selection of appeals because it reflects the degree to which sellers have real control over what appeals to offer. Some buyer or distributor requirements may be met in full simply because the supplier needs their selling support or buying volume. In such cases, the buyer or distributor can be viewed as more powerful than the supplier. Alternatively, buyers or distributors may be willing to accept a seller-determined appeal because of various sources of power possessed by the seller.

Theoretically, five bases of power exist. See Table 12-5 for a summary of the power bases available.[21]

1. One firm may have power because of its ability to *reward* the other. By offering an economically desirable appeal (such as a high gross margin), a

---

[20] David Szymanski, "Determinants of Selling Effectiveness: The Importance of Declarative Knowledge to the Personal Selling Concept," *Journal of Marketing*, January 1988, pp. 64–77.
[21] For an extensive discussion of the significance of power relationships, see Gary Frazier, "Interorganizational Exchange Behavior in Marketing Channels: A Broadened Perspective," *Journal of Marketing*, Fall 1983, pp. 68–78; and John F. Gaski, "The Theory of Power and Conflict in Channels of Distribution," *Journal of Marketing*, Summer 1984, pp. 9–29.

TABLE 12-5

ALTERNATIVE POWER BASES AVAILABLE TO MANUFACTURERS, DISTRIBUTORS, AND BUYERS

POWER BASE	TO A MANUFACTURER	TO A BUYER OR DISTRIBUTOR
Reward	Ability to offer product with low prices, quantity discounts	Ability to offer large buying volume
Coercive	Ability to withdraw product (with little loss in sales) when no comparable alternative is available to buyer or distributor	Ability to reject offer (with little loss in sales volume) when no equivalent distributors or buyers are available to seller
Expert	Ability to offer superior or needed technical assistance	Ability to provide unique distribution support
Referent	Ability to offer prestige brand name	Ability to offer image of quality retail outlet or to serve as prestige example of satisfied buyer
Legitimate	Contractual provision that requires distributor to carry full line	Contractual provision that requires seller to provide warranty, repair, exclusive distribution

seller may be able to induce a distributor to provide greater selling support or increase inventories.

2. Buyers or distributors that account for a large portion of a seller's volume may be able to demand specific appeals because of the *coercive* power they hold. That is, the fear of losing a key account may compel a seller to offer special delivery terms or service appeals. In the case of Gitano Group, Inc., Wal-Mart accounted for 26 percent of 1991 company sales. Wal-Mart set high standards for on-time delivery of defect-free apparel, which Gitano failed to meet. This resulted in the company recording over $90 million in losses from restructuring and inventory write-downs.[22]

3. Product or service appeals are often desirable to buyers or distributors because of the seller's *expertise*. Similarly, distributors may accept simplification appeals because they believe the manufacturer has a greater knowledge of final buyer needs or of appropriate merchandising techniques.

4. Certain appeals may be acceptable or desirable because of one firm's *referent* power. That is, a buyer or distributor may want the prestige of working with an established, well-known supplier, and thus be willing to forego some normal financial requirements in favor of product appeals.

5. *Legitimate* power usually exists when a seller and a distributor have a contractual relationship. For example, a franchiser's contract with the franchisee states the specific appeals (such as selective distribution, promotional aids) that will be used. When a supplier has legitimate power, the distributor fully accepts the legal or proprietary right of the supplier to specify certain levels of reseller support, and more or less standard appeals are established for all distributors.

To the extent that a supplier can measure the amount of power it holds relative to the amount buyers hold, some guidelines for selecting appeals can be developed. For example, if a supplier knows that it is perceived as having a unique technological advantage, management should emphasize its expertise by using product appeals. If a supplier has the ability to significantly reduce a buyer's costs or increase a distributor's profit by offering lower prices, management should use reward power by employing price appeals.

It is also important to recognize that power relationships can change over time. Indeed it appears that the relative power of manufacturers is in decline in many industries (both domestic and overseas) for a variety of reasons.

■ In wholesale distribution, larger professionally managed firms are displacing smaller family businesses at a rapid rate. Moreover, these larger wholesalers are establishing strong ongoing, long-term contractual relationships

---

[22] "Clout: More and More, Retail Giants Rule the Marketplace," *Business Week*, Dec. 21, 1992, p. 72.

with final buyers, making it difficult for manufacturers to avoid dealing with them.[23]

■ Large-scale retailers are also gaining a larger share of consumer-goods sales. This has enabled them to build their economic power base. But additionally, their expertise power is growing because of information technology. Expanded electronic scanning and computing capabilities combined with new statistical models for doing productivity analyses are allowing retailers to assess the profit performance of manufacturer brands more closely and to rely less on manufacturers' sales forces for advice on space allocation and in-store merchandising tactics.[24]

In Europe, grocery chains are merging and building stores outside their home countries, and buying decisions have been shifted to the home office. The establishment of the EC has led retailers to work together through alliances to buy a single product at the lowest cost. In the United States, there has been a consolidation of retailers, which has led to giant "power retailers" who use sophisticated information systems, tight inventory management, and competitive pricing to squeeze out weaker stores. The growth of these powerful retailers has brought about a power shift in the traditional relationship between manufacturer and retailer. Today, retailers such as Wal-Mart, Kmart, Target, Toys 'R' Us, and others dictate to even the largest manufacturers what goods to make and in what colors and sizes. In addition, shipping quantities and just-in-time deliveries, as well as discounts for new store openings and payments of fines for shipping errors, are being demanded. This has led to vendors' having to rethink to whom they sell and how they price and promote their products. In many cases this shift of power has led to restructuring the organization on the part of suppliers.

In addition to requiring on-time delivery and minimizing inventory, large power retailers are in a position to demand a variety of other special requirements from suppliers (see Table 12-6).

Historically, manufacturers have held a strong power advantage in Japan because of the dominance of small retailers. In that nation, 1.6 million small stores control 53 percent of sales. (In contrast, only 3 percent of sales go through small stores in the United States.) In large measure, this power is a result of legislation that allowed small retailers to determine whether large stores could be introduced in their trading areas. But in spite of this tradition, large-scale retailing now appears to be gaining ground in Japan.[25]

[23] James C. Anderson and James Narus, "A Model of Distributor Firm and Manufacturer Firm Working Partnerships," *Journal of Marketing*, January 1990, pp. 42–58.

[24] Brent Felgner, "Retailers Grab Power, Control Marketplace," *Marketing News*, Jan. 16, 1989, pp. 1–2.

[25] Bruce Hirobayashi, "Winds of Change," *Age of Information Marketing*, A.C. Nielsen Co., Chicago, 1989, pp. 9–12.

TABLE 12-6	REQUIREMENTS AND PRACTICES OF MAJOR RETAILERS

RETAILER	
Wal-Mart	Computerized reordering and electronic linkups with 5000 suppliers Wants to eliminate independent brokers and manufacturing reps and deal directly with suppliers Desires everyday low prices and avoids price promotions On-time delivery of defect-free merchandise
Kmart	Electronic links with 2600 of 3000 suppliers Provides major vendors with point-of-sale data that allow for automatic restocking of inventory
Toys 'R' Us	Involved in early design of new products Requires exclusive rights to some products
Home Depot	Requires lumber industry to place bar-code stickers on all wood pieces Provides input into supplier's new-product development—colors, names, warranties
Costco	Requires special package sizes and shipping procedures to minimize handling
Dillard's	Develops "hybrid exclusive labels" with suppliers

Source: Patricia Sellers, "How to Remake Your Sales Force," *Fortune*, May 4, 1992, pp. 98–103, and "Clout: More and More, Retail Giants Rule the Marketplace," *Business Week*, Dec. 21, 1992, pp. 66–73.

Power and Relationship Building

As the power of a manufacturer declines relative to the power of strong distributors or large buyers, there is a greater tendency to pursue long-term *relational exchanges*. These kinds of exchanges occur when both parties have a high degree of dependence on the other and when they operate in highly uncertain environments (such as those dominated by fast-paced technological change or extensive competition). A high degree of joint planning, well-coordinated activities, and mutual trust characterize these exchanges.[26] As a consequence, sales and distribution programs in these settings are geared toward implementing relationship marketing strategies (as we discussed in Chapter 7). Illustrative of such programs is the one developed at Black & Decker.

Black & Decker's U.S. Power Tool business established Wal-Mart and Home Depot divisions to cater to those large accounts. A vice president oversees a group composed of salespersons, a marketer, an information systems expert, a sales forecaster, and a financial analyst. This team has been responsible for creating specially designed packaging for drills and drill bits for the retailer. In addition, prior to introducing its new line of power tools in 1992, Black & Decker worked closely with retailers for 9 months, obtaining

---

[26] See F. Robert Dwyer, Paul Schurr, and Sejo Oh, "Developing Buyer-Seller Relationships," *Journal of Marketing*, April 1987, pp. 11–27, for a discussion of how these relationships develop.

input about the name, color, and development of a 30-day no-questions-asked return policy. As a result of this relationship, Black & Decker's new line had sales over $100 million during the first 10 months.[27]

Regardless of the nature of the relationship, however, a power base cannot be effectively employed nor a relational exchange established except through the sales force. To a large extent, the salesperson is the personification of the company. If a given salesperson demonstrates a lack of expertise, the company's image on this potential power base will suffer. Thus, both in selecting and in implementing appeals, the individual members of the sales force have a major role to play.

The Critical Role of the Sales Force

In selling to organizations (whether distributors or final buyers), it is important to maintain effective relationships with each account. That is, the salesperson generally faces the same buyer over and over, selling the same type of merchandise each time and becoming the major link between a supplier and its customer or distributor.[28]

Furthermore, the salespeople generally have a dual role. They are not merely the company's representatives to the customers (providing product information), but in addition, salespeople are the customers' or distributors' representatives to the supplier, because they help buyers obtain on-time delivery, special services, or special product designs.

These relationships are more or less continuous and involve the development of interpersonal relationships in which each individual (salesperson and buyer) is somewhat dependent on the other. Accordingly, the effectiveness of the salespeople is often dependent on the degree to which they are successful in communicating power.

TYPES OF SALESPERSON POWER

The primary bases of power available to the salesperson are expert power, referent power, and reward power.

Expert power exists to the extent that buyers or distributors believe that the salesperson has knowledge or skills that can be valuable to the buyer. Forms of salesperson expertise that may be valuable to buyers or distributors include knowledge of how a product can be effectively used, the ability to set up an effective display, and a knowledge of the products and models that will appeal to a distributor's customers. Consequently, appeals that employ the expertise of the salesperson may provide that salesperson with a basis for influencing the buyer.

---

[27] Sellers, op. cit., p. 102, and "Clout: More and More, Retail Giants Rule the Marketplace," *Business Week*, Dec. 21, 1992, p. 69.
[28] Benson Shapiro, "Manage the Customer, Not Just the Sales Force," *Harvard Business Review*, September–October 1974, p. 130.

Referent power will exist to the extent that the buyer is attracted to the salesperson out of friendship or a feeling of shared identity because the salesperson is viewed as having similar values or interests.[29] Because shared identity often leads to an increase in the buyer's willingness to trust the salesperson, referent power will provide the sales force with a source of influence that is useful even when a high degree of technical expertise is not needed.[30]

Reward power can also be employed by the sales force. Entertainment or special favors performed for the buyer (especially those related to the salesperson's role as the customer's representative to the supplier) are illustrative of the use of reward power. When a reward power is used over a period of time, the salesperson may, as a result, develop a referent power base as well, because the buyer will be more willing to trust the salesperson.

WHICH POWER BASE TO USE

Individual customers are likely to differ in their frequency of interaction with the salesperson, the size of their order, the amount of risk they perceive in a given buying situation, and the kind of decision process employed (as was discussed in Chapter 3). Accordingly, the selection of a type of appeal and type of power should depend heavily on the specific selling situation confronting the salesperson. Additionally, the technical skills and personal characteristics of salespeople will vary. While one may be adept at using expert power, another may rely on referent power. Accordingly, no single approach may be superior. Rather a given salesperson is likely to be most successful by adopting a behavior that is appropriate for his or her characteristics and skills as well as for meeting the buyer's or distributor's requirements.[31]

In sum, the salespeople must develop their own plan for the accounts they call on. A situation analysis should be performed for each customer, based upon that customer's requirements. An objective should be established for each account based on the current sales and distribution objective and on the salesperson's assessment of the opportunities for achieving that objective in each account. (This assessment will be based on competition, on the past level of success, and on whether the salesperson's company has the power to offer the necessary appeals.) Finally, the salesperson must adopt an influence strategy for each account based on his or her own capabilities and on the existing relationship with the buyer. Figure 12-3 portrays some of the elements involved in developing the individual account plan.

[29] See Gilbert Churchill, Robert Collins, and William Strang, "Should Retail Salespersons Be Similar to Their Customers?" *Journal of Retailing*, Fall 1975, pp. 29–42.
[30] Paul Busch and David Wilson, "An Experimental Analysis of a Salesman's Expert and Referent Bases of Social Power in the Buyer-Seller Dyad," *Journal of Marketing Research*, February 1976, pp. 3–11.
[31] See Barton Weitz, "Effectiveness in Sales Interactions: A Contingency Framework," *Journal of Marketing*, Winter 1981, pp. 85–103; and Thomas Leigh and Patrick McCraw, "Mapping the Procedural Knowledge of Industrial Sales Personnel: A Script-Theoretic Investigation," *Journal of Marketing*, January 1989, pp. 16–34.

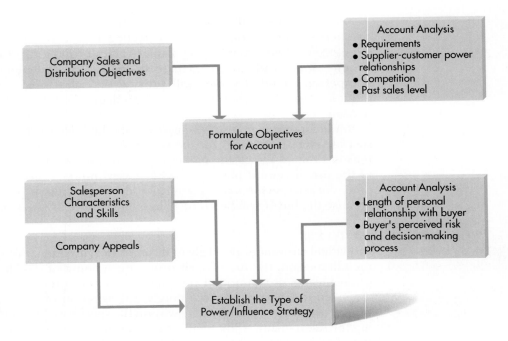

FIGURE 12-3
The salesperson's
planning process.

CONCLUSION

Sales and distribution programs provide the fundamental linkages between a firm and its buyers or distributors. The type of sales and distribution system a firm selects determines whether a product is sold direct or through wholesale or retail intermediaries and specifies the basic communication and customer service roles the sales force will play.

More specific direction for sales-force activities is provided by the program objectives that are established. These objectives should reflect the firm's marketing strategy and provide a basis for selecting the critical appeals offered to buyers or distributors. Additionally, managers must consider buyer requirements and the existing power relationships among manufacturers, distributors, and buyers in selecting appeals.

Although sales managers have an important role to play in designing the sales and distribution program, it will be up to the salespeople as well as sales managers to identify achievable objectives and to select appeals that will be effective in each buying situation. In effect, the sales-force members may become marketing strategists for their market areas. However, in order to assure consistency among salespeople, managers should set the overall program objectives and determine the range of appeals that can be offered before individual sales-force members design their own plans and tactics for influencing customers. In this chapter, we have examined the types of objectives and appeals that managers may choose, the process for selecting objectives and appeals, and some of the major considerations involved in implementing appeals. Figure 12-4 summarizes the relationship among the topics in this chapter and their relationship to the preceding and following chapters.

As with any marketing program, sales and distribution activities cost money and do not always lead to the achievement of objectives. Accordingly, it is important to understand the mechanisms for budgeting, allocating, and evaluating expenditures on these activities. These are the major topics in Chapter 13. However, before proceeding to the next chapter, consider the following example to review some of the major elements of a sales and distribution program.

FIGURE 12-4
Relationship of sales and distribution objectives and appeals to marketing strategy, situation analysis, and other marketing programs.

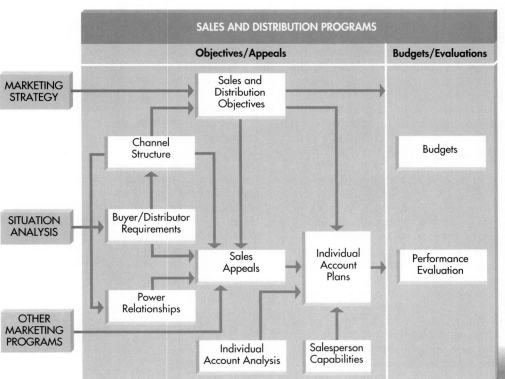

DELL COMPUTER: AN ALTERNATIVE DISTRIBUTION SYSTEM*

In 1984, Michael Dell moved the computer sales rep from the dealer channel to a telephone bank in Austin, Texas. The IBM-PC had set a standard that could be duplicated by others willing to buy the same microprocessors from Intel, disk drives from Seagate, and memory chips and miscellaneous control chips from Chips & Technologies. Soon, clones were being produced that matched IBM-PC's performance, and what had been a highly technological business suddenly became very easy to enter. Dell saw that the way to differentiate yourself in what was rapidly becoming a commodity business was through marketing innovations.

From its earliest days, Dell cut out the middleman and sold its computers directly to consumers via heavy advertising in the computer press and toll-free telephone numbers. IBM, Compaq, and other manufacturers paid little attention to this approach as they felt that nontechnical buyers would want the comfort of visiting a store prior to buying. In addition, it was felt that the dealer channel was necessary to provide the after-sale service required.

The Dell factory was, and remains, a screwdriver operation with little automation and almost a job-shop approach to manufacturing. With its low capital costs and flexibility, Dell was able to break into the market with low prices. However, Dell realized that others could cut prices too and developed a marketing strategy based upon reliability. Prior to Dell's entry, mail-order machines were often unreliable, risky for the consumer to buy. Dell's approach was to offer unlimited calls to a toll-free technical support line, a 30-day money-back guarantee, and next-day, on-site service through independent contractors, free for the first year.

Dell's sales were estimated to be $2 billion in 1992 with all but 15 percent of these made by telephone. Dell has a field sales force of 25 persons who call on business accounts and wholesale outlets such as Price Club. Dell's selling and administrative expenses are 14 percent of sales, compared to 24 percent at Apple and 30 percent at IBM. In addition, because it buys most of its components, Dell is able to support nearly $2 billion of sales revenues with just $55 million in land, property, plant, and equipment. For every dollar of fixed assets, Dell generates $33 in sales compared to IBM's $2. This allows Dell to turn over their inventory eight times a year and deliver a return on equity of 29 percent.

As large companies such as IBM, Apple, and Compaq began to sell direct, Dell responded by sending out Dellware, a catalog offering PC games, software packages, computer peripherals, printers, and disk drives. Dell will take an order over the telephone, then ask a software distributor to ship it to the customer with a commission paid to Dell. With product shipment within 5 days of order and 2-day delivery, Dell ranks first in customer satisfaction in its industry. By 1995, it is forecast that 30 percent of all PCs sold in the United States will be by direct mail. Not satisfied with their success in the United States, Dell announced in January 1993 that it will enter the Japanese market with the same distribution concept.

1. What would be the major obstacles facing firms such as IBM as they also add direct marketing to their existing distribution systems?

2. David Goldstein, president of Channel Marketing Corp., Dallas, says, "There will be a shift away from direct mail. It's a fad right now; everybody's trying to do it. But it's not a trend; it will go away." Do you agree with this? Why or why not?

3. Would you expect the many-tiered system of distribution in Japan to facilitate or impede Dell's entry into this market?

* Developed from "Computers by Mail: A Megabyte Business Boom," *Business Week,* May 11, 1992, pp. 93–96; Julie Pitta, "Why Dell Is a Survivor," *Forbes,* Oct. 12, 1992, pp. 82–91; "Mail-Order Madness," *Business Week/Quality,* 1991, p. 128; Carrie Goerne, "More Computer Marketers Taking the Direct Approach," *Marketing News,* Oct. 26, 1992, p. 6; and "A Surprise Lift for Computer Retailers," *Business Week,* Oct. 19, 1992, p. 63.

QUESTIONS AND SITUATIONS FOR DISCUSSION

1. What type(s) of sales and distribution system(s) would be appropriate in each of the following cases? Explain.

a. A firm produces an expensive and technically complex piece of diagnostic equipment for hospitals.

b. A firm produces paper for use in duplicating machines.

c. A firm sells a wide line of canned food products to institutional buyers (such as nursing homes, schools, and factory cafeterias).

d. A firm operates a lawn-care service for homeowners.

2. Wal-Mart accounts for over 20 percent of the sales of Mr. Coffee, Royal Appliance, and Gitano apparel. What advantages/disadvantages are there for both Wal-Mart and these suppliers to have such a heavy concentration of sales with one account?

3. Both firms that use trade sales forces and firms that use missionary sales forces employ distributors. Explain how these types of sales forces differ. Explain how the tasks performed by the distributors differ between channels in which the manufacturer uses each type of sales force.

4. Which type of sales and distribution objective would be most appropriate for each of the following firms?

a. A computer manufacturer operating at full capacity

b. A women's hosiery manufacturer with a product that is carried by a relatively small number of department stores

c. A bottler that wants to set up in-store retail displays for a new line of soft drinks

d. A manufacturer of automobile seat belts that is only one of several suppliers used by automobile manufacturers

5. What are the trade-offs that managers who are responsible for inventory need to consider when reordering merchandise?

6. In 1991, Wal-Mart's president sent a letter to manufacturers stating: "We have decided that our dealings should be directly with the principals of your company." This will lead to the elimination of manufacturer's representatives. What are the advantages/disadvantages for Wal-Mart and manufacturers?

7. "Wholesale clubs primarily buy leading brands, usually from whichever supplier gives them the best deal." If you are a supplier, are there ways you could avoid competing only on the basis of price?

8. Assume that you are a salesperson in each of the following situations. Which type of power do you think would be most effective for you to use? Explain why.

a. Your company has come out with a new product that has been so well received that there is not enough production to meet customer demand.

b. Your company manufactures a product that must be customized to meet each buyer's needs.

c. Your company sells a product through distributors, and customer demand for the product is highly sensitive to economic fluctuations.

d. Your product is essentially an undifferentiated commodity that is not very complex. A number of competitors offer equivalent products and delivery appeals.

9. Gus is an account representative for a major computer manufacturer and is responsible for all sales and customer service activities at a major New York bank. Besides Gus, two sales managers, four salespeople, two trainees, and thirteen technical service reps are assigned to this account by the computer firm. When major acquisitions are being contemplated, the decision-making process in this bank may well take a year.

a. What are the probable reasons for selecting a direct personal selling system in this case?

b. Which sales and distribution objective will Gus and his team likely emphasize most?

c. Which appeals do you think will be most effective in this situation?

d. Discuss the most important factors a salesperson should consider in this type of selling situation.

SUGGESTED ADDITIONAL READINGS

Calantone, Roger J., and Jule B. Gassenheimer, "Overcoming Basic Problems between Manufacturers and Distributors," *Industrial Marketing Management*, August 1991, pp. 215–221.

Dwyer, F. Robert, Paul Schurr, and Sejo Oh, "Developing Buyer-Seller Relationships," *Journal of Marketing*, April 1987, pp. 11–27.

Eisenhart, Tom, "Super Sales through Superstores," *Business Marketing*, December 1991, pp. T6ff.

Gaski, John F., "The Theory of Power and Conflict in Channels of Distribution," *Journal of Marketing*, Summer 1984, pp. 9–29.

Leigh, Thomas, and Patrick McGraw, "Mapping the Procedural Knowledge of Industrial Sales Personnel: A Script-Theoretic Investigation," *Journal of Marketing*, January 1989, pp. 16–34.

Magrath, Allan, and Kenneth Hardy, "Avoiding the Pitfalls in Managing Distribution Channels," *Business Horizons*, September–October 1987, pp. 29–33.

Shapiro, Benson P., V. Kasturi Rangan, and John J. Sviokla, "Staple Yourself to an Order," *Harvard Business Review*, July–August 1992, pp. 113–122.

Shipley, David, Colin Egan, and Scott Edgett, "Meeting Source Selection Criteria: Direct versus Distributor Channels," *Industrial Marketing Management*, November 1991, pp. 297–303.

Weitz, Barton, Harish Sujan, and Mita Sujan, "Knowledge, Motivation and Adaptive Behavior: A Framework for Improving Selling Effectiveness," *Journal of Marketing*, October 1986, pp. 174–191.

Yovovich, B. G., "The Direct Channel Booms," *Business Marketing*, December 1991, pp. T6ff.

CHAPTER 13

SALES AND DISTRIBUTION PROGRAMS: BUDGETS AND PERFORMANCE EVALUATION

OVERVIEW

In Chapter 12 we pointed out the importance of establishing sales and distribution objectives that would provide guidance for the design of specific sales and distribution appeals. We also discussed the importance of selecting appeals that would best satisfy the benefits being sought by the buyer-distributor. Those appeals should be chosen based upon careful analysis of buyer-distributor requirements as well as existing power relationships. It is important to remember that in today's competitive marketplace, a program that only maximizes sales or some other program objective (such as new product sales) may not be optimal from a profit perspective. Like all other marketing programs, sales and distribution activities cost money. With the median cost per sales call being approximately $200, sales managers must operate within a budget that is consistent with overall sales and profit objectives. It is the task of sales management not only to establish the budget necessary to support the expenses of the selling operation but also to match the available resources to the requirements of the markets.

In addition to assessing the cost of various programs, sales managers are responsible for evaluating program performance on both sales-volume and non-sales-volume dimensions. These evaluations usually are made at various levels: The performances of individual salespeople, distributors, or sales territories are examined in addition to overall program performance. Such evaluations are then used to identify possible program modifications for improving performance.

In this chapter we provide procedures for establishing the program budget as we examine the relationship between sales and distribution appeals and sales and distribution costs. Later in the chapter we also present a number of methods for evaluating sales and distribution performance. In Chapter 14 we will discuss some of the sales management actions that are directed toward enhancing the performance of individual sales-force members.

ESTABLISHING THE SALES
AND DISTRIBUTION BUDGET

In designing a program to achieve a sales and distribution objective, sales managers should attempt to estimate the budgetary consequences of the program. Specifically, managers should examine the costs a specific program will incur and the expected impact of the program on profitability. The importance of this can be illustrated by the general manager of the Health Care Division of Johnson & Johnson, who stated, "If [the departments] fail to meet the profit objectives of the division, the departmental budgets are reworked until they are brought in line."[1]

Managers can then determine if the budget is consistent with the product objectives. That is, a sales and distribution budget that will lead to increased sales and market share may be appropriate for a problem-child product even if a decline in total contribution is expected in the short run. For instance, with those types of products and services, it is not unusual for companies to pay additional incentives to open new accounts in order to increase market share. In addition, travel and entertainment expenses associated with the sale of low-share products in high-growth markets often are higher due to increased competitive activity. Alternatively, sales and distribution budgets for cash cows should normally result in an increase in total contribution.[2]

Figure 13-1 summarizes the elements in the budgeting process. As Figure 13-1 suggests, if the expected results of the proposed budget are inconsistent with the product objectives, revisions in objectives or in the appeals may be appropriate.

The first step in this process is to estimate the impact of the appeals on the profitability structure. As seen in Figure 13-1, sales and distribution programs can influence the direct costs of marketing a product or product line and the variable-contribution margin. Specifically, major budgetary factors that must be considered are

- Sales-force compensation costs
- Working-capital costs for credit and inventory
- Special transportation costs
- Prices and discounts (variable-contribution margin)

Sales-Force Compensation Costs

The salaries of sales and customer service personnel and the travel expenses necessary for supporting them are a major expense category for the firms

---

[1] "At Johnson & Johnson, the Sales Budget Gets the Best of Care," *Sales Management*, May 19, 1975, p. 10.
[2] The relationship between marketing budgets and their effect on market share is discussed in Robert D. Buzzell and Frederick E. Wiersma, "Successful Share-Building Strategies," *Harvard Business Review*, January–February 1981, pp. 135–144.

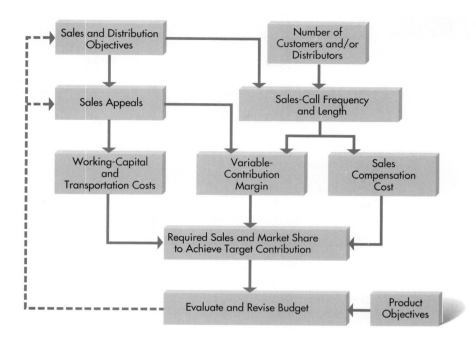

FIGURE 13-1
Establishing
a sales and
distribution
budget.

that employ company sales forces. Table 13-1 gives an indication of the cost per sales call associated with personal selling. The primary determinant of these costs is the size of the sales force.[3]

There are several ways in which the number of salespeople needed can be determined. Probably the easiest approach is simply to divide the dollars available by the costs necessary to support one salesperson. Although this method is simple to apply, it ignores the market conditions that should influence sales-force size. For instance, one would expect that early in the product life cycle it may be desirable to have more sales staff than would be necessary in the decline stage. Some firms hire as many salespersons as possible as long as the gross profit on the new business they generate equals the costs associated with the additional salesperson. This policy can readily lead to overstaffing, with too many salespersons calling on too few customers. In addition, both economic and market conditions are overlooked when such an approach is followed.[4]

A more logical and systematic approach is to determine the size of the sales force necessary by considering the number of customers or prospects and

---

[3] For a useful review of techniques for estimating the appropriate size of a sales force, see Arthur Median, "Optimizing the Number of Industrial Salespersons," *Industrial Marketing Management*, February 1982, pp. 63–74.

[4] Leonard M. Lodish, "A User-Oriented Model for Sales Force Size, Product, and Market Allocation Decisions," *Journal of Marketing*, Summer 1980, pp. 70–78.

| TABLE 13-1 | AVERAGE COST OF SALES CALL |

	TYPE OF SALES FORCE		
	CONSUMER GOODS	INDUSTRIAL GOODS	SERVICE
Average direct costs			
Compensation	60,500	58,500	64,000
Expenses	25,600	24,500	15,600
Total	86,100	83,000	79,600
Average calls per year*			
High-frequency areas or policies	841.5	748.0	1122.0
Low-frequency areas or policies	561.0	561.0	654.5
Average cost per call			
High-frequency areas or policies	143.59	137.62	100.00
Low-frequency areas or policies	215.38	202.54	197.43

* Assumes 187 selling days per year.
Developed from "1992 Sales Manager's Budget Planner," *Sales and Marketing Management*, June 22, 1992.

their requirements. A basic estimate of the number of salespeople needed can generally be made as follows:

$$\text{Size of sales force} = \frac{\text{number of accounts in target market} \times \text{required number of calls per year per account}}{\text{number of calls each salesperson can make}}$$

Note that managers may have to develop separate sales-force size estimates for different parts of the sales force. For example, when distinct selling tasks are required for different customers, specialized sales forces may exist. Managers may need to calculate separately the sizes of

- The sales force and the customer service force
- The new-prospect sales force and the sales force calling on established accounts
- The sales forces that call on accounts in different industries (when a specialized knowledge of industry production processes or technologies is important)
- The sales force for each territory

Whatever the relevant sales-force definition, the staffing plan must consider the number of accounts, the required sales-call frequency, and the call capacity of the sales and service representatives.

Estimating Required Call Frequency

Managers should consider each of the following factors in estimating the required number of calls per account:

- The size of the various buyer or distributor accounts
- The sales and distribution objectives
- The need for *unplanned* calls
- The estimated sales effects of increasing or reducing the number of calls per account

ACCOUNT SIZE

An important consideration in estimating the required number of calls is the size of the account, because the sales manager will want to minimize the risk of losing large accounts. Large accounts, moreover, may be more profitable because of the size of their orders.

The ABC rule of account classification holds that the first 15 percent of a firm's customers will account for 65 percent of the firm's sales, the next 20 percent will yield 20 percent of the sales, and the last 65 percent will produce only 15 percent of sales.[5] A recent study of 192 firms found that the top 20 percent of accounts produced 75 percent of the sales volume.[6]

It is a common practice of many firms to divide distributor or buyer accounts into account-size categories similar to the breakdown given in Table 13-2. As the table indicates, a small number of large accounts (the A accounts) generally represent a very large portion of sales. This is true whether the accounts are final buyers or distributors. Accordingly, those accounts will be called on more frequently than medium and small accounts, as seen in the case of Dictaphone:

> Dictaphone grouped its five-year historical sales data by the type of business sold to and the number of employees working in those businesses. Using the Dun & Bradstreet Market Identifiers database of 8.8 million U.S. businesses and Dictaphone's sales by type of business vs. number of employees at that business, they created values based upon what had historically been sold to each type and size of business. This provided Dictaphone with the potential dollar value that could be assigned to any size business. After eliminating businesses that offered too little potential, they created separate profile cards for each business, separated by territory. These were assigned to sales reps with rankings based upon sales potential. The company suggested that A accounts be called every two weeks, B accounts once a month, and C accounts once a quarter.[7]

An important issue in examining account size is whether to use *actual* sales or *potential* sales as the basis for classifying accounts. Firms that classify accounts on the basis of current sales are implicitly assuming the company has reached its maximum level of achievement in each account. Yet, for most

---

[5] Porter Henry, "The Important Few—The Unimportant Many," *1980 Portfolio of Sales and Marketing Plans*, Sales & Marketing Management, New York, 1980, pp. 34–37.

[6] William A. O'Connell and William Keenan, Jr., "The Shape of Things to Come," *Sales & Marketing Management*, January 1990, pp. 36–41.

[7] Bob Attanasio, "How PC-Based Sales Quotas Boost Productivity, Morale," *Sales & Marketing Management*, September 1991, p. 150.

firms, some of the C accounts are very likely to become A accounts if additional effort is applied.

SALES AND DISTRIBUTION OBJECTIVES

The sales and distribution objectives for a specific program may force a modification of the basic call-frequency pattern, however. Although the frequency patterns given in Table 13-2 may be appropriate for account maintenance, if managers establish other objectives, then revisions in call frequency may be necessary. For example, if an account-development objective is established, sales calls on new accounts must be included in the staffing plan. For instance, Goodyear requires each salesperson to open five new accounts a year and gives bonuses according to the size of the new accounts.[8] Similarly, some sales or customer service calls to existing accounts are designed to fulfill a specific objective (such as demonstrating a product's superiority in order to increase sales penetration in key accounts, or stimulating special reseller support on special programs).

UNPLANNED CALLS

Emergency repairs or follow-up of an order may require unplanned calls. Usually the ratio of unplanned-to-planned calls can be established from historical sales-call reports. However, in developing a staffing plan, the number of unplanned calls should be considered, because they take additional time from the sales force.

ESTIMATED SALES EFFECTS

As a final consideration in determining the required number of calls, managers should attempt to estimate the change in sales that will result from increasing or decreasing the current sales-call frequencies on each account. This analysis (which is incorporated in many computer-based systems for

[8] Bill Kelley, "How Much Help Does a Salesperson Need?" *Sales Management*, May 1989, p. 35.

TABLE 13-2 **AN ILLUSTRATION OF SALES-CALL FREQUENCIES BY ACCOUNT SIZE**

ACCOUNT GROUP	VOLUME PER MONTH	NUMBER OF ACCOUNTS	PLANNED FREQUENCY PER ACCOUNT	TOTAL CALLS
A	2000	100	24/year	2400
B	600	300	12/year	3600
C	50	600	6/year	3600
				9600

territory management) must usually be made on the basis of the joint judgment of the salesperson and the sales manager.[9] For example:

> Turner Warmack, Vice President of Sales and Marketing at Ziegler Tools, holds an annual meeting with each of his 18 salespeople to discuss previous year's sales, key accounts, account growth, and possible areas for new business. Warmack and his salespeople categorize accounts and decide how often to call upon them. If the salesperson believes he or she can get more business from an account by calling on that account more frequently, he or she is encouraged to increase the call frequency.[10]

As was the case with the judgmental estimates we discussed in Chapter 6 (response of sales to advertising) and in Chapter 9 (price-elasticity), managers should seek to answer certain specific questions to gain insight into the relationship between sales calls and sales volume. Among these questions are the following:

- How frequently are buying decisions made?
- Is there a significant opportunity for account penetration?
- How frequently do competitors call on this account?
- Are new competitors, new products, or new technologies anticipated?
- How important is it to maintain referent power through frequent contact?
- How difficult or time-consuming will it be for buyers or distributors to change suppliers?
- How frequently do buyers or distributors need customer service support?

ESTIMATING SALES-FORCE CALL CAPACITY

In most organizations it is not usually a difficult task to estimate the average length of a sales call. However, the length of a sales call may differ significantly from new to existing accounts and from large to small accounts and will also vary if the purchase decision is made by a buying committee rather than an individual. In addition to selling effort requirements, nonselling time considerations (telephone, paperwork, planning time, and so on) should be considered in the analysis. Further, the possible number of calls will depend on the time required to travel between accounts.

For instance, Diesel Supply Co. (DSC) has a seven-person national sales force, which calls on natural gas pipeline and refinery accounts. DSC salespeople can only make about four sales calls per day because accounts are seventy

---

[9] Leonard Lodish, "Vaguely Right Approach to Sales Force Allocations," *Harvard Business Review*, January–February 1974, pp. 199–214. The impact of sales-call length and frequency is also examined in Raymond LaForge and David Cravens, "A Marketing Response Model for Sales Management Decision Making," *Journal of Personal Selling and Sales Management*, Fall/Winter 1981–1982, pp. 10–16.

[10] Kelley, op. cit., p. 32.

to eighty miles apart. To assist field sales, DSC uses mapping software to construct sales call routing maps based upon highly specific client data.[11]

Accordingly, the sales-force call capacity will be significantly affected by the way the sales force is allocated to territories and to accounts. In turn, the number of salespeople and their travel costs will be determined by the allocation system.

Decisions regarding the assignment of *accounts to territories* are normally made only when several new territories are to be opened or when a major reorganization of the sales force is deemed necessary. In those situations, managers can use computer models to structure territories to minimize the cost per sales call. To implement these models, managers must first estimate the time and expense involved in calling on each account, the desired number of salespeople per sales manager, and the required call frequency.

Decisions regarding the *allocation of the sales force to territories* may be modified over time when management expects different territories to experience different rates of growth in potential. Accordingly, additions to the sales force should be allocated to territories in a manner that reflects these changes. (Indeed, it may even be necessary to shift salespeople from one territory to another.) The relative market potential of various territories may be a useful basis for allocating the sales force. However, in determining the size of the sales force actually required per territory, managers should also consider the required call frequency and the time per call on each account (old and new). Differences between territories in factors such as competition, travel time, and vulnerability to competitors are also often included in these decisions. It is important to keep in mind that although the goal of defining territories is usually to create comparable work loads and sales potentials while maximizing coverage and minimizing travel time, in some cases unequal territories and assignments may be desirable. For example, trainees may initially be assigned to small territories, whereas proven salespersons are assigned larger responsibilities.

Decisions regarding the *assignment of individual sales-force members to particular accounts* may be required in certain selling situations. That is, if two or more salespeople or customer service personnel are sharing a geographical area, accounts may be assigned to each salesperson on some basis other than simply minimizing travel time. In particular, managers may assign salespeople to individual accounts on the basis of special expertise (such as knowledge of the buyer's or distributor's industry) or simply for the purpose of maintaining the continuity of interpersonal relationships when referent power is important to sales success.[12]

---

[11] Richard Lewis, "Putting Sales on the Map," *Sales & Marketing Management*, August 1992, p. 29.
[12] For an expanded discussion of this issue see R. W. LaForge, I. E. Young, and B. C. Hamm, "Increasing Sales Productivity through Improved Sales Call Allocation Strategies," *Journal of Personal Selling and Sales Management*, November 1983, pp. 52–59.

Special Compensation Costs

Special compensation includes sales commissions, bonuses, and special incentives (such as merchandise and travel awards). These incentives are offered in order to achieve some specific type of performance on the part of sales-force members or distributors.

In the case of sales commissions, the incentive is directed toward sales-volume gains. Because the level of commission earned is determined as a percentage of sales or a fixed amount per unit of sales, the cost of this incentive is a *variable cost*. However, most special compensation costs represent increases in fixed direct costs and generally are tied to specific sales and distribution objectives. For example, bonuses or travel awards may be provided to salespeople who achieve a certain level of new-account openings or a certain level of retailer participation in a sales promotion.

Selling Costs and Manufacturer's Representatives

Because of the high cost of having a company sales force, a great many firms use manufacturer's representatives to perform the direct selling function. Manufacturer's representatives are independent businesses. Approximately 50,000 U.S. manufacturers use independent representatives; in 1992 there were over 30,000 representative firms in operation.[13]

These firms usually sell the product lines of a number of manufacturers within a specific industry and operate on a percent-of-sales commission basis. A study of the Manufacturer's Agent National Association showed that the typical independent agency represented an average of 10.1 different manufac-

[13] Lois C. DuBoise and Roger H. Grace, "The Care and Feeding of Manufacturer's Reps," *Business Marketing*, December 1987, p. 56; and Michael Marshall and Frank Siegler, "Selecting the Right Rep Firm," *Sales and Marketing Management*, January 1993, p. 46.

TABLE 13-3 **AVERAGE MANUFACTURER'S REPRESENTATIVES COMMISSIONS IN SELECTED LINES**

PRODUCT OR SERVICE	AVERAGE COMMISSION PAID
Advertising products and services	16.17
Building materials and supplies	7.65
Computers	9.99
Electronic consumer products	5.64
Food products and services	15.00
Marine	9.81
Paper industry	11.16
Plastics	6.18
Sporting goods supplies and accessories	8.18

Source: Manufacturers' Agents National Association, *Survey of Sales Commissions*, as reported in *1987 Survey of Selling Costs, Sales and Marketing Management*, Feb. 16, 1987, p. 59.

turers, employed 3.5 salespeople, and had $4,402,986 gross sales.[14] Table 13-3 gives some examples of the level of commission paid on net sales to manufacturer's reps in some selected industries.

From a cost perspective, the decision to use a company sales force or a manufacturer's rep revolves around the company's total sales volume. A company sales force is a fixed cost with respect to sales volume, while the manufacturer's rep commission is a variable cost. Thus, at very low sales volumes, the manufacturer's rep is the lower cost alternative. As sales volume (within a specific territory or market) grows, the fixed cost of the company sales force is gradually spread over more units.

Table 13-4 provides a comparison of direct sales and sales agencies costs. Figure 13-2 demonstrates how the costs of the two alternatives behave as sales volume increases. If the cost of a company sales force is $200,000 for a given

[14] Jon M. Hawes, Kenneth E. Mast, and John E. Swan, "Trust Earning Perceptions of Sellers and Buyers," *Journal of Personal Selling and Sales Management*, Spring 1989, p. 3.

TABLE 13-4 DIRECT SALES VS. SALES AGENCIES: A COST/RATIO ANALYSIS

NUMBER OF DIRECT SALESPEOPLE	TERRITORY VOLUME			
	$250,000	$500,000	$1M	$2M
One	$ 50,000 20%*	$ 50,000 10%	$ 50,000 5%	$ 50,000 2.5%
Two	$100,000 40%	$100,000 20%	$100,000 10%	$100,000 5%
Three	$150,000 60%	$150,000 30%	$150,000 15%	$150,000 7.5%
Four	$200,000 80%	$200,000 40%	$200,000 20%	$200,000 10%

SALES AGENCY COMMISSION	TERRITORY VOLUME			
	$250,000	$500,000	$1M	$2M
5%	$ 12,500 5%*	$ 25,000 5%	$ 50,000 5%	$100,000 5%
7.5%	$ 18,750 7.5%	$ 37,500 7.5%	$ 75,000 7.5%	$150,000 7.5%
10%	$ 25,000 10%	$ 50,000 10%	$100,000 10%	$200,000 10%

* Cost as a percent of total sales.

Notes: Annual cost figures for direct sales are based on a salary of $39,000 plus $11,000 expenses per salesperson. This doesn't include the cost of branch office facilities and personnel or fringe benefits normally paid to direct salespeople. The number of agency people covering the same territory may vary, but commissions as a ratio of sales would remain the same.

Source: Edwin E. Bobrow, "The Question of Reps," *Sales & Marketing Management*, June 1991, p. 34.

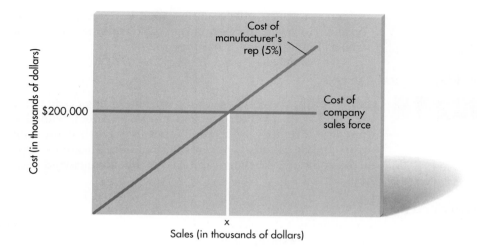

FIGURE 13-2
Relationship between sales volume and the cost of either a manufacturer's representative or a company sales force.

territory, and if a manufacturer's representative charges 5 percent of sales, the costs are equal when sales are equal to $4 million. The point of equal costs is derived as follows:

$$\text{Cost of manufacturer's rep} = \text{cost of company sales force}$$
$$.05x = \$200,000$$
$$x = \$4,000,000$$

In this example, therefore, the cost of a manufacturer's rep is lower at sales volumes below $4 million, but the cost of a company sales force is lower at sales volumes above $4 million. In addition to cost, other factors must be considered in the choice between a company sales force and a manufacturer's representative. Among the major arguments made on behalf of the two alternatives, the following points are the most widely accepted.[15]

■ Two critical advantages of manufacturer's reps are that they may have a better knowledge of customer or distributor needs and they may provide better coverage of small accounts. They are able to achieve these advantages because they combine the lines of several suppliers and thus can justify more calls on such accounts.
■ The critical advantage of the company sales force lies in control over performance. While manufacturer's reps do not get paid unless they make a sale, a company sales force can be motivated to perform nonselling or sales-development activities designed to build long-term growth or emphasize account maintenance. For instance, in Germany, industrial salespeople

[15] See Erin Anderson, "The Salesperson as Outside Agent or Employee: A Transaction Cost Analysis," *Marketing Science*, Summer 1985, pp. 234–254. For another view, see "Wal-Mart's War on Reps," *Sales and Marketing Management*, March 1987, pp. 41–43.

seldom prospect, infrequently expedite orders, and rarely follow up on orders. However, the Germans excel at training their clients' employees, as well as helping install what they sell.[16]

Working-Capital Costs

Until recently, the costs associated with providing credit to buyers and distributors and with inventory incentives were seldom related to sales budgets. However, inventory and credit appeals have become more important to buyers and distributors. As a result, more organizations have begun to evaluate the additional working-capital costs that are incurred because of the use of these appeals.[17]

CREDIT COSTS

In examining the costs of offering a credit appeal, managers must consider each of the following factors:

■ An estimate of the sales volumes generated under alternative credit policies
■ The annual rate of turnover of accounts receivable
■ The annual cost of providing trade credit (usually, the firm's cost of borrowing short-term capital plus costs of credit administration)
■ The variable-contribution margin

For example, assume a firm offers 30-day credit, a variable-contribution margin of 20 percent, and an annual cost of credit of 12 percent of the average amount of credit outstanding. If all credit customers pay their bills every month, and if expected credit sales under this policy are $20 million, then the annual rate of turnover is 12 (that is, 12 months in a year divided by 1 month), and the annual cost of credit is

$$\frac{\$20 \text{ million}}{12 \text{ turns}} \times .12 = \$200,000$$

Now, assume the same firm believes it can generate an additional $4 million in sales if customers are given 2 months to pay. Because the same credit terms must generally be offered to all customers, we can expect all credit customers to take the full 2 months to pay. Therefore, the account receivable turnover is now six per year (12 months divided by 2 months), and the cost of this credit policy is

$$\frac{\$24 \text{ million}}{6 \text{ turns}} \times .12 = \$480,000$$

---

[16] "How the Germans Do It," *Sales and Marketing Management*, Nov. 19, 1989, p. 25.
[17] William Crissy, Paul Fischer, and Frank Mossman, "Segmental Analysis: Key to Marketing Profitability," *Business Topics*, Spring 1973, pp. 42–49; also see R. D. Rutherford, "Make Your Sales Force Credit Smart," *Sales and Marketing Management*, November 1989, pp. 50–55.

Thus, credit costs will rise by $280,000 under the new policy. However, at a variable-contribution margin of 20 percent, the added $4 million in sales will increase the firm's dollar variable contribution by

$$\$4 \text{ million} \times .20 = \$800,000$$

Therefore, the net effect of the change in the credit policy will be

$$
\begin{array}{ll}
\$800,000 & \text{(increased variable contribution)} \\
-\$280,000 & \text{(increased working-capital cost)} \\
\hline
\$520,000 &
\end{array}
$$

Salespeople need to know the direct cost of delayed payment terms. When salespeople are paid commissions based on sales orders rather than on paid-up sales, they do not appreciate the direct cost to the company of delayed payment terms. However, many companies pay their salespeople when payment for the goods is received. In this way, salespeople quickly become as concerned about cash flow and the effect of credit terms on profitability as top management. Geolograph-Pioneer furnishes its salespeople with two statements each month. One shows collections from customers received during the prior month and the second shows all billings not paid. These two statements show each sales representative the status of each account every month, which leads to a closer working relationship between sales and credit.[18]

INVENTORY COSTS

Managers can employ a procedure similar to that used to examine the cost of credit appeals when they wish to identify the budgeting implications of inventory appeals. The major differences in the two analyses are that the annual rate of inventory turnover will be used in place of the annual accounts receivable turnover, and the annual cost of carrying inventory is used in place of the annual cost of providing trade credit. That is, for a given inventory policy,

$$\text{Inventory cost} = \frac{\text{annual sales}}{\text{inventory turnover}} \times \text{inventory carrying cost}$$

where

$$\text{Inventory turnover} = \frac{\text{annual dollar sales}}{\text{average dollar value of inventory held by the firm}}$$

Carrying costs generally incorporate short-term borrowing costs, adminis-

[18] Ibid., p. 54.

trative costs, product obsolescence, and breakage. Today these costs are being watched more closely than ever.

As in the case of accounts receivable, increases in inventory costs that result from sales and distribution appeals should be considered direct expenses, and managers should consider the amount of these expenses in evaluating the profitability consequences of the program.

As we suggested earlier, many firms do not yet incorporate these costs when developing sales and distribution budgets. However, as product obsolescence becomes more significant (a particular problem in fashion and high-technology industries), more firms have begun to consider the impact of these costs. Consider, for example, the problems experienced by Dynascan.

> Dynascan was originally a manufacturer of electronic testing equipment but moved into consumer and office products with its Cobra-brand citizens band radios in the 1970s. Subsequently, the company produced lines of cordless telephones, radar detectors, answering machines, and other electronics products. While the company was highly successful with all of these products from a sales standpoint, it had severe profit problems with the CB radio and cordless phone products: When sales leveled off, the company was awash in inventory. The company then recognized the impact of working-capital costs on its profits: $4 of working capital are needed to support every $10 of sales. So the company set up a system to analyze all sales programs continually for their impact on working-capital costs.[19]

Transportation Costs

Sales and distribution programs may cause increases in transportation costs when

- The sales force agrees to offer expedited (fastest-way) shipment of rush orders (requiring the most expensive transportation methods).
- More frequent delivery schedules (often entailing less-than-truckload or less-than-carload quantities) are offered.

Transportation costs are closely linked with customers' inventory policies. More manufacturers are adopting just-in-time inventory policies. These policies minimize the volume of inventory that needs to be kept on hand for the production process. Usually, the ability to help a customer implement a just-in-time policy is a prerequisite to obtaining a sale.

To the extent that transportation-cost increases result from sales or customer service programs, the increased direct cost should be charged to the sales and distribution budget. Moreover, because transportation costs usually represent a large portion of total costs for products that are bulky or that have a high package-to-product weight ratio, it will be difficult to pass the increased

[19] David Henry, "Death Wish," *Forbes*, Oct. 20, 1986, pp. 50–51.

transportation costs on to customers who require these appeals. Frequently, however, a change in the structure of the sales and distribution system may be useful in providing improved delivery at the same (or lower) prices. As an example, consider the changes initiated by IKEA.

> IKEA is one of Europe's largest furniture retailers. This Swedish firm distributes ready-to-assemble furniture and decorating accessories through a transnational distribution system. IKEA uses an innovative flat-pack technology that saves storage space and cuts shipping costs. Almost all of IKEA's 14,000 product offerings are sold knocked down in flat boxes and shipped from a central warehouse in Amhult, Sweden. This warehouse is staffed by only three people using computerized fork lifts and thirteen robots. IKEA had seven U.S. stores in 1991 with plans to expand to eight huge stores in the New York and Los Angeles markets by 1993. These stores are serviced by distribution centers on the East and West coasts, with future plans calling for a system of five regional distribution warehouses. IKEA has 1500 suppliers in 45 countries, and its unique distribution and packaging technology allows it to have retail prices up to 50 percent lower than those of its competitors.[20]

Variable-Contribution-Margin Effects

Managers often use price appeals (such as cash and quantity discounts or price shading) to achieve the program objectives. However, each of these appeals results in a reduction in the variable-contribution margin. Accordingly, to the extent that sales personnel have a role in setting prices, the profitability impact of price appeals should be closely evaluated.

CASH DISCOUNTS

Firms in most industries employ cash discounts as sales appeals. In fact, cash discount policies are often established more by industry tradition than through analysis. A wide variety of terms are available. Liz Claiborne, for instance, has terms of 10/10 EOM: Retailers get a discount of 10 percent if they pay for merchandise in the first ten days after the month in which they receive the goods. Full payment must be made by the end of the month after the goods are received.[21]

Although cash discounts may encourage faster payment of invoices (thus reducing working-capital costs), the costs of the discount often exceed the working-capital costs. For example, a firm that offers a 2 percent discount to buyers or distributors who pay in 10 days rather than 30 days is really paying 2 percent to get its cash 20 days sooner. This translates into an annual interest

[20] Barbara Soloman, "A Swedish Company Corners the Business: Worldwide," *Management Review*, April 1991, pp. 10–B; Bill Saporito, "IKEA's Got 'Em Living Up," *Fortune*, Mar. 14, 1991, p. 72; and Jeffrey A. Tracktenberg, "IKEA Furniture Chain Pleases with Its Prices, Not with Its Service," *The Wall Street Journal*, Sept. 17, 1991, pp. A1, A5.
[21] "An SA Surprise: Claiborne Hikes Trade Discount," *Women's Wear Daily*, July 30, 1990, pp. 1, 19.

rate of about 36 percent. (That is, 2 percent times 365 days divided by 20 days equals 36 percent.) Since most firms can borrow money at rates well below 36 percent, then the cash discount policy really increases total cost.

QUANTITY DISCOUNTS

The seller may save in many ways through quantity discounts:[22]

- A possible shifting of inventory burdens and costs to the buyer or distributor
- Reduced sales-contact and order-processing costs
- More economical shipping costs because of increases in volume per shipment
- Improved production scheduling because larger, more economical production runs can be made

For instance, assume a firm has a buyer that orders 1200 units per year in monthly orders of 100 units each. Also assume the seller's sales-contact and processing costs per order are $400, the inventory-carrying cost is 20 percent, the unit-variable-production cost is $80, and the price is $100 per unit. Further assume the buyer will purchase in orders of 200 units if the price is lowered to $98 per unit. This means the firm must obtain and process only six orders per year (1200 units divided by 200 units per order). From the seller's viewpoint the two alternatives can be compared in terms of margin reductions and order costs, as indicated in Table 13-5.

[22] An analytical approach for establishing quantity discounts is available in James P. Monahan, "A Quantity Discount Pricing Model to Increase Vendor Profits," *Management Science*, June 1984, pp. 720–726.

TABLE 13-5   **EVALUATING THE PROFIT IMPACT OF A QUANTITY DISCOUNT**

	AT NORMAL PRICE	AT QUANTITY DISCOUNT
Price	$100/unit	$98/unit
Variable cost	$80/unit	$80/unit
Unit variable-contribution margin	$20/unit	$18/unit
Sales volume	1200	1200
Dollar contribution margin	$24,000	$21,600
Order cost	$400/order	$400/order
Number of orders	12	6
Total order cost	$4800	$2400
Reduction in margin:		$24,000 − $21,600 = $2400
Savings in order cost:		$ 4,800 − $ 2,400 = $2400
Net profit impact		$ 0

The reduced direct cost of obtaining and processing orders offsets the lost contribution margin in this example. Note that this analysis does require several key assumptions:

- That order rates are fairly constant over the year
- That order-processing costs are actually lowered (that is, the sales calls are reduced and reductions in order-processing costs are actually made)
- That buyers will perceive a gain from the lower prices that exceed their increased carrying costs

However, the seller is very likely to obtain additional benefits from reduced transportation costs and, in some cases, from reductions in the amount of inventory that must be held by the seller in order to satisfy customer requirements.

CUMULATIVE QUANTITY DISCOUNTS

These discounts (also known as *volume rebates*) are given on the basis of the total volume of purchases over a period of time (usually 1 year) regardless of average order size. Some firms justify these discounts by showing that selling costs for large-volume accounts are proportionately less than for smaller accounts. However, the motivations for employing volume rebates are usually competitive. Customers may demand volume rebates because competitors offer them. However, firms may offer the rebates because the rebates give better account penetration: With volume rebates, there is more incentive for a buyer or distributor to reduce the number of sources of supply.[23]

PRICE SHADING

Price shading appeals are used when a lower price will enable the sales force to close a sale to a particular customer. Frequently, the lower price results in additional sales that otherwise would not be made. This is true especially when opening a new account or attempting to gain a larger share of the business of an existing account (account penetration). In those cases, price shading will increase profitability as long as excess capacity exists and as long as the price exceeds the variable costs plus the cost of delivery. However, the excessive use of price shading may mean the sales force is not emphasizing other nonprice appeals to an adequate extent. By employing price shading on a broad scale, managers may ultimately find dollar-contribution margins begin to decline and competitors begin to expand their use of price shading. Accordingly, some firms have begun to eliminate shading except for new accounts or very large buyers, and others have put greater limits on the sales force's author-

---

[23] See Ashak Rao, "Quantity Discounts in Today's Markets," *Journal of Marketing*, Fall 1980, pp. 44–51, for a more extensive discussion.

ity regarding price, in order to ensure minimally acceptable margins are realized.[24]

Finalizing the Budget

After a manager has identified the costs and margin reductions associated with providing a given set of appeals, a sales budget can be established. As indicated in Figure 13-3, several steps are involved in developing this budget:

1. Determining the required levels of sales and market share needed based on (a) increases in direct costs, (b) changes in variable-contribution margins, (c) the target contribution desired, and (d) the industry sales forecast

[24] In one study, researchers found that salespeople with the greatest degree of pricing authority generated the lowest sales and profit performance. See P. Ronald Stephenson, William L. Cron, and Gary L. Frazier, "Delegating Pricing Authority to the Sales Force: The Effect on Sales and Profit Performance," *Journal of Marketing*, Spring 1979, pp. 21–28.

FIGURE 13-3
Finalizing the sales and distribution budget.

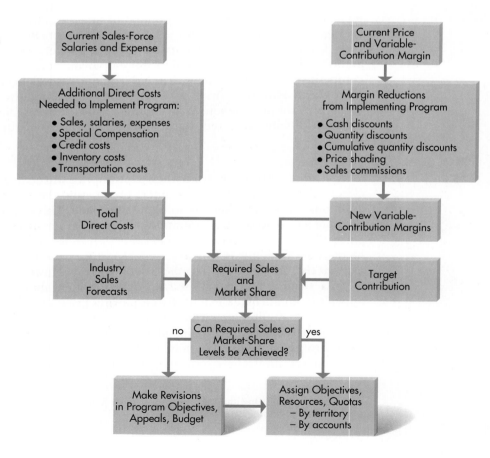

2. Determining whether the required sales and market share can be achieved on the basis of productivity judgments
3. Making revisions, if necessary, to the program objectives (such as the level of achievement required) or to the appeals in order to develop a more realistic budget
4. Assigning specific levels of achievement, if appropriate, for program objectives and sales quotas to individual sales territories, salespeople, and, perhaps, to individual accounts, and allocating human and financial resources to each sales territory in a manner consistent with territorial potential, objectives, and quotas.

Note that steps 1 through 3 deal with the total sales and distribution budget. In assessing the likelihood that the required sales and market-share levels will be reached, the impact of other programs (such as advertising) must be known.

Consequently, the sales managers may not be the only managers involved in making the assessment about the reasonableness of the budget. (The process of coordinating program budgets is discussed in detail in Chapter 15.)

Managers may also have to develop separate budgets for different portions of the sales force. For example, a number of organizations separate the sales and customer service functions and budgets. That is, in some firms, customer service is viewed as a separate profit center—particularly when direct service charges are made to customers receiving maintenance, repair, and operating services.

Finally, as indicated in step 4, separate budgets may be established for individual sales territories and for specific customer or distributor accounts. Sales quotas may be established to indicate specifically the share of required sales that must be achieved in each territory or account in order to meet the budget requirements. Human and financial resources may be allocated to territories or to accounts to reflect differences in the potential for achieving the program objectives or for achieving sales-volume gains.

As the budget becomes finalized, then, the sales manager has effectively established a number of standards for monitoring and evaluating performance.

EVALUATING PERFORMANCE

In order to measure the effectiveness of sales and distribution programs and to identify opportunities for improved resource utilization, managers must employ some procedure for performance evaluation. Of course, measures of sales volume and total profit contribution are useful for measuring performance, but these measures may reflect the overall effectiveness of the marketing effort.[25] In evaluating sales and distribution performance, sales managers need measures and procedures that focus on the specific objectives, activities, and costs for which they are responsible. Further, sales managers usually need to evaluate performance at one or more of the following levels:

- Individual salesperson performance
- Individual distributor performance
- Sales territory performance
- Sales segment performance

By examining performance at these various levels (as well as total performance), sales managers will be better able to understand the reasons for the overall total program results. Specifically, they will be able to identify the sales segments, territories, salespeople, and distributors that are strong and weak performers. Additionally, if the evaluation procedure is sufficiently detailed, managers should be able to understand the reasons for differences in performance and prescribe some corrective actions.

Individual Salesperson and Distributor Performance

Managers must evaluate the performance of individual sales and customer service personnel and individual distributors with several purposes in mind:

- Awarding incentives and bonuses
- Identifying personnel or distributors who may need additional training
- Identifying *problem* accounts or *problem* geographical areas covered by individual salespeople or distributors
- Determining whether new or additional distributors are needed

To be as widely useful as possible, measures of salesperson or distributor performance should help managers to determine whether the performance is due to individual or distributor actions or whether it is due to noncontrollable market forces. This means performance evaluation should include *results-oriented* and *effort-oriented* measures. Tables 13-6 and 13-7 present some of the typical performance measures that are widely used by sales managers.[26]

When results-oriented measures are being used, the measure should have a logical and equitable basis. For example, if dollar-sales volume is being used, individual quotas should be established only after the sales potential in each distributor's or salesperson's account has been considered. Similarly, if the number of new accounts opened is the performance measure, then the num-

---

[25] Robert J. Freedman, "For More Profitable Sales, Look Beyond Volume," *Sales and Marketing Management*, August 1989, pp. 50–53.

[26] The frequency with which managers use these various measures is examined in Donald Jackson, Janet Keith, and John Schlacter, "Evaluation of Selling Performance: A Study of Current Practices," *Journal of Personal Selling and Sales Management*, November 1983, pp. 43–51.

TABLE 13-6	**RESULTS-ORIENTED MEASURES FOR EVALUATING DISTRIBUTORS OR SALESPEOPLE**

1. Sales volume (total or by product or model)
2. Sales volume as a percentage of quota
3. Sales profitability (dollar gross margin or contribution)
4. Number of new accounts
5. Number of stockouts
6. Number of distributors participating in programs
7. Number of lost accounts
8. Percentage volume increase in key accounts
9. Number of customer complaints
10. Distributor sales-inventory ratios

TABLE 13-7	**EFFORT-ORIENTED MEASURES FOR EVALUATING DISTRIBUTORS OR SALESPEOPLE**

1. Number of sales calls made
2. Number of MRO calls made
3. Number of complaints handled
4. Number of checks on reseller stocks
5. Uncontrollable lost job time
6. Number of inquiries followed up
7. Number of demonstrations completed

ber of potential accounts in each salesperson's or distributor's territory should be considered in evaluating performance.

The most appropriate effort-oriented measures are those most directly related to the sales and distribution program. For example, the number of inquiries followed up will be the most appropriate effort measure to use if the sales and distribution objective is to increase the number of accounts. However, the number of complaints handled will be a more appropriate measure of effort when an account-maintenance objective has been established.

In general, however, management's primary concern is with results. Effort-related measures are primarily useful for diagnosing why performance is above or below average. That is, by comparing efforts and results, managers should be better able to assess whether poor performance is due to inadequate effort or misdirected effort. For instance, a salesperson or distributor may have a low performance measure in terms of account development because of a rush of customer complaints that had to be handled or because an inadequate number of sales calls were made. In the latter case, management can ascribe poor performance to a weak effort. But in the former case, the effort may have merely been misdirected because of circumstances beyond the distributor's or salesperson's control. Many companies are in the process of attempting to develop customer satisfaction measures that can be used in measuring individual salesperson performance. Nevertheless, because the customer may be unhappy for reasons out of the salesperson's control (such as prices, competition, or credit policies), performance and effort measures relating to customer satisfaction have not been widely used.[27] By combining results-oriented and effort-oriented measures, therefore, sales managers can better diagnose the reasons for variations in performance and take the necessary remedial actions.

Sales-Territory Performance

Individual sales territories will differ in terms of sales potential and in terms of the resources they require for the firm to remain competitive. For example, some territories will have several well-established, high-volume accounts concentrated in a small area (so sales volume will be high and travel costs low). But other territories may have a large number of small accounts that are widely dispersed geographically, leading to a lower sales potential and higher travel costs. Because of these kinds of differences, managers cannot easily compare performance in several territories. However, each territory can be evaluated in terms of the degree to which sales and distribution objectives are achieved and in terms of profitability measures.

ACHIEVEMENT OF OBJECTIVES

Measures of the achievement of objectives compare the level of performance of each territory with the objectives specified in the sales and distribution program. As we suggested earlier in this chapter, sales managers will usually assign specific levels of the program objective (such as the number of new accounts opened) to each sales territory.

Although managers often use these measures for awarding bonuses and other incentives, they also use them as diagnostic devices for identifying low performance territories. Once the low-performing territories have been identified, the sales manager can attempt to determine the causes of low performance. For instance, Frito-Lay found sales declining in their South Texas market. Closer analysis revealed this was occurring because a competitor had gained more shelf space at Frito-Lay's expense in specific Houston and San Antonio supermarkets. Based on this discovery, a head-to-head strategy using computerized analysis and inventory planning to regain shelf space was developed by the district sales manager.[28]

In some cases the territory objectives may have been set arbitrarily without adequate consideration of market potential and competitive conditions. Alternatively, inadequate effort, unexpected changes in local economic conditions, or a lack of necessary resources may be the cause of poor performance. On the other hand, some territories may have reached their sales and distribution

[27] "Taking Aim at Tomorrow's Challenges," *Sales and Marketing Management*, September 1991, pp. 66–80.
[28] Jeffrey Rothfeeder, Jim Bartimo, Lois Therrien, and Richard Brandt, "How Software Is Making Food Sales a Piece of Cake," *Business Week*, July 2, 1990, pp. 54–55.

objectives simply because of excessive reliance on price appeals or delivery appeals, which may have resulted in negative profitability. Accordingly, sales-territory performance should also be evaluated from a profitability perspective.

PROFITABILITY

Measures of profitability at the sales-territory level can take several forms. Managers may compare territories to identify any variations in margins and traceable fixed selling costs as a percentage of sales. Additionally, margins and fixed selling costs may be related to sales and distribution objectives. For example, managers may want to measure the total dollars of selling cost per new account.

In addition to margins and selling costs, certain assets may be managed at the sales-territory level. Accordingly, territorial profitability may also be measured in terms of the return generated on those assets. Return-on-assets-managed ratios for different territories can be compared to find opportunities to improve allocation procedures regarding assets and direct expenses or to modify territorial budgets. Typically, accounts receivable, inventories, and warehouse assets are the assets that might be employed for calculating *assets managed*. To the extent that the sales territory determines credit policy and has its own warehouse for holding inventory, the assets managed may be substantial enough to warrant using this measure. Sales and cost analysis identifies the results achieved and the costs of obtaining those results. However, it is also necessary to consider the assets that are necessary to obtain those results. The formula for return on assets managed (ROAM) considers both the contribution margin for a given level of sales and asset turnover.

$$ROAM = \text{contribution as percentage of sales} \times \text{asset turnover rate}$$

Table 13-8 provides an illustration of the use of territorial profitability measurement.

By comparing profitability results and levels of achievement of program objectives in different territories, managers can obtain several insights on territorial performance. For example,

- A low percentage-variable-contribution margin may indicate excessive reliance on price appeals.
- A high ratio of shipping costs-to-sales or a low ratio of sales-to-average inventory may indicate excessive reliance on logistical appeals.
- A territory in which account-development objectives are not being met may have a high ratio of new accounts per dollar of salary expense. The current sales force is doing an adequate job of generating new accounts, but is failing to capitalize on the total market opportunity, indicating that the territory may be understaffed.

TABLE 13-8	CALCULATING TERRITORIAL PROFITABILITY MEASURES

Sales	$1,500,000
Less variable costs	900,000
Variable-contribution margin	$ 600,000
Less direct costs	
Salaries of sales and customer service personnel	$ 200,000
Travel expense	50,000
Point-of-sale material	30,000
Expediting of shipments	20,000
Contribution to indirect costs and profit	$ 300,000
Assets managed	
Accounts receivable	$ 140,000
Warehouse	600,000
Finished-goods inventory	160,000
Total assets managed	$ 900,000
Contribution as a percentage of sales	$\dfrac{\$\,300{,}000}{\$1{,}500{,}000} = 20\%$
Asset turnover	$\dfrac{\$1{,}500{,}000}{\$\,900{,}000} = 1.667$

$$\text{ROAM} = 1.667 \times 20\%$$
$$= 33\,^1/_3\%$$

In sum, the combined use of profitability-performance measures with a measure of the achievement of program objectives will enable managers to evaluate sales territories more fairly and will permit managers to diagnose the problems and opportunities in each territory more effectively.

Sales-Segment Performance

Frequently, managers find major differences in sales and profitability patterns when comparing different types of distributors and different types of customers. By recognizing these differences, managers can often identify possible improvements in the allocation of sales and customer service resources. For example, call frequencies, delivery policies, and discount policies may be adjusted for different types of sales segments. Two approaches can be used in examining these segment differences: sales analysis and distribution cost analysis.

SALES ANALYSIS

Sales analysis is a term that covers a variety of procedures for examining sales performance and sales opportunities across various territories, customer groups, or distribution channels. There is no one best measure of sales and distribution effectiveness. Because there are multiple goals and objectives, it is necessary that any performance evaluation consider several factors. Typically, managers use sales analysis to answer questions such as:

- How are sales distributed across sales segments?
- In which segments did sales exceed or fail to meet expectations?
- How effectively are sales resources being allocated to sales segments?
- Which products are being sold to which segments?

Essentially, sales analysis is the process of aggregating the sales reports of individual salespeople in a variety of ways. Consider, for example, the data in Table 13-9.

In this sales analysis report, each salesperson's unit sales results for the period October–December 1993 are aggregated by one of three model types and by customer group. (Note that this company sells direct to some customers, such as government agencies and banking and financial institutions, and indirectly through distributors to other buyers.)

The managerial value of sales analysis can best be examined by first inspecting the total sales figures for each model for the three customer groups and then examining the figures within customer groups. For example, Series 99

TABLE 13-9

EXAMPLE OF A SALES ANALYSIS REPORT

CUSTOMER GROUP AND COMPUTER SERIES	UNIT SALES OF HIGH-SPEED PRINTERS				
	ACTUAL OCT.–DEC. 1993	PLANNED OCT.–DEC. 1993	PERFORMANCE* INDEX	ACTUAL OCT.–DEC. 1992	PERCENT† CHANGE
1. Government agencies					
Series 60	8,000	6,000	133	4,000	100
Series 90	2,000	5,000	40	4,000	−50
Series 99	2,000	4,000	50	4,000	−50
Total	12,000	15,000	80	12,000	0
2. Banking and finance					
Series 60	3,000	3,500	86	3,000	0
Series 90	4,000	2,000	200	2,000	100
Series 99	1,000	1,500	67	1,000	0
Total	8,000	7,000	114	6,000	33
3. Distributors					
Series 60	23,000	18,000	128	18,000	28
Series 90	13,000	16,000	81	10,500	24
Series 99	4,000	2,000	200	1,500	167
Total	40,000	36,000	111	30,000	33
4. Total for 3 groups					
Series 60	34,000	27,500	123	25,000	36
Series 90	19,000	23,000	83	16,500	15
Series 99	7,000	7,500	93	6,500	8
Total	60,000	58,000	104	48,000	25

* Calculated as: (Actual 93 − Planned 93) × 100
† Calculated as: (Actual 93 − Actual 92) − (Actual 92) × 100

sales grew by only 8 percent over the preceding year and fell just shy of expectations. (Note that the performance index is just below 100, a level at which planned and actual sales would be equal.) However, these results mask some important sales results. When Series 99 sales are compared across customer groups, it is apparent the sales of this model were well below expectations in the government and banking and finance groups. Similarly, the banking and finance customer group is decidedly different from the other two in the sales performance for the Series 60 and Series 90 models.

This type of information permits management to identify more readily areas in which performance is distinctly different from expectations or from past trends. Armed with such information, managers can focus their attention on these particular sales segments to determine whether changes in objectives, appeals, or sales-force effort should be considered. For example, the manager using the data in Table 13-9 would likely be concerned with determining why banking and finance customers are shifting from the Series 60 to the Series 90 while government agencies seem to be moving in a different direction.

It is important to recognize, however, that sales analysis only provides information on one dimension. As we suggested at the outset of this chapter, managers must also examine the costs involved in generating these sales and the profit implications of using alternative sales appeals. The most comprehensive approach for analyzing sales and distribution costs is known as *distribution cost analysis*.

DISTRIBUTION COST ANALYSIS

Distribution cost analysis is a procedure for comparing the profitability of sales segments and for identifying possible approaches for improving profitability. The emphasis in distribution cost analysis is on assessing the costs incurred to generate the achieved level of sales. Specifically, distribution cost analysis can be used to identify changes in sales and distribution appeals and budgets or in the structure of sales and distribution systems that may enhance the profitability of one or more sales segments. Although this procedure can be used for examining the profitability of sales territories, it is more widely used when the sales segments to be analyzed are

- Alternative systems (for example, direct response versus direct personal selling versus trade selling)
- Alternative distribution channels (for example, department store versus discount chains or wholesale versus direct to retail channels)
- Alternative customer types (for example, buyers in different industries)
- Alternative account-size (sales-volume) classes

The basic procedure employed in performing a distribution cost analysis is to identify the sales revenues and costs attributable to each sales segment. Typically, managers allocate three types of costs to the various sales segments:

- Variable costs associated with manufacturing or selling the product (including sales commissions).

- Direct fixed costs that would not be incurred if a given sales segment were eliminated. (For example, if one or more salespeople sold only to a given sales segment, the salaries and travel expenses of those salespeople would be directly assignable to that segment.)
- Traceable indirect costs that can be allocated (traced) to various segments on some logical, nonarbitrary basis. Operationally, firms will only allocate those indirect costs for which the level of costs can be influenced by the sales and distribution effort or appeals assigned to each sales segment.

The procedures and uses of distribution cost analysis can be illustrated by the analysis developed by Classic Apparel, Inc.

Classic sold a line of fashion-oriented lace blouses through quality department and specialty stores, using a small sales force. Each member of the sales force called on both large department store buyers and small independent women's apparel stores in a given geographic area. In 1993, Classic also began selling blouses via a direct response campaign in which mail-in order forms were distributed through a direct mail service targeted to higher-income households. Classic paid for shipments made to its retail distributors. However, direct response customers paid for the shipping costs of their orders. Table 13-10 presents a distribution cost analysis of Classic's sales and distribution systems.

The analysis revealed some significant differences in the relative profitability of the various systems.

- The percentage-variable-contribution margin on manufacturer sales for the direct response system was 60 percent, as opposed to 50 percent for the

TABLE 13-10

DISTRIBUTION COST ANALYSIS: CLASSIC APPAREL, INC.
(Sales in Thousands)

	DEPARTMENT STORE CHAINS	SPECIALTY APPAREL STORES	DIRECT RESPONSE SALES	BASIS FOR ALLOCATION
Sales	$12,000	$ 4,800	$1,500	Sales receipts
Labor	−2,000	−800	−200	Unit cost
Material	−4,000	−1,600	−400	Unit cost
Variable contribution	$ 6,000	$ 2,400	$ 900	
Shipping	−800	−600	0	Delivery records
Order taking/billing	−10	−30	−60	No. of orders
Personal selling	−400	−800	0	Sales-call reports
Direct mail	−0	−0	−50	Invoices
Credit	−300	−200	−50	Average amount outstanding
Total contribution	$	$ 770	$ 740	
Total contribution per $ sales	$ .374	$ .160	$ .493	

indirect channels, reflecting the elimination of retail margins in the direct response channel.

■ Shipping, selling, and order-taking costs as a percentage of manufacturer sales were much higher for specialty stores than for department stores. A major reason for this was that specialty stores were large in number but purchased in smaller volumes. Department stores were able to order in quantities that were large enough to ship economically.

On the basis of these results, Classic's sales manager was able to identify some possible actions to take in order to improve profitability.

1. Classic could establish minimum order volumes for free delivery or impose delivery charges for small orders.
2. Classic could require cash payments on small orders to reduce credit costs.
3. Classic could reduce the frequency of sales calls on smaller accounts and thereby either reduce the size of the sales force or shift more selling effort to department store chains.
4. The fact that percentage-variable-contribution margins are identical for the two indirect channels suggests that no quantity discounts are being offered. Classic might elect to raise prices but offer quantity discounts to large-volume buyers.
5. Classic might attempt to hire manufacturer's representatives to sell to specialty stores. Currently, personal selling, order taking, and credit costs account for over 20 percent of specialty store sales. If these functions could be performed at a lesser cost by using a second intermediary, profitability could be enhanced.
6. Classic could separate the specialty apparel segment into multiple subsegments based on purchase volume levels. This analysis might reveal that some accounts should be eliminated. It is important to note that a distribution cost analysis is useful in diagnosing where the profitability problems are but not necessarily in choosing the actions to be taken. That is, each of the alternatives under consideration would reduce or eliminate a sales and distribution appeal. Accordingly, before implementing any of these actions, Classic's marketing manager must analyze the sales consequences as well as the cost consequences. In other words, Classic must review the importance of these appeals in the context of distributor requirements and power relationships (as discussed in Chapter 12) in order to determine how specialty apparel stores will respond.

The sales budget is used as the benchmark for evaluating costs. The general approach is to compare the actual costs incurred with those planned as defined in the budget. The ultimate purpose of selling costs is to generate sales. The objective is not to minimize selling costs but to see that a specified relationship between sales and those selling costs is maintained. It is useful to calculate various selling costs as a percentage of sales achieved. This provides a means for evaluating whether the cost-sales relationship has been maintained even when actual costs may exceed the level provided for in the selling budget.

In our discussion of distribution cost analysis we have not taken into consideration what it costs to replace a lost customer. The Sandy Corporation has estimated the costs of replacing a customer can exceed $400 in the service industry. For instance, banks lose about $80 in unrealized revenue every time they lose a customer. Other studies have shown companies can increase profits by almost 100 percent by retaining just 5 percent more of their customers. In addition, for those businesses that lose 15 to 20 percent of their customers each year, cutting these defections in half will more than double the average company growth rate.[29] For these reasons, some companies use "number of lost accounts" as a measure of sales performance.[30] Development Dimensions International (DDI) has gone so far as to eliminate sales bonuses for bringing in new clients. This has been done because they believe such bonuses motivate their salespersons to develop new business rather than service the existing customer base.

CONCLUSION

Sales and distribution programs incorporate a variety of activities linking the sales force, the customer service force, and distributors. Further, a number of different objectives and appeals may be employed by sales managers, and

[29] Frederick F. Reichheld and W. Earl Sasser, Jr., "Zero Defections: Quality Comes to Services," *Harvard Business Review*, September–October 1990, pp. 105–111.
[30] "How Much Is a Customer Worth?" *Sales and Marketing Management*, May 1989, p. 23.

FIGURE 13-4
Relationship of sales and distribution programs with situation analysis, marketing strategy, other marketing programs, and coordination and control activities.

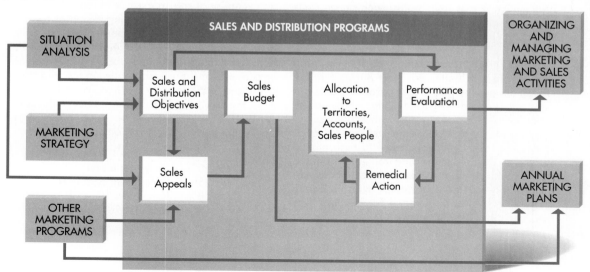

these objectives and appeals will affect the firm's cost and profitability structure in many ways.

The complexity of these programs does not mean they are unmanageable, however. The purpose of Chapters 12 and 13 was to present a logical approach for developing and implementing these programs and to identify some of the conceptual and analytical approaches managers can use to achieve effective sales and distribution efforts. The relationship among these conceptual and analytical approaches and the relationship of sales and distribution programs to the other chapters in this book are summarized in Figure 13-4.

Because most marketing jobs fall into the sales and customer service categories, and because the cost and effectiveness of these programs are critical to marketing success, an understanding of these approaches, concepts, and tools is of paramount importance not only to sales managers but to the members of the sales force as well. It is vital that managers recognize and use the various tools and concepts discussed in this chapter, as the following situation demonstrates.

BBB OF CENTRAL INDIANA: ANALYZING A SALES PROGRAM

The Board of Directors of the Better Business Bureau of Central Indiana requested a review and analysis of the sales operations of the bureau at their October 1992 meeting. The primary objective of this review was to analyze the strengths and weaknesses of the present sales operations. It was anticipated such an analysis would result in recommendations that would strengthen the sales branch of the bureau in the future.

The Central Indiana Better Business Bureau was one of 180 Better Business Bureaus in the United States. The BBB is a nonprofit association of business and professional firms, with an overriding goal to foster business self-regulation by working with individual firms and trade groups to develop and gain adherence to high ethical standards of advertising and selling. It concentrated its marketing in five counties where approximately 40,000 businesses were located. The major source of revenue for the BBB was membership dues (84 percent).

The National Council of BBB's studies indicated that effective salespeople needed to earn at least $20,000 a year. If they were paid less, they quit, or were generally not effective. Most bureaus expected to pay about 50 percent of all first-time revenues to their salespeople, and only an exceptional salesperson sold more than four new accounts per week. Selling expenses for the top twelve BBBs were 27 percent of member dues income in 1991. The Central Indiana BBB dues schedule was based upon the number of employees of the member businesses and had averaged $190.36 in 1991. (See Table 13-11.)

In the past, the BBB had recruited salespersons who were thought to be "lean, mean, and aggressive," and paid them on straight commission. Commission rates were:

40–50%	New memberships
25%	Delinquent accounts
10%	Renewals
5%	Manager override

After a brief training period, new salespersons were provided with a new member sales kit and supporting materials and turned loose to recruit members in the five-county area.

During the 1992 year, there had been sixty-two salespersons who had earned commissions. As of November, there were nine active salespersons. Five individuals accounted for 66 percent of the total commissions. The commissions and salaries paid to these individuals amounted to approximately 25 percent of revenues attributable to new and renewal memberships. (See Table 13-12.)

1. How could the BBB use the above information to further analyze performance and make recommendations for improvement?
2. Given the above information, what areas would you identify as needing further analysis?
3. What additional information would be necessary to analyze membership segments, cost of sales, and individual salesperson performance?

TABLE 13-11

MEMBERSHIP DUES SCHEDULE
Effective April 1, 1991

# EMPLOYEES	ANNUAL DUES
1–3	$175.00
4–7	$225.00
8–15	$300.00
16–30	$425.00
31–50	$575.00
51–100	$775.00

Over 100 employees: $775.00 plus $1.00 per employee.

- Plus $25.00 one-time application fee
- Branches (extra locations): Fee based on total number of employees at all locations, plus $50.00 per extra location

---

TABLE 13-12

NAME	GROSS INCOME	PERCENT NEW AND RENEWAL MEMBER REVENUES	PERCENT OF TOTAL COMM.
R. Robinson	$54,068	9%	23.4%
W. Kolesar	$44,637	7.5%	19.3%
K. Kolesar	$22,166	3.7%	9.6%
J. DeVries	$19,582	3.1%	8.5%
C. Robinson	$12,306	2.1%	5.3%

(Certain names and figures have been adjusted to preserve confidentiality.)

TABLE 13-13

BETTER BUSINESS BUREAU OF CENTRAL INDIANA, INC.: OPERATING RESULTS

YEAR	1985	1986	1987	1988	1989	1990	1991	9 MO.
Income								
Membership Income	$107,381	$182,781	$284,428	$364,910	$433,063	$537,497	$570,996	$545,740
Other	$ 27,563	$ 97,827	$ 80,305	$100,448	$ 97,362	$116,311	$111,967	$ 73,520
Total	$134,944	$280,608	$364,733	$465,358	$530,425	$653,808	$682,963	$619,260
Expenses								
Cost of Membership	$ 43,423	$ 65,123	$ 98,451	$116,358	$129,793	$141,361	$207,450	$234,373
Operations	$ 30,956	$ 73,837	$131,850	$170,566	$219,293	$276,593	$281,954	$220,034
Administration	$ 32,129	$ 76,461	$ 93,919	$128,518	$187,832	$212,204	$231,177	$163,899
Total	$106,508	$215,421	$324,220	$415,442	$536,918	$630,158	$720,581	$618,306
% Membership Income to Cost of Sales	40%	36%	35%	32%	30%	26%	36%	43%

BETTER BUSINESS BUREAU OF CENTRAL INDIANA, INC.: 1990 BUDGET

1992 BUDGET		1992 JULY	1992 AUGUST	1992 SEPTEMBER	BUDGET SEPTEMBER	$ MONTHLY VARIANCE	ACTUAL YTD	BUDGET YTD	$ VARIANCE YTD	% VARIANCE YTD
	Revenue									
$ 429,400	Membership-new	$31,760	$27,720	$19,225	$40,401	($21,176)	$246,775	$334,749	($47,874)	−26%
$ 455,500	Membership-renewal	$31,848	$37,563	$33,681	$35,251	($1,570)	$298,965	$350,458	($51,483)	−15%
$ 8,000	Interest	$ 507	$ 643	$ 508	$ 667	($150)	$ 5,054	$ 5,995	$941	−16%
$ 137,500	BBB Care	$ 6,088	$ 9,036	$ 4,725	$11,317	($6,592)	$ 68,016	$103,030	($35,014)	−34%
$ 51,700	Other	$ 400	$ 0	$ 0	$ 8,000	($ 8,000)	$ 450	$ 42,484	($42,034)	0%
$1,082,100	Total Revenue	$70,603	$74,962	$58,139	$95,636	($25,033)	$619,260	$836,716	($213,874)	−26%
	Expenditures									
	Membership									
$ 429,100	Commissions/salaries	$25,778	$25,545	$19,159	$40,401	($21,242)	$209,632	$326,611	($116,979)	−36%
$ 16,000	Support salaries	$ 1,025	$ 1,025	$ 1,025	$ 1,333	($308)	$ 9,597	$ 12,005	($2,408)	−20%
$ 36,500	Payroll taxes	$ 1,116	$ 1,740	$ 1,077	$ 3,042	($1,965)	$ 10,865	$ 27,388	($16,523)	−60%
$ 9,000	Sales materials	$ 191	$ 0	$ 152	$ 750	($598)	$ 4,280	$ 6,753	($2,473)	−37%
$ 490,600	Total membership	$28,110	$28,310	$21,413	$45,526	($24,113)	$294,374	$372,757	($138,383)	−37%

TABLE 13-14

BETTER BUSINESS BUREAU OF CENTRAL INDIANA, INC.: MEMBERSHIP TRENDS

1987	JAN	FEB	MAR	APR	MAY	JUN	JUL	AUG	SEPT	OCT	NOV	DEC
New Memberships								$19,800	$14,950	$18,000	$17,677	$17,625
Renewals								$16,125	$17,250	$12,400	$16,150	$14,900
Total Income								$43,664	$37,566	$40,166	$40,443	$40,920
1988												
88 New Members	$15,275	$19,275	$16,775	$17,735	$14,115	$15,000	$17,500	$11,950	$15,250	$15,398	$11,795	$14,605
88 Renewals	$11,550	$15,125	$24,275	$26,015	$21,075	$26,725	$21,400	$22,200	$21,850	$18,350	$18,925	$21,475
88 Total Income	$35,038	$43,402	$48,853	$50,485	$42,620	$50,434	$46,031	$45,266	$45,343	$41,879	$36,910	$44,838
1989												
89 New Members	$15,500	$16,925	$18,450	$17,075	$15,800	$20,100	$24,100	$18,400	$23,210	$ 7,650	$14,975	$22,623
89 Renewals	$19,950	$27,325	$27,000	$35,925	$29,650	$31,675	$27,160	$26,400	$26,276	$28,305	$22,075	$22,050
89 Total Income	$45,499	$52,192	$55,058	$61,419	$57,996	$59,777	$59,883	$53,931	$56,064	$46,467	$44,186	$61,038
1990												
90 New Members	$19,552	$12,300	$17,350	$26,005	$22,350	$23,275	$17,075	$24,650	$15,050	$17,158	$12,425	$16,825
90 Renewals	$26,725	$29,538	$30,632	$34,816	$31,825	$31,678	$30,538	$26,310	$25,685	$30,189	$25,545	$25,900
90 Total Income	$59,483	$51,625	$63,042	$62,652	$64,877	$62,006	$56,780	$58,284	$47,903	$56,194	$48,534	$54,125
1991												
91 New Members	$20,892	$29,377	$27,856	$32,198	$23,150	$35,150	$31,760	$27,720	$19,225			
91 Renewals	$28,580	$27,850	$30,116	$32,076	$45,772	$31,479	$31,848	$37,563	$33,681			
91 Total Income	$57,805	$65,913	$68,786	$72,547	$76,196	$74,945	$70,603	$74,961	$58,139			

QUESTIONS AND SITUATIONS FOR DISCUSSION

1. "In many companies, managers concentrate on ratios that indicate substandard performance. Given enough information, it is possible to find ratios that will make any unit of analysis look bad." Do you agree or disagree with this statement? Should this be the focus of sales and cost analysis?

2. After completing an analysis of their accounts, the M&N company found that many of their small accounts were unprofitable. Under what conditions would you recommend that they stop selling to these accounts and instead concentrate their resources on the more profitable medium and large customers?

3. Alpha Corporation sells $50 million worth of industrial repair parts to manufacturing companies each year, earning a 50 percent variable-contribution margin. Recently, customers representing 10 percent of Alpha's sales told Alpha that it must guarantee delivery in 2 days on all parts if it wants their business. Alpha's managers have figures that indicate they will have to increase inventory levels at their regional warehouses from an annual average of $12.5 million to $20 million in order to provide this service. Currently, Alpha's cost of carrying inventory is 25 percent of average inventory.

    a. Determine Alpha's inventory cost of both average inventory levels.

    b. Should Alpha submit to this request?

4. A manufacturer is reviewing its policy of offering discounts of 1 percent to distributors who pay invoices within 10 days rather than within the normal 30-day period. What specific issues should the manufacturer consider before making this decision?

5. At the beginning of Chapter 12, it was suggested that sales volume was generally inadequate as a program objective. However, in Chapter 13, we have indicated that sales volume is an important consideration in budgeting and in performance evaluation. Explain the relationship between sales volume and the four types of objectives established in Chapter 12. Then explain the roles of sales volume and of the types of sales and distribution objectives in the budgeting and performance-evaluation processes.

6. The Wicker Chair Co. allows its salespersons to vary the price of some products as much as plus and minus 5 percent. What specific types of sales analysis would be useful to management when evaluating this policy?

7. The national sales manager for your company has asked you to begin evaluating working-capital requirements in assessing the performance of sales territories. You have received the following data for the year just ended for two territories, A and B.

    a. Compare the two territories in terms of return on assets managed.

    b. Assume the firm's cost of carrying inventory and accounts receivable are 15 and 10 percent, respectively. Treating inventory and accounts receivable as direct costs, compare the total contribution of the territories.

    c. Which territory is the better performing one, and what factors account for the differences in performance?

	TERRITORY	
	A	B
Sales	$5,500,000	$6,800,000
Variable costs	3,300,000	4,488,000
Direct selling costs	300,000	350,000
Average inventory	2,040,000	2,125,000
Average accounts receivable	440,000	450,000

SUGGESTED ADDITIONAL READINGS

Anderson, Erin, "The Salesperson as Outside Agent or Employee: A Transaction Cost Analysis," *Marketing Science*, Summer 1985, pp. 234–254.

Finkin, Eugene F., "Expense Control in Sales and Marketing," *Journal of Business Strategy*, May–June 1988, pp. 52–55.

Gates, Michael, "New Measures of Sales Performance," *Incentive*, November 1988, pp. 45–52.

Good, David J., and Robert S. Stone, "How Sales Quotas Are Developed," *Industrial Marketing Management*, February 1991, pp. 51–55.

Jackson, Donald, and Lonnie Ostrom, "Grouping Segments for Profitability Analysis," *Business Topics*, Spring 1980, pp. 39–44.

Kaplan, Robert S., "One Cost System Isn't Enough," *Harvard Business Review*, January–February 1988, pp. 61–66.

LaForge, Raymond, and David Cravens, "A Market Response Model for Sales Management Decision Making," *Journal of Personal Selling and Sales Management*, Fall/Winter 1981–1982, pp. 10–16.

Lambert, Douglas M., and Jay U. Sterling, "What Types of Profitability Reports Do Marketing Managers Receive?" *Industrial Marketing Management*, November 1987, pp. 295–304.

Levy, Michael, and Michael Van Breda, "A Financial Perspective on the Shift of Marketing Functions," *Journal of Retailing*, Winter 1984, pp. 23–42.

Lodish, Leonard M., "A User-Oriented Model for Sales Force Size, Product, and Market Allocation Decisions," *Journal of Marketing*, Summer 1980, pp. 70–78.

Monahan, James P., "A Quantity Discount Pricing Model to Increase Vendor Profits," *Management Science*, June 1984, pp. 720–726.

Parasuraman, A., and Ralph Day, "A Management-Oriented Model for Allocating Sales Effort," *Journal of Marketing Research*, February 1977, pp. 23–33.

Ross, William T., Jr., "Performance Against Quota and the Call Selection Decision," *Journal of Marketing Research*, August 1991, pp. 296–306.

Schiff, J. S., "Evaluating the Sales Force as a Business," *Industrial Marketing Management*, April 1983, pp. 131–137.

PART FOUR

CORPORATE MARKETING PLANNING

SITUATION ANALYSIS

MARKETING STRATEGIES AND PROGRAMS

COORDINATION AND CONTROL

COORDINATION AND CONTROL

In Part 3 we examined the various marketing strategies and programs that managers use to achieve product or product-line objectives. More specifically, we noted that product development, price, advertising, sales promotion, and sales and distribution programs can be used jointly or individually to stimulate demand in the desired fashion.

Because a variety of programs may be employed to carry out a marketing strategy and because more than one individual may be involved in managing these programs for a product or product line, some method of coordinating the programs is necessary. Further, the effectiveness of marketing strategies and programs will depend on how well they are executed. Nevertheless, even a well-designed, closely coordinated, and properly executed plan may fail to achieve the product objectives because of uncontrollable factors such as economic forces or competitors' actions.

In Chapters 14 and 15 we provide tools and procedures for

- Improving the coordination and execution of strategies and programs
- Monitoring results
- Modifying strategies and programs as necessary on the basis of performance or because of major environmental changes or both

Specifically, in Chapter 14 we present alternative approaches for structuring the organization and for managing human resources in order to achieve effective coordination and execution of strategies and programs. In Chapter 15 we demonstrate how managers can use annual marketing plans for coordinating the allocation of resources among marketing programs, for monitoring performance, and for adjusting the plan in response to gaps between planned and actual levels of performance.

CHAPTER 14

ORGANIZING AND MANAGING MARKETING AND SALES ACTIVITIES

OVERVIEW

A central theme of this book is that managers should select strategies and programs that are consistent with the situation analysis and are designed to achieve specific objectives. However, a well-chosen strategy will still be ineffective if it is not properly executed. It is much easier to think up marketing strategies than it is to make them work under company, competitive, and customer constraints.[1]

As will be shown in Chapter 15, by coordinating the various marketing programs through annual plans, managers can improve the likelihood that the marketing strategy will be properly implemented. However, though the strategy may have been the appropriate one, given the situation, poor execution may have resulted in poor market performance. Therefore, it is important to coordinate and control marketing practices as well as the persons responsible for implementing these decisions.

Additionally, the success of the marketing effort will depend in large part on the degree of coordination achieved between marketing and the other functional areas of a business.

Over the past two decades, a number of important changes have had major impact upon the marketing role within the company. New forms of business organizations have developed in response to competitive and market conditions. This has led to a transformation of the marketing function and its traditional functional role within the organization. Accordingly, the organizational structure a firm uses to achieve coordination and the effectiveness of interpersonal relationships among managers in the various functional areas will have a major influence on the success of the firm's strategies.

In this chapter we will examine some of the problems associated with executing marketing strategies. Since organizational design may be one of the

[1] The importance of paying attention to execution is discussed in Thomas V. Bonoma, "Making Your Marketing Strategy Work," *Harvard Business Review*, March–April 1984, pp. 68–76.

key factors in determining the effectiveness of people in the firm, we will examine some of the types of organizational structures as well as factors considered in selecting the most appropriate type. Subsequently, we will examine the relationships among other functions of the business and discuss some ways of managing interfunctional conflict to improve coordination. Additionally, because the successful execution of marketing strategies is determined at the level of the individual salesperson, some of the actions managers can take to improve sales-force execution and effectiveness will be discussed.

The role of the sales force is particularly important in the execution of strategy. As we indicated in Chapter 12, the sales function will be effective only if appropriate sales appeals are communicated and if the sales force is structured for maximum efficiency in calling on customers or distributors. Accordingly, management must be sure that these human resources are effectively used if the strategy is to be properly executed.

EXECUTING MARKETING STRATEGY

Marketing practitioners know successful performance depends both on strategy and on the execution of that strategy. Consider, for example, the case of Tandy Corporation.

In 1986, Tandy Corporation's sales of personal computers showed strong growth. Sales of Tandy's low-priced home version PC were increasing, while at the same time PC clones were gaining share from IBM. This was viewed by Tandy executives as an opportunity to increase sales further by selling direct to businesses. Tandy's strategy called for designating selected Radio Shack stores for direct computer sales and recruiting a direct sales force of 1500 persons. Radio Shack managers were assigned the responsibility for recruiting, training, and managing this direct sales force. Many of these retail managers initially hired the wrong people as trainees. These errors resulted from the managers' inexperience and their inability to perform sales management activities effectively while at the same time continuing to be responsible for day-to-day store operations.

Trainees were given sales training over a period of eight Saturdays. This meant they were selling for two months before they had completed their training. Within a year, all 200 college graduates hired for direct sales had left Tandy, and the annual turnover of those remaining approached 65 percent. In an attempt to correct the situation, Tandy hired experienced direct sales managers to supervise those designated Radio Shack computer stores as well as assistants to handle administrative details. However, this did not result in increased performance. Tandy thus closed 103 computer centers and consolidated the remaining direct sales people under the most effective center managers. Experienced Regional Managers were assigned responsibility for hiring, and a month-long sales training program was initiated. In addition, compensation programs were adjusted and a dozen sales veterans were recruited to concentrate on major corporations.[2]

[2] Todd Mason and Geoff Lewis, "Tandy Finds a Cold, Hard World Outside the Radio Shack," *Business Week*, Aug. 31, 1987, pp. 68–70.

Marketing strategy and the execution of this strategy have a reciprocal effect on each other. Thomas Bonoma, a former professor at the Harvard Business School, has concluded that strategy obviously affects actions; and execution also affects marketing strategies over time.[3] Problems in implementation can often disguise a good strategy. If the execution of the strategy is poor, it may cause marketing management to attribute the failure to a poor strategy and permanently change its approach. However, at the other extreme, one may find inappropriate strategies compensated for by excellent execution. In this situation, management may have time to recognize its strategic mistakes and adjust its strategy. At other times, it is possible that good execution of a poorly designed strategy can accelerate failure. Because poor execution may disguise whether the strategy was appropriate or inappropriate, it is necessary that managers look to marketing practices before immediately making strategic adjustments. These problems and practices can occur with either marketing functions, programs, systems, or policy directives.

Often poor execution is the result of the failure of management to pursue marketing fundamentals or to follow up on their implementation. Another cause of problems or failure comes about from the lack of a clear focus or from trying to concentrate on too many functions at one time, resulting in what Bonoma has called "global mediocrity." In contrast, successful execution often derives from excellence in performing one function well.

Marketing programs combine both marketing and nonmarketing functions for a certain product or market. Management attempts to blend functions such as sales promotion and production to sell a particular product or penetrate a target market. The combining of these various functions into effective marketing programs is often done poorly. Poorly executed programs may result from a company trying to go beyond its functional capabilities or from a lack of direction. Pepperidge Farm's decision to introduce Star Wars cookies, which didn't fit their upscale, high-quality image, was a strategy that didn't match either marketing identity or product direction.

Poor marketing practice may be due to errors in formal organization, inadequate resource commitment, or failure to depart from tradition. For instance, a few years ago IBM was one of the world's most profitable companies, and reputedly one of the best managed. IBM's success had been built upon market domination for large mainframe computers. These machines were built to proprietary standards so they didn't work with those of other manufacturers. Once a customer was committed to IBM, there was little payoff in scrapping millions invested in hardware and customized software to switch to an unfamiliar supplier. However, in the mid-1980s the increasing power and falling prices of personal computers transformed the industry. In

---

[3] Professor Bonoma has argued that more often than not it is poor implementation rather than poorly designed strategies that results in failure to achieve marketing objectives. This section is based on Bonoma's investigations as described in Thomas V. Bonoma, "Making Your Marketing Strategy Work," *Harvard Business Review*, March–April 1984, pp. 69–76; and in Thomas V. Bonoma, *Managing Marketing*, The Free Press, New York, 1984, p. 552.

the late 1980s new integrated circuits and a new variety of desktop machines (workstations) made it possible to tie these units together in a network as a cheap alternative to minicomputers and mainframes. IBM failed to see the threat that PCs and workstations posed to its mainframe business. On January 19, 1992, it announced a loss after taxes and charges of $4.7 billion.[4]

The lack of adequate information may also result in poor execution. Too frequently, marketing managers lack the necessary information to determine profitability by segment, product, or individual account—even though such information is requested from other functional departments.

Several distinct characteristics seem to differentiate companies that execute marketing effectively from those that do not. First, in the best organizations there seems to be a sense of identity and direction. A clear theme and vision are present, and there is little uncertainty as to what the company represents and where it is going. For instance, Mag Instruments manufactures and markets state-of-the-art flashlights. Mag has been built on a philosophy and strategy of pushing quality to the limits. Premium quality permeates every aspect of the company's operations, from its uniquely designed products to its manufacturing process and entire marketing effort. As a result, the company can sell its best-selling flashlight for a retail price of $16.95, double the price of most flashlights. Mag products consistently appear in lists of best American-made products as well as on those that illustrate the finest in American design.[5]

Second, concern for customers, including retail and wholesale distributors, exists with those firms that consistently execute their strategies effectively. These firms view end users and distributors as partners and expect them to profit in terms of the value they receive as well as the lasting partnership that develops. For instance, Black & Decker Corp. has divisions with staffers from a variety of functions, such as logistics and finance, dedicated to serving such customers as Home Depot. In developing its new heavy duty professional power tools, Black & Decker executives spent three months visiting more than 200 retailers to solicit feedback.[6]

Finally, in those companies that consistently seem to execute marketing well, employees are encouraged to challenge and question upper management.[7] For example, lower level managers are encouraged to provide suggestions for improvements to existing methods of operation. Delta Airlines, for instance, is known for its open-door policy for employees and its willingness to make substantial policy changes as a result of employee suggestions.

[4] "What Went Wrong at IBM," *The Economist*, Jan. 16, 1993, pp. 23–26; and Carol J. Loomis and David Kilpatrick, "The Hunt for Mr. X: Who Can Run IBM?" *Fortune*, Feb. 22, 1993, pp. 68–72.
[5] Paul B. Brown, "Magnificent Obsession," *Inc.*, August 1989, pp. 79–84.
[6] "New Selling Tool: The Acura Concept," *Fortune*, Feb. 24, 1992, p. 88.
[7] Thomas V. Bonoma, "Market Success Can Breed 'Market Inertia'," *Harvard Business Review*, October 1981, p. 115.

TYPES OF ORGANIZATIONAL STRUCTURES

Essentially, an organizational structure accomplishes two things:

1. It defines the formal allocation of work roles to identify the members of the organization who will perform each activity.
2. It establishes the lines of authority for integrating and coordinating activities.

In this section, our major concern is with the impact of traditional organizational structure on the execution of marketing activities. Specifically, we examine the ways in which a given structure can enhance or limit the coordination of marketing activities.

Firms have organized along one of three dimensions: the *functions* performed, the *products* and product lines offered, or the *markets* to be served. Although certain combinations of these forms can be used to fit the specific situation facing an individual firm, the primary basis for organization will be along one of these three dimensions.

Organizing by Function

The functional organization structure is a common approach to grouping marketing activities, especially among companies that offer a limited variety of products or services. In this type of structure, marketing activities are organized according to the type of duties performed, and decision-making authority and coordination are highly centralized. Because all functions are centralized, this structure is most applicable when the product line is relatively limited; when the products have similar manufacturing, research, and advertising requirements; and when the same sales force and distributors can easily be used for all the firm's products.

Although the centralization of the marketing effort reduces problems in coordinating marketing programs, it places a major responsibility on the chief marketing executive for coordinating marketing with the other functional areas. Additionally, when all decisions are centralized, decision making is often slow. Further, in large firms, the chief marketing executive may have difficulty in keeping abreast of market developments for every product. As a result, many firms have found that, as product lines expand, a completely centralized functional organization becomes unwieldy. For example, consider the changes initiated by Xerox.

When Japanese producers introduced low-price copiers in the mid-1970s, Xerox was unprepared to compete for this market segment. Because of this competition, Xerox's share of U.S. copy revenues declined from 96 percent in 1970 to less than 45 percent in 1983. Product planning, design, service, and manufacturing had reported to separate executives at corporate headquarters, and no one had the primary responsibility for seeing that new products were completed and introduced. To correct this, Xerox reorganized the copier business into four strategic business units. General managers of each unit set long-range strategy and oversaw product development while reporting to the head of the Reprographics Business Group, who in turn answered to only one executive at headquarters. This resulted in an immediate 10 percent productivity gain. Further, engineering cycles for some new products were shortened by 10 percent.[8]

Essentially decentralization can be accomplished by organizing on the basis of products or markets. The previous Xerox organizational form was in place until 1992, when Xerox created nine businesses aimed at markets such as small business systems, engineering systems, and office document systems. Each business now has its own profit responsibility and an identifiable set of competitors. Manufacturing layouts have been reorganized to be dedicated to specific businesses. A new Customer Operations Group, consisting of sales, shipping, installation, service, and billing, has been created. Businesses negotiate contracts with Customer Operations to ensure that information about market forces and customers extends into all areas of each business.[9]

Organizing by Product

To the extent that a firm has a large array of products, and to the extent that the products are dissimilar in terms of their marketing requirements (so that each product requires specialized attention), a product-oriented organization can be structured in two ways: through product-manager systems and through autonomous product divisions.

THE PRODUCT-MANAGER SYSTEM

In a product-manager system, individual managers are assigned to coordinate the marketing programs of one or more products or brands. The key to the successful use of this form of organization is the effectiveness with which the product manager coordinates marketing programs with manufacturing and logistics. The product manager will develop and administer marketing programs; analyze and report on a business's progress; administer budgets; oversee sales, product development, and manufacturing functions; and train personnel. Although product managers have no line authority over the field sales force, they work closely with them to accomplish the necessary sales goals for their product. Although the product-management job differs from organization to organization, a frequently used arrangement is for the product or brand manager to be given a budget for the marketing of the brand and then

---

[8] "How Xerox Speeds Up the Birth of New Products," *Business Week*, Mar. 19, 1984, p. 58; and "The New Lean, Mean Xerox: Fending Off the Japanese," *Business Week*, Oct. 12, 1981, pp. 126–132.
[9] Thomas A. Stewart, "The Search for the Organization of Tomorrow," *Fortune*, May 18, 1992, pp. 92–98.

to purchase sales support, advertising, marketing research, or other services the brand requires from the company.

The product-manager organization is not without its deficiencies, however. For example:

- The product manager may be knowledgeable about the product while lacking the expertise needed to make appropriate decisions in the technical areas of product research, manufacturing, and even sales and media.
- Product managers generally lack the authority commensurate with their responsibilities. For example, they must attempt to coordinate sales promotions with sales-force and manufacturing schedules, but they have no authority over either activity. Accordingly, they must rely on their persuasive capabilities to gain the necessary cooperation.
- Many product managers find little time to perform the planning activities so critical to success because of the extensive time and effort involved in their daily interactions with other functional areas.
- Product managers spend considerable time on research and analysis, refining and executing minor changes, and balancing quarterly marketing expenditures, but much of this activity deals with issues on which they can have only limited impact.
- If the product or brand manager has profit responsibility and is rewarded based on the profit performance of the brand, there may be no incentive to invest to build market share, because this may reduce short-term profits.

Product management is undergoing a fundamental change for several reasons. Technology has provided brand managers with increasing amounts of information, and mass markets are becoming more fragmented. The advent of tracking technology has changed brand marketing's focus from broad national programs into numerous regional and subregional campaigns. Perhaps more important has been the growth of the retailer's influence, as we discussed in Chapter 13. Retailers want companies to talk to them with one voice rather than several. This has led to the development of category management in companies like Procter & Gamble, Clorox, and Ralston Purina. At Ralston Purina, brand managers set the trade promotion budget and calendar, and the trade marketing organization controls day-to-day decisions in the field, including how the budget is spent. At some companies, such as Coca-Cola Foods in Houston, brand managers have been eliminated and replaced with regional trade and consumer marketing groups.[10]

THE MULTIDIVISIONAL PRODUCT ORGANIZATION

Firms that have a very large number of products that differ in their manufacturing and R&D requirements as well as in their marketing requirements often employ a multidivisional product organization. In this organizational

---

[10] Laurie Petersen, "Brand Managing's New Accent," *Adweek's Marketing Week*, Apr. 15, 1991, pp. 18–22.

structure, separate divisions are formed, with products grouped into divisions containing similar products. Each division will have its own functional organization and, very frequently, will contain a product-management system.

In many firms, each division will be treated as a unique, autonomous business. Additionally, a recent study indicates that in well-managed companies, divisional managers are usually given responsibility for replenishing the new-product array and are usually allowed to reinvest earnings from the division's own products within the division. Although this practice appears inconsistent with the product portfolio approach (in which cash cow divisions provide the resources for divisions with greater growth potential), managers can still use the product portfolio concept to determine allocations of resources and product objectives among products within each division. More important, many of these firms believe managers will not develop entrepreneurial skills in corporations that "give the fruits of one manager's labor to someone else."[11]

This organizational approach has some limitations. In some cases, divisional lines can inhibit coordination and increase costs. For example,

> Sara Lee made its first European acquisition in 1962 when it obtained a Dutch producer of canned foods. Since that time, Sara Lee has made numerous other international acquisitions, including Douwe Egberts (Dutch coffee, tea, and tobacco company), Nicholas Kiwi Ltd. (the Australian maker of shoe polish), Akzo N.V. (consumer products division), and DIM (French hosiery and underwear). Cornelius Boomstra, chairman of the company's main European unit, in preparation for the European Community after 1992, initiated a program of standardization and reorganization. Douwe Egberts coffee was previously sold under different brand names in seven countries. Standardized packaging sizes and colors and a global advertising campaign was initiated to develop a European identity. By integrating the management structures of Akzo, Douwe Egberts, and other European units, Sara Lee expected profits to improve by $40 million a year. To avoid interdivisional disputes with existing megabrands, specialty products have been emphasized for Eurobranding. For instance, instead of expanding *Prudent*, its top selling Benelux brand, Sara Lee selected *Zendium*, a Danish enzyme toothpaste that cost more. By combining administration and developing a coordinated approach, Boomstra anticipates Sara Lee will be better prepared to develop the European market and at the same time save enormous amounts of money.[12]

Organizing by Market

When customer groups have dramatically different needs, and when these groups are large enough to justify individual attention, the organizational structure often includes market managers and separate sales forces. Note that the various market managers may share common manufacturing and research facilities because essentially the same product is being sold to different mar-

---

[11] Thomas J. Peters, "Putting Excellence into Management," *Business Week*, July 21, 1980, p. 200.
[12] Steve Weiner, "How Do You Say L'Eggs in French?" *Forbes*, Nov. 27, 1989, pp. 73–77.

kets. However, there may be major differences in the quantities purchased, the appropriate channels of distribution, or the technical usage needs of the various customer groups. Accordingly, different packaging and pricing programs, sales forces, and customer service activities may be needed for each group. In these situations, many firms have begun to adopt these market-based organizational structures.

For example, Procter & Gamble has assigned employees from other areas of the company—marketing, finance, distribution, operations—to coordinate with sales and work with key buyers. A group of P&G executives were even moved to Arkansas to work every day with Wal-Mart, P&G's largest account. Borden, Inc., at one time had twenty-eight different people calling on Wal-Mart to sell a variety of snack-food brands. Borden has combined its eight sales organizations, six distribution operations, and five information systems into one to deal with large customers.

As in the case of product managers, market managers seldom have authority over all the functional areas that are essential for implementing the marketing programs. Rather, market managers are responsible for planning and coordination, and sales managers are responsible for implementation. Mergers of large retailers have created a number of regional giants with immense distribution power. These large retailers require specialized attention, such as Gillette's Safety Razor Division provides. Gillette chose to concentrate on the regional level rather than expand their national accounts department. Regional key account managers not only call upon headquarters but also upon chain division offices, even if they are outside of the region. The regional sales manager's job expanded into that of a business unit manager. This was accomplished by putting merchandising and sales planning under the regional sales manager. Salespeople, as a result of this restructuring, are now prepared to talk to their accounts about pricing, distribution, promotion, and display.[13]

Factors Influencing Marketing Organization

Marketing as a management function was centralized well into the 1970s. Marketing was related to the other functions of the business primarily through the budgeting and financial reporting process. This centralization provided for specialized expertise as well as economies in the purchase of marketing services. In addition, it was useful for maintaining control of marketing efforts for individual product groups and brands as well as the sales effort.

In the 1980s, more and more organizations found it necessary to downsize and become more flexible in responding to changing competition and market conditions, including advances in telecommunications, transportation, and

---

[13] "Gillette Hones Salespower to a Fine Edge," *Sales and Marketing Management*, June 1987, p. 59.

information. In addition, global competition led to consumers having better alternative products at lower costs. In most companies, these changes resulted in pressures to reduce costs through technological improvements in products, better manufacturing processes, and reorganization.

The new organizations took on a variety of forms to respond to changes in technology, competition, and consumer demands. One trend was the emphasis on partnerships between previously competing firms, such as General Motors and Toyota, Ford and Mazda, and IBM and Apple Computer. Other responses were to develop multiple types of ownership and partnering within the organization, such as IBM displayed in reorganizing itself into more autonomous operating units (such as Lexmark International, its former desktop printer and typewriter business). Others, such as Nike and Reebok, whose strengths are in design and marketing, farm out the production of their shoes to efficient, low-cost factories in the Far East. Regardless of the form, these new organizational responses are characterized by flexibility, specialization, and an emphasis on managing relationships rather than just market transactions.[14] Although market forces are a major factor in conducting business and determining prices, equally important are ongoing relationships and negotiation.

These relationships take the form of either a strategic alliance, a joint venture, or a network. A strategic alliance takes place in the context of a company's long-term strategic plan and seeks to improve or dramatically change a company's competitive position. Joint ventures are a kind of strategic alliance but unique in that they create a new firm with its own capital structure and sharing of other resources. Networks result from multiple strategic alliances and are usually combined with other forms of organization either within or outside the existing company. Although there is no single best way to organize, the presence or absence of certain conditions can influence the effectiveness of a given organizational structure.

Corporate Strategy

A major purpose of structure in an organization is to assist in the implementation of corporate strategies. Accordingly, one type of structural form may be superior or inferior, depending on the strategic situation. A market-development strategy, for instance, might require a functional or customer-oriented organization if new markets are to be effectively developed. For example,

> Digital Equipment Corporation (DEC) was organized by product line for nineteen years. Product managers were responsible for profitably developing and marketing one product line. However, introducing the VAX superminicomputers, which were intended to be capable of automating entire corporations, required a highly unified

[14] For an excellent discussion, see Frederick E. Webster, Jr., "The Changing Role of Marketing in the Corporation," *Journal of Marketing*, October 1992, pp. 1–17.

and coordinated marketing effort. To accomplish this marketing effort DEC dismantled the product-line organization and organized along functional lines. The development of the VAX 9000, which directly competes with IBM mainframes, brought additional organizational changes in 1989. In an effort to target specific industries, regional managers were put in charge of all employees—programmers, system engineers, and salespeople—who serve a given industry.[15]

In 1992, the company reorganized into nine business units, focusing on specific industries and product markets. In addition, DEC is seeking a partner to help design future processors for its Alpha AXP line of computers based on a reduced-instruction-set computing chip.[16]

Note that DEC's structure has changed as its strategy has changed. Consequently, management should allow the strategy to dictate the structure rather than the reverse.[17] For instance, Sony is working with Panavision, Inc., on a lens for a high-definition TV; with Compression Labs, Inc., on a new video conferencing machine; and with Alphatronix, Inc., on rewritable optical disk storage technologies. In none of these cases has Sony assumed equity or formed a joint venture. They simply share staff, production facilities, engineering concepts, and marketing research and plans.[18]

Needs of Target-Segment Customers

A firm's organizational structure should provide management with the most effective way to meet customer needs quickly. St. Regis Paper reorganized their Bag Packaging/Consumer Products Divisions for this reason. As competition became more aggressive, target market customers demanded faster response times on bids and answers. Previously, bag packaging, the industrial side, had been combined with consumer products. Under the reorganization, five autonomous business units were established within the division: (1) consumer goods—school, home, and office-supply products; (2) retail packaging—grocery bags; (3) specialty packaging—stretch film and semibulk containers; (4) multiwall east; and (5) multiwall west. The multiwall east and multiwall west divisions have complete operational control, including marketing, sales, and manufacturing for industrial products, and are responsible for profit and planning growth for their divisions.[19]

Customer considerations are the major focus in Sony Medical, which makes printers and other peripherals used with medical imaging equipment. Sony personnel spend lots of time with doctors and HMOs and constantly search

---

[15] Peter Petre, "America's Most Successful Entrepreneur," *Fortune*, Oct. 27, 1986, pp. 24–32; and "DEC Has One Little Word for 30,000 Employees: Sell," *Business Week*, Aug. 14, 1989, pp. 86–88.
[16] "DEC's Comeback Is Still a Work in Progress," *Business Week*, Jan. 18, 1993.
[17] For further discussion, see Alfred Chandler, *Strategy and Structure*, MIT Press, Cambridge, 1962.
[18] Allan J. Magrath, "Collaborative Marketing Comes of Age—Again," *Sales and Marketing Management*, September 1991, p. 62.
[19] "St. Regis Divides to Conquer," *Sales and Marketing Management*, Oct. 10, 1983, pp. 39–42.

the rest of Sony for technologies that might serve these customers. When they find a possible technological application, they start a group of about ten people from different disciplines to develop the idea. In 1992, using Sony's Touchscreen and laser-disk technology, they created an interactive system that helps patients learn about their afflictions. Sales are projected to total $40 million within four to six years. Sony Medical is constantly creating and then eventually destroying the organization as the market demands.[20]

In sum, to the extent that customer needs differ among products and customers, the organizational structure should enable the firm to develop and execute marketing strategies to meet the needs of target customers. Further, the more dynamic a firm's markets, the greater the importance of being able to respond to customers' needs.

Management Philosophy and Resources

Management attitudes regarding concepts such as participative decision making, decentralization, and innovation will also influence the effectiveness of an organizational design. For example, in discussing Henry Ford II's decision to retire as chief executive officer of the Ford Motor Company, *Business Week* emphasized his desire to build a decentralized management structure similar to that of General Motors.[21] However, because of the strong personality of Henry Ford and his inability to relinquish control over certain decision areas, this effort was less than successful.

Unilever, which was formed in a 1930 merger of Britain's Lever Brothers Ltd. with Holland's Margine Union Ltd., was one of the first true global marketers. Most of Unilever's United States business is done by Lever Brothers. Unilever's unusual Anglo-Dutch structure gave it a multinational culture, which resulted in a highly decentralized management. For the most part, Unilever's top management lets local executives of its 500 subsidiaries in 75 countries run things as they chose. However, in the United States, the company set unrealistic profit objectives that led Lever Brothers managers to reduce advertising spending at the same time competitors were increasing expenditures and introducing new brands.

After Lever Brothers lost a total of $100 million from 1981 to 1986, Unilever took a more active role in the U.S. operations. One of Unilever's three cochairmen came to the United States and essentially dismantled Lever Brothers, leaving it with only household products. The personal products division was shifted to Chesebrough-Ponds Inc., and the food division was made into a separate unit called VanderBurgh Foods. Each division now reports directly to Europe. This eliminated several layers of management and

[20] Brian Dumaine, "The New Non-Manager Managers," *Fortune*, Feb. 22, 1993, pp. 83–84.
[21] "Ford After Henry II: Will He Really Leave? Absolutely," *Business Week*, Apr. 30, 1979, pp. 62–72.

resulted in faster adoption of new ideas. Subsequently, Unilever's share of the U.S. household products market rose from 15 percent in 1980 to 25 percent in 1989. In addition overall operating profit increased 69 percent during this period.[22]

To summarize, the marketing organization must be structured so that corporate and marketing strategies can be effectively and efficiently carried out to meet customer needs. In addition, top management must be aware that both its philosophy and attitudes about the role of marketing and the availability of qualified middle managers can lead to the choice of an improper structure.

However, the structure of the total organization and of the marketing organization can never ensure the successful execution of strategies and programs. Organization charts do not coordinate activities—people do. And because of marketing's integrative role with the other functional areas, the ability to manage interorganizational relationships is essential, especially for product and market managers.

MANAGING ORGANIZATIONAL RELATIONSHIPS

In Chapter 1 we discussed the various ways in which marketing was related to the other functional areas of the organization. Because of these interrelationships, marketing managers must develop interpersonal skills to be successful in dealing with managers over whom they have no direct authority. Managers consistently cite the importance of their interactions with others, especially in coordinating efforts with other departments. In particular, marketing activities must be closely coordinated with R&D, manufacturing, physical distribution, and finance. We will now discuss the importance of achieving coordination with each of these functions.

Research and Development

In most product-development programs, marketing and R&D must work closely together. Accordingly, marketing managers should have an understanding of the technical problems and processes involved in the various stages of product development. Additionally, managers must be aware of the inevitable frustrations and exacting nature of the R&D activity and should share fully their knowledge of the needs of the market to provide useful guidelines for the work of R&D. Consider, for example, the experience of Colgate.

In 1985, Colgate started to adopt a system whereby managers of product

---

[22] Walecia Konrad, "The New, Improved Unilever Aims to Clean Up in the U.S.," *Business Week*, Nov. 27, 1989, pp. 102–106.

categories would have direct profit responsibility. To provide them with the necessary authority, these category managers were given some control over other functions such as research, finance, and manufacturing. This system was designed to promote better planned and faster new-product introductions. A. Courtenay Shepard, Colgate's president in the United States, says that "by surrounding the marketing people with these multidisciplinary skills we make them instantly effective." This approach has been attributed as the reason the company could take FAB 1 Shot detergent and fabric softener from the idea stage to national introduction in only eleven months.[23]

But these two functions often don't share knowledge. One author has suggested four reasons for the lack of coordination between marketing and R&D.

1. *Product-oriented company philosophy:* In many companies the orientation is an inward-looking one, dominated by products, properties, and processes. This attitude leads to the development of products that are designed around the organization's technological capability rather than around market needs.

2. *Deference toward R&D:* Marketing managers' lack of knowledge regarding the tools and techniques of the "scientists" may lead to permissiveness or great deference to R&D. As a result, some R&D efforts may lead to products that have little chance for commercial success.

3. *Search for perfect products:* R&D often attempts to achieve product perfection. But a technically perfect solution to the problem may be more than the market desires. Technically superior products may be unmarketable because the complexity of these products may preclude high reliability or ease of maintenance. Alternatively, such products may have to be priced too high because of excessive production costs.

4. *Science versus art:* Although market satisfaction is derived from *benefits* (which are usually intangible), R&D is concerned with the tangible *attributes* of products.[24]

Because there is a tendency in most companies for marketing and R&D to view their jobs as very different from one another, it is almost impossible to get them to cooperate. In a study of German small and mid-size companies having world market shares in the range of 70 to 90 percent, it was found that these firms viewed the market and technology as equal driving forces. These companies believe that when technology dominates, engineers become remote from customers. Likewise, when marketing dominates, technology suffers. The ideal would be for technical people to have a thorough understanding of consumer needs. Direct contact by people in R&D with consumers is critical.

[23] Zachary Schiller, "The Marketing Revolution at Procter & Gamble," *Business Week*, July 25, 1988, p. 76.
[24] Mack Hanan, "Effective Coordination of Marketing with Research and Development," in Victor Buell (ed.), *Handbook of Modern Marketing*, McGraw-Hill, New York, 1970, pp. 3-17–3-28.

Wurth & Company, for instance, requires all its managers to see a customer at least once a month.[25] Physically locating departments next to one another and holding combined departmental meetings have worked for some firms. The key is having someone coordinate the effort—someone who has the necessary authority to get the two groups to cooperate.[26]

Manufacturing

Probably the most frequent conflicts between functions are those between marketing and manufacturing. Table 14-1 summarizes the various kinds of conflicts that typically occur between these two functions.

Although these conflicts can seldom be fully resolved, the level of conflict between these two groups can be made more manageable so that greater cooperation is achieved. Among the actions managers may employ to manage these conflicts are the following.

- Clearly specified corporate strategies and marketing strategies should be developed to provide a common set of rules for both functions. For example, when the markets to be served are clearly specified, the number of models or product lines to be produced can be agreed upon more easily.
- Management can modify the evaluation and reward system to include interfunctional performance. For instance, marketing managers may be evaluated on sales forecasting performance and manufacturing managers on order response time as well as on inventory levels.
- By having manufacturing personnel attend sales meetings or marketing managers do "internships" in manufacturing positions, managers in each functional area may gain better insights into the problems facing managers in the other functional areas.[27]

Physical Distribution

An effective and well-integrated physical distribution system can provide a firm with a significant competitive marketing advantage. Because a substantial share of the final price of a product is accounted for by physical distribution costs, any reduction in price resulting from more effective coordination will lead to more competitive prices or higher margins. In addition, companies are finding that the speed with which they respond to changes in the market is the most crucial element in being more competitive.

Allegheny Beverages' computerized order-entry system provides this type of advantage for its field sales force and production scheduling system. Alle-

[25] Herman Simon, "Lessons from Germany's Midsize Giants," *Harvard Business Review*, March–April 1992, p. 120.

[26] Michael Duerr, *The Commercial Development of New Products*, The Conference Board, New York, 1986.

[27] Benson Shapiro, "Can Marketing and Manufacturing Coexist?" *Harvard Business Review*, September–October 1977, pp. 111–113.

| TABLE 14-1 | MARKETING, MANUFACTURING AREAS OF NECESSARY COOPERATION BUT POTENTIAL CONFLICT |

PROBLEM AREA	TYPICAL MARKETING COMMENT	TYPICAL MANUFACTURING COMMENT
1. Capacity planning and long-range sales forecasting	"Why don't we have enough capacity?"	"Why didn't we have accurate sales forecasts?"
2. Production scheduling and short-range sales forecasting	"We need faster response. Our lead times are ridiculous."	"We need realistic customer commitments and sales forecasts that don't change like wind direction."
3. Delivery and physical distribution	"Why don't we ever have the right merchandise in inventory?"	"We can't keep everything in inventory."
4. Quality assurance	"Why can't we have reasonable quality at reasonable cost?"	"Why must we always offer options that are too hard to manufacture and that offer little customer utility?"
5. Breadth of product line	"Our customers demand variety."	"The product line is too broad—all we get are short, uneconomical runs."
6. Cost control	"Our costs are so high that we are not competitive in the marketplace."	"We can't provide fast delivery, broad variety, rapid response to change, and high quality at low cost."
7. New product introduction	"New products are our life blood."	"Unnecessary design changes are prohibitively expensive."
8. Adjunct services such as spare parts inventory support, installation, and repair	"Field service costs are too high."	"Products are being used in ways for which they weren't designed."

Source: Reprinted by permission of the *Harvard Business Review* from "Can Marketing and Manufacturing Coexist?" by Benson Shapiro, September–October 1977. Copyright © 1977 by the President and Fellows of Harvard College; all rights reserved.

gheny's Desk and Furnishings Division's sales representatives are each equipped with a Hewlett-Packard Portable Plus laptop computer that allows them to dial into the headquarter's HP 3000 mainframe. Individual salespersons can check on the order status as well as shipment schedule for any customer. In this way they can assure customers of delivery dates or suggest alternatives. In addition, they can reserve inventory as well as place orders almost instantaneously.[28]

[28] Thayer C. Taylor, "Laptops and the Salesforce: New Stars in the Sky," *Sales and Marketing Management*, April 1987, pp. 50–55.

As we noted in Chapters 12 and 13, logistical appeals are becoming more desirable to customers, but the cost of providing these appeals is also increasing. Just about every business is looking for ways to cut distribution costs. Accordingly, coordination between sales programs and physical distribution is essential to building profitable sales-volume levels. Helene Curtis' Suave shampoo has cut its price to the consumer by 10 percent over the past two years. Over one-half of that cut was made up by savings in distribution and inventory costs. Helene Curtis' overall distribution costs have been cut by 40 percent, in large part due to its modern automated and computerized distribution warehouse. This facility has no paper order tickets or shipping tags and uses computer-controlled forklifts to place packages on conveyors. Once they are on the conveyor, lasers read bar codes and sort the packages by destination. This one facility can handle twice as many goods as the six older warehouses it replaced. On the other hand, Sun Microsystems has outsourced its distribution system to Federal Express, because Sun wanted distribution to be primarily a variable rather than fixed cost in the manufacturing process.[29]

Finance

The marketing plan includes major financial inputs, such as the cost and profit history for the business, pro forma financial statements, budgets, and the related marketing strategies. In developing and selecting the appropriate marketing strategies, management requires certain financial inputs. Many marketing decisions should be viewed as investment decisions. For instance, as discussed in Chapter 8, new-product alternatives should include a financial evaluation of the required investment and revenue stream. However, this shouldn't be limited to new products, as the financial aspects of promotion, distribution alternatives, and pricing decisions must be considered by marketing management as well. In addition, financial considerations can often act as a significant constraint on the strategic options open to the marketer.

The failures of the computer ventures of RCA and General Electric in the 1970s are examples of the constraints financial considerations can place on marketing strategy. The market-share and growth objectives of both companies required a capital commitment to finance a large and rapidly growing leased-equipment inventory. However, the capital-generating ability of the marketing effort was inadequate in both cases.

Often, marketers fail to recognize the impact their decisions have on such variables as inventory level, working-capital needs, financing costs, debt-to-equity ratios, and stock prices. Too often these are thought of as purely the responsibility of finance. Marketing management needs to be particularly sensitive to the impact various marketing strategies can have upon the financial well-being of the company. The development of financial plans involving capital requirements, cash flow, and credit policies all require marketing input

---

[29] Rita Koselka, "Distribution Revolution," *Forbes*, May 25, 1992, pp. 54–61.

to work effectively with the finance department. It may be necessary for marketing to provide alternative strategies and environmental-condition scenarios to assist in financial planning. In addition, marketers must be willing to make the trade-offs necessitated by various financial considerations. This requires close cooperation and contact with the finance function as well as an understanding of the concepts and approaches utilized.

In sum, although an effective organizational structure can assist managers in the execution of corporate and marketing strategies, the development of interorganizational coordination ultimately will depend on the attitudes and actions of the managers in the firm. Essentially, marketing managers must "market the marketing strategies and programs" to other functional areas in order to obtain coordination. To be effective in performing this task, an understanding of the needs and aspirations of other managers, and an awareness of the constraints limiting their actions (such as the reward system they face), is essential. If marketing managers can develop this kind of understanding, they are more likely to develop programs that will receive support from managers in the other functional areas.

MANAGING THE FIELD SALES FORCE

Managing human resources is an important task in all functional areas. But within marketing, this task is primarily important for sales managers. This is true for three reasons. First, the largest number of marketing personnel are in sales positions. Second, the cost of personal selling is extremely high because sales salaries and other compensation are usually relatively high and because of the expenses associated with travel, training, and sales demonstrations. As shown in Table 14-2, these selling expenses as a percentage of total sales range from 9.1 percent for industrial goods to as high as 21.4 percent for services.

Finally, effective sales-force management is important because the responsibility for execution of sales and distribution is highly decentralized. That is, the effectiveness of these programs depends on the performance of a large number of people. In contrast, other marketing programs (such as advertising) are normally executed by a relatively small number of people who have the opportunity to work closely with the managers responsible for the programs. Accordingly, sales managers must generally be far more concerned with human resource management than other middle-level marketing managers.

There are three kinds of sales-force performance sales managers can influence in order to improve the execution of sales and distribution programs. First, sales managers can attempt to influence the *total number of sales calls* made in order to maximize the total selling effort. Second, sales managers can attempt to influence the *quality of the sales calls* by taking actions that enhance the expert and referent power of salespeople. Finally, sales managers can

| TABLE 14-2 | SALES-RELATED COSTS BY INDUSTRY |

INDUSTRY GROUP	SELLING EXPENSES*	ADV./PROMO. EXPENSES**	MEDIAN SALES BY INDUSTRY***
	(As a percentage of total sales)		
Consumer Goods	14.3%	5.0%	$30,000,000
Industrial Goods	9.1%	2.7%	$ 9,500,000
Services	21.4%	3.8%	$14,000,000

* **Selling Expenses** include compensation, benefits, travel and entertainment expenses, meeting costs, recruiting and training costs, support materials, staff and administrative expenses, and commissions to outside reps and distributors.

** **Advertising and Promotional Expenses** include direct costs of materials and media (print, radio, TV, and so on), as well as any associated costs related to research, preparation, and execution.

*** **Median Sales by Industry** is calculated by examining the entire range of responses to this year's survey and selecting the midpoint in each set of ranges (that is, half the responses were above, and half below, this figure).

Source: "1992 Sales Manager's Budget Planner," *Sales & Marketing Management.*

attempt to improve each salesperson's *allocation of selling effort.*[30] Table 14-3 summarizes the kinds of management actions that relate to each of these sales-force dimensions.

In Chapter 13, we reviewed some of the considerations involved in determining the number of sales calls, the size of the sales force, and sales-force allocation. In the remaining portion of this chapter, we examine sales-management actions that are directed more toward enhancing the performance of individual members of the sales force—especially regarding the quality of the sales call.

Selecting Salespeople

In many firms, efforts to recruit, select, and train sales-force members are almost continuous because of market expansion, promotions of salespeople into management, and resignations or retirements. A large investment of time and money is required to recruit and train new salespeople. Accordingly, it is important to develop selection procedures that enable a firm to hire people who will be successful. An improper selection can cost an organization $150,000 or more when all the efforts involved in selecting, training, developing, and managing are calculated. For example, consider the case of Dow Chemical.

[30] Porter Henry, "Manage Your Sales Force as a System," *Harvard Business Review*, March–April 1975.

TABLE 14-3	**HOW MANAGERS CAN INFLUENCE THE EXECUTION OF SALES AND DISTRIBUTION PROGRAMS**

THE SALESPERSON CAN TAKE THE FOLLOWING ACTIONS:	THESE ACTIONS OF THE MANAGER INFLUENCE THE SALESPERSON:
NUMBER OF SALES CALLS	NUMBER OF SALESPEOPLE
	Training in territory coverage, routing, and time management
	Standard operating procedures for sales-force organization, territory coverage, and routing
	Tools for time saving
	Motivation and compensation
QUALITY OF SALES CALLS	
1. Message content	Training in product knowledge and customer operations
	Information flow on customer status, industry trends, and call planning
2. Communications effectiveness	Salespeople selection
	Training in sales skills, communications, listening, and group presentations
	Standard operating procedures for sales-force organization and call planning
	Visual sales aids
3. Interpersonal relationships	Salespeople selection
	Sensitivity training
	Motivation and compensation
ALLOCATION OF SALES EFFORT	
	Training in territory coverage, time management, and market planning
	Standard operating procedures for sales-force organization and territory coverage
	Motivation and compensation

Dow Chemical recruits almost exclusively from college campuses. Over the years, Dow has selected a group of about thirty-five colleges and universities, primarily in the Midwestern and Southern parts of the United States. The company has developed relationships with these institutions similar to those of a business partner. All recruits are processed through a year-long program, followed by actual field selling. Dow calculates that after about four years with the company, the investment in each recruit is in the hundreds of thousands of dollars.[31]

Selecting salespeople would not be a difficult task if the characteristics that made a good salesperson could be readily identified. Moreover, each sales job has its own unique requirements. Formal tests, extensive interviews, and weighted applications are finding increasing use as firms attempt to improve their recruiting processes. Increasing use is being made of psychological assessment services in an attempt to reduce turnover.

In 1991, turnover was greater than 20 percent for 24 percent of the companies in the services industry.[32] Acme Fabrication estimates that they lose about $25,000 in salary, training, and recruiting cost each time they have to replace a salesperson. Each year they interview approximately 500 persons and hire 100 of them. Of these 100, about 20 will be terminated during the first year, resulting in a loss of $500,000. In an attempt to improve this performance, Acme has started to utilize a psychological assessment service. After preliminary interviews are conducted, they refer the best 200 candidates to an assessment firm to review at a cost of $150 a candidate. Acme feels that if the assessment service can reduce turnover by 2 percent, they get full payback in three-fifths of a year: two people times $25,000 (turnover cost) equals $50,000 as opposed to 200 times $150 equals $30,000 (cost of assessment).[33]

Training Programs

To the extent that training provides the salesperson with product knowledge, customer knowledge, and special skills, the expertise power of the salesperson can be enhanced. Similarly, training in interpersonal relations can improve a salesperson's ability to use referent power. Additionally, training sessions may help salespeople to manage their time better and thus be more productive.

Training can be costly and time-consuming, but more and more companies are recognizing the importance of this activity. For example,

> Bell Atlantic introduced its Top Gun program intended to position account executives to be better prepared for emerging technologies in the telecommunications-information services market. Bell selected sixty top sales producers for an intensive thirteen-week course to equip them better with solutions to solve customer problems. Goodyear has initiated a training center in which sales recruits spend approximately three months in training and veteran salespersons are brought back at

---

[31] "Dow Makes It Big by Thinking Small," *Sales and Marketing Management*, September 1991, p. 46.
[32] "1992 Sales Manager's Budget Planner," *Sales and Marketing Management*, June 22, 1992, p. 71.
[33] Lester L. Tobias, "Making Tests Pay," *Sales and Marketing Management*, Aug. 12, 1985, p. 80.

regular intervals for refresher courses (because the tire business has become more technical).

Every member of Hewlett-Packard's sales staff receives basic training in strategic selling and account management, using custom-training videos. H-P also uses interactive TV/satellite training sessions to train sales groups on specific projects or on regional groups whose customers would benefit from specific H-P products. Industry-specific training that relates new technologies to customer needs has become a major component of H-P's training and development effort.[34]

Standard Operating Procedures and Selling Tools

Standard operating procedures are used to develop routines for those aspects of the sales function that lend themselves to standardization. If managers can routinize certain aspects of the sales function, more of the salesperson's time can be freed for the creative part of the selling task. Increasingly, firms are using automation and computerization for this purpose.

A variety of audiovisual sales aids and literature can be used to increase the communications effectiveness of the salesperson. In addition, technology is providing new ways of performing many selling activities. This has led to increased efficiency and improved quality of the selling function. Videodisc players, compact portable computers, telemarketing, and other electronic tools are becoming widely used in an effort to boost sales productivity. Video presentations, for example, can quickly and precisely show a complicated product's features. Gould Incorporated's Medical Products Division used video in selling a new product (called a "disposable transducer") that translated blood pressure into readable electronic impulses. Two videotapes—a 6-minute sales presentation and a 9-minute user training film—were produced at a cost of $200,000. An additional $75,000 was spent on video recorders for salespeople to take with them on calls. Gould claims this approach captured 45 percent of the $75 million transducer market in less than a year. This was a market Gould had previously been unable to penetrate because some salespeople couldn't convey the exact message the inventor and manufacturer had in mind when the product was designed.[35] All of Nabisco's 2800 sales reps carry hand-held computers, used to collect sales data for individual accounts. In addition, two-thirds use laptop computers to help retail buyers configure their shelf space in the most productive manner. Computer models then tell

---

[34] Al Urbanski, "America's Best Sales Forces," *Sales and Marketing Management*, June 1988, pp. 24–45; and "Hewlett Packard Strives to Connect with Its Customers," *Sales and Marketing Management*, September 1991, p. 48.

[35] "Rebirth of a Salesman: Willy Loman Goes Electronic," *Business Week*, Feb. 27, 1984, pp. 103–104.

the salesperson the best display method for each account for each Nabisco product. This focus on their clients' needs helped Nabisco double its profit over a 3-year period while at the same time winning it recognition as the best customer-focused sales organization in the packaged goods industry.[36]

Motivation and Compensation

A central concern of any top- or middle-level manager is how to motivate people to achieve the desired level and type of performance. Unfortunately, research on motivation has not provided management with simple guidelines for selecting the best way of motivating the sales force.

In fact, most studies indicate that performance does not depend solely on motivational devices such as bonuses, awards, and promotions. Rather, performance also depends on factors such as quality of supervision, the realism of the selling objectives and quotas, the salesperson's need for achievement, the type of selling task (such as new-account development or account mainte-nance), and the type of sales job (such as trade selling versus missionary selling). Accordingly, the effectiveness of incentives will differ among indus-tries, firms, and even salespeople within a firm.

It is clear that noncompensation-related forms of motivation should be a part of the motivational package in most firms. IBM wants its employees to feel like winners and has a 100-percent Club for those salespersons achieving their sales quota. About 70 percent of the sales force make the 100-percent Club. The reward for this is a 3-day trip that includes a recognition dinner, a blue and gold lapel pin, and the names of recipients posted on their respective branch office's wall.[37] Recognition is critical and, after a fair level of compen-sation, is a major motivational tool in many companies.[38]

Compensation-based incentives are also widely employed and are ex-tremely effective in many industries. However, when incentive compensation plans are to be used, they should be designed to support the firm's particular sales-program objectives. An incentive based on dollar volume alone may encourage the sales force to emphasize low-margin products and may also lead to inadequate attention to any customer service or account-development objectives that have been established. In an attempt to overcome such prob-lems, many firms in a variety of industries moved away from straight commis-sion schedules and fixed salaries during the 1970s. Too much protection in a pay plan tends to favor the least productive salespeople and provides little stimulus for putting forth the extra effort to reach the sales objectives that have been established.

[36] Patricia Sellers, "How to Remake Your Sales Force," *Fortune*, May 4, 1992, p. 100.
[37] Patricia Sellers, "How IBM Teaches to Sell," *Fortune*, June 6, 1988, pp. 141–146.
[38] "Rewarding the Troops," *Inc.*, October 1991, p. 156.

In a study of compensation plans, it was found the most frequently used was some combination of base salary plus incentive pay in the form of commissions, bonuses, or both. Only 14.8 percent of the companies studied used only salary, and only 7.5 percent of the compensation plans were based on full commission.[39]

In order to serve customers better, many firms have worked to increase teamwork and collaboration both within the sales force and between the sales force and other functions of the company. This has led to difficulties in determining compensation, and companies are starting to test and implement new forms. For instance, G.D. Searle plans to give salespeople bonuses based partially on "assists." In this plan, the person who provided the assistance to the individual actually making the sale would also be rewarded. Eastman Kodak is now evaluating its reps on how well they coordinate with co-workers to help the customer, and Pepsi Cola General Bottlers is developing a formalized process to measure customer satisfaction in a way that will be useful for compensation purposes.

CONCLUSION

An essential ingredient to success in any business, government, or other type of organization are the individuals (and groups of individuals) who make and execute plans. Accordingly, if people are to be effective, managers must design an environment that will facilitate—not hinder—the efforts of individuals and enhance the coordination of efforts. Marketing strategy and the execution of this strategy have a reciprocal effect on each other. Inappropriate strategies can sometimes be compensated for by excellent execution. On the other hand, good strategies can often fail because they are poorly implemented. Several distinct characteristics differentiate those companies that seem to do a good job of implementation from those that do not. A well-defined direction, concern for customers' needs, and managers who encourage subordinates' ideas are among those major characteristics.

In this chapter we discussed the impact of the organizational structure in facilitating the execution of strategies and programs. But we also recognized that no structure will ensure coordination. Interpersonal skills and cooperative attitudes must be developed to ensure effective coordination. Further, managers must learn to understand the factors that can hinder the performance of people within their own function. In marketing, this problem is most critical with respect to sales-force performance, because if programs are to be effectively implemented, the sales force usually has a major role to play. Although there is no "magic formula" for effective sales-force management,

---

[39] "Compensation: How Do You Pay Your Sales Force?" *Inc.*, August 1991, p. 82.

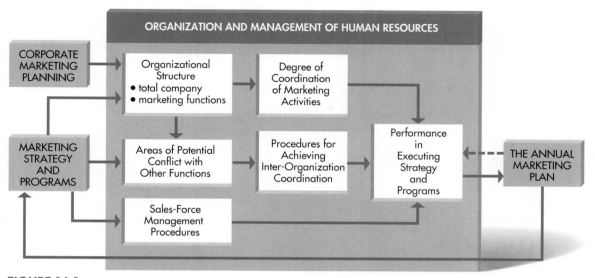

FIGURE 14-1

Relationship of organizing and managing human resources to the other elements of the marketing planning process.

managers must consider the issues discussed in this chapter in order to build and maintain a quality sales effort.

It is important to be aware that organizing and managing human resources are essential parts of the planning process. Different organizational structures, different approaches for coordinating activities, and different devices for directing the sales-force effort will be necessary depending upon the types of strategies and programs selected. The relationships between these decisions and the other elements of the planning process are summarized in Figure 14-1.

It is particularly important to recognize that the corporate strategy and the product objectives have a special relationship to decisions regarding organization and human resources management. In fact, some managers believe products require different managerial skills at various stages of the product life cycle.

In sum, an effective organizational structure and sound human resource management procedures can be of immense value in executing a marketing strategy. However, because a complex array of marketing programs are often employed to implement the marketing strategy, annual marketing plans should be developed for defining and coordinating program plans. As we indicate in the next chapter, the specific type of plan will depend in part on the organizational structure selected. Before proceeding to the chapter, however, consider the following situation in light of the issues discussed in the present chapter.

COMPAQ COMPUTER: RESPONDING TO A CHANGING MARKET*

Compaq Computer was founded in 1982 by a group of former Texas Instruments engineers. Compaq pioneered the market for PC clones by copying IBM's personal computer technology. They were one of the few PC makers to build their own power supplies and casings, and their pricing strategy was to match IBM's prices but with more innovative PCs. Compaq's engineering culture placed a premium on developing and producing new products quickly rather than making them inexpensively. The PC division head described the manufacturing director as "probably the only manufacturing guy in a Fortune 200 company who doesn't have a P&L. He never had it. If he did, he'd always want long runs and stable design—which means little innovation. He wouldn't be interested in a feature-rich product that's hard to build, and he'd want longer lead times so he could work longer with suppliers to get low costs."

The pricing umbrella created by IBM and Compaq made it possible for cheaper clones like Dell and AST to enter and compete in the market, primarily through distribution and farming out manufacturing. However, by 1986 Compaq had introduced the first 386 system (a full year before IBM) at a premium price, and they soon were seen as establishing the pace in the personal computer market. Compaq was able to manage a price differential between their high-quality machines and low-priced clones of 35 percent. In 1990 Compaq reached its peak performance with profits of $455 million on sales of $3.6 billion. However, in October 1991, Compaq announced its first-ever quarterly loss and planned to lay off 1700 employees, 14 percent of the total. At the October board meeting, the founder and CEO was replaced by the board of directors.

Two factors accounted for this sudden change. First, Compaq had not responded to newcomers like Dell, which had cut prices and introduced the basic and reliable PCs customers were demanding. In addition, AST research had

delivered the first 486-based PC in December 1990 with a machine almost $2000 cheaper than the comparable one Compaq later brought to market. AST's sales had tripled since 1987, and Dell's had doubled since 1989, partly at Compaq's expense.

Eckhard Pfeiffer, Compaq's new CEO, quickly determined the major problems facing him. These were the high cost of design, high product cost, premium pricing, excessive overhead and expenses, lack of customer support, narrow distribution focus, and poor communications with the marketplace. Compaq had to lower cost quickly and permanently. Suppliers were required to bid for contracts, which saved $165 million through October 1992. The cost of components dropped about 30 percent. Four separate PC engineering organizations were reorganized into two—one for product development and one for production. Managers in manufacturing had to work closely with marketing and vice versa. Members of a product-development strategy team from all parts of the company meet weekly to work out conflicts.

Pricing practices were totally changed. Previously, product designers totaled up the cost of all the features, determined which sole supplier would provide what parts at what price, and then added on a margin of 40 percent. The total was the price to the dealers, who would then add on another 15 percent. Under the new system the process is reversed. Managers first establish what the customer price should be based on competitive factors. They then assume a

---

* This case developed from "Duel," *The Economist*, Jan. 30, 1993, pp. 57–58; David Kirkpatrick, "The Revolution at Compaq Computer," *Fortune*, Dec. 14, 1992, pp. 80–88; "Compaq: How It Made Its Impressive Move Out of the Doldrums," *Business Week*, Nov. 2, 1992, pp. 146–151; Julie Pitta, "Identity Crisis," *Forbes*, May 25, 1992, p. 82; "The Datamation 100," *Datamation*, June 15, 1992, p. 46; and David P. Hamilton, "Compaq Plans to Intensify Japan PC War," *The Wall Street Journal*, Feb. 3, 1993, p. B6.

continued

dealer markup, subtract Compaq's gross profit margin (about 30 percent), and instruct various departments to resolve among themselves how to allocate the remaining costs.

On June 15, 1992 Compaq announced an expanded line of PCs, including forty-five new models, and across-the-board price cuts of up to 32 percent. In addition, the advertising budget was increased by 60 percent and distribution outlets were increased from 3300 to 8300 worldwide. Compaqs are also sold through catalogs and telemarketing. A newly created position of vice president of worldwide logistics was created to cut Compaq's $800 million inventory by at least 10 percent.

Compaq signed up Merisel Corp. and Tech Data Corp. to sell Compaq products to specialized resellers. Anderson Consulting and Electronic Data Systems were authorized to sell Compaq products as part of their systems integration business. Compaq authorized Tandy Corp. to sell selected low-end Compaq models in their new Computer City Superstores chain. A customer support center was established, and two third-party service providers were contracted to handle on-site service. In addition, in Japan, Compaq's subsidiary offers its customers 3-year service warranties free of charge, with free repair on customer's machines at their homes and office.

On January 26, 1993, Compaq announced revenues were up by 25 percent to a record $4.1 billion, and net profit had increased by 63 percent to $213 million. Compaq's share of the world PC market was expected to reach 10 percent, up from 6.6 percent in 1992.

1. Dell, unlike Compaq, contracts out almost all its manufacturing to other companies and then assembles the components in its own factories. This results in Dell's operating costs being 14.5 percent of sales, versus 16.4 percent for Compaq'. What factors seem to influence Compaq's and Dell's different approaches to manufacturing and marketing?

2. Would a product manager or category manager system be appropriate for Compaq Computer?

3. What different organizational forms did Compaq utilize in their rapid response to changing market and competitive conditions?

QUESTIONS AND SITUATIONS FOR DISCUSSION

1. Pioneer Hi-Bred International produces and markets hybrid seeds that are hardier and more productive than varietal seeds. Pioneer's 4500 commissioned salespeople in the past called on every farmer in a sales area. Now they concentrate on sophisticated, large-scale farmers who plant 1000 acres or more. Agronomists and specialists are called in to provide preferred customers with detailed information on new kinds of seeds or assist those having crop problems. This "customer focus" marketing approach is credited with Pioneer's recent market-share increases. What compensation problems would you expect with such an approach?

2. Some manufacturers of pharmaceuticals prefer to hire and train inexperienced salespeople, while others attempt to hire experienced people from competitors. What would be some of the reasons for these two different approaches?

3. A leading marketing manager recently said that "as markets become more fragmented and companies keep developing multiple products, the key technical, manufacturing, and sales issues will become line-oriented rather than brand-oriented, making the involvement of product managers inefficient." Why would these factors prompt him to make such a prediction?

4. "As retail customers become fewer and more sophisticated, the balance of power is shifting to the customer's favor." How would you expect this to affect the job of sales management?

5. A medium-sized manufacturer of machine tools uses a top-management group for all major decisions. This group consists of the president and vice presidents of finance, marketing, manufacturing, personnel, and research and development. Assume you are the vice president of marketing and the top-management group is considering the following issues:

a. Whether to expand warehouse capacity for finished goods at the existing home manufacturing facility or to establish four regional warehouses across the United States.

b. Additional requests have been made for increasing staff by the research and development manager and by the sales manager. The vice president of finance indicates that only one of these requests can be funded at this time.

c. A new alloy that is cheaper and more compatible with manufacturing processes has been proposed for use in a majority of products in the existing product line.

Would there be any difference(s) in the position you took if you approached these issues from the best interest of the company as a whole as opposed to those of your own function? Explain.

SUGGESTED ADDITIONAL READINGS

Avlonitis, George J., Kevin A. Boyle, and A. G. Kouremenos, "Matching Salesmen to the Selling Job," *Industrial Marketing Management*, Vol. 15, February 1986, pp. 45–54.

Blerke, Joel, and David Ernest, "The Way to Win in Cross Border Alliances," *Harvard Business Review*, November–December 1991, pp. 127–135.

Bonoma, Thomas V., "Making Your Marketing Strategy Work," *Harvard Business Review*, March–April 1984, pp. 68–76.

Lorange, Peter, and Johan Roos, "Why Some Strategic Alliances Succeed and Others Fail," *Journal of Business Strategy*, January–February 1991, pp. 32–35.

Lyons, Michael Paul, "Joint Ventures as Strategic Choice—A Literature Review," *Long-Range Planning*, August 1991, pp. 130–144.

McAdams, Jerry, "Rewarding Sales and Marketing Performance," *Management Review*, April 1987, pp. 33–38.

Morgan, James, "Strategic Sourcing Rises to the Top," *Purchasing*, Apr. 12, 1992, pp. 54–55, 57, 59.

Ruekert, Robert W., and Orville C. Walker, Jr., "Marketing's Interaction with Other Functional Units: A Conceptual Framework and Empirical Evidence," *Journal of Marketing*, January 1987, pp. 1–19.

Simon, Herman, "Lessons from Germany's Midsize Giants," *Harvard Business Review*, March–April, 1992, pp. 115–123.

Strahle, William, and Rosann L. Spiro, "Linking Market Share Strategies to Salesforce Objectives, Activities, and Compensation Policies," *Journal of Personal Selling and Sales Management*, August 1986, pp. 11–18.

Vaccaro, Joseph P. "Organizational Issues in Sales Force Decisions," *Journal of Professional Services Marketing*, No. 2 1991, pp. 69–80.

Webster, Frederick E., Jr., "The Changing Role of Marketing in the Corporation," *Journal of Marketing*, October 1992, pp. 1–17.

Yovovich, B. G., "Partnering at Its Best," *Business Marketing*, March 1992, pp. 36–37.

CHAPTER 15

THE ANNUAL MARKETING PLAN

OVERVIEW

For virtually all organizations, the most basic planning mechanism is an annual plan that describes the goals or objectives the organization expects to achieve in the coming year and the budget required to realize these objectives. As we have indicated at several points in this book, many corporate and marketing strategies will take a long time (at least more than a year) to be implemented fully. Nevertheless, because the financial results for the total organization must be presented annually, budgets and the rationale for these budgets must also be developed within this time frame.

In this chapter we examine the annual *marketing* plan, which is the mechanism by which the objectives, activities, and budgets for the various marketing programs (discussed in Chapters 8 through 13) are integrated. These plans serve three basic purposes.

- Like the various program plans, annual plans serve as a communications device. They indicate clearly to the personnel involved in marketing what the planned objectives and programs are, and thus should provide guidance to personnel on what activities to pursue.
- In an organization with multiple products, markets, or other divisions, annual plans serve as important inputs to the resource allocation process. Top management usually will review each annual plan within an organization, assess the corporate resources available, and approve or modify budgets based on an assessment of each unit's needs and contributions.
- Finally, once approved, the annual plan serves as a mechanism for control. That is, the annual plan establishes standards of performance against which the organizational unit's progress can be evaluated. Periodic checks of the performance-evaluation gap can be useful in making timely modifications to the plan. Additionally, the overall achievement of the unit is assessed largely on annual performance relative to the plan.

The major goal of this chapter is to identify the basic elements of a typical annual marketing plan, to demonstrate the use of the marketing plan for purposes of control, and to present some of the most important organizational issues associated with effective planning. Because managers must also assess the impact of environmental factors in setting standards and in evaluating performance, we also examine the process of environmental monitoring and its relationship to the marketing planning process. Before examining these concepts and procedures, however, we distinguish three major types of annual marketing plans and we indicate the various types of objectives that can be selected for the annual plan.

TYPES OF ANNUAL MARKETING PLANS

Organizations may have one annual marketing plan or several annual marketing plans. Additionally, the scope of the annual plan is not the same for all companies. Basically, the number of plans and the scope of the plans will depend on the diversity of the firm's products and markets and on the firm's organizational structure.

The Business Level Annual Marketing Plan

Often an organization with a single product or a single line of highly related products sells through a sales force responsible only for that product or line. Not only is this situation typical of many small- and medium-sized manufacturing firms, but it also may typify strategic business units or business categories within a large diversified firm. In such cases, a single annual marketing plan is developed for that particular "business" (whether the business is an entire company, a division, or some other strategic unit). Usually such plans are designed by the general sales manager or by the marketing manager for the business. Similarly, limited-line retailers who specialize in a product category may develop a single storewide plan under the guidance of a merchandise manager or a store manager. Finally, a total marketing plan may be developed by a marketing director of a consumer services company (such as a bank or a health maintenance organization). These firms offer a large number of highly related services and do not normally employ sales forces.

Annual Product or Department Plans

Firms organized by product lines may require separate plans for each product (or, in retailing, for each department). In these situations, the number of programs included in the scope of the plans is limited. For instance, a product manager typically develops the advertising and sales-promotion elements of a plan. But if a common sales force is used for several separately managed products, the product manager often has no control over the size of and expenses incurred by the sales force. In such cases, the sales budget may not be a part of the annual product plan. Finally, large service companies (such as large banks) may employ product plans if some products require special attention. For example, many banks develop separate annual plans to market services used only by corporate customers (such as certain pension trust services).

When individual product plans are developed, these plans must be integrated into other plans at higher levels in the organization. For example, in an organization with several divisions, each of which has several products, a divisional manager must develop plans reflecting the sum of the product plans. Subsequently, corporate plans and divisional plans must be consistent with the corporate marketing planning objectives discussed in Chapter 2.

Annual Sales Plans

A third type of plan is the annual sales plan. If a sales force is responsible for several products in a division, a separate plan and budget covering only sales-force responsibilities may be developed by the sales manager. Sales-force salaries, commissions, and expenses will typically be the major elements in such budgets. However, to the extent that the sales force has decision-making power regarding discounts, credit, special-delivery terms, warranties, and merchandise returns, these may also be included in the scope of the plan. The annual sales plan will then be integrated with the various product plans in the divisional plan.

Because sales plans have already been discussed in Chapter 13, our discussion of the annual plan will center on the total marketing plan and the product plan. However, it is important to recognize that in multiproduct companies, each annual plan will be reviewed at the divisional or corporate level, or both.

Figure 15-1 indicates how the various types of middle-management-level marketing plans may be integrated at higher organizational levels. As we suggested in Chapter 2, these product plans must be consistent with the product objectives established at the top-management level. However, the plans must also be developed in a way that reflects the situation analysis. In the next section we briefly review the major considerations influencing the marketing plan.

DEVELOPING THE PLAN

There is no single format or formula that is universally agreed on for every annual planning situation. In practice, each firm will develop a method, outline, or form that seems to fit its own needs best. However, there are two basic kinds of inputs to the planning process that should be a part of every plan: (1) a comprehensive situation analysis and (2) a statement of overall performance objectives.

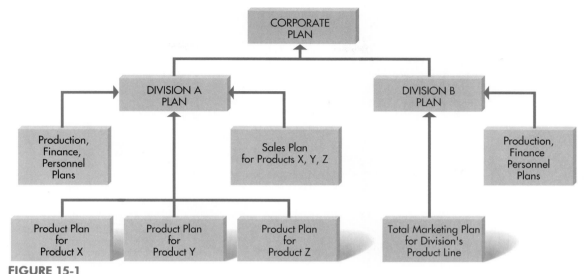

FIGURE 15-1
Relationship of annual marketing plans, product plans, and sales plans to divisional and corporate-level planning.

Comprehensive Situation Analysis

As we discussed in the early chapters of this book, a firm should perform a situation analysis before designing its marketing strategy and programs. Specifically, we argued that a marketing strategy should be based on a detailed market analysis, a competitive analysis, market measurements, and profitability and productivity analysis.

For an annual plan, it is not usually necessary to repeat each of these analyses (unless the annual plan will present a new marketing strategy). Assuming a firm is continuing with its basic marketing strategy, the emphasis of the annual plan will be on the choice of and funding for individual marketing programs. Consequently, the situation analysis for an annual plan will focus on competitors' activities, industry trends (such as shifts in industry sales growth), and the productivity of the most recent marketing programs.

Consider, for example, Figure 15-2, which portrays a process that has been used at Procter & Gamble. In this figure, we see that the annual planning process begins about 12 weeks before approval with a review of the sales performance of a given brand and of competitive activity. Over the following weeks, the product manager develops estimates of the level of budgetary commitment required to achieve various unit sales volume and market-share levels. These productivity estimates (which are based largely on the analysis of historical ratios and judgments of competitive activity) are critical inputs to the budgeting process. In addition, however, managers involved in the planning process must have a clear sense of the objectives they are expected to achieve.

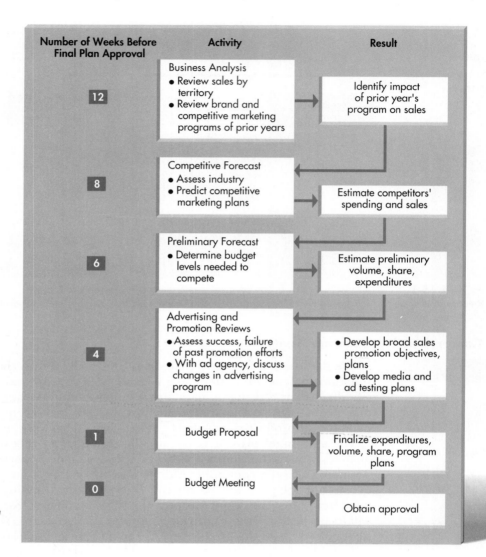

FIGURE 15-2
An example of the annual planning process.

Annual-Plan Objectives

In Chapter 2 we examined *corporate objectives* and the process of establishing corporate strategies. On the basis of these corporate strategies and the product portfolio analysis, *product objectives* are used to provide guidance to middle managers who develop the marketing strategies and programs that are needed to achieve the product objectives.

Because an annual plan must be developed for each product or product line, the plan must be consistent with the product objective. However, product objectives are usually stated in general terms (such as "increase market share"). Because a marketing plan must be expressed in detail, management must express the annual marketing-plan objective (or the annual product-plan objective) in specific terms regarding *time* and *level*. For example, a product objective stated as "increase the market share of product X" might be specified in an annual plan as "increase the market share of product X from 17 to 20 percent in 6 months, and to 22 percent in 1 year." When stated in this way, the objectives can provide more specific guidance on budget development and more measurable standards for evaluating achievement.

Essentially, there are three types of objectives managers can establish for an annual plan: market-share objectives, sales-volume objectives, and profitability objectives.

MARKET-SHARE OBJECTIVES

When management believes a high market share will mean high profits, market-share objectives will be established. As suggested in Chapter 2, market-share growth is typically a product objective for problem-child products and for new products entering an established market. If the markets are growing rapidly, an increase in market share will lead to rapid sales growth and long-run profitability for these products. Further, growth in market share may be essential in order to achieve or maintain adequate distribution, because distributors may prefer to carry only the fastest selling brands.

Market-share maintenance may be the appropriate objective for stars. Because these types of products already have high market shares, it is usually costly and difficult to expand market share. However, because the market-growth rate is high, sales (and, it is hoped, profits) should be increased just by maintaining the current market-share level.

SALES-VOLUME OBJECTIVES

Sales objectives are clearly related to market-share objectives. That is, if a firm has a market-share objective and an industry sales forecast, then a sales objective can be calculated by multiplying the industry sales forecast by the market-share objective. The primary reason for converting a market-share objective into a sales-volume objective is that a unit sales-volume objective is needed to develop a complete budget. Without some estimate of the units to be sold, production costs cannot be calculated, and therefore profitability cannot be estimated. Accordingly, when a market-share objective is established, the sales volume that reflects that market-share objective should also be determined. Additionally, sales-volume objectives are appropriate when market share cannot be reliably measured because of a lack of industry sales data, as well as when the annual plan is for a new product form (where the market share is 100 percent).

PROFITABILITY OBJECTIVES

As we discussed in Chapter 2, new products and problem-child products generally must receive extensive marketing support in order to build sales volume and market share. In the short run, this means profitability must be sacrificed in order to achieve a strong market position and long-run profitability. For these kinds of products, market-share and sales-volume objectives will take precedence over profitability objectives. However, cash cows and dogs are presumed to have few opportunities for sales growth. Thus profitability objectives are usually paramount in these cases. Additionally, although stars are often not heavy cash generators, they are expected to be profitable. Finally, even in the case of new products and problem-child products, profitability cannot be totally ignored. There will be limits to the short-run losses management can take on these products. In general, then, profitability will be either a primary objective or a secondary objective on all products. Any annual plan for a product, product line, or department will be expected to achieve some minimum target contribution (or some maximum negative contribution in the case of new products and problem-child products) to overall divisional or company profitability.

Returning to Figure 15-2, it is important to recognize that, in this particular process, all preliminary forecasts are submitted to top management so that the sum total of budget requests are known and can be prioritized before final budget meetings are held. Significant differences of opinion on budget levels between top management and the brand manager could well result in a directive to provide substantially revised goals or plans in the final budget proposal prior to the budget meeting.

To illustrate the development of an annual plan, we will return to the case of Linkster Inc., first discussed in Chapter 6.

An Annual Product Plan: Linkster, Inc.

Linkster's marketing manager has developed an annual product plan for jackets. Table 15-1 summarizes the basic elements of the plan. (As indicated in Chapter 6, this plan is likely to have some influence on umbrella and sweater sales. Those effects might be captured in the overall business plan, which would also incorporate marketing plans for other Linkster products.)

The essence of Linkster's plan is to build volume through a price promotion during April and a magazine advertising campaign. The advertising campaign will emphasize two distinctive benefits: the jackets (1) are warm as well as rain repellant and (2) were designed by golfers specifically for golfers. The price promotion will involve a $15 discount on any Linkster jacket at all golf course pro shops. The promotion will be announced in the magazine advertisements. The plan suggests that the combined effects of these programs will yield a 40 percent increase in jacket sales.

Specific features of the plan merit special discussion:

■ Total promotional sales are expected to be 8000 units, with 3000 of these expected to be displaced sales. (Without the price promotion, management's expected gain in sales from the advertising campaign alone was 3000).

TABLE 15-1	LINKSTER: 1994 PRODUCT PLAN FOR JACKETS

ANNUAL PERFORMANCE OBJECTIVES

1. Increase unit sales of jackets to 28,000 (from 20,000 in 1993)
2. Increase total contribution on jackets to $300,000 (from $250,000 in 1993)

MARKETING STRATEGY

Acquire new customers from differentiated positioning (warm and rain repellant; designed just for golfers).

MARKETING PROGRAMS

PROGRAM	OBJECTIVES	BUDGET
1. Magazine ads: Jan.–March	Achieve 40 percent awareness among readers of golf magazines by March 30.	$176,000 for 4 insertions in *Golf Magazine* plus production costs of $8000.
2. September promotion: $15 savings in golf course pro shops.	Achieve sales of 8000 units.	$10,000 in point-of-purchase displays; $15 discount on 3000 displaced sales.

■ Because Linkster's prior advertising has been modest, the company's goal for 1994 is to begin building greater brand awareness as a base for the future. The target audience will be golfers who subscribe to *Golf Magazine*, which has a circulation of about 1 million. Linkster's ad agency believes it must generate 800 GRPs by the end of March to establish 40 percent awareness. Since the target audience is 1 million, and since one GRP is achieved by reaching 1 percent of the target audience one time, it takes 1 percent times 1 million or 10,000 impressions to generate one GRP. (Refer back to Chapter 10 to review the relationship between gross rating points and gross impressions.) The agency thinks it can purchase space in *Golf Magazine* at a cost per thousand of $22. Therefore, Linkster can obtain the required GRPs for $176,000, as calculated in Table 15-2.

The process of putting the annual plan together is not a simple one because a variety of combinations of prices, program budgets, and costs may have to be considered. Consequently, managers will often go through a number of tentative plans before coming up with one that is satisfactory. However, the complexity and time involved in this process are substantially reduced if a manager uses one of the popular interactive electronic spreadsheet programs (such as Lotus 1-2-3) available on personal computers.

Finally, the plan should not assume results will be achieved at a constant rate throughout the year. Seasonality of demand and variations in the timing of alternative programs are likely to exist in most plans. Where possible, therefore, monthly or quarterly breakouts should be established to let all

TABLE 15-2	CALCULATION OF LINKSTER'S REQUIRED ADVERTISING BUDGET	
	Size of target audience	1,000,000
	× 1%	× 1%
	Number of people to be reached for 1 gross rating point (GRP)	10,000
	× Number of GRPs required	× 800
	Total impressions required	8,000,000
	÷ 1000	÷ 1000
	Thousands of impressions required	8,000
	× Cost per thousand (CPM)	× $22
	Required media budget	$176,000

managers know when the various results are expected to be achieved and to facilitate control. (Table 15-3 provides monthly benchmarks for Linkster's product plan.)

USING THE PLAN FOR CONTROL

If managers were simply to forget about a plan once it was adopted, they would be failing to take full advantage of the planning process. That is, the annual plan serves not merely as a tool for coordination but also as a control device.

In fact, seldom will results go precisely according to plan. Changes in competitive actions, in buyers' willingness and ability to buy, or in other environmental factors may occur. Also, managers can seldom be absolutely certain of how productive the marketing programs will be in influencing sales—even in the absence of competitive reactions or other environmental changes. Finally, even costs are sometimes difficult to project.

Managers should recognize that there are at least two approaches to control. *Postaction* control can be used at the end of the planning period to review the degree of success achieved and to isolate the causes of any gaps between planned and actual performance. For example, at the end of 1994, Linkster could review its results, compare these to the planned sales and profit objectives, and try to determine why any performance-plan gaps resulted. The major purpose of this type of control system is to use the knowledge obtained from this analysis in developing future plans.

As an alternative, organizations can adopt *steering-control* models. This approach assumes that if performance deviations from the plan can be identified sufficiently early, managers can take corrective actions—that is, the plan can be adjusted (steered) to meet the original objectives.[1] From a marketing

[1] Subhash Sharma and Dale Achabal, "STEMCOM: An Analytical Model of Marketing Control," *Journal of Marketing*, Spring 1982, pp. 104–113.

TABLE 15-3

LINKSTER, INC.: BIMONTHLY PROJECTIONS FOR 1994 FOR JACKETS

	JAN–FEB	MAR–APR	MAY–JUN	JULY–AUG	SEPT–OCT	NOV–DEC	BUDGET TOTAL
Jacket sales at regular prices	2000	6000	4000	2000	3000	3000	20,000
VCM-regular sales	$76,000	$228,000	$152,000	$ 76,000	$114,000	$114,000	$760,000
Jacket sales at promotion prices	0	0	0	0	8000	0	8000
VCM-promotion sales	0	0	0	0	$184,000	0	$184,000
Total sales (cumulative)	2000	8000	12,000	14,000	25,000	28,000	28,000
Total VCM (cumulative)	$76,000	$304,000	$456,000	$532,000	$830,000	$944,000	$944,000
Advertising expense (cumulative)	$52,000	$184,000	$184,000	$184,000	$184,000	$184,000	$184,000
Promotion expense (cumulative)	0	0	0	0	$ 10,000	$ 10,000	$ 10,000
Other direct expense (cumulative)	$75,000	$150,000	$225,000	$300,000	$375,000	$450,000	$450,000
Total contribution (cumulative)	($51,000)	($30,000)	$ 47,000	$ 48,000	$261,000	$300,000	$300,000

management standpoint, the steering-control approach certainly has important short-run advantages because the effectiveness of marketing programs in producing sales is always somewhat uncertain. Consequently, managers would prefer to have the opportunity to make adjustments to the marketing plan as soon as possible when it becomes apparent annual objectives may not be achieved.

In order to implement the steering-control approach, managers must take the following steps:

1. Select the performance measures to be monitored.
2. Compare actual and planned performance at appropriate time intervals.
3. Specify the acceptable degree of deviation.
4. Identify implications of the deviations.
5. Modify the plan to steer it toward the objectives.

Selecting Performance Measures

Because the primary objectives of a marketing plan are stated in terms of sales, market share, or profitability, managers would naturally want to monitor these performance measures. However, managers are likely to find that these measures are inadequate for a steering-control model for two reasons. First, information on these measures may not be available quickly enough. For example, manufacturers who sell through distributors often experience a lag between the timing of retailer sales and retailer purchases. Additionally, information on market shares may not be available on a regular basis. Second, and more important, managers who use the steering-control approach need information on *how* to change the plan to meet sales, market-share, or profit objectives. Consequently, it is important to monitor program performance because deviations in program performance may serve as indicators that annual objectives are not being achieved. Table 15-4 lists some of the more common performance indicators that managers should monitor.

In many companies, the kind of information portrayed in Table 15-4 is also not available in a timely manner. In such cases, experienced managers often resort to developing their own measures using whatever data are available. For example, one consumer-goods manager devised a weekly "Gimme Index," which was computed as the ratio of trade-promotion expenditures to consumer-promotion expenditures. The index served as a warning either of increased competitive activity to get shelf space (when the ratio is very high) or of weakening consumer sales (when the ratio declines). As a result, it signaled the manager that there was likely to be a deviation between planned and actual performance on either the level of distribution achieved or on sales.[2]

Increasingly, some measures of customer satisfaction are being used in assessing performance. For one thing, more firms are realizing that long-

[2] Thomas Bonoma, "Marketing Subversives," *Harvard Business Review*, November–December 1986, pp. 113–118.

| TABLE 15-4 | **SOME POSSIBLE PERFORMANCE MEASURES TO BE MONITORED FOR CONTROL** |

OVERALL PERFORMANCE MEASURES

1. Unit sales
2. Dollar sales
3. Sales in specific market segments
4. Marketing costs
5. Production costs
6. Market share
7. Customer ratings of product quality
8. Customer ratings of servicing provided

PROGRAM PERFORMANCE MEASURES

1. New-product programs	a. Rate of trial
	b. Repurchase rate
	c. Cannibalized sales
	d. Number of customer returns
2. Pricing programs	a. Actual price charged
	b. Price relative to industry average
3. Advertising programs	a. Awareness levels
	b. Attribute ratings
	c. Actual expenditures
4. Sales-promotion programs	a. Redemption rates
	b. Displacement rates
	c. Stock-up rates
5. Sales and distribution programs	a. Direct response rates
	b. Number of sales calls
	c. Number of new accounts
	d. Number of lost accounts
	e. Number of distributors carrying the product
	f. Number of customer complaints
	g. Travel costs

term, repeat sales are primarily a function of the customer's experience with the product and (especially for complex purchases, such as automobiles) with the purchase experience itself.[3] In such cases, customer satisfaction measures (such as the number of reported product problems or likelihood of repurchasing the same brand in the future) can serve as important indicators of overall performance as well as diagnostics for explaining poor sales and market-share results.

COMPARING ACTUAL PERFORMANCE WITH PLANNED PERFORMANCE

Performance comparisons should be made as frequently as possible so that managers can have the greatest opportunity for steering the plan. However,

[3] Larry Armstrong, "Who's the Most Pampered Motorist of All?" *Business Week*, June 10, 1991, pp. 90–91.

the intervals used to compare performance should be long enough to be meaningful. For example, because advertising programs generally work slowly, it will be more difficult to get useful indicators of advertising performance in a short period of time. On the other hand, sales promotion and direct response marketing work more quickly and can meaningfully be monitored on a monthly basis (or even more frequently if desired). Additionally, effort-based performance measures (such as the number of sales calls or product demonstrations) can also be measured frequently. Finally, differences do exist across industries in terms of customer purchase frequencies. Consequently, sales performance may be meaningfully measured on a monthly basis in some markets, whereas in others quarterly comparisons may be more reasonable.

Specifying Acceptable Degrees of Deviation

The annual plan should also specify the acceptable degree of deviation from the performance standards. As noted earlier, managers do not really expect every performance standard to be fully attained. However, managers do want to identify significant deviations from the sales, market-share, and cost standards that have been set. Accordingly, it is generally useful to specify the acceptable range of performance in advance, so that management attention can be focused on the most important deviations. (For example, one firm may consider a 5 percent deviation in actual sales from planned sales acceptable, whereas another may consider only 1 percent acceptable.)

Additionally, the acceptability of a deviation should be considered in the context of the degree of reliability of the performance standard. For example, if managers want to impress their superiors, there is always the chance they will set performance standards in too pessimistic a fashion so that the likelihood of achieving a standard (and any resulting bonus) is enhanced. On the flip side, some high-level managers push planners to set certifiably high-performance expectations. This may occur because top management is hoping for a good result (perhaps to justify an earlier decision) and thus is too optimistic, or because these managers believe the middle managers doing the product and sales plans have been setting conservative sales and profit goals so they can more easily meet them. While this problem is not easily solved, it can sometimes be made more manageable by getting managers to articulate their degree of certainty about various performance levels. For example, managers might be asked: "For a given budget, what share of market is 50 percent likely? 80 percent likely? 100 percent likely?"[4]

---

[4] For a discussion of these and other issues related to goal setting on marketing plans, see Thomas Bonoma, "Marketing Performance—What Do You Expect?" *Harvard Business Review*, September–October 1989, pp. 44–47.

Identifying Implications of Deviations

Depending on the specific performance indicators being monitored, managers will be faced with analyzing deviations in either sales performance, program performance, or cost performance.

Observed deviations from planned sales performance may be due to uncontrollable factors, such as changing market conditions leading to a decline in industry sales or unanticipated competitive actions. But if managers find no evidence that either type of uncontrollable factor is responsible for performance deviations, then the logical next step is to analyze the performance of the marketing programs. (Additionally, as noted earlier, managers may want to examine indicators of program performance even before useful sales results are available.)

Program performance should be examined at two levels, where possible: the degree to which program *objectives* are being achieved and the degree to which planned program *effort* is being achieved. If levels of effort (such as actual sales calls or advertising coverage) are not being achieved as planned, then neither program objectives nor sales-performance objectives are likely to be achieved. However, if the planned level of effort is being achieved but program objectives (for example, number of new accounts or brand awareness levels) are not being achieved, then either the *design* of the program (for example, sales appeals, price level, advertising copy, value of coupon, and so on) is ineffective or the *budget* is inadequate. Further, managers may find that the performances of the various programs are all proceeding according to plan, but sales performance is still below the planned level. Assuming the manager has ruled out uncontrollable factors as a cause of sales deviation, the manager must conclude that the sales productivity of the various programs has been overestimated. (Figure 15-3 summarizes the steps involved in analyzing sales deviations.)

Finally, the actual direct marketing costs and variable costs may deviate from planned costs. Accordingly, reasons for these deviations should be identified. These reasons may include cost increases dictated by suppliers, inadequate estimates of the cost of reaching program objectives, or simply, faster achievement of program objectives than anticipated. For example, the sales force may call on some customers earlier or more frequently than planned. If so, sales costs may exceed the budget during the early periods of the plan.[5]

Regardless of the type of deviation being examined, managers must be able to distinguish environmental causes from controllable causes of poor performance. This is often very difficult because not all environmental changes are immediately recognized. Accordingly, a system for monitoring environmental

---

[5] Methods for identifying the sources of cost variance are presented in James Hulbert and Norman E. Toy, "A Strategic Framework for Marketing Control," *Journal of Marketing*, April 1977, pp. 12–20.

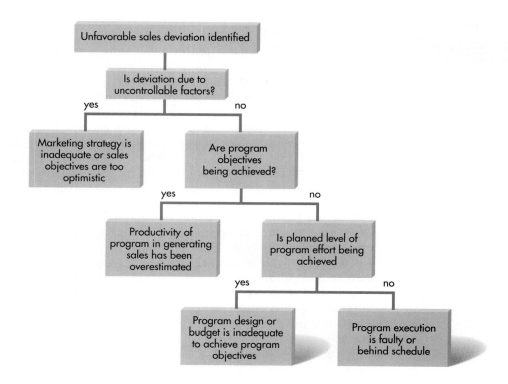

FIGURE 15-3
Analyzing sales
deviations.

trends and forces will assist managers in identifying uncontrollable effects and in attempting to make modifications to the plan. Some procedures and approaches to environmental monitoring are discussed later in this chapter.

Making Modifications to the Plan as Needed

Managers should make any marketing program modifications that are needed to get the firm back on track toward achieving the annual-plan objectives. If deviations between the plan and actual performance are relatively minor, then this is usually the only type of remedial action managers must take. However, if the deviations are fairly large and if the likelihood of making up for these deviations during the rest of the year is relatively small, management may have to revise the annual-plan objectives. (Of course, if actual performance exceeds planned performance, it may be desirable to revise objectives upward.) Finally, in the case of serious unanticipated competitive, cost, or other environmental changes, the entire marketing strategy and even the product objectives may have to be revised.

To illustrate the process of controlling the marketing plan, let us return to the case of Linkster, Inc. Table 15-5 summarizes the overall performance of the product plan as of the end of June. Halfway through the year, Linkster is lagging far behind its sales and profit plan.

In assessing the reasons for the failure to meet performance standards, management discovered the following:

- *Uncontrollable factors:* The spring weather was unusually warm in the South and unusually wet in the North. Thus, demand for jackets was lower than usual in the South and many Northern golfers were forced to delay the start of their season.
- *Program objectives not achieved:* By tracking brand awareness, management was able to determine that only 25 percent of the target audience was aware of the brand by mid-June. The program execution was on schedule, leaving poor advertising strategy or inadequate spending as the problem.
- *Cost overruns:* Initial estimates of advertising design costs proved to be low, resulting in a modest overrun in the advertising budget. This was partly offset by lower-than-planned fixed production costs.

Based on this analysis, Linkster's management decided on the following actions.

- The annual sales goal for jackets at nonpromotion prices was revised downward by 2000 units in recognition of the sales lost due to weather conditions.
- Advertising spending of $45,000 was added for September to coincide with the promotion. Management hoped this would increase promotion sales in September by 2000 units and also stimulate an extra 500 units in sales during the postpromotion period.

Table 15-6 presents the revised plan. Note that if Linkster can achieve the levels of performance stipulated in the revision, the company will make up all of the shortfall in sales and part of the shortfall in total contribution. In other

TABLE 15-5

LINKSTER, INC.: ACTUAL VS. PLANNED PRODUCT PERFORMANCE—JANUARY–JUNE 1994

PERFORMANCE MEASURES	ACTUAL	PLANNED
Total jackets at regular price	9500	12,000
Total jackets at promotion price	0	0
Total jackets	9500	12,000
Total VCM	$361,000	$456,000
Advertising expense	$197,000	$184,000
Other direct costs	$220,000	$225,000
Total contribution	($56,000)	$ 47,000

TABLE 15-6	LINKSTER, INC.: REVISED PLAN FOR JULY–DECEMBER 1994		
	ORIGINAL JULY–DEC.	REVISED JULY–DEC.	NEW TOTAL* FOR 1994
Total jackets at regular price	8000	8500	18,000
Total jackets at promotion price	8000	10,000	10,000
Total jackets	16,000	18,500	28,000
VCM—regular price	$304,000	$323,000	$684,000
VCM—promotion price	$184,000	$230,000	$230,000
Total VCM	$488,000	$553,000	$914,000
Advertising expense	0	$ 45,000	$242,000
Promotion expense	$ 10,000	$ 10,000	$ 10,000
Other direct costs	$225,000	$225,000	$445,000
Total contribution	$253,000	$273,000	$217,000

* Includes January–June actual and July–December revised plan.

words, management will have begun the process of steering the plan toward the original objectives. Although the initial profit objective is no longer viewed as achievable, the process at least enabled management to spot the effects of uncontrollable factors and an ineffective program before the entire year was wasted. Clearly, the earlier the detection of such problems, the more effective a steering-control system will be.

It is also important to note that the effectiveness of steering control will depend in part on the degree to which a firm can be effective in making modifications. If deviations are primarily due to noncontrollable environmental factors, managers cannot modify their strategies without thorough consideration of the effects of further environmental changes. Thus, the process of environmental monitoring is an important adjunct to the process of steering control.

ENVIRONMENTAL MONITORING

Environmental monitoring consists of searching for and processing information about changes in an organization's environment. While some analysis of the environment is a prerequisite for the development of corporate and marketing strategies, the marketing environments faced by most firms are dynamic. Thus, in order to analyze deviations in performance from the basic plan and in order to make any necessary adaptations in strategy, managers should have access to systems that continually monitor the environment.

Strategic Environment Monitoring Systems

Strategic environmental monitoring systems are formalized approaches for monitoring change on a continuous and systematic basis. Such a system can be effective if management has clearly defined its purpose to ensure that crucial information will not be overlooked.

Montgomery and Weinberg have proposed three kinds of purposes for such systems.[6]

1. *Defensive:* This intelligence is obtained in an effort to avoid surprises. That is, the purpose of environmental monitoring is simply to determine if the implicit and explicit assumptions upon which current strategies are based will remain valid.
2. *Passive:* This intelligence is used to provide benchmark data for an objective evaluation of a firm's policies. For example, a firm might gather industry sales compensation data in order to reward sales performance in a manner comparable to the firm's competitors.
3. *Offensive:* This kind of intelligence is designed to *identify* opportunities.

By establishing the purpose of a strategic environmental monitoring system, management can be more certain to collect the kinds of information they require and to avoid what is irrelevant. Once the information sources and needs have been established, the participants who need this environmental information must be identified. Since a variety of individuals and departments are involved in providing the necessary strategic information, definite assignments for the acquisition of specific types of intelligence must be made.[7] Figure 15-4 summarizes the major elements that would be necessary in a strategic environmental scanning system.

Environmental Information Sources

In establishing a formal environmental monitoring effort, managers must identify the information sources likely to be of most use for its stated purposes. In Chapter 4 we discussed some sources that were especially pertinent to competitive analysis, and in Chapter 5 we identified some sources for general market-measurement data. Additional useful sources are presented in the Appendix.

[6] David B. Montgomery and Charles B. Weinberg, "Toward Strategic Intelligence Systems," *Journal of Marketing*, Fall 1979, p. 42.
[7] David B. Baker, "Organizing a Strategic Information Scanning System," *California Management Review*, January 1983, pp. 76–83.

FIGURE 15-4
Organizing a strategic environmental scanning system.

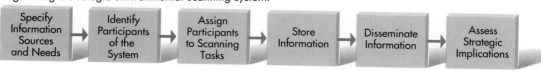

Specify Information Sources and Needs → Identify Participants of the System → Assign Participants to Scanning Tasks → Store Information → Disseminate Information → Assess Strategic Implications

TABLE 15-7	**MAJOR DATA BASE DISTRIBUTORS OF BUSINESS INFORMATION**

SERVICE AND DISTRIBUTION	DESCRIPTION
DIALOG Information Services	More than 200 data bases containing over 55 million records; article indexes and financial data; annual reports of publicly held U.S. corporations.
Dow Jones News Retrieval	Business and economic news, stock quotes, investment information, complete and unabridged articles from *The Wall Street Journal*, *Barron's*, and Dow Jones News Service.
The Source	General news, air schedules, retail catalogs, market quotes, research tools, employment data bases.
Compuserve Information Service	Financial information, banking, encyclopedia, newspaper abstracts.
Bibliographic Retrieval Service	Multiple data bases covering agriculture, business, management, engineering, and other academic indexes.
Data Resources	Business and economic data and Japanese Economic Information Service.
PROMPT	Citations and abstracts on new products, technology, markets from over 2000 U.S. and foreign publications.
DRI-VisiCorp	Fifty-eight data bases, economic forecasts, foreign exchange, individual industries.

Perhaps the most important development in recent years with regard to environmental monitoring is the on-line information bank. Some of the better-known organizations and the data they make available are listed in Table 15-7.

Other Sources of Intelligence

In addition to data-based sources of intelligence, there are several sources that are reliant on the skills and expertise of human experts.

TECHNOLOGICAL FORECASTING

Technological forecasting includes a variety of procedures managers may use to predict the probability, timing, and significance of future technological developments regarding products or processes. Among the procedures firms use for technological forecasting are Delphi probes, scenarios, and trend extrapolation.

The *Delphi probe* is a systematic method for analyzing independent expert opinion. A panel of experts are questioned individually about some future event or trend. All responses are combined and summarized, and the results are returned to the participants. After the results have been communicated to all participants, the experts are asked to respond again to these questions. This process is repeated for three or more rounds until a consensus is reached. The Delphi method may be used not only for identifying relevant changes but also for identifying the most appropriate actions the firm should take.

Scenarios are composite descriptions of possible future technological events or conditions that may have an effect on the decisions made by an organization. Usually multiple scenarios are developed to represent possible alternative environments. In effect, scenarios are "what if" exercises that force managers to consider certain technological challenges they may face. Given a set of alternative scenarios, strategic planners can then develop and evaluate the alternative strategic responses the firm should be prepared to make if a given technological development materializes.

Another method of technological forecasting is to *extrapolate historical trends*. The primary assumption is that the trend of technological advances in the past will remain fairly constant in the future. Particularly in very high technology industries such as electronics, past rates of advance (such as cost per bit of information processed) can be projected into the future with some degree of reliability.

SOCIAL TREND ANALYSIS

Individuals, groups of individuals, and society at large are constantly changing in terms of what is considered a desirable and acceptable way of living and behaving. These changes can have a profound impact on individuals' attitudes toward products and toward marketing activities. In particular, it is important for managers to understand and predict changes in consumer values and changes in the social issues that groups within society feel are important. To track such changes, several independent research firms, measure social and value trends on issues such as materialism, sexual freedom, and religion. Organizations, such as Arthur D. Little's Impact Service, Predicasts, Inc., and The Future Group, also provide subscription services for monitoring social trends and related economic trends.[8]

ORGANIZING FOR PLANNING

Because the annual marketing plan may involve different program elements in different organizations, there is no single best way to assign responsibility for the annual marketing plan for an individual product.

[8] Myron Magnet, "Who Needs a Trend Spotter?" *Fortune*, Dec. 9, 1985, pp. 51–56.

Although a number of larger firms have planning staffs, these individuals are primarily involved in long-range planning and in providing information regarding short-run forecasts and market conditions. Thus, the role of a planning staff in developing the annual plan is to provide basic inputs into the short-run situation analysis and objective setting. Additionally, these individuals may participate in the process of reviewing proposed plans to ensure the key market assumptions (and sometimes the manufacturing cost assumptions) are reasonable.

Most planners seem to feel planning should be delegated as far down the organization as possible, so that one person is responsible for achieving each program objective. The reasoning behind this view is that the manager most closely involved with a program is in the best position to estimate the costs and productivity of the program and to identify possible changes in market conditions.

However, in many firms this will mean planning for an individual product will rest in the hands of more than one person. That is, unless the plan is confined strictly to one marketing program (such as sales), some organizational mechanism is needed to coordinate program plans into the overall annual plan. In firms with a broad product line, the product manager or brand manager will typically assume this role, and that manager's plans will be reviewed by a higher level marketing manager. In other firms, the sales manager may perform this role—especially when selling costs dominate the budget, when the sales manager is responsible for sales promotions (often the case in industrial marketing), and when advertising focuses on the corporation as a whole rather than on individual products and thus is managed at the corporate level. Finally, the senior marketing manager may perform this role when program responsibilities are widely dispersed among a number of managers.

It is clear, however, that in the modern, large organization the marketing planning process is bidirectional. Research on how firms develop marketing plans indicates it is rare to find a situation where the total marketing budget is developed simply by summing the requests of various product or sales managers. More typically, these requests are reviewed and revised to fit total corporate needs. In still other cases the total marketing budget is decided centrally (usually with excessive influence by the finance department) and allocated to individual products or departments.[9]

CONCLUSION

Because of the array of different programs that managers may employ to implement the marketing strategy for a product or a line of related products, the annual plan is a critical element of coordinating activities and budgets.

[9] Nigel Piercy, "The Marketing Budgeting Process: Marketing Management Implications," *Journal of Marketing*, October 1987, pp. 45–59.

Further, because the marketing environment is dynamic and because the effectiveness and costs of marketing programs are always somewhat uncertain, annual plans are necessary for monitoring results and directing corrective actions. Individual programs must also be monitored, because in most cases each program makes only a partial contribution to product objectives such as sales or market share or total profitability. Consequently, the annual plan is necessary in order to evaluate the total marketing effort as well as the contributions of the various program elements. (Figure 15-5 shows the relationship of annual planning to other aspects of the marketing planning process.)

Moreover, because program performance is heavily influenced by environmental changes, an effective control system cannot be developed unless managers have access to strategic intelligence regarding customers, competitors, or other relevant environmental forces.

Ultimately, the effectiveness of the annual marketing planning process depends on the quality of the efforts made by those who do the plans. But the degree to which the organization facilitates market-driven planning is also important. In organizations that are truly market-oriented (as discussed in Chapter 1), not only is the annual marketing plan likely to be viewed as a very important management activity, it is also likely that the plan is primarily designed by the manager most knowledgeable about the market. To gain more insight regarding this process, reconsider the situation facing NBC as it began to develop its plan for the Triple Cast.

FIGURE 15-5
Relationship of annual marketing planning to other elements of the marketing planning process.

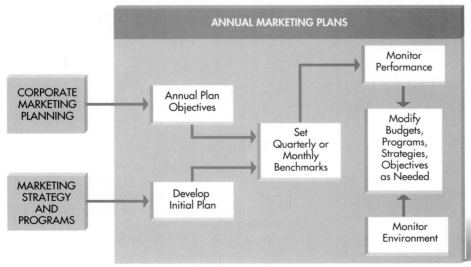

NATIONAL BROADCASTING CORPORATION: DEVELOPING A MARKETING PLAN FOR THE OLYMPICS*

As discussed in Chapter 5, the National Broadcasting Corporation (NBC) counted heavily on revenue from pay-per-view television of the Triple Cast to offset the costs of broadcasting the 1992 Summer Olympics.

In January of 1992, NBC established a sales target of 3.5 million homes on the assumption that cable systems would make pay-per-view technically accessible to 35.9 million households. The costs for the Triple Cast were expected to be $40 million in promotion and $55 million in production costs, split between the local cable companies and NBC.

NBC actually began its promotional campaign in December 1991, eight months before the Olympics were to be held, even though previous cable company experience with pay-per-view sports broadcasts suggested that 90 percent of all orders for a special event are placed in the final week before the event. Christmas season ads were placed on NBC and through the cable channels, and NBC marketing officials claimed these generated 100,000 inquiries. Further, NBC was planning monthly promotions beginning in February for each month prior to the Olympics. For example, a free remote control was to be offered for each purchase of the complete pay-per-view package (priced at $125 for the full 15 days) in February, and a free VCR-plus for each sign-up made in March.

Industry observers noted that the extensive promotional campaign was designed to build a level of consumer demand that would overcome the resistance of cable operators who needed to clear these channels to provide Triple Cast coverage.

1. What program performance measures could NBC have used for control?
2. Given that pay-per-view customers tend to wait until the last minute to order, would there be any point in tracking sign-ups for purpose of control?
3. Following the general format presented in Figure 15-3, lay out the list and sequence of questions NBC should have been asking as it became obvious that sales would be below expectations.

---

* Developed from Mark Lewyn and Mark Landler, "Why NBC's Triple-Cast Never Made a Run at the Gold," *Business Week*, Aug. 17, 1992, pp. 34–35; "Triple Cast Success Lies in Unknowns," *Electronic Media*, July 13, 1992, p. 1; "Financial Evaluation of the 1992 Summer Olympics Triplecast," *Mediaweek*, Mar. 16, 1992, p. 26; "NBC High on Triplecast," *Television Digest*, Jan. 13, 1992.

QUESTIONS AND SITUATIONS FOR DISCUSSION

1. Explain why a market-share growth objective should be accompanied by a sales-volume objective and a target-contribution objective.
2. Explain the difference between postaction control and steering control.
3. In each of the following situations, would you tend to establish performance benchmarks at short intervals (such as weekly or monthly) or at long intervals (such as quarterly)? Explain your answers.

a. A consumer-goods firm relies heavily on sales-promotion programs to achieve a sales-volume objective for its line of cookies.

b. A manufacturer of copy machines is introducing a new line of products for its commercial and industrial buyers. Advertising in industrial magazines and personal selling are the primary programs being used to achieve a sales-volume objective.

c. A food company is attempting to improve the profitability of the product line it sells to institutional customers. The marketing effort is primarily designed to increase the volume purchased by large, existing accounts through more frequent sales calls and the use of quantity discounts.

4. What differences, if any, are there between a strategic environmental monitoring system and marketing research?

5. In some firms, marketing budgets are primarily determined by top management and in others by middle managers. In what circumstances should top management be the initiator of the budget as opposed to acting primarily as a reviewer of the budgets submitted by middle management?

6. In February of 1990, Time Warner Inc. launched *Entertainment Weekly*, a magazine designed to review movies, videos, records, books, and television shows. In addition to reviews, several in-depth features on the entertainment business were to be part of each issue.

After 2 years of direct mail testing, the company was able to identify the market to which it had the greatest appeal. The expected profile of the readership was 36.8 years of age, equally divided between male and female, 72 percent college educated, with a median income of $41,800. The magazine was priced at $1.95 per issue or $51.48 for an annual subscription. Because magazine revenues come from two sources—subscriptions or newsstand sales and advertising sales—Time Warner needed to develop two separate yet consistent plans. The size of the circulation base (which was targeted at 600,000 per week for the first year) would obviously have an impact on magazine sales revenue. But the circulation base, along with the profile of the readers and the actual number of readers (which might be five times the circulation), would all be important to prospective advertisers.

To get subscribers, Time Warner offered a sales promotion involving four free issues of the magazine. The promotion was bolstered by $30 million in advertising through television and Time Warner's other magazines. Simultaneously, the advertising sales force was making calls on potential advertisers and advertising agencies, with a goal of signing up 100 advertisers to 2-year commitments.

a. Develop a list of the annual performance objectives that could be included in the annual plan(s).

b. What program performance measures should Time Warner use for control?

7. The Bramble County Credit Union had been established in 1963 to serve employees of Bramble County government and the Bramble County schools. By 1990, 6320 employees had become members of the credit union.

The credit union offered share savings accounts, share draft (checking) accounts, certificates of deposit, and a variety of types of loans. At the end of 1990, the board of directors voted to offer a VISA credit card to the membership.

During January of 1991, a subcommittee of the board met with the executive director of the credit union to construct a marketing plan for the VISA credit card. The executive director, Ms. Ingram, had developed some data on the cost of a credit-card program. She believed the credit union could attract nearly 2000 members to the credit-card program during the first year based on the experiences she had heard about from other credit union directors. To do this, she expected the credit union would need to offer a rate of 10 percent on the unpaid monthly balance and avoid any annual fixed fees to cardholders. This would provide a 2 percent interest rate advantage against local banks.

Ms. Ingram also was planning a direct mail advertisement campaign for March, April, and May, designed to achieve 90 percent awareness that Bramble County Credit Union now offered a credit card and 80 percent awareness of the 10 percent interest rate. The target market included all members and all 8000 county employees who were still nonmembers. Based on the experience of other credit unions, Ms. Ingram anticipated that approximately 15 percent of members and 5 percent of potential members would sign up once they were aware of the availability of a VISA card, as long as the price was competitive.

A telephone campaign was planned for the period June 1 to October 30. The telephone campaign was designed to remind members and potential members of the availability and price of the card and to get the member or potential member to agree (at least) to receive the application packet. Employees would be used to do the telephoning and would receive overtime pay as applicable. It was expected that 100 calls per week would be completed, that 60 percent of the calls would result in the mailing of a packet, and that half of these application packets would actually be completed and returned.

Based on industry averages, Ms. Ingram estimated the credit union's fixed operating cost for this product would be $10,000 per year. Additionally, the variable cost per account was expected to be $54 per year. Marketing costs were projected as $1500 for direct mail and $200 per week for the telephone campaign. In August of 1991, one new clerical person would need to be hired in the operations department at a salary of $1300 per month to help in processing these accounts. Monthly revenue per account was expected to average $6.72 after the account was established for one month.

Develop a marketing plan for the VISA card for the period March 1 to December 31, 1991, following the general approach given in Tables 15-1 and 15-2. State the reasons behind your estimates of the number of accounts the credit union will have at the end of each month.

SUGGESTED ADDITIONAL READINGS

Bonoma, Thomas, "Marketing Performance—What Do You Expect?" *Harvard Business Review*, September–October 1989, pp. 44–47.

Cooper, A. C., and Daniel Schendel, "Strategic Responses to Technological Threat," *Business Horizons*, February 1976, pp. 61–69.

Daniells, Lorna M., "Sources on Marketing," *Harvard Business Review*, July–August 1982, pp. 40–43.

Hulbert, James, and Norman E. Toy, "A Strategic Framework for Marketing Control," *Journal of Marketing*, April 1977, pp. 12–20.

McLeod, Raymond, Jr., and John Rogers, "Marketing Information Systems: Uses in the Fortune 500," *California Management Review*, Fall 1982, pp. 106–118.

Piercy, Nigel, "The Marketing Budgeting Process: Marketing Management Implications," *Journal of Marketing*, October 1987, pp. 45–59.

Sharma, Subhash, and Dale Achabal, "STEMCOM: An Analytical Model for Marketing Control," *Journal of Marketing*, Spring 1982, pp. 104–113.

Stasch, Stanley F., and Patricia Lanktree, "Can Your Marketing Planning Procedures Be Improved?" *Journal of Marketing*, Summer 1980, pp. 79–90.

APPENDIX

SELECTED SOURCES OF INFORMATION FOR MARKETING MANAGERS

Source Description Code

A General industry conditions, competitors, trends
B Consumer market characteristics/buying power
C Consumer purchasing patterns
D Advertising and promotion statistics
E Sales tracking and marketing effectiveness studies

ABI/INFORM:(A)
UMI/Data Courier, Inc.
620 S. Third St., Louisville, KY 40202-2475; (502) 582-4211
On-line service. Provides access to business information. Contains abstracts of articles on accounting, economics, information science, marketing, and other related subjects. Magazine express, periodical abstracts.

ADTRACK:(D)
Corporate Intelligence, Inc.
P.O. Box 16073, St. Paul, MN 55116
A computerized index to advertising appearing in major consumer and business magazines. Advertisements of 1/4-page size or larger are indexed by fourteen data items. Data coverage includes company name, product name, description, color, date, page number, magazine name, and spokesperson.

Advertising Age-100 Leading National Advertisers:(D)
Crain Communications
740 Rush St., Chicago, IL 60611; (312) 649-5200
Marketing reports for each company provide useful facts about their marketing operations, such as sales and earnings, leading product lines and brands, how they rank nationally,

share of market, advertising expenditures; also names of marketing personnel and agency account executives, both for print company and for principal divisions (found in the mid-September issue).

Advertising and Marketing Intelligence (AMI):(C,D)
New York Times Information Service, Inc., and J. Walter Thompson Co.
Mt. Pleasant Office Park, 1719 Route 10, Parsippany, NJ 07054
Includes abstracts from advertising, media, and marketing covering new products, consumer trends, people, research, media planning and buying, and sales promotions. Each entry consists of a brief statement on the subject, product, or person with the relevant bibliographic citation.

Adweek's Marketer's Guide to Media:(B)
ASM Communications, Inc.
1515 Broadway, New York, NY 10036; (212) 536-5336
Quarterly. Includes audience data for various kinds of media.

American Profile:(B)
Donnelley Marketing Information Services
P.O. Box 10250, 70 Seaview Ave., Stamford, CT 06904;
(203) 353-7266; FAX (203) 353-7276
Profiles over 70 million households. Coverage includes household population, income, dependents, and other demographic variables. This data base also maintains an excellent array of socioeconomic data including number and type of businesses, number of employees in area, banking activity, and other demographic area profiles.

American Statistics Index:(A,B)
Congressional Information Service, Inc.
4520 E-W Highway, Bethesda, MD 20814; (800) 638-8380,
(301) 654-1550
This is a comprehensive guide and index to the statistics published by all government agencies, congressional committees, and statistics-producing programs.

Annual Study of Advertisers:(D)
Provides information on the 100 U.S. firms that spend the most on advertising. For each advertiser, provides estimates of total advertising and promotional expenditures, total sales, and total earnings. Contains extensive descriptions of each firm's products, markets, corporate planning, and strategy.

Ranks the top 100 advertising spenders, and includes general descriptions of trends in advertising spending, strategy, and techniques of these firms.

BAR (Broadcast Advertising Reports):(D)
BAR, Inc. (owned by ARBITRON)
142 W. 57th St., New York, NY 10019; (212) 887-1300
Maintains monthly data on network television commercial activities and expenditures by product, network, parent company, and mean estimate per commercial minute. Includes the relationship between a particular commercial and the others aired in the preceding and succeeding time slots.

Brand Preference Change Measurements:(E)
Audience Studies, Inc. (ASI)
The ASI measurements are made during and after exposure of the test commercials to a recruited, captive audience gathered in a theater. Various aspects of viewer response to television commercials are measured.

CACI Marketing Systems:(B)
1100 N. Glebe Rd., Arlington, VA 22201; (800) 292-2240;
FAX (703) 243-6372
This service provides demographic information and is accessible on nine time-sharing networks. Offers a sales potential system that measures consumer spending in any area of the United States. Information can be used for site selection, market-entry planning, market-share and penetration decisions, promotional planning, store performance analysis, and so forth. Updates U.S. Census data regularly and provides many specialized reports.

Consumer Economic Service Data:(B,C)
Data Resources, Inc.
24 Hartwell Ave., Lexington, MA 02173; (617) 863-5100
Offers vast amount of detailed demographic and economic data in five report areas: (1) Current Population Survey Annual Demographic File; (2) Consumer Expectations Survey—a diary and interview of 40,000 households; (3) TGI-Brand specific purchasing and media penetration data; (4) Longitudinal Retirement History Survey; and (5) Consumer Markets Services—personal consumption, retail sales, and associated prices.

Consumer Expenditure Study:(C)
Bureau of Labor Statistics, Department of Labor
2 Mass Ave., NE, Washington, DC 20212; (202) 606-7808

Bulletins and/or reports. Annual. These studies are based on personal interviews from a sample of 20,000 consumer units and record-keeping by a sample of 23,000 consumer units. These samples offer income and expenditure analysis by income class, family size, and several other demographic parameters.

Consumer Expenditure Survey:(B)
> National Technology Info Service, U.S. Dept. of Commerce,
> 5285 Port Royal Rd., Springfield, VA 22161; (703) 487-4600
>> Report. Eight volumes. Covers seven demographic parameters and presents consumer expenditure statistics for each area by demographic type. Coverage includes family income, size, age, race, education, tenure, and composition.

Demographic Research Company:(B)
> 233 Wilshire Blvd., Suite 995, Santa Monica, CA 90401;
> (310) 452-7587, 451-8583
>> This data base provides demographic, marketing research, and multivariate analysis assistance as well as a ZIP Code Data Base that organizes U.S. Census data in terms of income, occupation, and housing in ZIP code areas.

DIALOG:(A,B)
> 3460 Hillview Ave., Palo Alto, CA 94303-0993; (800) 334-2564;
> (415) 858-3785; FAX: (415) 858-7069
>> This on-line service covers more topics than almost any other data base. The DIALOG Business Connection is a menu-based information service that offers quick and easy access to high-quality business information from a collection of respected sources. Available information includes share of market data, analysts' reports on industries, sales prospecting, and much more.

Dow Jones News Retrieval
> Dow Jones and Company
> Box 300, Princeton, NJ 08543-0300; (800) 522-3567, Ext. 141

Comprehensive Company Reports:(A)
> On-line service that provides detailed financial and business information on public companies.

Dunn & Bradstreet Financial Profiles and Company Reports:(A)
> In-depth historical, financial, and operational reports for public and private companies.

Statistical Comparisons of Companies and Industries:(A)
>Offers comparative stock prices, volume, and fundamental data on companies and industries.

Editor and Publisher's Market Guide:(B,C)
>11 W. 19th St., New York, NY 10011; (212) 675-4380
>>Useful for market planning and selection, setting sales quotas, planning advertising and merchandising programs, and selecting store/plant/warehouse locations; this guide contains standardized fourteen-item surveys of market data for over 1500 daily newspaper markets in the United States and Canada. Also includes estimates of total and per household disposable income and offers current retailing data for nine sales classifications based on U.S. Census of Retail Trade. Published annually.

Government Market Studies:(A)
>Washington Researchers Publishing
>2612 P St., NW, Washington, DC 20007; (202) 333-3533
>>Book. Provides information on how to find and obtain over 5000 industry studies and reports. 1980.

Industry Reports:(A)
>U.S. Dept. of Commerce, Superintendent of Documents, U.S. Government Printing Office
>Washington, DC 20402; (202) 783-3238
>>Reports. Quarterly. Presents summaries on selected industry trends.

Information Access Corporation
>362 Lakeside Dr., Foster City, CA 94404; (800) 227-8431

America Buys:(C)
>>Annual book. Indexes information on over 40,000 products, including evaluations, brand name references, consumer buying information, and brand comparisons.

Business Index:(A)
>>This data base indexes and abstracts information from more than 300 business periodicals, *The Wall Street Journal* (cover to cover), *Barron's* (cover to cover), *The New York Times* (Financial Section), business articles from more than 1000 general and legal periodicals, and business books from the Library of Congress' MARC data base. It provides extensive special indexing of information on corporations, their divisions, executives, and profits.

International Media Guide:
>   Directories International, Inc.
>   150 Fifth Ave., Suite 610, New York, NY 10011; (212) 807-1660
> >   Comprehensive source of rate lists for business publications, newspapers, and consumer magazines. Complete set includes six volumes: IMG Business Publications-Europe, Latin America, Middle East/Africa, and Asia/Pacific; IMG Newspaper Worldwide; IMG Consumer Magazines Worldwide.

Leading National Advertiser, Inc. (LNA)
>   11 W. 42 St., New York, NY 10036; (212) 789-1440

>   Company Brand Report:(D)
> >   Records the advertising expenditures of national advertisers. Lists parent companies alphabetically, showing total advertising expenditures by brand along with expenditures in each of the following media: magazines, newspaper supplements, network television, spot television, network radio, and outdoor advertising. Also lists the leading national advertisers, the top-ranking spenders in each of the six media, media tools for the ten previous years, magazine totals by group, total industry class expenditures, and industry class expenditures in each of the six media.

>   Multi-Media Report Service:(D)
> >   Quarterly. Analyzes advertising expenditures of about 15,000 companies.

>   Publishers Information Bureau:(D)
>   PIB/LNA Magazine Advertising Analysis
> >   Three volumes (monthly service). This is a service that provides detailed month-by-month advertising expenditures and linage by brand and by name of specific magazine. It is arranged in the following sections: volume 1 contains data for apparel, business/finance, and general/retail; volume 2, drugs/toiletries, food/beverages, home building, transportation, and agriculture; volume 3 gives magazine totals, class totals, and an index.

Market Profile Analysis:(B)
>   Dun & Bradstreet, Inc.
>   299 Park Ave., New York, NY 10171; (212) 593-6800
> >   Annual. Loose-leaf. Detailed profiles of U.S. metropolitan areas.

Market Statistics, Inc.:(B)

    355 Park Ave. South, New York, NY 10010; (212) 592-6250

        This data base includes demographic and retail sales information on each of 3100 American counties, including data on income, buying power, demographic profiles, and more. Four basic data packages are available: (1) Demographic Data Base I (basic demographic information); (2) Demographic Data Base II (basic demographic information plus ethnic characteristics); (3) County Commercial and Industrial Data Base (covers industrial and business characteristics); and (4) Planner's Data Base (includes television, geographic, and market information necessary for strategic planning and forecasting).

Mead Data Central, Inc:(A,B)

    P.O. Box 933, Dayton, OH 45401; (800) 227-4908; (513) 865-6800

        Through one of its two main data base families known as Lexis, Mead Data Central provides electronic access to the full text of hundreds of business data bases. Available information includes wire services, company annual reports, investment firm reports, periodicals, newsletters, and selected newspapers.

Media Market Guide:(B,D)

    322 East 50th St., New York, NY 10022; (212) 832-7170

        Published by Conceptual Dynamics, Inc. Provides marketers, media sellers, media buyers, and advertising executives with a description of the physical dimensions, population characteristics, and major media opportunities in each of the top 100 metro markets.

Merrill Lynch Economic Regional Database:(A,B)

    Merrill Lynch Economics, Inc.

    One Liberty Plaza, 165 Broadway, New York, NY 10080;

    (212) 449-1000

        Maintains demographic and economic data for individual statistics and SMSAs on labor-force trends, population, tax payments, individual profiles, retail sales, construction, income, and housing starts.

MRI:(C,D)

    Mediamark Research, Inc.

    708 Third Ave., New York, NY 10017; (212) 599-0444

        This is a syndicated research organization that compiles information showing relationships between media use, product use, and demographics. Advertising agencies, magazines, and other media utilize the information to guide strategy and target markets. Reports include those on magazine audiences, multimedia audiences, and product volumes.

NEXIS

Mead Data Central, Inc.
9393 Springboro Pike, P.O. Box 933, Dayton, OH 45401;
(800) 227-4908

Marketing:(A,B,C)

Information from trade publications and other sources on advertising, marketing, marketing research, and public relations. Also consumer attitudes, product announcements, demographics, and reviews.

Promt/Plus:(A,E)

Presents overview of markets and technology. Analyzes specific companies and industries, tracks competitors, identifies and monitors trends. Various advertising and promotional technologies are assessed and summarized.

Nielsen, A. C.
Nielsen Plaza, Northbrook, IL 60062-6288; (708) 498-6300

Retail Index:(C)

This index measures the buying patterns of consumers by store type, brand/product, sales area or region, and price. Data are indexed by major media advertising expenditures, in-house advertising support, retailer's gross profits, and retail inventory profiles.

Station Index:(B)

This index keeps track of family viewing habits by tracking the results of each family's diary. The results are used by advertisers in buying time and stations for program evaluation.

TV Index:(B)

The Nielsen Television Index measures the number of homes in which television sets are in use, the channels to which these sets are tuned, and reports these measures in terms of total homes and percentage ratings and shares. Data are developed for those demographic characteristics that reflect household data such as geographic area, county size, household size, household income, and presence of nonadults. The NTI reports measurements of 4-week cumulative program audience and frequency, in addition to many other breakdowns and analyses.

NPD Research:(C)

    9801 W. Higgins Rd., Rosemont, IL 60018; (312) 692-6700

        Offers four syndicated research services: (1) The CREST Report (Consumer Reports on Eating Share Trends) on consumer buying habits in restaurants; (2) The Gasoline Market Index on national and regional gasoline and allied products; (3) Textile Apparel Market Index on household textile, apparel, and home sewing markets; and (4) The Toy Market Index on the national toy market.

Online Site Evaluation System (ONSITE):(B,C)

    Urban Decision Systems, Inc.

    2040 Armacost Ave., P.O. Box 25953, Los Angeles, CA 90025; (310) 820-8931

        Provides trade-area demographic data of more than 600 aggregate data items. Coverage includes such demographics as consumer expenditures, updated income, population, and household equipment and figures.

Predicasts

    Predicasts, Inc.

    11001 Cedar Ave., Cleveland, OH 44106; (800) 321-6388

Basebook:(A)

        Comprehensive, loose-leaf volume containing approximately 29,000 time series, arranged by modified 7-digit SIC code; and including statistics for economic indicators. The industry statistics usually include production, consumption, exports/ imports, wholesale price, plant and equipment expenditures, wage rate.

PROMT:(A)

        Monthly. Quarterly and annual cumulation. Abstracts of market information grouped into twenty-eight major industry sections. International coverage.

Terminal System (PTS):(A)

        This data base contains over 3 million summaries of information taken from over 2500 U.S. and foreign trade journals, newspapers, and general business publications. It offers article summaries, statistical data, and one- or two-line indexing services to provide users with background information on companies, products, industries, or marketing trends.

Prospects:(B)
 The Futures Group
 80 Glastonbury Blvd., Glastonbury, CT 06033; (203) 633-3501
   A data base for consumer forecasting. Sample data coverage includes households, families, marriage, divorce, education, labor-force, population, and lifestyle indicators. Forecasts are accompanied by a list of projected events based on historical trends and related events. Forecasts may contain over 100 indicators used to describe American consumers and their behavior. Also used for forecasting the hospital supply and pharmaceutical industries.

Rand McNally's Commercial Atlas and Marketing Guide:(B,C)
 Rand McNally & Company
 8255 Central Park Ave., P.O. Box 127, Skokie, IL 60076;
 (800) 284-6565; (708) 673-9100
   Of particular use in allocating sales effort, this volume presents detailed maps of the United States and provides information about population, households, retail sales, auto registration, sales for consumer goods, food stores, drug-stores, and other census statistics for counties, principal cities, and Standard Metro Statistical Areas. Published annually.

Rezide/1980 Update:(B)
 Claritas Corp.
 1911 N. Fort Meyer Dr., Arlington, VA 22209
   1981. National edition (ten volumes). For each ZIP code in the United States, shows population, number of households, household income in seven intervals, and median household income.

Sales Manager's Budget Planner
 Sales & Marketing Management Magazine
 633 Third Ave., New York, NY 10017; (800) 554-2754; (212) 986-4800
   Presented in the June issue, this guide contains information on compensation and expenses by industry, salesperson and sales-support personnel average compensation, media cost per call by industry, trade show exhibit costs, and automobile operating expenses. Also profiles metro markets giving meal and lodging costs, hotels, and conference centers with tele-phone number and rates.

Simmons Study of Media and Markets:(B,C)
   Simmons Market Research Bureau
   420 Lexington Ave., 8th Floor, New York, NY 10170; (212) 916-8900; FAX: (212) 916-8918
   > Consists of detailed descriptions of the characteristics of users of individual products, brands, and services and of audiences of individual media. Descriptions include detailed information regarding age, sex, education, occupation, income, geographic location, household description, lifestyle and psychographic data (including hobbies, recreational and leisure activities), respondent self-concept, buying style, and social position.

Site Potential:(B,C)
   Caci, Marketing Systems
   1100 N. Glebe Rd., Arlington, VA 22201; (800) 292-2240; FAX: (703) 243-6272
   > Provides estimates of the demand (consumer expenditures) by residents within a defined area for approximately 140 product and service items. This data base generates reports covering sixteen different retail stores and three financial institutions. Coverage includes apparel stores, appliance stores, auto service stores, department stores, drugstores, footwear stores, grocery stores, hair salons, home improvement stores, ice cream stores, optical centers, commercial banks, financial companies, and savings and loan associations.

Social Indicators:(B)
   Government Printing Office, Washington, DC 20402
   > Triennial. Charts and tables on population; the family; housing; social security and welfare; health and nutrition; public safety; education and training; "work," income, wealth, and expenses; culture, leisure, and the use of time; social mobility, and participation. International data are provided for comparison. Extensive technical notes accompany each section. Includes references for further reading and a subject index.

SRI Values and Lifestyles (VALS):(E)
   SRI International
   333 Ravenswood Ave., Menlo Park, CA 94025; (415) 326-6200
   > SRI International-VALS is a research service that tracks marketing-relevant shifts in the beliefs, values, and lifestyles of a sample of the American population. The VALS system divides the population into segments consisting of three major groups of consumers, in turn divided into nine specific segments. Tracking the shifts in the values and behavior of these

segments can help in understanding the target segment one is appealing to.

Standard & Poor's Industry Surveys:(A)
Standard & Poor Corp.
25 Broadway, New York, NY 10004; (212) 208-8000

> Separate pamphlets for thirty-three industries, updated quarterly and annually. This is a valuable source for basic data on thirty-three industries, with financial comparisons of the leading companies in each industry. For each industry there is a "Basic Analysis" (about forty pages) revised annually, and a short "Current Analysis" (about eight pages) published three times per year. Received with this is a four-page monthly on "Trends and Projections," which includes tables of economic and industry indicators, and a monthly "Earnings Supplement," giving concise, up-to-date revenue, income, and profitability data on over 1000 leading companies in these thirty-three major industries.

Starch Recognition Tests of Print Advertisements:(E)
Starch INRA Hooper, Inc.
566 E. Boston Post Rd., Mamaroneck, NY 10543; (914) 698-0800

> Starch Readership Studies make three basic measurements among persons who claim readership of specific magazine issues: the noting score, the seen associated score, and the read most score.

Statistical Abstract of the United States:(A,B)
U.S. Bureau of Census, Department of Commerce, Public Info. Office, Federal Office Bldg., 3 Silver Hill, Rm. 2705, Suitland, MD 20233; (202) 482-3263

> This guide provides a general overview of statistics collected by the federal government and other public and private organizations. Some of the topics covered include geography and environment, labor force, communications, population, employment and earnings, business enterprises, vital statistics, transportation, energy, manufacturers, foreign commerce and aid, standard metro area statistics, and more.

Statistics Reference Index:
Congressional Information Service, Inc.
4520 E-W Highway, Suite 800, Bethesda, MD 20814;
(301) 654-1550; (800) 638-8380

> Monthly in two parts, with annual cumulations. A comprehensive, selective guide to American statistical publications available from sources other than the United States govern-

ment, such as trade, profit, and other nonprofit associations and institutions; business organizations; commercial publishers (including trade journals); independent and university research centers; state government agencies.

Survey of Buying Power:(B)
    Sales & Marketing Management Magazine
    633 Third Ave., New York, NY 10017; (800) 543-3000;
    (212) 986-4800
        Presented in the July issue, this guide contains information on all Standard Metropolitan Statistical Areas in the country and covers population, households, effective buying income, retail sales, and a "Buying Power Index" useful in allocating marketing and promotional efforts. Also includes national and regional summaries; and metro areas, county, and city rankings. Published annually.

Survey of Current Business:(A)
    Bureau of Economic Analysis, Department of Commerce,
    Tower Bldg., 1401 K Street, NW, Washington, DC 20230
        This publication presents monthly and quarterly statistics on several business indicators for national income, from income and marketing, inventories, industrial production, commodities, advertising, and wholesale and retail trade by product category. Published monthly. Order from: U.S. Government Printing Office, Superintendent of Documents, Washington, DC 20402.

Survey of Media Markets
    Sales & Marketing Management Magazine
    622 Third Ave., New York, NY 10017; (800) 554-2754;
    (212) 986-4800
        Presented in the October issue, this guide contains population, income, and retail sales data for Media Market as well as projections. Breakdowns of Media Markets (ADIs) and ranking as well as 1996 projections for states and regions and U.S. totals. These are given for population, EBI, Retail Sales, and Buying Power Index.

Target Group Index:(B,C)
    Axiom Market Research Bureau, Inc.
    666 Fifth Ave., New York, NY 10103; (212) 541-3811
        Report. Supplies sample demographic data for users and non-users of various products and services. Includes market shares for such things as product brands, TV programs watched, and magazines read.

U.S. News & World Report's Study of American Markets:(B,C)
  2400 N St. NW, Washington, DC 20037; (202) 955-2000
    It covers customer characteristics, buying behavior, purchase influences, and media exposure for such products as liquor, life insurance, hand-held electric calculators, automobiles, watches, cameras, home entertainment products, travel.

ZIP Code Demographic Database (ZDDB):(B)
  Demographic Research Co.
  233 Wilshire Blvd, Suite 995, Santa Monica, CA 90401;
  (310) 451-8583
    Provides completion of the latest statistics on population, education, income, and housing by postal ZIP code.

Acknowledgments

FIGURES

Fig. 1.1   From John C. Narver and Stanley F. Slater, "The Effect of a Market Orientation on Business Profitability," in *Journal of Marketing,* October 1990, p. 23. Copyright © 1990. Used by permission of the American Marketing Association.

Fig. 2.4   Reprinted by permission from p. 174 of *Analysis for Strategic Market Decisions* by George Day; copyright © 1986 by West Publishing Company. All rights reserved.

Fig. 4.7   Reprinted by permission of the *Harvard Business Review.* An exhibit from "How Competitive Forces Shape Strategy," by Michael Porter (March/April 1979). Copyright © 1979 by the President and Fellows of Harvard College; all rights reserved.

Fig. 4.8   From George S. Day and Robin Wensley, "Assessing Advantage: A Framework for Diagnosing Competitive Superiority," in *Journal of Marketing,* April 1988, p. 3. Copyright © 1988. Used with permission of the American Marketing Association.

Fig. 4.9   From David Aaker, *Strategic Market Management,* 2nd ed., p. 86. Copyright © 1988. Reprinted by permission of John Wiley & Sons, Inc.

Fig. 5.2   Developed from data presented in W. R. Dillon, T. J. Madden, and N. H. Firtle, *Marketing Research in a Marketing Environment* (St. Louis: Times Mirror, Mosby, 1987, pp. 705–706). With permission of Richard D. Irwin, Homewood, Illinois.

Fig. 6.2   From "Advertising Research at Anheuser-Busch," By L. Ackoff and J. R. Emshoff, the *Sloan Management Review,* Winter 1975, p. 4, by permission of the publisher. Copyright © 1975 by the Sloan Management Review Association. All rights reserved.

Fig. 9.2   From Thomas T. Nagle, *The Strategy & Tactics of Pricing: A Guide to Profitable Decision Making,* © 1987, p. 280. Reprinted with permission of Prentice Hall, Englewood Cliffs, New Jersey.

TABLES

Table 4.1   G. L. Urban, J. R. Hauser, N. Dholakia, *Essentials of New Product Management,* © 1987, p. 117. Adapted by permission of Prentice Hall, Englewood Cliffs, New Jersey.

Table 4.5   Adapted from G. L. Urban, *et al.,* "Market Share Rewards to Pioneering Brands: An Empirical Analysis and Strategic Implications," in *Management Science,* June 1986, p. 654. © 1986. Used by permission of The Institute for Management Sciences and the author.

Table 5.8   Adapted from F. Beaven Ennis, *Marketing Norms for Product Managers,* Association of National Advertisers, New York, 1985, p. 27. © 1985. Used by permission of the Association of National Advertisers.

Table 5.9   Tables from *The Clustering of America* by Michael J. Weiss. Copyright © 1988 by Michael J. Weiss. Copyright © 1988 by Michael J. Weiss. Reprinted by permission of Harper-Collins Publishers.

Table 7.3   Reprinted from *The Value Side of Productivity,* American Association of Advertising Agencies, New York, 1989, p. 18. This table was developed from *Advertising Age,* and Boston Consulting Group analyses. Copyright © 1989. With permission of the American Association of Advertising Agencies.

Table on p. 226   From Betsy Sharkey, "The People's Choice," *Adweek's Marketing Week*, Nov. 27, 1989. © 1989 Adweek. Used by permission.

Table 9.11   Adapted from J. Barry Mason and Hazel F. Ezell, *Marketing: Principles and Strategy,* Business Publications, Plano, Texas, p. 392.

Table 10.2   From *Business Marketing Magazine,* November 1991, pp. 111–113. © 1991. Used by permission of Business Marketing Magazine.

Table 10.3   From Michael L. Rothschild, *Advertising: From Fundamentals to Strategies.* © 1987. Used by permission of DC Heath and Company.

Table 11.1   From Roger Strange, *The Relationship between Advertising and Promotion in Brand Strategy,* Marketing Science Institute, Cambridge, MA. Report No. 75-119, p. 13. Reprinted by permission.

Table 12.2   Adapted from "Twenty-Sixth Survey of Sales Force Compensation," The Dartnell Corp., Chicago, IL, 1990. © 1990. Used by permission of The Dartnell Corporation.

Table 13.1   From the 1992 Sales Managers Budget Planner, in *Sales and Marketing Management,* June 22, 1992. © 1992.

Table 13.3   From Manufacturers' Agents National Association, *Survey of Sales Commissions,* as reported in 1987 Survey of Selling Costs, in *Sales and Marketing Management,* February 18, 1987, p. 59. © 1987.

Table 13.4   From Edwin L. Bobrow, "The Question of Reps," in *Sales and Marketing Management,* June 1991, p. 34. © 1991.

Table 14.1   Reprinted by permission of *Harvard Business Review.* An exhibit from "Can Marketing and Manufacturing Coexist?" by Benson P. Shapiro (September/October 1977). Copyright © 1977 by the President and Fellows of Harvard College; all rights reserved.

Table 14.2   From the 1992 Sales Managers Budget Planner, in *Sales and Marketing Management,* June 22, 1992. © 1992.

Table 14.3   Reprinted by permission of *Harvard Business Review.* An exhibit from "Manage Your Sales Force as a System" by Porter Henry (March/April 1975). Copyright © 1977 by the President and Fellows of Harvard College; all rights reserved.

INDEX